History Without a Subject

NEW PERSPECTIVES IN SOCIOLOGY

Charles Tilly and Scott McNall, Series Editors

History Without a Subject

The Postmodern Condition

David Ashley
University of Wyoming

WestviewPress

A Division of HarperCollins*Publishers*

For Guy Debord, Raoul Vaneigem, and their generation

New Perspectives in Sociology

All rights reserved. Printed in the United States of America. No part of this publication may be reproduced or transmitted in any form or by any means, electronic or mechanical, including photocopy, recording, or any information storage and retrieval system, without permission in writing from the publisher.

Copyright © 1997 by Westview Press, A Division of HarperCollins Publishers, Inc.

Published in 1997 in the United States of America by Westview Press, 5500 Central Avenue, Boulder, Colorado 80301-2877, and in the United Kingdom by Westview Press, 12 Hid's Copse Road, Cumnor Hill, Oxford OX2 9JJ

A CIP catalog record for this book is available from the Library of Congress.
ISBN 0-8133-1732-0 (hc).—0-8133-1733-9 (pbk)

The paper used in this publication meets the requirements of the American National Standard for Permanence of Paper for Printed Library Materials Z39.48-1984.

10   9   8   7   6   5   4   3   2   1

Contents

9 Postmodernity and the New Class 210

The Contemporary Economy of Signs, 210
The New Class of Cultural Intermediaries, 217
New Marketing Strategies, 219
Postmodern Consumer Culture, 225
Postmodern System-Lifeworld Exchanges, 234

10 Conclusion 236

Acknowledgments

A Flittie Award from the University of Wyoming gave me the time to work on this project. I thank the members of my department for nominating me.

Part of this book was completed at the University of York during a sabbatical leave. I am grateful to Andy Tudor, head, and the members of the Sociology Department at York for providing me with an office and with other facilities.

Several people—Chet Meeks, Pem Davidson Buck, Charles Tilly, David L. Harvey, David Dickens, Richard Machalek, and Lynne Berg—read the book in manuscript form and helped me alter or remove some of the weaker parts of the argument. They will not be entirely satisfied with the result, but they did help me write a better book. Earlier versions of various chapters were shared with students in my graduate theory seminar, and they, too, helped me formulate my ideas a little more clearly.

Dean Birkenkamp, Jess Lionheart, Melanie Stafford, Jill Rothenberg, and Lisa Wigutoff gave me every assistance at Westview. It was a pleasure to work with them.

My wife, Yarong Jiang Ashley, gave me continuous support and encouragement. I could not have finished this book without her help.

David Ashley

What can one expect from man, considering he's such a strange creature? You can shower upon him all earthly blessings, drown him in happiness so that there'll be nothing to be seen but the bubbles rising to the surface of his bliss, give him such economic security that he won't have anything to do but sleep, nibble at cakes, and worry about keeping world history flowing—and even then, out of sheer spite and ingratitude, man will play a dirty trick on you.

—**Fyodor Dostoyevsky, *Notes from Underground* (1961, 114)**

1 Postmodernism in America: An Introduction

Over the past couple of decades, the number of books and articles on postmodernism has increased exponentially. Although the topic is popular among many younger academics and intellectuals, it is not always regarded as enthusiastically by the older generation.[1] As the late Ernest Gellner (1992, 22), professor of social anthropology at Cambridge University and a self-proclaimed stickler for "Enlightenment Rationalist Fundamentalism," complained: "Postmodernism is a contemporary movement. It is strong and fashionable. Over and above this, it is not altogether clear what the devil it is." Yet whatever it might be, postmodernism has transformed intellectual and academic debate—particularly in Britain, Canada, Australia, and the United States. In the West at least, postmodernism appears to have affected the whole of culture. According to one authority, there is "hardly a single field of intellectual endeavour which has not been touched by the spectre of 'the postmodern'" (Docherty 1993, 1). Indeed, the topic "has become a shibboleth for tendencies in film, theatre, dance, music, art and architecture; in philosophy, theology, psychoanalysis and historiography; in new sciences, cybernetic technologies, and various cultural lifestyles" (Hassan 1987, xi).

Some have claimed that postmodernism reflects a new era. David Harvey (1989a, vii), for instance, believes that "since about 1972" western societies have experienced "a sea-change in cultural as well as political-economic practices." According to Stephen Crook, Jan Pakulski, and Malcolm Waters (1992, 36), the effects of such change are now obvious; "postmodernization," they warn, "is well under way and . . . the denouement of modernity is imminent." Somewhat inconsistently, Crook et al. adopt familiar sociological concepts and theories, thereby implying that "postmodernization" can be grasped in modern terms. By contrast, Zygmunt Bauman (1992) argues that postmodernism has undermined all confidence in universal projects of intellectual exploration—including modern sociology. For Bauman (1993, 134), postmodernity means the "end of . . . ultimate truth, . . . the end of the political or missionary am-

1

bitions of art, the end of dominant style [and] of artistic canons." Steven Seidman (1994a, 299) agrees: "Central to postmodernity," he insists, "is the abandonment of any basis for claiming certainty or for appealing to universal standards of truth, goodness, and beauty."

Unlike Harvey or Crook and colleagues, Jean-François Lyotard (1984; 1991, 34) has denied that "postmodernism" is some new "stage" in human history, and he points out that the issue in any case is largely irrelevant, for theorists who choose to describe something as "pre" or "post" something else still have to examine that "now of the present from which one is supposed to be able to achieve a legitimate perspective on a chronological succession" (1991, 24). According to Lyotard (27–28), postmodernism can be defined as the extension and elaboration of playful, experimental, and nonserious forms of expression, examples of which can be found among all leisured classes, even in the pagan world.

If theorists have been unable to determine whether postmodernism reflects the end of an epoch, they have nonetheless agreed that postmodernism has transformed action and experience in quite diverse spheres. Postmodernism, for example, has supposedly transformed medicine (Fox 1993), influenced criminology (Schwartz and Friedrichs 1994), challenged theology (Cox 1984), touched engineering (Platten 1986), and helped to develop new models of spatial organization (Scott 1988; Soja 1989). In legal studies it has created "postmodern legal feminism" (see Greensberg 1992, xxvii; Frug 1992). In theater it has eclipsed both character and plot (Fuchs 1983; Eco 1984). In dance it has created a radically "changed political and social context for performers and spectators alike" (Daly 1992, 55). Whereas some intellectuals have tied postmodernism to new theories of economic value (Mirowski 1991), others have argued that its main outcome has been to break the effect of modern architecture on the built environment (Jencks 1987; Porphyrios 1989). For Paul Rabinow (1986), postmodernism has radicalized anthropology. Yet for at least one business professor, it has "infiltrated the academic study of management and organizations" (Wilmott 1992, 58). According to Nancy Fraser and Linda Nicholson (1993, 429), "A postmodern-feminist form of critical inquiry [is] the theoretical counterpart of a broader, richer, more complex and multilayered feminist solidarity." Postmodernism, above all, is associated with the emergence of the "gender-flexible and playful subjects" (Hennessy 1995, 271) who have allegedly replaced the old-fashioned "centrifugal self" (McHale 1992, 259).

The onset of postmodernity has been associated with new bodies (Kroker and Cook 1986), new modes of physical fitness (Glassner 1990), new cultural and social specialists (Betz 1992), a new middle class (Featherstone 1991; Kellner and Heuberger 1992), new kinds of social organization (Clegg 1990), new politics for "New Times" (Jacques and Hall 1989), new types of economic organization (Gilbert, Burrows, and Pollert 1992), new literary forms (Ruccio 1991), new knowledge (Lyotard 1984), new types of planned "auto-ethnographic" communities (Dorst 1989), and new recreational opportunities, including the popular leisure pursuit of the 1990s: "post-tourism," or tourism for ironists: what Guy Debord (1994, 120) once described as the chance to go and see what has been made banal.

How can postmodernism be expressed in so many different activities? How has it been able to affect so many different life spheres—economic, political, personal, intellectual? In this chapter I suggest an answer to such questions.

"Postmodernism": The Basics

First, however, let me try to give a general description of postmodernism's cultural outlook. Among other things, this entails:

- A fascination with the convoluted mechanisms and dynamics of symbol systems
- A rejection of realist or objective theories of knowledge
- A form of hyperreflexivity that is self-absorbed but not critically self-reflective
- An emphasis on leisure and on "aristocratic" expressiveness, not on work
- An abandonment of universal narratives of progress
- A sense of fragmentation as well as an acknowledgment that "total" philosophical or religious systems are no longer believable
- A kind of hypersophistication that reflects the subject's ironic involvement with its knowingly manufactured environments (Eco 1986, 67–68)

Both modern and postmodern cultural orders create subjects who recognize to a historically unprecedented extent that language itself does not immediately reflect or mirror the *non*linguistic. This shift in perception can be illustrated by means of the following rather general typology of forms of signification (Baudrillard 1983b, 11; see also 1990b, 65ff).[2]

1. *Premodern:* Signs express a "natural law of value" reflecting a reality that appears to exist in its own right and on its own terms. Symbols map an order that is extrinsic to language and culture. Example: Holy Scripture (signifier) reveals God's Law (as object

or referent). By definition, the "Word" cannot be a human artifice.

2. *Early modern:* Signs modify or screen reality, which is thereby acknowledged to be at least partially artificial or contingent. Observers concede that symbolic forms of mediation do not immediately touch or mirror reality-in-itself. Example: There is a growing recognition among intellectuals that theological disputes are an unavoidable part of deciphering the *enigma* that is "God."

3. *Modern:* Signs dissimulate—that is, they conceal the presence of absence. Example: We begin to understand that God does not exist (absence), that he was always a figment of our too-fertile imaginations. Nevertheless, we concede that religious belief should perhaps be tolerated because it gives people hope and a reason for living.

4. *Postmodern:* Signs no longer claim to depict, mirror, or even disguise an objective reality. Consequently, symbolic modes of representation become pure "simulacra": copies (or copies of a copy) that have no original (Baudrillard 1983b, 146). The simulacrum embodies nothing but a knowingly manufactured and contrived reality. Hence, culture must be faked before it can be recognized. Example: A McDonald's commercial shows a little girl supposedly enjoying a hamburger with her father.[3] Such a commercial is neither "true" nor "false." Both at the point of production and at the time of consumption, it is judged merely in terms of whether it is attention-worthy.

In Jean Baudrillard's (1983b, 2) terms, postmodern simulation "is the generation by models of a real without origin or reality: a *hyperreal.*" The ad just described is not therefore compromised by viewers' awareness that what they are seeing is perfectly contrived, for postmodern subjects feel quite at home in a world where everything around them is already faked. Indeed, precisely because their lives lack stable or reliable meaning, postmodern subjects are often characterized by a desperate need to be seduced (Baudrillard 1990c, 1990b). Note, too, that a clever or successful ad will interest both the simpleton incapable of ironic detachment *and* the sophisticate cynically enjoying the commercial on its own terms. We must accordingly conclude that neither intelligence nor perspicacity gives us the resources to resist postmodernism. The modern intellectual believed that critical intelligence armored the individual against the seductions of eloquence. By contrast, postmodern subjects fail to achieve critical distance from what they perceive.

By successfully collapsing the distinction between what signifies and what is signified, postmodernism makes it increasingly difficult to take either a realistic or a transcendent ("God's-eye") view of things. Because postmodern culture involves the "overproduction of signs and the loss of referents" (Featherstone 1991, 114), its subjects lose their bearings. The ability to locate themselves is lost. From the vantage point of the isolated (and terminally confused) postmodern subject, culture shatters into a multitude of relatively self-contained, relatively self-referential simulacra, each of which appears to be about as attention-worthy as any other.

From Modernism to Postmodernism

Whereas modernity is a historical state or *condition* (entailing, most notably, industrialism, bureaucracy, urbanization, and secularization), "modernism" is a cultural, intellectual, and aesthetic *orientation* that attained its maturity during the first third of the twentieth century (Lash 1990, 14ff; Huyssen 1986; Bürger 1984; Lunn 1982). Some theorists see postmodernism as a radically new and exciting departure from modern forms of expression (see, for instance, Young 1991). Yet according to Craig Calhoun (1993b, 79, 80), the "broad themes of postmodernism are not new and do not mark any sharp break with modernity or modernism." Lyotard (1984, 79), for his part, slyly claims that postmodernism "is not modernism at its end but in the nascent state, and this state is constant." This suggests that modernism and postmodernism are very close indeed.

What Was Modernism?

By about 1900 modern avant-gardists had begun to accept that "flux and change, ephemerality and fragmentation" had become "the material basis of life" (Harvey 1989a, 20). As sociologist Georg Simmel (1858–1918) noted at the time, modern individuals were confronted with a flux of experience that created a perpetual feeling of dynamic ambiguity (Simmel 1978). Modernity fostered a sense of "disintegration and renewal, of struggle and contradiction" that was experienced not just as something external but also as a splintering of self (Berman 1982, 15). Thus, "to be modern is to find ourselves in an environment that promises us adventure, power, joy, growth, transformation of ourselves and the world—and, at the same time, that threatens to destroy everything we have, everything we know, everything we are . . . . To be modern is to be part of a universe in which, as Marx said, 'all that is solid melts into air'" (15).

Responding to the loss of certainty that modernity wrought, modern art tried to capture the "inner" experience of people's shattered and contradictory life worlds. At the leading edge of modernism, art attempted to impose a temporary and highly abstracted pattern onto a mosaic of sensation and feeling.[4] By contrast, postmodernism melds a chaotic, incomprehensible, and random universe with the experience of subjects who no longer believe it is possible to identify foundations for personal or "inner" autonomy. Modernism presumes that aesthetic order expresses the will of the heroic subject, who is thereby reflected in culture; postmodernism, in contrast, recognizes that pattern (or synchronicity) will be "fatal" to its observers because what is thereby felt or expressed can never be made humanly tractable.

Modernism, however, did not just react to modernity; it also tried to *resist* modernity. Among other things, modernism condemned what the poet William Blake (1979, 78) called the "dark Satanic Mills" of the Industrial Revolution and what Max Weber saw as bureaucracy's measured parceling out of the soul. Modernism was a cry of protest from those who still believed that aesthetic expression could express the "soul" of increasingly "soulless conditions," the "sentiment of a heartless world," as Karl Marx (1986, 46) once put it in quite a different context. As a result, modernism was always "oppositional and marginal" (Jameson 1984a, 195), "scandalous and offensive to the middle-class public—ugly, dissonant, bohemian, sexually shocking . . . critical, negative, contestatory, subversive" (1985, 123–124, 125). Modernism did nonetheless try to touch and to express the *Innerlichkeit:* the "inner," self-reflective subject foregrounded by the painful and terrible modern condition.

The Intersection of Modernism and
Postmodernism (Dadaism)

To examine how modernism and postmodernism both differ and yet still overlap, let us examine "dadaism," which began in a Zurich nightclub during World War I. "Dada," a meaningless word chosen in the well-founded hope that it would be annoying, was a critical reaction to the dehumanizing excesses of modernity, and to this extent at least it was modernist in outlook. Like postmodernists, the dadaists recognized that art could no longer represent some absolute or autonomous ideal. Rejecting this possibility, revolutionary artists such as Hugo Ball, Tristan Tzara, and Hans Ruelsenbeck took aesthetic expression out of the domain of pure representation and private contemplation and into the streets, where they thought it belonged.

Like the nineteenth-century romantics (e.g., William Wordsworth in England and, somewhat later, Stefan George in Germany), the dadaists decried the vulgarity and small-mindedness of their masters. Recognizing that a whole "generation was being massacred in the names of culture, honour, reason and civilization," the dadaists "set out to destroy . . . the fine sensibilities, impeccable good taste, and implacable confidence of the bourgeoisie" (Plant 1992, 41). Unlike nineteenth-century romantics, however, the dadaists recognized that artists could no longer escape modernity's effects—including, for instance, the culture of industrial mass production. They grasped that artistic expression could no longer match, let alone surpass, what modernity itself had already accomplished. Can the painter hope to depict something more beautiful or more evocative than the sight of Manhattan by night? Is it possible for "art" to capture the sublime destructiveness experienced by some during the first day of the Battle of the Somme?

The dadaists perceived that the era of the beautiful illusion was over. They saw that in the modern era aesthetic expression could hope only to be "a stratagem by which the artist can impart to the citizen something of the inner unrest which prevents the artist himself from being lulled to sleep by custom and routine" (quoted in Marcus 1989, 200).[5] Believing that art had become inseparable from the very processes it claimed to express, Tzara made poetry by cutting words out of newspapers and then randomly scattering these fragments across a page. Following a similar logic of experimentation, other dadaists used cigarette butts, discarded concert tickets, and other bits and pieces of rubbish to construct highly politicized collages designed to make an ironic commentary on the trivia, litter, and castoffs of urban living.

Like postmodernists, the dadaists rejected aesthetic objectivity (the belief that art can authentically capture or represent an autonomous, timeless moment of beauty and truth). In addition, they erased the distinction between aesthetic and political modes of expression. According to the *Dada Almanach,* the politicization of aesthetics would prevent us from being "lulled to sleep" by custom and routine (quoted in Marcus 1989, 200).[6] Yet what the dadaists failed to recognize was that the aestheticization of politics would likely reduce the "political" to little other than the production and management of spectacle (see Benjamin 1973). Nevertheless, like the student activists of the 1960s (whose activities to some extent dadaism anticipated), the dadaists were less interested in changing the world than in establishing the right to have fun in the meantime. Unlike postmodernists, the dadaists hoped to use the "freedoms"—or, more exactly, the chaos, uncertainty, and dislocation that modernity itself had unleashed—as a *weapon* not just against the bourgeoisie but also against all forms of institutional authority. As far as the dadaists were concerned, aesthetic expression should be the worm in the tequila bottle at the cocktail party, the toilet rigged to erupt outward, not flush inward. A generation later, their spirit resurfaced in Jerry Rubin's successful attempt to disrupt the New York Stock Exchange by throwing money into the trading pit. And as recently as 1987, dadaist principles were invoked by the Orange Alternative in Poland, which marked its country's "Official Day of the Police and Security Service" by organizing "an enthusiastic march in Wrocław to 'thank' the police" in which the security forces "were showered with flowers, and embraced by the participants who were later arrested" (Plant 1992, 149).

For young revolutionaries such as Henri Lefebvre (1901–1991), who introduced Baudrillard to sociology in the 1960s, dada was the only possible response to the destructiveness and nihilism that modernity itself had created. Lefebvre recalled toward the end of his life that what had attracted him to dada fifty years earlier was its ability to grasp that modernity, as he expressed it, "carries within itself, from the very beginning, a radical negation"—its own (quoted in Marcus 1989, 200).[7]

Postmodernism

Unlike the dadaists, who went to their graves in the 1960s and 1970s, contemporary postmodernists have lost all sense of opposition to capital and to what used to be called the "bourgeois" order. The reasons for this are not hard to discern. Few people worry about the "bourgeois" proprieties anymore—least of all those with any power or standing. Moreover, whereas modernism viewed popular culture with suspicion and disdain, postmodernism blandly absorbs it, allowing "aesthetic production" to "become integrated into commodity production generally" (Jameson 1984b, 56). Instead of expressing a spirit of resistance, postmodernism contents itself with "pastiche, blankness, a sense of exhaustion; a mixture of levels, forms, styles; a relish for copies and repetition; a knowingness that dissolves commitment into irony, acute self-consciousness about the formal, constructed nature of the work; pleasure in the play of surfaces; a rejection of history" (Gitlin 1989, 347).

We can see, then, that, unlike modernism, postmodernism manages to be self-absorbed without even pretending to be critically self-reflective (Ewen 1988). It compliantly reproduces extant modes of cultural and political disorientation, itself revealing that its subjects are unable "to map the great global and decentered communicational network" in which they are caught (Jameson 1988b, 25). Postmodernism accordingly is not so much "a thought in its own right but rather . . . a significant symptom, a function of the increasing difficulties in thinking of such a set of interrelationships in a complicated society" (Jameson 1988a, 356).

Postmodernism, in brief, emerged at the point where modernism's raison d'être—its contestatory possibilities—were exhausted. By the

1960s (during which time postmodernism supposedly took root), "the classics of high modernism" (e.g., Pablo Picasso's paintings, James Joyce's novels) had all become part of the established canon of official cultural expression. Once they were displayed in museums, boardrooms, banks, and city halls, they were, of course, emptied "of their older, subversive power" (Jameson 1985, 124; see also Guilbaut 1983). One way of marking the break between modernism and postmodernism is therefore to locate "the moment . . . in which the position of high modernism and its dominant aesthetics become established in the academy by a whole new generation of poets, painters and musicians" (Jameson 1985, 124).

By the 1950s, the work of abstract expressionists such as Jackson Pollock was being funded by the Central Intelligence Agency as part of an official state effort to demonstrate that American artists were more "advanced," more imaginative, and more "progressive" than their Soviet counterparts (Saunders 1995). This propaganda effort, which was funded by the Fairfield Foundation and other CIA-financed organizations, was additionally intended to win the hearts and minds of avant-garde intellectuals, many of whom stubbornly continued to insist that Marxism had more to offer the world than Dwight Eisenhower's America.

Postmodernity

As we have seen, postmodernism is an orientation that is unable to comprehend the bases of its own cultural production. Thus, if we are to understand postmodernism, we must first create some distance from it—a "daunting task," according to Mike Featherstone (1991, 34ff), that, as Bryan Turner (1993, 72) suggests, social theorists have hardly yet begun. So before we, too, fall into the vortex and are lost forever, let us quickly distinguish between (1) postmodernism (the all-embracing, uncritical orientation) and (2) the condition of postmodernity. Although postmodernism cannot be comprehended in its own terms, we might still be able to say something coherent about postmodernity.[8]

Unfortunately, the pomo glitterati are of little assistance here. Baudrillard, for instance, has discarded even the possibility of critical theory, and Lyotard (1984, 37–41) believes that "total" explanations or narratives are too closely identified with the "failed" and "discredited" project of modernity to have any credibility. Yet it is one thing to claim that one has access to a privileged and untestable metatheory and quite another to hypothesize that certain historical processes (e.g., the organization of work) are produced as part of a "total" or globalized system of domination. Characteristically, many postmodernists (of which Lyotard is but one example) fail to note this rather crucial distinction. As a result, they do not distinguish between total epistemologies, on the one hand, and globalizing historical processes, on the other.

The Spectacle-Commodity Economy

I asked earlier how we could explain why postmodernism has revealed itself in so many different spheres of life—not just in aesthetic but also in political, intellectual, and personal spheres. To provide an answer to this question, we must turn to a critical movement that developed in France more than three decades ago.

In 1967 Guy Debord (1931–1994)—an associate of Baudrillard's and a major, if generally unacknowledged, influence on him—suggested in *The Society of the Spectacle* that capitalism was becoming, as we now can say, hyperreal. As Debord noted at the time, commodities were increasingly expressed as sign (e.g., "fashionware") or were sold as sign (e.g., "revolutionary new washing-machine") (Plant 1992, 36). Instead of informing us about a world of useful products, "spectacular" advertising invoked a universe that had become its own justification. It thus realized a general political economy in which "the commodity is immediately produced as a sign, as sign value, and where signs (culture) are produced as commodities" (Baudrillard 1981, 147; emphasis removed). The relationship of the subject to such a political economy is immediate. As expressed by the commercial for Nike Air Jordans, this relationship is mediated by little other than impulse: "Get some get some get some get some."

According to Debord, commodification was always destined to liberate the money form from its long-standing connections with physical needs, labor power, and the calculated or rationalized exchange of use values.[9] First, as production is automated the need for labor falls; second, cultural goods bestowing symbolic distinctions become increasingly important in consumer capitalist societies; third (and related to this second point), consumerism weakens the correlation between the value of a commodity and the amount of labor that went into its production. The most desirable commodities today (e.g., the coolest fashionware or the most striking images) do not necessarily take the longest time to produce. On the contrary, they are often what can be placed into circulation most rapidly.

In "late" or "advanced" capitalist societies, capital steadily marginalizes the instrumentalist and productivist orientations it once helped institutionalize, apparently liberating the form of value "from any of its former concrete or earthly content" (Jameson 1994, 25). Once unleashed, such value ceases to represent the fruits of production and instead comes to signify attention-worthy fashion, style, object-image, leisure, rebellion even (e.g., Snoop Doggy Dogg's "gangsta rap"), all of which are sold back to us by dominant corporations. As a result, what Debord (1994, 12) called the "spectacle-commodity economy" seems to be little other than a continuous and unfolding spectacle of consumption—not so much a "collection of images" but a social relationship among people mediated by commodified signs and images. The consequent emphasis on "spectacularization" buries history in commodified culture and reconfigures society without a sense of community (137). The spectacle-commodity economy thus "manifests itself as an enormous positivity, out of reach and beyond dispute. . . . It is the sun that never sets on the empire of modern passivity. It covers the entire globe, basking in the perpetual warmth of its own glory" (15).

Following Debord (1994, 29), we can define postmodern culture as the unexamined expression and reproduction of the "historical moment at which the commodity completes its colonization of social life": the point at which consciousness and awareness are themselves almost fully commodified. We thus arrive at a most important point: Once the noncommodified means to resist commodification are successfully undermined, little remains to prevent culture from being merchandised as entertainment in all spheres of life. As Jean Baudrillard (1988b, 19) has emphasized, once the public space of communal self-reflection and historical memory is undermined, "advertising invades everything." As a consequence, the "private space" of the old "bourgeois" individual becomes little other than "the potential grazing ground of the media" (20–21).

What the "conservatives" of postmodern America have thus failed to grasp is that it is not a "decline of values" or a "failure of character" that is responsible for the cultural tendencies they so loudly condemn. Rather, it is the unopposed incursion of the spectacle-commodity economy into areas of life that earlier had managed to resist the encroachment of the commercial domain. Nineteenth-century market societies doggedly (and slowly) sold useful articles to calculating buyers. Postmodern consumer capital is far more ambitious. Whereas market societies sold articles that promised instrumental efficacy (e.g., candles, bread, machine tools), contemporary capitalism offers far more abstracted and intangible commodities (e.g., image, diversion, identity, fashion). This is such a major shift that it transforms not just business but life as a whole. Entertainment Tonight replaces the CBS Evening News with Walter Cronkite, presidential candidates are known (and judged) on the basis of their media campaigns, and college teachers are evaluated on their ability to sell the simulation of an education. Even the wrathful God of the Old Testament loses his long-standing and transcendent authority and is ignominiously downsized and repackaged as yet another user-friendly lifestyle choice.

Epitaph for Dada

After Lefebvre's early involvement with dada, he joined the French Communist Party (Parti Communiste Français, or PCF) in 1928. Much later he became a prominent academic and one of the most influential Marxist theorists in France. In the 1960s, he taught sociology at the new University of Nanterre to Debord and Daniel ("Danny-the-Red") Cohn-Bendit, both of whom played a prominent role in the 1968 student and worker rebellion. This uprising, however, made little impact on the coercive system that Lefebvre and the other members of his group had earlier mocked so relentlessly.

By the 1960s, dada's bricolage of meaning had been successfully appropriated by capital, which effortlessly recuperated (or neutralized) its nonserious and ironic sense of style.[10] As a result, collage, pastiche, and irony were used by business not, of course, primarily to critique or to deflate institutional authority but to valorize commodities in new and creative ways. Today, a "dadaist" collage of signifiers is more likely to be seen in ad copy and on T-shirts than on revolutionary posters.

Postmodern consumer culture is not yet absolute, but in New York, Shanghai, São Paulo, Tokyo, Berlin, or Hong Kong 1 million disembodied bits of commercial neon reflect back to us the fragmented pieces of our commercially mediated lives. To the extent that art can still shock, this, too, has been absorbed by the market. For instance, Benetton, the Italian fashionware company, has worked into its commercial art photographs of a bloodied baby leaving the birth canal, a black African mercenary clutching a human thighbone, and a man dying of AIDS.

In late 1994, Benetton was filming in Bosnia-Herzegovina—the site of the greatest conflict Europe has seen for more than a generation. In a gesture more radical than anything Tzara ever anticipated, Benetton's publicists integrated a picture of a slain Croatian soldier's bloody tunic into a publicity campaign for the company's overpriced fashionware.

Like heroic modernism, dada is dead. But its corpse feeds postmodern industrial culture.

Resistance to Postmodernism?

Postmodernism is resisted most strenuously by Marxists and by those who characterize themselves as "cultural conservatives." The more revolutionary the Marxist, the more likely it is that he or she will find common cause with such conservatives. As we shall see (and as might be expected), postmodernity makes for strange bedfellows.

Neo-Marxists and Critical Theorists

Postmodernism has been analyzed most seriously by neo-Marxists and by critical theorists such as Ben Agger, Stanley Aronowitz, Douglas Kellner, Steven Best, Fredric Jameson, and David Harvey—the whole pack of whom, if the postmodernists have it right, should have been put out to pasture long ago. Yet we should not be surprised by this development. Ironically, Marxist theory is one of the few theoretical approaches still capable of subjecting culture to a critical examination.

The response of most leftist critics to postmodernism has been ambivalent. On the one hand, they understand that postmodernism is too important to ignore; on the other, they loathe its effects. Yet some of them have tried to see some good in the phenomenon. Hal Foster (1985), for instance, was one of the first to try to separate a "postmodernism of resistance" from a "postmodernism of reaction," and Scott Lash (1990, 37) has similarly distinguished between an "oppositional" and a "mainstream" postmodernism. Todd Gitlin (1989, 359) has claimed that "there is an intelligent variant [of postmodernism] in which pluralist exuberance and critical intelligence reinforce each other," and Ben Agger (1992, 74, 284) even suggests that "the more theoretical versions of postmodernism" are sometimes subversive and can "seriously engage with world-historical issues of social theory and social change."

Agger (1992, 291) nonetheless comprehends that postmodernism and commodification are inseparable, and he condemns the spreading influence of the corporate dadaists who promote what he calls the "New Individualism." This, he suggests, is centered on a "glitsy, Manhattanized postmodernism" that replaces "substance with style, installing ironic detachment as the central social value" (75, 79). "Strolling through Soho and Tribeca in New York or along Queen Street West in Toronto, one discovers the cultural hegemony of postmodernism. Hipsters dressed in black wander and shop and dine under the zeitgeist of the postmodern, whatever that is supposed to mean. Postmodernism does mean something in these formulations and manifestations: it represents a thoroughgoing aversion to political discussion and contention, embodying . . . narcissism" (75).

Following Ernest Mandel (1978), Fredric Jameson (1984a, 207) suggests that postmodernism is to some extent a consequence of capital's newfound ability to extend its mode of domination to areas previously uncolonized and uncommodified, such as "the Third World and the unconscious." In his terms, the "purer capitalism of our time consequently eliminates the enclaves of precapitalist organization it had hitherto tolerated and exploited in a tributary way" (1984b, 78). Like Harvey, Jameson (1991, 6) recognizes that postmodernism is a reflection of "the bewildering new world space of late or multinational capital." Hence, it must be "grasped as a symptom of the deeper structural changes in our society and its culture as a whole—or in other words in the mode of production" (1994, xii). Jameson (1991, 46) points out that if postmodernity is indeed "a historical phenomenon, then the attempt to conceptualize it in terms of moral or moralizing judgments must . . . be identified as a category mistake." In short, whether we like it or not—and whatever we happen to think of postmodernism—we are now inescapably within its orbit.

Moralists, Revolutionary Marxists, and Other "Old Conservatives"

Taking quite a different tack, Christopher Norris (1990, 44) suggests that postmodernism has "served as an escape-route from pressing political questions" and has given intellectuals "a pretext for avoiding any serious engagement with real-world historical events." As Norris (16) pointedly observes, "Theoretical activity on the left tends to assume ever more rarefied, abstract or sophisticated forms as the real-world situation offers fewer opportunities for direct political engagement."

Like Norris, the revolutionary socialist and political sociologist Alex Callinicos (1989, 170–171) claims that postmodernism is the ideological product of "a socially mobile intelligentsia," forced to "articulate its political disillusionment and its aspiration to a consumption-oriented lifestyle" during "the Reagan-Thatcher era." Callinicos (174) emphatically condemns western intellectuals' failure to seek revolutionary change and their willingness, "like Lyotard and Baudrillard, to fiddle while Rome burns."

In trying to account for postmodernism, Callinicos (1989, 168) emphasizes that the "1968 generation" began to reach positions of influence and authority during the "postmodern epoch" of the 1980s. As he poignantly notes, this was the decade "when those radicalized in the 1960s and early 1970s began to enter middle age. Usually, they did so with all hope of socialist revolution gone" (168). This observation hits the spot, but it also resonates in surprising accord with the positions staked out by conservative commentators such as Roger Kimball. He (1990) savages the faddish affectations of the "sixties generation": the "tenured radicals," as he puts it, now occupying positions of responsibility and authority within the American system of higher education. Yet even though they both condemn the posturing of college professors, neither Callinicos nor Kimball asks how these creatures support or reflect broader, material social processes. Such an omission is to be expected of someone like Kimball but is somewhat surprising in Callinicos's usually more critical observations.

For an "old conservative" such as Kimball, the academy should be a repository of timeless values and classical truths. Callinicos, for his part, believes that younger intellectuals have abandoned the attempt to create a better, more just world. Both the old conservative and the old leftist look back in anger. According to Kimball, the barbarians are no longer at the gate; they are inside the sanctuary—and they are trashing it. In turn, Callinicos can only helplessly look on as the world for which he and his comrades struggled recedes into the past. His fate perhaps is the crueler, for history (that final arbiter and judge) has made something of an old conservative out of him.

Postmodernism as a Contemporary Version of Philosophical Idealism

Following in Jameson's and Harvey's footsteps—and developing many of the ideas Debord advanced earlier—I tie postmodernity (the condition) with global transformations in the overall process of capitalist accumulation. As I see it, this process does not so much alter what Marx described as the formal logic of capitalist accumulation as create the kind of internally differentiated and localized spaces within which "postmodern culture" can flourish.

Like Harvey (1989a, 328), I believe that postmodern transformations are "within the grasp of historical materialist inquiry, even capable of theorization by way of the meta-narrative of capitalist development that Marx proposed." Although I can see that the world has changed over the last 150 years, I believe we still inhabit a system wherein the imperatives of capitalist accumulation are overwhelming and determining. Moreover, I do not accept that we have as yet entirely broken free from the processes of modernization classically defined by Marx and Weber. Thus, I believe that the "postmodern" tendencies of the current era are not so much ruptures as incremental shifts in development. Nonetheless, I do think that rapidly expanding fissures between modernity and postmodernity can now be discerned.

Capital and power in their present incarnations provide the "infrastructural" or larger determining context that makes the postmodernism of the intellectuals a meaningful and "ideological superstructure." Like Louis Althusser (1971), I treat ideology not so much as a set of beliefs or as a body of ideas but as a material practice that is lived unreflectively. Following Marx (1970, 47), I do not set out from what people say, imagine, or conceive or from people as narrated, thought of, imagined, or conceived. Rather, I begin with real, active persons and on the basis of real and contemporary life processes attempt to explain the (postmodern) ideological reflexes and echoes of the condition of postmodernity.

For Marx, philosophical idealism (or the idealist mode of thinking) was the common illusion that consciousness thinks itself into existence: the fantasy that thought and values are not mediated by power, interest, or other extrinsic factors. Opposing the instinctive confusion of intellectuals, Marx's "materialist" explanation was "mainly directed against the *separation* of 'areas' of thought and activity . . . and against the related evacuation of specific content—real human activities—by the imposition of abstract categories" (Williams 1977, 78). Marx, in short, abandoned idealist philosophy and turned to a "materialist" analysis of "real life processes" because he understood that language or "practical consciousness" "is saturated by and saturates all social activity" (37). In this context it must be noted that Marxism does *not* seek to separate "ideas" from a "material base." It merely presumes that thought cannot pull itself up by its own bootstraps or manage to be in attendance at its own birth. Consciousness, in short, is always mediated by something other than itself.

Most postmodernists, however, tend to be aggressively idealist. They write as if Karl Marx's and Friedrich Engels's *The German Ideology* had never been penned. According to Henry Kariel (1989, 44), "The language of postmodernism" is "elaborately circular"; it "assumes no definitive points of arrival or departure; it seizes nothing decisively." "In the end," Kariel (44) giddily announces, "postmodernists are in possession of nothing but their own sheer consciousness." In a similar vein, Linda Hutcheon (1986, 182) suggests that postmodernism allows us "to contest the very possibility of there ever being 'ultimate objects.'" For John Murphy (1989, 162), "Postmodernists provide an educational program that allows persons to return to themselves." These subjects, Murphy affirms, "can live their lives without accepting or rejecting reality" (162). The prince of the postmodernists, Jean Baudrillard (1991), assures us, in turn, that the Gulf War never took place (because it was only a simulation);[11] moreover, "the Vietnam war never happened" because "it was only a dream, a baroque dream of napalm and the tropics" (1987a, 17). We learn, too, that the realities of Auschwitz and Dachau were a "mythic reconstruction—a media reconstruction" (1988c, 16). In fact, according to Baudrillard, "the more we have pored over Nazism and the gas chambers in an effort to analyze those things, the less intelligible they have become, and we have in the end arrived quite logically at the improbable question: 'When it all comes down to it, did all those things really exist?'" (16).

As far as I know, the idealist philosophers skewered by Marx (1970, 41) for refusing "to inquire into the connection of German philosophy with German reality" never asserted that the battle of Austerlitz had not taken place because (like Bonaparte) it had been only a simulation. Nor did they suggest that humans should "live their lives without accepting or rejecting reality." Although Marx (99) did admittedly criticize Immanual Kant for trying to disconnect "theoretical expressions" from "class material interests," he never doubted that Kant had made a major contribution to philosophy. Conservative reactionary and "bourgeois idealist" though he might have been, Kant did not stake his reputation on the claim that everything was sheer disembodied consciousness, nor did he take leave of his senses by suggesting that reality had become irrelevant. Marx condemned his opponents for failing to make dialectical connections between thought and practice, consciousness and reality. Yet these idealists were not so detached from real life that they could conclude that "domination," "exploitation," or "injustice" had become empty terms, lacking all possible application.

Accepting that there have indeed been significant historical and empirical transformations in the advanced capitalist societies over the last two or three decades, I argue that these changes should be analyzed in their own right, not celebrated mindlessly, contemplated fatalistically, or condemned moralistically. Above all, I want to assert that postmodernity is as much ingrained in real life processes as postmodernism is reflected in popular culture and transmitted by the neural circuitry of intellectuals. What I am suggesting, then, is that the scope and penetration of postmodernism are even greater than those claimed by its most ardent supporters. My thesis, in short, is that postmodernity *is* tractable as a material practice and deeply embedded in the way we live; it has not just arrived from Neptune, without a past, without identity papers, and without support from existing authorities.

To borrow a phrase from Marx (1967a, 20), we must extract the "rational kernel" of postmodernity from the "mystical shell" of postmodernism. This requires us to examine processes that are global in scope. In addition, we must examine "the carriers and distributors of postmodern culture and the processes that have led to their rise" (Betz 1992, 96). The development of postmodern culture is connected, for instance, with "the expansion in the number of specialists and intermediaries engaged in the production and circulation of symbolic goods" and with "the formation of audiences, publics and consumers for postmodern cultural goods" (Featherstone 1991, 126; 1989, 132).

Postmodernity as a Material Reality

Turning first to global changes, we can note a recent dramatic transformation in modes of political organization that were first institutionalized at the end of World War II and that seemed entrenched as recently as two decades ago. In part, this transformation involves the collapse of the much-copied, if short-lived, Stalinist model of centrally planned state socialism, together with the demise of "Eurocommunism," but it also refers to the increasing irrelevance of the modern, relatively autonomous nation-state; the intensification of ethnic and cultural divisions in many parts of the world; the rise of the so-called new social movements (of which more later); and an overall fall in support for institutionalized politics. From 1960 to 1988, for example, the proportion of blue-collar workers who cast their vote in American presidential elections fell by one-third (Hobsbawm 1994, 581).

The reduction of politics to the marketing of imagery is another tendency often described as postmodern. As one spokesperson for the Ross Perot campaign pointed out in 1992: "Back in the 70s, the parties lost to television advertising their role as the main source of the nation's political information. Reaching voters through emotion-based image-making became far more efficient than trying to enlist them as party members" (Squire 1992, A20). Even though there is nothing very new about the use of mass media to manufacture consent, the absolute reduction of political electioneering to consumer research is innovative and novel. Coupled with the abandonment of the idea of rational political representation, we can witness a surprising reversal of some of the processes of bureaucratization, objectification, and rationalization that were previously regarded as unassailable. The ideal-typical Weberian bureaucracy, for instance, seems far less applicable to formal organizations than it was fifty years ago. In America at least, people seem increasingly less inclined to believe that formal law can transcend particularistic divisions.

A third major cluster of features associated with "postmodernity" involves "deindustrialization" in the West—that is, capital flight and the loss of manufacturing capacity. Related to this phenomenon are the declining significance of vertically integrated, nationally coordinated modes of industrial production and their replacement with a new global division of labor involving the more flexible forms of accumulation favored by the North America Free Trade Agreement, the General Agreement on Tariffs and Trade, and Asian Pacific Economic Cooperation. Little, if anything, opposes capital today. Since the early 1980s, China has been increasingly integrated into the capitalist world order. What used to be the USSR is more postcivilizational than postmodern.

The global economic restructuring that has occurred since the early 1970s has spawned new class alignments, affected hundreds of millions of families in scores of countries, and created new political alignments in the West and uprisings in the South. Linked to these changes is a seemingly permanent crisis of overproduction coupled to levels of unemployment and underemployment that are increasingly hard to explain away as "cyclical" or "temporary." Associated with these economic developments, moreover, is the perception that capital is fatal: something that must be endured, not humanized.

Americans now confront an economy that seems to have turned against them. Although the "Clinton boom" that began in 1992 created millions of new jobs, two-thirds of these paid less than $25,000 a year (Bartlett and Steele 1996, 38A). The number of part-time jobs in the United States has doubled since 1980 and now amounts to one-third of the total. Many employers are increasingly relying on temporary workers. If deindustrialization set the tone for 1975–1985, the years since have been marked by "downsizing," "decruiting," "total quality management," "work redesign," and "process engineering." In short, Americans are working longer hours for less money, and layoffs are increasing as a result.

In Europe chronic underemployment has demoralized a whole generation of people who were unlucky enough to be born after 1965 and has had a much greater impact on culture than is generally acknowledged. In 1996 over 30 million people were officially unemployed in the European Community (EC) alone, and more than 70 million were without paid work in Europe as a whole. The marginalization of labor—particularly male labor—in many parts of western (and now eastern) Europe has completely transformed the outlook of many youths and has dramatically increased the rate of crime and antisocial activity in countries, such as Britain, that used to think of themselves as "law-abiding."

As far as the emerging global economy is concerned, not only has "production [become] 'uncoupled' from employment," as Peter Drucker (1986, 768) suggests, but also "the 'real' economy of goods and services" seems to be "moving [even] further and further apart" from "the 'symbol' economy of money, credit and capital" (783). Among other things, this decoupling helps create the impression that business now has little or no relationship with production, "need," or use and not much connection with anything "real" at all. Strengthening this perception is the fact that financial markets today are less interested in "down-to-earth assets" such as stocks, bonds, commodities, currencies, mortgages, precious metals, real estate, and bank certificates of deposit and are more involved with "out-of-this-world derivatives" (Greenwald 1994, 23). According to one popular news magazine, "Wall Street seems to be rushing headlong into financial cyberspace" (22).

A fourth development associated with postmodernity is the acceleration of cultural relativism—a *"Relativismus über Alles,"* as Gellner (1992, 40–71) grumpily complained (see also Gross and Levitt 1994). In this regard, the traditional verities of the academic establishment are undermined, and the opportunities for expanding and developing new kinds of expression and inquiry (and with them new kinds of expertise) are endlessly developed—particularly within the already fragmented, hyperdiversified, and hyperdisoriented American system of higher education. Within the larger culture, consciousness of ethnic and racial particularities appears to be increasing, not diminishing. Some public colleges have even developed special courses for "minorities" only. Who among us still believes that civic responsibility or the idea of "citizenship" transcends allegiance to postmodern group or tribe?

Fifth, as part of a widening of commodification processes we can see a continuing erosion of the line between "high" culture (i.e., culture that is sanctioned by an honored elite) and mass culture, which responds to the logic of the marketplace: "If it sells, it's right." The increasing importance of the cultural intermediaries who promote the habitus or lifestyle of the boutique bourgeoisie is itself linked with a further aestheticization of social existence. According to Featherstone (1991, 83), "We are moving toward a society . . . in which the adoption of styles of life (manifest in choice of clothes, leisure activities, consumer goods, bodily dispositions) which are fixed to certain groups has been surpassed."

Finally, I think, we can see a meltdown in the more repressive, disciplined, routinized, or "inner-directed" modes of identity formation generally associated with the early modern period (e.g., by Weber 1958; Riesman 1970). This development is tied to the much-discussed "end-of-the-individual" thesis, dramatized in Michel Foucault's (1973, 308, 387) alarming assertion that just as "before the end of the eighteenth century, *man* did not exist," this entity will, with the crumbling of the modern era, "be erased, like a face drawn in sand at the edge of the sea." In terms of this thesis, the emergence of the relatively autonomous, relatively self-reflective modern *individual* was—so it turns out—just a temporary blip in what Weber (1974, 122), following Friedrich Nietzsche, saw as "the ethical irrationality of the world" and the subsequent need for subjects to determine their own meaning.

Perhaps, then, the formation of the modern morally cohesive social individual was not the irreversible or "evolutionary" breakthrough in which Talcott Parsons (1966) and other midcentury American liberals so earnestly believed. Instead, it was a historical peculiarity or cultural mutation triggered by short-lived, unsustainable, and rather odd religious orientations. As Foucault (1973, 308) has coolly observed, "man" seems "quite a recent creature, which the demiurge of knowledge fabricated with its own hands less than two hundred years ago: but he has grown old so quickly that it has been only too easy to imagine that he had been waiting for thousands of years in the darkness for that moment of illumination in which he would finally be known."

All of these trends (which are discussed in more detail later) are real and significant enough in their effects. They do, I believe, lend some weight to the idea that *something* is happening out there that is undermining and transforming many of the social, political, and economic relations that were institutionalized in the West by about 1900 and attained maturity in the 1940s and 1950s.

1968 and After

During the late 1960s, the emergence of new kinds of popular expression in the developed world marked a sudden weakening of modern versions of authority, which were also challenged politically by a wave of "antisystemic protest" in many countries (Wallerstein 1990). The cultural and political upheavals of the 1960s initially were opposed to the dominant order. Before long, however, most were successfully contained.

Britain was perhaps most vividly and dramatically affected by the cultural transformations of the 1960s. At the start of the decade, England was still very much a "postwar" society. Food rationing had ended just a few years earlier, and an aura of gray conformity pervaded everyday life. It was life lived in black and white, or life as it was seen through minuscule TV screens. Not that television was a major part of people's existence: No programs were broadcast during the day, and none was transmitted in the early evening, a time when the nation's children were supposedly doing their homework.

In the early 1960s, the British Broadcasting Corporation (BBC, a state-controlled entity) had a total monopoly on all radio broadcasting in the United Kingdom. The BBC did not like "pop music." Yet by 1966 Londoners could tune into the numerous illegal "pirate radio stations" that broadcast from ships off the coast of southeast England and what *Time* magazine called Swinging London had become a tourist attraction and a major spectacle in its own right. During the late 1960s, English pop groups such as the Beatles and the Rolling Stones became more popular (and far more profitable) than the black artists in America who had created rhythm and blues in the first place. English pop was subsequently exported back to the United States, where it was enthusiastically purchased by affluent white teenagers.

The political upheavals of 1968 had the greatest impact in France, where a major student and worker revolt had far-reaching consequences. Absorbing the lessons of this revolt, most French leftists had acknowledged by the 1970s that it was no longer possible to identify a "single locus of great Refusal," a "soul of revolt," a "source of all rebellions, or pure law of the revolutionary" (Foucault 1978, 94). Once power was recognized as insidious and multidimensional, Marxist-Leninist strategies of resistance were hopelessly undermined. If, as the French poststructuralist Michel Foucault now insisted, the multiplicity of points of resistance was present everywhere in the "power network," the source of social domination could no longer be reduced to one single hegemonic force.[12]

Let us look at May 1968 in more detail. What did it end, what did it express, and what did it portend?

May 1968

During World War II, the communists in France—as in the rest of occupied Europe—played the leading role in combating fascism. Partly as a result, support for the Parti Communiste Français peaked in 1945. In 1956, however, the PCF's standing, together with that of the other communist parties in Western Europe, was badly damaged by Nikita Khruschev's report to the Twentieth Congress of the Communist Party of the Soviet Union, which described Joseph Stalin's abuse of power.

Because the PCF initially resisted "de-Stalinization," its relationship with many intellectuals was thrown into turmoil. In 1958 Henri Lefebvre was expelled, after thirty years of party membership, for "lack of discipline" and for participation in "factional" anti-Stalinist tendencies. This expulsion demonstrated quite vividly that the most influential communist party in the West no longer had any use for one of the leading Marxist philosophers of the postwar period—a longtime activist who had founded France's first Marxist theoretical journal in 1928. Unsurprisingly, the rift had a significant impact on younger Trotskyist intellectuals such as Cornelius Castoriadis, Claude Lefort, Pierre Canjuers, and Lyotard (all members of the Marxist group Socialisme ou Barbarie) and on acolytes such as Baudrillard, Nicos Poulantzas, and André Gorz.[13]

In France the slow decline of the PCF throughout the 1970s and 1980s was foreshadowed by the mass rebellion that occurred during May 1968. Although short-lived, the sudden uprising against established authority had a major impact on the upcoming generation of intellectuals—including, most notably, Rudolph Bahro, the "post-Marxist" Gorz, Alain Touraine (who taught at Nanterre with Baudrillard and Lefebvre), Chantal Mouffe (a student of Althusser's), Gilles Deleuze, Félix Guattari, Foucault, and two of the most familiar names in the postmodern business: Baudrillard and Lyotard, both of whom were involved in the uprising.

Beginning with protests at Nanterre on the outskirts of Paris, half a million demonstrators brought the Gaullist regime to a standstill on May 13, the tenth anniversary of the founding of the Fifth French Republic. On the night of May 24, the Paris Bourse, the French stock exchange, was set on fire. For a time, it seemed that President Charles de Gaulle would use the army to "restore order." Ultimately, however, his government managed to buy peace from the strikers by using union bosses to broker deals between workers and management. Public demonstrations were banned, and "extremist" organizations were dissolved. In the elections that de Gaulle called in June 1968, the PCF won only 34 seats in the National Assembly against 73 before. The Gaullists captured 295 seats.

Who Were the 1968ers?

Many of the leaders of the 1968 revolt were strongly influenced by the ideas and political program of the "Situationists," an anarchistic and artistic group that Debord and others had founded in Paris in 1957. The Situationists traced their origins to sans-culottism, Louis-Antoine de Saint-Just (the revolutionary who sent King Louis XVI to the guillotine), the young Marx, the dadaists of the 1920s, and Georges Bataille, "the patron saint of post-structuralism" (Richardson 1994, 135). Their platform advocated the hanging of the last bureaucrat in the guts of the last capitalist, and their journal, *Internationale Situationniste*, promoted "intellectual terrorism" and anarchy in the streets as the only credible opposition to a system dedicated to the absorption of all possible foci of opposition. The Situationists saw the 1965 Watts riots and the subsequent looting in Los Angeles as a *critique de l'urbanisme*[14]—a "direct realization" of the warped principle "To each according to his *false* needs" (quoted in Plant 1992, 30).[15] Enthused by the lead taken by the American Negro underclass, the Situationists hoped for similar conflagrations in France. As Debord explained, "Where there was fire, we carried gasoline" (quoted in Marcus 1989, 176).

The revolt at Nanterre initially was sparked by the Enragés, a group that had noticed that "capitalism demands the mass production of students who are not educated and have been rendered incapable of thinking" (quoted in Plant 1992, 94).[16] Prominent among the Enragés were several Situationists, many of whom had been attracted to Nanterre by what at the time was the most radical sociology faculty in France. But in April 1968, the university came to a virtual standstill as students abandoned their classes. Leftist professors were themselves condemned for their "bourgeois" characteristics—"the cretins of submissive thought," as one student described them, "the knaves of recuperation, the modernist nullities of social integration, the Lefebvres and Touraines" (Viénet 1992, 21). On May 2 the academic authorities closed the campus and initiated disciplinary proceedings against the student leaders, and it was this crackdown that triggered widespread demonstrations in Paris.

Instead of welcoming the revolt against a despised system of authority, the PCF reacted with hostility and alarm to the subsequent social disorder. Although the party had long advocated the wholesale transformation of society, it had never scripted a role for "emotional" and "nonrational" nonfunctionaries. According to the general secretary of the party's Confédération Générale du Travail (Trade Union Organization, or CGT), the student leaders were "trouble makers and provocateurs who denigrate the working class" (Gross 1969, 102). Completely befuddled by events, *L'Humanité*, the party newspaper, which was itself targeted by strikers, announced at one point (to the unqualified delight of the students), "Government and Employers Prolong Strike!" The CGT did finally authorize a one-day work stoppage against police brutality and offer belated support to the resistors, but PCF leaders were unable to exercise much leverage over the multiple forms of protest.

In short, the 1968ers rejected all institutional authority and used popular modes of expression to foment a broad-scale and multidimensional revolt. Accepting Debord's (1984, 89) admonition that it is impossible to "combat alienation by means of alienated forms of struggle," the radicals maintained a flexible form of organization, aestheticized the idea of struggle, and refused to define themselves through a "charismatic leader" or a "revolutionary vanguard" (Nagel 1969). Their political program was written on subway walls:

> The More You Consume, the Less You Live.
> Live Without Dead Time.
> They're Buying Your Happiness. Steal It!
> Art Is Dead. Don't Consume Its Corpse.
> Everything Disputable Must Be Disputed.
> Move Quickly, Comrade. The Old World Is Behind You.
> (and, most famous of all, a slogan later expropriated by "spectacular" advertising)
> I Take My Desires for Reality Because I Believe in the Reality of My Desires.

The Significance of May 1968

As street theater and as a popular mode of entertainment, May 1968 was a ringing success. Yet in more conventional political terms, it was, of course, a failure. As Sadie Plant (1992, 106) has pointed out, 1968 "seemed to indicate that, in spite of the extraordinary uprising against it, capitalist society was resistant to revolutionary upheaval." As she (111) suggests, it was in part the experience of 1968 that helped justify "the postmodern insistence that criticism is impossible, subversion futile, and revolution a childish and reactionary dream." We must remember, however, that the 1968ers had acknowledged the impossibility of total societal transformation from the very beginning. And because they were looking for heterotopias, not utopia, May 1968 was not, as Harvey (1989a, 38) has suggested, a complete "failure . . . in its own terms." After all, the organization that historically had represented "total" disciplined transformation was the PCF, and, as we have seen, the student radicals were as much opposed to the Communist Party as they were to the Gaullist authorities.

Yet as Situationist Raoul Vaneigem (1994, 26) has recently acknowledged, 1968 did nothing to slow the absorption of the "economy of production" by the "economy of consumption." Indeed, the 1968ers were always fated to "go where the economy beckoned"—to *its* benefit, as he put it, but "to ruin for them" (12). By undermining the bases for disciplined class resistance, by splintering into a thousand points of resistance, by using mass media as a main weapon of the strike, and by depending on popular modes of communication, the student rebels presented a front that was easy to absorb and still easier to recuperate.

Although May 1968 did ultimately serve to flush some of the detritus of modern political authority (including de Gaulle and the Communist Party), it did not oppose mass mediation, nor did it undermine what Gilles Lipovetsky (1994, 217) subsequently called the "narcissistic individualism" of the 1968ers. Instead of resisting the trajectories of postwar society, the activists of May 1968 helped facilitate and advance a cultural dynamic that was already under way, motored by forces that the students themselves could never hope to master. As Vaneigem (1994, 9) himself admitted: "A mutation of the economy took hold [during the 1960s] whose effects are increasingly evident today. . . . I can now see much more easily how I was able to take advantage, in effect, of a kind of interregnum—during which the old authority was losing its grip but the new had still not thoroughly consolidated its power." But

in the end the economy picks up whatever it has put in at the outset, plus appreciation. This is the whole meaning of the notion of "recuperation." . . . The revolution of 1968 was no exception to this rule. The commodity system finding generalised consumption more profitable than production itself speeds up the shift from authoritarianism to the seductions of the market, from saving to spending, from puritanism to hedonism, from an exploitation that sterilizes the earth and mankind to a lucrative reconstruction of the environment, from capital as more precious than the individual to the individual as the most precious capital. (10)

The Political and Intellectual Aftermath of 1968

Foucault (1991, 40), toward the end of his life, acknowledged how critical May 1968 had been in forcing him to change his own way of thinking. Without it, he acknowledged, "I would never have done the things I'm doing today; such investigations as those on the prison, sexuality, etc., would be unthinkable." Not all leftists viewed May 1968 so positively, however. According to Perry Anderson (1988, 32), for instance, although France from 1945 to 1968 enjoyed "a cosmopolitan paramountcy . . . that recalls in its own way something of the French ascendancy in the epoch of the Enlightenment," by 1976 Paris had become "the capital of European intellectual reaction." In the United States and in Britain, the rejection of Marxism by an intelligentsia that had been *marxisant* for a generation was trumpeted as proof that Gallic intellectuals had finally come to their senses. Nevertheless, even as they purged themselves of their illusions, "post-Marxists" such as Gorz (1988, 96) nonetheless insisted that the "condition of post-Marxist Man is that the meaning Marx read in historical development remains for us the only meaning that development can have, yet we must pursue this meaning independently of the existence of a social class capable of realizing it."

Jean Baudrillard's shifts in orientation from the 1960s to the 1990s followed a fairly well-trodden path. Until the mid-1970s, the most influential "postmodernist" of them all had been a fairly conventional, if minor, member of the Left-intellectual establishment. Baudrillard's early interests were mainly literary and philosophical, and he did not turn to sociology until his thirties. In 1968 Baudrillard followed ultraleftists such as Debord and Vaneigem,[17] but immediately after 1968 Baudrillard concentrated on academic critiques of Marxist orthodoxy. In the 1970s, Baudrillard's outlook shifted from a critique of Marxism to a rejection of it in toto. As Kellner (1989, 216) has suggested, Baudrillard's later work was largely a reaction to the 1968ers' failure "to bring about significant social change" and a measure of his "subsequent disillusionment."

For Anderson (1988, 57), the "collusive" turn among the French anti-Marxist intellectuals of the 1970s, together with their adoption of Cold War rhetoric and their support for "technocratic functionalism" and liberalism, was more striking for its "fatuity" than for its iniquity. This did not, however, stop U.S. academics from using many of the ideas that initially emerged from this collusive turn to conjure up what they subsequently claimed was a novel and innovative intellectual movement. During the 1980s, the work of "post-Marxists" such as Jacques Derrida

(who subsequently turned out not to be so "post-Mar̟
Derrida 1994]) was enthusiastically plumbed by the ne'
preneurs, who saw it as a means to advance their own
sult, what I call the "postmodernism industry"—the un¢
astic *endorsement* of postmodern culture among int
institutionalized not in France (where it would have mᾱᴜᴄ ᴵᴵᵗᴵᴱᴱ, ᴵᴵ any,
sense) but in the American system of higher education. We should remember, however, that, unlike Disneyworld, Mormonism, or the Hollywood Minute, postmodernism itself is not all-American.

Postmodernism in America

During the 1980s, the increasingly jaded worldview of the American
postmodernists was itself aided and abetted by an unorthodox executive
hell-bent on dismantling much of the institutionalized political consensus that had been part of U.S. political life since the 1940s. As they debated the emergence of the "hyperreal," these American postmodernists
discussed (often with approval) the rise of a popular U.S. president who
had established his identity on a proved ability to sell himself as a fictive
reality. During the 1980s, postmodernism turned out to be quite compatible with Ronald Reagan's New America, and to this extent at least it
must be regarded as reflecting something *real* about political life and
popular culture during the 1980s—most obviously, that there was little
to choose between the two.[18]

By 1992 America had so blurred the distinction between the medium
and the message that without a hint of irony *Advertising Age* awarded
the title "Adman of the Year" to Ross Perot, a major presidential candidate (see Colford 1992). In the same year, the line between image and reality became so confused that TV viewers were able to watch a sitcom
character ("Murphy Brown") pose as a real journalist criticizing an allegedly real vice president (Dan Quayle) for condemning her fictional
pregnancy. (The baby's TV shower was, of course, attended by "real" re-
porters.) Viewers were subsequently treated to the spectacle of Quayle
discussing with "real" journalists Murphy Brown's criticism of him as if
this attack had been launched by a real newswoman on a real news
show. Needless to say, the vice president's increasingly bizarre behavior—which included persistent attempts to send flowers to a character
he seemed not to understand was fictional—was itself covered as a major news event about which the public needed to be kept fully informed.

In the "classic" postmodern text *The Postmodern Condition* (published in France in 1979), Lyotard suggested that the slogan for knowledge in the future would be "performativity": a measure of knowledge's
ability to provide outputs at the lowest possible cost. According to Lyo-

ard (1984, 65ff), the *grands récits* (grand narratives) of history and science had had their day in the sun, and it was no longer possible to believe in the Enlightenment ideal of a revisable consensus accessible to all. In the classical era, knowledge had been tested by the old-fashioned yardstick of "truth," but according to Lyotard, the "postmodern condition" bypassed such a clumsy procedure. In the future, Lyotard warned (5), knowledge will cease "to be an end in itself; it [will lose] its 'use-value.'" "[It] will be produced in order to be sold" (4).

Noting the growing resemblance between postmodernism, on the one hand, and the Thatcher and Reagan administrations, on the other, Terry Eagleton (1986, 134) wryly observed: "It is not surprising that classical models of truth and cognition are increasingly out of favor in a society where what matters is whether you deliver the commercial or rhetorical goods. Whether among discourse theorists or the Institute of Directors, the goal is no longer truth but performativity, not reason but power."

Basic Banalities:
Reagan and Postmodernism

Shortly before dying, Foucault declared that the modern obsession with grounding or legitimating the individual subject's right to speak was finally coming to an end.[19] As Foucault (1984, 118) saw it, modern intellectuals had taken for granted (1) that language can mirror or represent an extrinsic object-domain that exists in its own right and on its own terms and (2) that because subjects *precede* language, they can turn this medium to their own ends. Modern intellectuals had accordingly wrestled with the following (old-fashioned) kinds of questions:

- How can a free subject penetrate the substance of things that are *extrinsic* to discourse and give them meaning?
- How can this subject activate the rules of a language from within and create designs of its *own* making?

Foucault (1984, 118), however, suggested that the important questions had become:

- How—under what conditions and in what forms—can something like a subject appear in the order of discourse?
- What place can it occupy in each type of discourse? What functions can it assume, and what rules must it obey?

This distinction does, I think, shed some light on some of the major differences between the forces that created modern leaders such as

Thomas Jefferson, James Madison, or Abraham Lincoln, on the one hand, and postmodern artifacts such as Reagan or Quayle, on the other. For most of Reagan's backers, he was not so much the inspired leader as "the ultimate presidential commodity . . . the right product," as James Lake, press secretary of the Reagan-Bush 1984 campaign, put it at the time, perhaps rather too cogently (quoted in Hertsgaard 1988, 6). As far as Reagan's handlers were concerned, the president did not have to focus on anything beyond the perfectly controlled, electronically mediated world of the spectacle.[20] After all, "if everyone agrees it is morning in America, then indeed it is. Reagan had no illusions about the role of evidence, argument and rationality in this war [of the words]. He saw that the world obeyed discourse, not the other way around; he saw that reason was of very little help in creating communities of discourse" (Jamiesen 1991, 592).

Like those of all the major presidential candidates who came after him, Reagan's speeches and appearances were expertly manicured to be attention-worthy. His political commercials were produced by some of the leading experts in the field, including Richard Wirthlin ("Adman of the Year" for 1984) and Phil Dusenberry (who made the popular Michael Jackson Pepsi spots), and the focus groups that previewed the candidate's canned sound bites and one-liners were polled and wired with hand-held sensors, so that the rather more focused minders could quantify what might work and what would flop. Reagan's America, in short, succeeded in *realizing* one of Baudrillard's (1988b, 23) more cynical theses: In mass-mediated society the message or referent is irrelevant; it "no longer exists." Instead, "it is the medium that imposes itself in its pure circulation," in a kind of "ecstatic communication" that is without bounds, without privacy, without sense, and without any resistance (23).

Political rhetoric has been around a very long time. Yet traditional forms always worked most effectively when they dissembled, when they used the intricacy of language to obscure an argument that might otherwise be challenged. In contrast, the marketing of Reagan and the televisualization of politics throughout the 1980s did not so much try to disguise falsehood as showcase the triumph (and ultimate vindication) of postmodern political aesthetics. Reagan's commercials did not generate falsifiable or even testable claims. Rather, like the Pepsi ads they could only aspire to be, they were spectacles that were either more or less successful. At the time, most journalists were content merely to provide some color and background to the antics of the "spin doctors" and PR strategists responsible for the whole sorry charade. By interviewing many of those involved in the packaging of Reagan, Mark Hertsgaard (1988) has shown just how complicit these creatures were, eager to make an official record out of whatever bits and pieces of rubbish happened to be passed to them.[21]

During the 1980s, what Americans got from the "Great Communicator"—as Reagan was described by an increasingly Orwellian press—was not straight talk but a successful simulation.[22] It is not surprising, then, that political content became almost irrelevant and that as many as 40 percent of the people who voted for Reagan discovered that they were against his programs after finding out what they were. Nearly everyone who liked the Great Communicator learned about him from television, and as long as the TV show was seamless and self-contained, the simulation was beyond critique; the viewers, in other words, were unable to attain any kind of independent or objective purchase on the glossy surface of the video simulation.

Like Baudrillard, Reagan's media hounds focused on the image and the simulacrum and on "the dissolution of TV into life, the dissolution of life into TV" (Baudrillard 1983b, 55). This strategy seemed to work. In the eighteen-minute movie Dusenberry made for the 1984 Republican Party Convention, he taped one young woman enthusing: "I think he's [Reagan] just doggone honest. It's remarkable. He's been on television, what have I heard, 26 times? Talking to us about what he's doing? Now that's— he's not doing that for any other reason than to make it *real* clear. And if anybody has any question about where he's headed, it's their fault. Maybe they don't have a television" (quoted in Slansky 1989, 105).

So there we have it: The unexamined life is worth living after all. In fact, don't even bother to get a life; just get a television.

If—as Georg Lukács is said to have remarked—Stalin made a realist out of Franz Kafka, the Great Communicator topped this. He managed to turn Baudrillard—the disappointed and embittered 1968er—into a theorist of vision and insight.

2 Postmodernism and Social Theory

This chapter addresses postmodernism's influence on theory. As the "cultural dominant" of consumer capitalism, postmodernism is not exclusively, or even primarily, an intellectual movement. It has nonetheless significantly affected academic practice, particularly in the United States.

In this chapter, I first describe how "modernity" has been conceptualized by sociologists. Next, I examine how classical sociology responded to the complexities of modernity by trying to turn it into a reflexive project that promised to make us masters of our social environment. The *failure* of this project, I argue, had two interrelated consequences. First, it was devastating for classical sociology. Second, it undermined what Jean-François Lyotard has called the emancipatory narrative or "metanarrative" of modernity. According to Lyotard (1984, 35), this metanarrative told a story about a "practical subject" ("humanity") that was poised to emancipate itself from everything that prevented it from governing itself. Sociology not only was part of this narrative during its "classical era" (circa 1880–1920); sociology also promised to play the key role in helping realize this narrative.

After describing how sociologists have defined modernity, I discuss the cleavage that developed between theorists such as Karl Marx (1818–1883) and Émile Durkheim (1858–1917), on the one hand, who believed (albeit in different ways) that the emancipatory narrative of modernity could be realized, and theorists such as Max Weber (1864–1920) and Friedrich Nietzsche (1844–1900), on the other, who concluded that intellectuals could never repair the cultural fragmentation, differentiation, and complexity that modernity itself had wrought. The contemporary version of this dispute is represented in the debate between critical theorist Jürgen Habermas (b. 1929) and the rapidly increasing number of post- and antimodern theorists.

We have heard a great deal recently about how postmodernism reflects the end of the Marxist project of universal enlightenment. In this chapter, however, I also want to look at how the failure of Durkheimian sociology helped give birth to postmodernism via poststructuralists such as Georges Bataille (1889–1962), Michel Foucault (1926–1984), and Jacques Derrida (b. 1930). Whereas poststructuralism was a *critical* response to modernity's favored account of itself, the postmodernism industry is largely a noncritical endorsement of postmodernity. Postmodernism, in other words, is a form of acquiescence in, and approval of, the dissolution of the cultural forms that could challenge or resist postmodern consumer capitalism.

At the end of this chapter, I return to the question of whether historical materialism has anything to offer in the way of interpreting and explaining postmodernity. On the face of it, the fate of Marxist theory seems to be the same as that of classical sociology. Like sociology, historical materialism promised to help realize the emancipatory narrative of modernity. Yet it has retained more of a critical bite than sociology. In part this is because Marx had a better empirical grasp of the dynamic of modernization than the sociologists. But it is also because historical materialism was more willing to challenge modernity's grandiose pronouncements about what it had already accomplished.

Modernity

In terms of classical sociological theory, modernity involves several factors:

- Industrialization
- Urbanization
- Rationalization of work and growth-oriented economic planning
- Bureaucratization—"*the* means of transforming social action into rationally organized action" (Weber 1978, 987)
- Pluralist political systems
- Secularization and the decline of established religion
- Increased differentiation of institutions and roles
- Individuation (i.e., the development of individual selves) and the expansion of multiple dimensions of personal choice

The foregoing factors are the products of three fundamental processes, which are integral to modernization. These are

1. The use of the symbolic medium of money to reorganize labor and rationalize the productive use of time (Marx 1967a; Thompson 1982). Modernity thus promotes capitalism, which Marx defined as the measured use of mechanically assisted labor power

to optimize the continuous expansion of quantified value. As Marx's conception of capital is discussed in more detail later, we can defer further exploration of the topic until then.

2. The rationalization of action and culture according to formal, technical, and instrumental norms (Weber 1978, 71–74; 1951; 1969). Cognitive life spheres (i.e., scientific and technological practices) are most responsive to such rationalizing tendencies. In the early stages of modernization, moral and aesthetic life spheres (i.e., morality and art) are comparatively more resistant.

3. The replacement of total, cosmological, or religious worldviews with decentered and differentiated social institutions. These are relatively permanent and specific clusters of roles, groups, organizations, customs, and activities that perform increasingly specific social functions—political, educational, religious. Modern, differentiated social institutions are less inclusive and hence are more specialized than their predecessors (Parsons 1951, 1966, 1967). Like highly specialized bodily organs (e.g., the heart or the lungs), these institutions organize internally complementary patterns of action that create greater autonomy for the social "organism" vis-à-vis its larger environment.

Theorists who have emphasized the rationalizing/differentiating tendencies of modernity tend to fall into one of two groups.[1] In the first are those, such as Weber, who reject the idea that modern rationalization and differentiation will culminate in some kind of emancipatory and holistic resolution among the diverse life spheres. Because Weber believed that science, morality, and art could no longer be reconciled, he concluded that science and technology could never resolve conflicts of value or taste, let alone the overarching "problem of meaning." As he (1949, 57) put it, "The fate of an epoch which has eaten of the tree of knowledge is that it must know that we cannot learn the *meaning* of the world from the results of its analysis, be it ever so perfect; it must rather be in a position to create this meaning itself." Like Jean-Paul Sartre, Weber (1946, 143) concluded that modern individuals were, in a sense, *condemned* to "freedom": sentenced to live in a world that responds with silence and indifference to the all-important question "What shall we do, and how shall we live?" Rather than resist such a fate, however, Weber embraced it because he decided that it bestowed on us the only kind of "freedom" we are ever likely to experience.

In the second group of intellectuals who have emphasized the rationalizing, differentiating tendencies of modernity are theorists, such as Habermas, who recoil from the nihilism Weber appears to advocate. For Habermas (1987b, 117), culture is "rationalized" (1) when the life spheres just described are subjected to critical self-scrutiny in their own right and on their own terms and (2) when the communicative lifeworld of meaning, commitment, and expression is afforded some autonomy from the instrumentalist and objectified demands of the "system media" of money and power. If we put this another way, we can say that Habermas believes that contemporary subjects are confronted with a choice between either the invasion and dissolution of aesthetic and moral domains by the kind of abstracted commodification entailed by postmodern consumer capitalism or aesthetic and moral resistance to the kind of instrumental domination institutionalized by advanced forms of capitalism.

Habermas's "defense of modernity" therefore presumes that modernity "allows crucial differentiations of validity claims, spheres of value and the institutionalization of appropriate forms of argumentation" (Roderick 1986, 121). It also requires that the "lifeworld"—"society" as "conceived from the perspective of acting subjects" (Habermas 1987b, 117)—be granted some independence from objectified or routinized systems of purposive-rational action. To state this more accessibly: Habermas acknowledges that modern, rationalized societies must "steer" themselves in terms of the media of money and power, but he does not believe that these media should be used to organize or to develop moral reason or artistic expression. In short, Habermas's theory of communicative rationality seeks to reconstruct modernity's metanarrative by showing how the three life spheres can coexist in a state of mutual respect and reciprocity, each adhering to its own internal and quite specific rules of normative validation.

Habermas is an important intellectual—not least because he is perhaps the last human alive still trying to reconstruct modernity's metanarrative, albeit in a highly modified form. I return to his theory of communicative rationality later and attempt to show how it is implicated in the discussion about postmodernity. First, however, I want to examine what was perhaps the most ambitious sociological effort to make a reflexive project out of modernity: Durkheimian structuralism. As mentioned earlier, the poststructuralist reaction to this failed project was a major influence on the intellectuals who later embraced postmodernism.

Modernity and Reason: Durkheim Versus the Poststructuralists

Émile Durkheim invented modern sociology, in part because he thought it could provide a reasoned comprehension of the overarching principles of social order. Unlike Weber (1946), who saw sociology as itself part of a process of modern disenchantment, Durkheim claimed that his new discipline was both scientific *and* value orienting.[2] He believed, in other words, that sociology could uncover new (social) facts and serve as a moral compass, strengthening and revitalizing civic or public culture in the process.

Durkheim argued that the individual was bound to the collectivity by shared moral sentiments, not by reason or atomized self-interest. As far as he was concerned, the most fundamental or "elementary" institutions in premodern, prerationalized societies are those that deal with religion or sacred matters. These emotionally reproduce what the societal community believes is of ultimate importance. Durkheim (1915, 470) claimed that no society can "create itself" or "recreate itself without at the same time creating an ideal" that maintains "at the necessary degree of intensity" the "sentiments" that are necessary for the society in question to "assemble and concentrate itself." In an argument that is obviously circular, if not outrightly tautological, he (1974, 35–62) suggested that *some* comprehension of a sacred ideal (e.g., "God," "Nation," "Humanity," "Progress") was both the end and the cause of the social or moral order. Yet regardless of the formal defects of Durkheim's program, it strongly influenced many American sociologists—including liberal theorist Talcott Parsons (1902–1979), who claimed that Durkheim's "discovery" that normative obligation was the heart of the social had paved the way for a scientific understanding of culture (see Durkheim 1974, lxiii–lxiv). Toward the end of his life, Durkheim planned to supplement his earlier study of the "elementary forms" of religion with an analysis of secular moral universalism that would show how modern, civic education could similarly integrate complex, modern societies. Such societies, he acknowledged, were not as tightly assembled or as "concentrated" in their sentiments as "primitive" societies. Unfortunately, he died before he could complete this project.

Durkheim and his nephew Marcel Mauss (1872–1950) were both eager to show that even "economic" practices were subordinate to sociomoral forces, and they both insisted that systems of economic exchange were not just the summation of atomized expressions of self-interest. In *The Gift* (1925), for instance, Mauss (1967) attempted to demonstrate that the "primitive" "economy of gift-exchange" created a circulating and expanding sense of reciprocal obligation that functioned to implement and reproduce normative (hence, social) structures. Although "gift-giving" is supposedly voluntary, disinterested, and spontaneous, because it produces a sense of reciprocal obligation, it also reinforces social solidarity. As Claude Lévi-Strauss (1969, 51) suggested, men's "gift" of their daughters to other men allows the "donors" in question to claim legitimate title to their own wives. Whereas modern, rationalized economies are not based exclusively or even partially on the exchange of gifts, Mauss (1967, 70) insisted that modern market activity still had a precontractual *moral* basis that was both "obligatory and efficacious." He accordingly argued that sociology could show how even economically differentiated societies institutionalized not merely "a science of manners" but also "ethical conclusions—'civility,' or 'civics' as we say today. Through studies of this sort we can find, measure and assess the various determinants, aesthetic, moral, religious and economic, and the material and demographic factors, whose sum is the basis of society and constitutes the common life" (81).

Durkheim and Mauss (1963) additionally argued that "society" structured cognitive as well as moral forms. In these terms, society "was not simply a model which classificatory thought followed; it was its own divisions which served as divisions for the system of classification" taken as a whole (82). Even the most fundamental categories of thought—those of "time" and "space," for instance—were, as a result, "closely connected with the corresponding social organization" that had produced them (88). Employing this classically structuralist model, Durkheim and Mauss elegantly claimed that the categories that provided the awareness of objects or "things" in the world mirrored the underlying forms of social sensibility that had created such knowledge in the first place.

Because Durkheim and Mauss (1963, 88) recognized that *modern* structures "progressively weakened" the concentrated force of "social affectivity," they acknowledged that modern societies left "more and more room for the reflective thought of individuals." Modern individuals consequently had a unique capacity for self-reflective or sociological insight. By way of contrast, "primitive" consciousness was emotional and unstructured, "fluid and inconsistent" (87). Because it lacked distance from itself, "primitive" thought functioned merely to obscure and to mystify the "social sensibilities" that had brought it to life. In short, Durkheim and Mauss believed that, whereas modern individuals could be knowledgeable (i.e., self-reflective) about the causal influence of the social, the simple creatures of *les sociétés inférieures* had to experience the collectivity's effect on them unreflectively. "Primitive" thought was thus "haunted" by the modern science that lay in readiness to master and disperse it (Foucault 1973, 339). By contrast, as far as Durkheim and Mauss were concerned, modern subjects turned modernization into a reflexive project of collective self-discovery.

For Foucault (1973, 303–343), Durkheimian sociology exemplifies the modern structuralist search for what he calls "Man and his Doubles": the quixotic search for a form of knowledge incarnate that not only "knows" it is the reflection of a particular form of life but also succeeds in apprehending *how* it came into being. What is particularly poignant about the modern outlook, however, is that while it does accept that language is not inherently or immediately representational, it nevertheless fails to acknowledge that humans will never succeed in isolating the structures that mirror consciousness. The reason for this inability is not difficult to explain: Such structures do not exist. This fact has not, however, prevented modern intellectuals from searching for them. During the modern era, sociology and Marxism exercised such a hold on intellectuals precisely because these outlooks promised to give them what they craved: the ability to show how they could mirror themselves as "enlightened" subjects in a "locus of a discourse" that was transparently self-mastered.

As we have seen, Durkheim and Mauss (1963, 86ff) believed that the "locus of discourse" *was* society. For Durkheim (1915, 470), society is a self-producing entity; "it is not made up merely of the mass of individuals who compose it . . . but is above all the idea which it forms of itself." Sociology, in these terms, was *the* scientific discipline that could show modern, self-reflective subjects how they could grasp the "mode of production" through which their civilized being was mirrored.

At this stage, the following questions emerge:

- Are the horizons of human understanding constrained by the idea that society forms of itself? (Such a conception of human potential seems socially overdetermined.)
- Is it correct to assume that modernity gave us a privileged vantage point? If so, what are its limitations, if any?
- If we assume that modern social anthropology and sociology can show how "primitive" or premodern forms of life are structured, do these structures represent an order that exists in itself (in their own right), or do they mirror the categories that modern intellectuals imposed on their own thought processes?
- Is modern knowledge, then, so benign and so enlightening? Or, as Foucault suggested, does it reflect an underlying need to impose some kind of order on the "primitives" who can never be allowed to be the executors of their own meaning? At root, does modern knowledge both represent and disguise little else than *power:* the will to dominate, to control, to sweep the Other into the net of one's own comprehension?
- Is normative obligation (or, in Maussian terms, the norm of reciprocity) a timeless and universal template that structures social relations both in "primitive" and modern settings? Have modern intellectuals projected onto "savages" an elementary, unformed,

and unfinished version of the "civilized" order they need to believe they *alone* were fit to accomplish?

Whereas Weber was cautious and gloomy about what sociology could accomplish, Durkheim believed that the new discipline could steer modernity in terms of principles that sociology alone could master. In reaction to this, *anti*moderns such as the poststructuralists Bataille, Foucault, and Derrida rejected the axioms of Durkheimian sociology *and* the version of modernity posited by such theory. However, Bataille, Foucault, and Derrida did not advocate something called "postmodernism," nor did they ever claim to be "postmodernist." What poststructuralists share with the intellectual outlook of postmodernism (which is not a great deal) is a certain sensitivity to the kinds of issues just bulleted. In essence, poststructuralists (1) reject "the tyranny of [modern] globalizing discourses" (Foucault 1980, 83); (2) refuse to accept that signifiers mirror or reflect referents according to some necessary, naturalistic, or consistent formula; and (3) believe that "incommensurability and fragmentation" can be "liberating" (Best 1994b, 29).

But unlike the postmodernists, Bataille, Foucault, and Derrida celebrate "incommensurability and fragmentation" because they refuse to accept modernity's imperialistic claim that its point of view is inherently more reasonable than any conceivable alternative. In contrast, the postmodernists, as we have seen, embrace "incommensurability and fragmentation" not so much because they have scrutinized or questioned modernity but because they are unable to resist postmodernism.

Postmodernism is now strongly identified with American popular culture, but, as mentioned earlier, its intellectual roots are French. In this regard, Baudrillard is a pivotal figure because he bridges (1) a poststructuralist tradition that includes Nietzsche, Bataille, and Foucault and (2) the postmodernism industry in this country. It is important to get the relationship between poststructuralism and postmodernism straight, however. Poststructuralism is an antimodern intellectual movement with continental roots. Postmodernism is a far more diffuse cultural orientation that reflects (1) the spectacle-commodity economy and all it entails, together with (2) the uncritical perspective of many western intellectuals (see, for example, Murphy 1989; Kariel 1989; Seidman 1991, 1994, 1995).

My thesis is that the poststructuralist critique of modernity that Bataille initially developed intellectually anticipated a trajectory of disintegration that consumer capitalism is *materially* realizing today. Postmodernism, in these terms, is an expression and uncritical acceptance of the dissolution, fragmentation, and exhaustion of previously differentiated and autonomously rationalized life spheres that are now quite overwhelmed.

From Poststructuralist Critique to Postmodernist Acquiescence

We now turn to a discussion of Jean Baudrillard's (1993b, 1990b) contribution to the debate about postmodernism. Baudrillard's work is important for several reasons. First, it is a continuation of Bataille's radical attack on classical sociology (or on modernity's own account of itself). Second, Baudrillard continues (and recuperates) themes that Debord and Vaneigem first explored in the 1960s. Third, although not as original as is often assumed, Baudrillard's writings pointedly address contemporary developments in mass media, popular culture, and consumer society. Finally (and most important), by showing how consumer capitalism replaces economic (commodity) exchange with "symbolic exchange" (explained later), Baudrillard shows how *capital itself* is implicated in the dissolution of the "world-historical process of societal rationalization" described by Weber. As Baudrillard (1993c, 199) emphasizes, "If it was capital which fostered reality, the reality principle, it was also the first to liquidate it in the extermination of every use-value."

Georges Bataille

Habermas (1987a, 229) has noted that Bataille made it his "scientific ambition" to show how the world-historical process of societal rationalization described by Weber could be "overturned into freedom." Like dadaist Richard Huelsenbeck, who complained that the "chronic disease" poisoning the modern world was the total "inability of a rationalized epoch and of rationalized men to see the positive side of an irrational movement" (quoted in Dachy 1990, 188), Bataille believed that modern individuals were little other than prepared corpses: routinized zombies programmed to sustain the kind of instrumentalities guaranteed to make life not worth living.

As a student, Bataille initially pursued a fairly conventional career in sociology, which he studied under Mauss. After dabbling in surrealism and Left communism during the 1920s, Bataille helped found the neo-anarchistic and ultraradical Collège de Sociologie (1937–1939). It was dedicated to a "critique of sociology, not of sociology in general and in every aspect, but sociology understood as totally represented by the sociological school of the French university system and illustrated by Durkheim and Lévy-Bruhl" (Hollier 1988, 369–370).

The members of the Collège refused to accept that the horizons of human existence were bound by the depressing vision that the modern, rationalized, and differentiated social order had formed of itself. As far as they were concerned, such an outlook denied human will its creative impulse. Because Bataille (1988b, 219; emphasis supplied) believed that modern science (including modern sociology) "is made by men in whom the *desire* to understand is dead," he viewed Durkheim's and Mauss's work as statist and totalitarian in orientation. With Michael Leiris and Roger Caillois, Bataille condemned science as a monstrous fantasy that tried to harden, consolidate, and legitimate a social domination that modern forms of rationalization had already achieved.

As we have seen, Durkheim (1915, 52, 257) claimed that the "sacred" was what *society* deemed "superior in dignity and power," and he accordingly concluded that the familiar distinction between the "sacred" and the "profane" was a representation of the structural order reproduced by systems of social solidarity. In opposition, Bataille and the other members of the Collège de Sociologie defined "the sacred" as "the forbidden element of society that exists at the margins where different realities meet" (Richardson 1994, 34). Access to this "sacred" order accordingly demands transgression and the search for "limit-experiences": a deliberate flouting of the boundaries.[3] Because he insisted that the sacred must be taken on its own terms, Bataille rejected the functionalist claim that the rites, rituals, and ceremonies of "primitive" people could be explained through a second-level interpretation that showed how these practices contributed to social solidarity. According to Bataille, the sacred could never be measured or tamed: It was "something prestigious . . . something unusual . . . something dangerous . . . something ambiguous . . . something forbidden . . . something secret . . . something breathtaking . . . something that, all in all, I can hardly conceive of except as marked by the supernatural" (quoted in Hollier 1988, 31).

Durkheim acknowledged that modern individuals could no longer experience the sacred as an undifferentiated force. Yet he nonetheless persuaded himself that modern societal institutions could still sustain a more diffuse sense of their symbolic power by means of the reproduction of an "organic" (i.e., differentiated) solidarity. For Bataille, however, modernity (and, by association, sociology) expunges all sense of the sacred. He noted that sociology cannot even touch the sacred; there is no common ground. "Scientific sociology" thus fails to grasp that a sense of the sacred enables subjects to express what is for modern science *inexpressible*.

As well as rejecting Durkheim's conception of the sacred, Bataille and the other members of his group also jettisoned (1) the notion that thought was determined by the structures of society and (2) the idea that normative templates of obligation and reciprocity were at the heart of human existence. For Bataille, the Durkheimian school had a distinctly oversocialized view of humans. In opposition, he advanced "a version of Nietzsche's 'aristocratic,' 'master morality,' in which value articulates an excess, an overflow and an intensification of life energies" (Kellner 1989, 43). In these terms, much of liberal, functionally oriented sociology is based on a fundamental misconception. What humans want are not structured opportunities to achieve "nomic integration"—marriage, a nice home, a steady job (the whole tragedy, in other words)—but the chance to regain what modernity stole from us: an exuberant sense of being alive.

In a larger context, the aristocratic "discharge of excess" that Bataille believed was so central to human modes of expression could be seen as reflective of a fatal flaw in human design. This is best illustrated by a comparison of human and nonhuman organisms. For the most part, nonhuman animals are hardwired to match effort with need: Barring the presence of a "super stimulus," lions, for instance, stop chasing wilde-beest once they have feasted sufficiently. Yet humans are condemned to dispose of what Bataille called the "accursed share": the surplus they produce over and above basic "needs" because of their inability to recognize "natural" limits. As a result, humans must dedicate much of their energies to participating in the "useless" symbolic expenditure of the unnecessary resources they have so pointlessly husbanded.

Bataille pointed out that, unlike "primitive" economies, modern, rationalized capitalist production is based on a system of endless deferrals. Instead of allowing people to enjoy the surplus they have produced, capitalist production neurotically seeks to amplify wealth. As a result, the individual becomes fixated on growth for growth's sake, on what Vaneigem (1994, 33–34) sardonically described as "the pleasure of business," "the dignity of labor," "restrained desires," and "survival"—"the filthy tub that human faculties have been bubbling in for nearly two centuries."

Bataille (1988a), in seeking to make his ideas more concrete, turned to a description of what he claimed was the "General Economy" of "primitive" societies. This, he argued, follows the example of the sun, which expands its warmth and energy on everyone without obligation and without any hope of return. In an inversion of Durkheim's well-known distinction between "mechanical" (homogenized) primitive and "organic" (heterogeneous) modern forms of solidarity, Bataille claimed that it is modern societies that are homogenized or inflexibly cohesive and "primitive" life that is open-ended and vital. By promoting symbolic (as opposed to economic or commodity) exchange, General Economy encourages wealth or surplus to be exchanged for prestige: what Thorstein

Veblen (1979) a century ago called "conspicuous consumption." One illustration of such symbolic exchange is the "potlatch" ceremonies of the Pacific Northwest Indians who gave away or even destroyed goods at elaborate festivities that created "big men."

We can illustrate symbolic exchange as follows. Let us imagine a yuppie who purchases her cosmetics from the Body Shop and her clothes from The Gap (sewn by children who are paid twenty cents an hour by Taiwanese businessmen in El Salvador). Our yuppie purchases "green" products only and would never buy anything tested on animals. She basks in the knowledge that the label on her butt tells the world that her jeans cost five times as much as the generic product in K-Mart. We can say that our yuppie is not seeking to optimize instrumentally rational behavior but is enjoying—at others' expense, of course—an expensive semiotic privilege. In purchasing such "privilege," she uses money not as a token of utility but as something sacrificed to the greater glory of showing that (unlike the riffraff at DollarSave) one is a person of quite superior bearing. Our yuppie, in short, is a consumeratti; she is attuned to symbolic modes of expression, not focused on economic modes of rationalized commodity exchange.

Unlike "pure" commodity exchange, which produces relations of utility, *symbolic* exchange creates cultural distinctions. These include those between the fashionable and the honored, on the one hand, and the dowdy, the nondescript, the irrelevant, and the ignored, on the other. As an infinitely revisable and extendible practice, sumptuary consumption demands waste, prescribing only that its subjects consume needlessly. In a contemporary form, this goal is achieved through the costly purchase of semiotic privilege: a degree from an elite liberal arts college, not Texas Tech; a BMW or Lexus, not a battered pickup; an anorexic "trophy wife," not a woman who is humdrum, sturdy, and obviously used to labor.

Like Bataille, Baudrillard (1993b) contrasts the spontaneity of "primitive" symbolic exchange with the routinized forms of economic exchange that exist in modern capitalist economies. Following Bataille, Baudrillard claims that the real divide in symbol systems is between symbolic and economic exchange, not, as Marx insisted, between production and exchange. Citing Veblen, Baudrillard suggests (1981, 31–32) that the "commerce of everyday goods" (i.e., economic exchange) involves a completely different logic of value than that entailed by the circulation of prestige (i.e., symbolic exchange). What economic or commodity exchange is to productive capitalism, symbolic exchange is to consumer capitalism.

As we have seen, whereas symbolic exchange allows being or existence to precede and thereby freely to shape the attainment and enjoyment of status, modern rationalized economies reproduce rigidly prescribed systems of lifeless, impersonal, and quantified obligation.[4] This raises the possibility that capitalist societies were always fated ultimately to experience not economic but cultural disintegration. As Baudrillard (1975, 143) once suggested, capitalism's "fatal malady" "is not its inability to reproduce itself economically and politically, but its incapacity to reproduce itself *symbolically*. It is this fatality of symbolic disintegration under the sign of economic rationality that capitalism cannot escape."

Baudrillard's View of the Modern Social

Baudrillard (1983a, 73–74) believes that the modern period (which he suggests emerged in western Europe at the end of the sixteenth century) replaced living expressions of "symbolic integration" with dead forms of "functional integration" that took "charge of the residue from symbolic disintegration." Once "the dead and institutionalized relations" of bureaucracy and capital displaced the subjective thrust and organic vitality of earlier forms of open-ended symbolic expression, the formal-rational institutions of "modern society" were what was left as "excremental" remainder: a dried-out substitute for forms of life long since departed (Baudrillard 1983a, 72ff). The modern "social" is, in these terms, not a reflexive project of collective self-discovery but rather the accumulation of dead (rationalized) forms that were "laid down one after the other on the ruins of the symbolic and ceremonial edifice of former societies . . . " (65; 1993b). For Baudrillard (1983a, 78), these lifeless forms (e.g., complex formal organizations, economic institutions) function to "take care of the useless consumption of remainders so that individuals can be assigned the useful management of their lives." *Fex urbis, lex orbis* (Saint Jerome)—The law of the world is made out of the feces of civilized life.

Looking backward, Baudrillard (1990b, 182; 1993c, 356) sees modernization as "the abduction, rape, concealment and ironic corruption of [a lost and forgotten] symbolic order": an Original Sin that he manages to equate with "the principle of Evil" itself. For Baudrillard, the modern era of Kafka and the civil servant signified "a culture of death" in which we are all to some extent still entombed. Modern institutions, he insists, are melancholic and "hypochondrial." Employing a vivid and unforgettable metaphor, Baudrillard (1990a, 11) suggests that such institutions survive only by managing and ingesting "their own dead organs."

Baudrillard's outlook is fanciful and overstated but does perhaps help explain how and why "postmodern culture" emerged. It implies that the spectacle-commodity economy reflects the slow demise (or at least the steady marginalization) of rationalized, routinized, differentiated practices and their replacement with open-ended versions of symbolic exchange based on sumptuary practices. Postmodernism, in short, expresses the replacement of a rationalized, mastered cosmos with an "order of fatality" that is refreshingly indifferent to everything for which Weberian rationalization or Marxian Enlightenment once stood.

Like Lyotard, then, Baudrillard does not mourn the end of the modern era. As a post-Marxist, he nevertheless retains a modicum of nostalgia for the heroic emancipatory narrative that died around 1968, at the end of the postwar period. Baudrillard is not the only one who feels nostalgic about the end of what historian Eric Hobsbawm (1994) has called the "short twentieth century" (the period from 1914 to 1991). As World War II recedes from memory, each anniversary of the "victory to save democracy" (thirtieth, fortieth, fiftieth) becomes increasingly more impassioned—particularly within those spaces (Britain?) most affected by postmodernism. The resulting spectacles eerily invoke Vaneigem's (1994, 90) prediction, made thirty years ago, that the "Nation" would soon become "no more than a few thousand war veterans."

As Baudrillard (1994, 74) observes, "It is because we are moving further and further away from our history that we are avid for signs of the past, not, by any means, in order to resuscitate them, but to fill up the empty space of our memories." Solidarity and community in what Habermas calls "Old Europe" can be invoked now only through pseudo-festivals such as the Olympics or the 1989 Bicentennial Celebration of the French Revolution, which the "socialist" French government put together in a desperate and much-ridiculed effort to show that there was still some connection between it and revolutionary passions long since throttled. From Baudrillard's (1987b) perspective, the functionaries responsible for this ghastly spectacle have about the same relationship to the event they are commemorating as a vulture does to a carcass.

Resistance to Commodified Mass Culture?

At the beginning of the 1960s, Situationist Raoul Vaneigem (1994, 110–111) declared: "Humanity has never been short of justifications for giving up what is human. . . . With what passivity, what inertia, we can accept living or acting for some *thing*—'thing' being the operative word, a word whose dead weight always seems to carry the day." Vaneigem's dream was that modern humans might yet learn how "to live without dead time." In the early 1960s, he still had some hope. As he (1994, 111, 110) stirringly declared in *The Revolution of Everyday Life* (written from 1963 to 1965): "Thousands of workers around the world are downing tools or picking up guns. . . . Revolution is made everyday despite, and in opposition to, the specialists of revolution. . . . These movements are carnivals in which the individual life celebrates its unification with a regenerated society."

With Baudrillard, however, all hope lies crushed. Not only is there no longer any basis for opposition to "spectacular" consumption (Baudrillard 1983a, 44), but also such opposition in any case will immediately be recuperated by a system that subverts high seriousness as it commodifies new pleasures. Yet in a somewhat twisted sense, Baudrillard does manage to see some good in consumer capitalism. Admittedly, consumerism will never undermine or even slow the circuit of capital described by Marx (1967b) in the second volume of *Capital*. Nonetheless, as consumerism encourages the "hyperconformity" of mindless expenditure, it does allow us to escape the "filthy tub" of "pleasurable business" and "dignified labor" that Vaneigem sarcastically described. Baudrillard (1983a, 46) thus gives two cheers for the refreshingly nihilistic ethic of the postmodern mass: "You want us to consume—O.K., let's consume always more, and anything whatsoever; for any useless and absurd purpose."

Like Debord, Baudrillard (1983a, 27) sees that spectacularization emerged at the point where it became necessary for capital to produce not goods but "consumers, to produce demand." Yet Baudrillard welcomes "hyperconformity"—largely because he sees it as the only chance the masses have to turn the spectacle against itself. Baudrillard seems to have persuaded himself that as American popular culture broadens "useless" symbolic exchange, it invokes, in Charles Levin's (1981, 21) words, "a world before Weber's disenchantment and the coming of the white man." Perhaps, then, we can see why Baudrillard (1988a, 7) whimsically calls America "the only remaining primitive society," the "primitive society of the future." With the possible exception of Foucault, who spent many happy months exploring the S/M bars and gay bathhouses of San Francisco before his untimely death in 1984 (see Miller 1993), Baudrillard is probably the first French intellectual who claims to prefer this country to his own. (The claim is not meant to be taken seriously.)

Besides arguing that consumer capitalism is undermining rationalized commodity exchange, Baudrillard also suggests that "postmodern" tendencies are destroying the very basis for power. In the 1940s and 1950s, American corporate power and American popular culture (and, as we have seen, the CIA) helped finish off modernism. According to Baudrillard (1988a, 8), the sights have been raised and the cross-hairs are now forming on "Historical Reason, Political Reason, Cultural Reason, Revolutionary Reason," the "Reason of the Social." Guy Debord observed in 1989 (1991, 20) that "once the running of a State involves a permanent and massive shortage of historical knowledge, that State can no longer be led strategically." Pursuing this same line of thought, Baudrillard links the rise of postmodern culture with the waning leverage of the modern political. As he (1983a, 9–10) emphasizes, both the "conservative" and "radical" version of the project of modernity did at least try "to keep the masses *within reason*"; both versions had "an imperative to produce meaning that takes the form of the constantly repeated imperative to moralize information, to better socialize, to raise the cultural level of the masses, etc."

In the past, "historical knowledge" attempted to produce a reasoning and reasonable political constituency. Today, however, the hyperconforming masses "scandalously resist this imperative of rational communication" (Baudrillard 1983a, 10). Fascinated by scandal, corruption, and decay (and wanting only more of the same), they are beyond redemption. As Baudrillard (1990b, 65) happily observes, the postmodern masses are completely out of control; "voyeurs without illusion" mindlessly absorbed in the minutiae of the O. J. trial (or whatever happens to be the spectacle of the week), they are "resistant to all pedagogies, to all socialist education." No longer Durkheim's "mirror of the social," they are what shattered this mirror (Baudrillard 1983a, 9). Baudrillard (5) notes that programs of political repair are unlikely to appear today, for "there is no longer any social signified to give force to a political signifier." Modern, radical "politics" centered on the hope that humans could plan a "subversion and dislocation of the social" (Laclau 1990, 61). Yet for Baudrillard, such a measurable (and hence reformable) "social" is increasingly difficult to locate. Under the circumstances, we should not be surprised that modern politics is coming apart at the seams.

As far as Baudrillard is concerned, consumer culture is so all-encompassing, so detached from material and earthly contact, and so immune to any kind of critique that all we can do now is encourage it to gag on its own vomit. As he (1984b, 39) makes plain, "If being nihilist is to take, to the unendurable limit of the hegemonic system, this radical act of derision and violence, this challenge which the system is summoned to respond to by its own death, then I am a terrorist and a nihilist in theory as others are through arms." If Baudrillard has a coherent picture of "postmodern America" (and a coherent picture of how postmodernism might be resisted), this is it.

Fex Urbis, Lex Sociologis

Baudrillard (1983a, 4) agrees with Durkheim that sociology was the "mirror" of the social and of its "vicissitudes," and he acknowledges, moreover, that sociology "survives only on the positive and definitive hypothesis of the social." Yet if the organized "social" is disappearing—erased in the excesses of the mindless spectacle—the scope for the kind of knowledge Durkheim once envisioned must now be quite limited. Whereas Durkheim believed that a civilized modernity could be guided, shaped, and redeemed by the reflexive project of sociology, Baudrillard understands that because modern forms of rationalization conspired from their very beginnings to deny us our being as humans, it was always a fallacy to insist that modernity would be "humanized" one day.

According to Baudrillard (1983a, 67), the "social" that sociology addressed had "only an ephemeral existence, in the narrow gap between the symbolic formations and our 'society' where it is dying." Like Foucault, Baudrillard argues that sociology could flourish only during the brief period that produced subjects who were prepped to believe that their social environment could be "humanized." As we now can recognize, Weber was right and Durkheim was wrong: Classical sociology only reinforced but did not revivify the desiccated and disenchanted (and increasingly marginalized) residues of a dying social. While critical sociology promised to reform modernity, positivistic sociology dutifully measured and thereby normalized and solidified modernity's "excremental remainders." Today, however, sociology is losing its grip. As the crisis deepens, dead institutions pile up on one side of the equation and superannuated sociologists characteristically unable to explain even their own sorry existence jam up on the other. Under the circumstances, it is hardly surprising that a discipline that promised so much during its "classical era" has since become so banal, so fragmented, so disoriented, and so pointless.

Few western intellectuals have yet learned to adjust to these changes. The increasingly irrelevant humanists are still trying to "humanize" their social environment, still demonizing mass media and insisting that they "distort" or "conceal" the truth. Yet as Baudrillard (1983a, 105) insists, instead of being "on the side of power" in manipulating the masses, the media are really "on the side of the masses in the liquidation of meaning." The media have become so promiscuously nondiscriminatory, so mindlessly sensationalistic, so attuned to spectacularization, that only an idiot could still believe they still respond to truth in some sense, or understand, let alone shape, Debord's "historical knowledge." Yet if the humanists are threatened, so, too, according to Baudrillard, are the positivists. The problem they face is that the masses are no longer tractable as socially defined objects: They are no longer "a referent because they no longer belong to the order of representation. They don't express themselves, they are surveyed. They don't reflect upon themselves, they are tested" (1983a, 20). They are, in other words, merely an echo of whatever talk show or survey is used to locate them.

Baudrillard thus does offer some kind of an explanation (overstated though it may be) of the fix in which sociology finds itself. Active sociologists tend to fall into one of two main groups, neither of which wants much to do with the other. In one corner we find the would-be civic reformers and moralists: the Marxist-puritans; the liberal humanists; the multiculturalists; the professionally affronted First World feminists; the loony, intense, badge-covered activists; and all the other outmoded nuisances. In the other we see the missing band of surveyors: the quants and number crunchers who have long forgotten why they were once put to work but who, like Sisyphus, labor unendingly.

Because the masses are immune to their blandishments, the professional do-gooders experience permanent frustration. In a desperate attempt to recoup some leverage over those who "have no history themselves, no meaning, no consciousness, no desire" (Baudrillard 1986, 20), these reforming busybodies encourage and define increasingly more implausible versions of victimhood. Yet life is no more rewarding for the plodding statisticians who ritualistically prolong the circularity of sociological research as they measure and objectify the "residues" of a dead modern (Baudrillard 1983a, 31ff). At the end of the twentieth century, sociologists, it seems, have little left to do and can find fewer and fewer humans with whom to do it.

Baudrillard and the Postmodernism Industry

Because few English-speaking sociologists know much about Bataille, Nietzsche, the radical versions of poststructuralism, the dadaists, the surrealists, the 1968ers, or the Collège de Sociologie, it was easy for them to conclude that Baudrillard was the first to break with the classical traditions of modernity and offer deep new "postmodern" insights about a distinctly overripe and fin-de-millennium America. Yet few French theorists would find much about which to be startled in Baudrillard's musings. Foucault, for instance, refused to acknowledge the importance of Baudrillard's existence, even though Baudrillard unsuccessfully tried to get a rise out of him on more than one occasion.

Baudrillard's pronouncements about "postmodernism" (which are few and far between) are ambivalent and dishonest. On the one hand, he has claimed (seductively, of course) that he is not a postmodernist (see Gane 1990). Certainly, he has shown no interest in responding to the careful critique of his work that American neo-Marxists such as Kellner have developed (see Kellner 1989; Best and Kellner 1991). These studies bore Baudrillard; they are too serious. On the other hand, Baudrillard has been more than willing to play the star at American festivals of postmodernism (see Stearns and Chaloupka 1992; Bennahum 1997), where those at the cutting edge of theory can bask in his reflected glory and enjoy his musings about a world that intellectuals can only approach ironically.

In a sense, however, Baudrillard is an odd sort of creature to be patronized by American liberals. Many seem not to have noticed that the Poster Boy of the Postmodernism Industry is not a big supporter of humanism, "soft feminism," "liberal Marxism," or "green politics." For Baudrillard, such orientations are "enfeebled ideologies" suitable only for American "yuppies" (Gane 1990, 323). Like most really important intellectuals, Baudrillard has never found it necessary to respond to those who have made out of him what they want. Nonetheless, he (1994, 24) has mused in passing on "the suicidal compulsion of certain members of the cultural and intellectual elite to exalt thinkers . . . [like] Nietzsche and Bataille . . . who have only scorn for that elite and are its living condemnation."

In recent years, Baudrillard has managed to become the drag queen of the postmodern Left—a living embodiment of Debord's (1994, 143) worse nightmare, which was that "the critical concept of the spectacle" would in the hands of the "pro-situs" (compliant) intellectual become "just another empty formula of sociologico-political rhetoric . . . so serving to buttress the spectacular system itself."[5] In the last decade, Baudrillard's main career interest has not surprisingly centered on his own notoriety (and hence his marketability). The effort has born fruit. As Mike Gane (1993, ix) notes, Baudrillard has now become one of "the leading half-dozen French intellectuals in terms of citations and translations."

In this regard, the contrast between Baudrillard—"a sharp-shooting Lone Ranger of the post-Marxist left," as the *New York Times* explained to its readers (Markham 1988)—and Debord, who died in obscurity, is revealing. In a compelling study of the Situationist International, Sadie Plant (1992, 165) notes that although Baudrillard remained "engaged with situationist theory all his life,"[6] his "postmodern" phase "marks . . . the complete inversion" of the original Situationist attempt to show "that struggles against alienation would reveal a new world of immediacy and participation." In short, unlike Debord, who anticipated most of Baudrillard's critique of mass-mediated society, Baudrillard has adjusted quite comfortably to the "spectacle's own account of itself" (169).

Baudrillard, in brief, must be regarded as a jester: While he expresses the age in thought, he cannot explain it. In failing to grasp that he is a clever ironist and *not* a critical or even a very serious theorist, many Americans have managed only to confirm Baudrillard's view of them. Doug Kellner, for instance, has perhaps not entirely recognized that it is not only pointless but also counterproductive to moralize about Baudrillard's calculated excesses. By accusing him of "ecstatic chauvinism" and by pointing out that "regressive metaphysics is connected all too often with retrograde social attitudes," Kellner (1989, 171) has managed only to pump the bladder on the end of Baudrillard's stick. To list Baudrillard's numerous "provocations" against leftists and feminists (Kellner 1989, 122–152) or to accuse him of being "dangerous" (Callinicos 1989; Norris 1992) or being a man who launched a "rabid attack" on feminism (see Gallop 1987) only plays into the jester's game. By the same token, it is quite wrong to describe Baudrillard as the instigator of "a postmodern theory" (Kellner 1988, 242; 1989, 94ff), a "postmodern social theory" (Ritzer 1997, 1ff), or a "sociology of postmodernity" (Best 1994b, 40).[7] And it is, of course, quite amazingly beside the point to accuse the jester of writing books that are "totally outrageous to a liberal humanist sensibility," as one feminist complained recently (see Gallop 1987, 111).

Like the Great Communicator, Baudrillard may reflect the times, but it is difficult to see anything novel in his description of our predicament. It is not, for instance, particularly original to suggest that the arrival of mass society heralds the demise of Enlightenment hopes or to claim that that the dominant order has become so all-encompassing that all opposition to it is captured. At the end of the day, then (and after much tomfoolery), Chief Inspector Baudrillard rounds up just the usual suspects. As the "old leftist" Stanley Aronowitz (1988, 53) has noted, these turn out to be "consumer society, technology," and "the absence of a public in which critical debate about important issues can take place."

Nevertheless, even though Baudrillard is a jester, he manages not to be a complete fool. As Aronowitz (1988, 49–50) notes, Baudrillard's efforts to link a strategy of political denial with the emergence of "consumer society," together with his emphasis on the "withdrawal of the masses from participation in the sham of parliamentary democracy," identifies a form of "political terrorism" that is likely to be "more damaging than any deed against the symbols of hierarchical power, for it deprives global capitalism of the legitimacy" it perhaps still craves. According to Aronowitz (53), Baudrillard's theoretical efforts bear "the ineradicable stamp of Critical Theory." This is a trifle overstretched, however, for, like most contemporary intellectuals, Baudrillard is more a casualty than a critic of postmodernity. As the jester himself (1984a, 24, 25) observes, there is little left to do in a "deconstructed" and "destroyed" universe save "play with the pieces." All that is left is "pleasure in the irony of things, in the game of things." All that remains is "to reach a point where one can live with what is left."

A Requiem for Baudrillard

Baudrillard's "postmodernism" (which is more an invention of Baudrillard's American fans than of the jester) is a contemporary recuperation of the antimodern, antistructuralist, anti-Durkheimian critique developed earlier by poststructuralists such as Bataille and Foucault. In the middle third of this century, some intellectuals (e.g., members of the Collège de Sociologie, the Situationists, some poststructuralists) did try to critique some of the deadening impulse of modernity. Baudrillard, however, manages to get about as close to critical theory as Oprah Winfrey or the artist formally known as Prince. He seems to have turned himself into the living instantiation of Plant's (1992, 150) description of "postmodern philosophers" as "sold-out situationists who wander without purpose, observing recuperations with a mild and dispassionate interest and enjoying the superficial glitter of a spectacular life."

In the decade after 1968, Baudrillard did manage to produce a radical critique of the sign. In the last ten to fifteen years, however, he has luxuriated in (and profited from) his insistent claim that popular or consumer culture has now realized many of the nihilistic tendencies that Lefebvre and the other dadaists first recognized were immanent in modernity's trajectory. If we want to understand (but not necessarily fix) postmodernity as a historical phenomenon, we must leave the jester to his devices and return to Habermas.

The Counterdiscourse of Modernity: Habermas Versus the Post- and Antimodernists

According to Habermas (1981a; 1987a, 238–293), the "New Critique of Reason" developed by French "postmodernists" and poststructualists such as Bataille, Baudrillard, Lyotard, and Foucault aims to suppress a "200-year-old counterdiscourse inherent in modernity itself" (1987a, 302). Because Habermas believes that the two promises of modernity need to be revitalized, not abandoned, he reacts quite negatively to Bataille, Foucault, and Baudrillard—not because they are "*post*modern" but because, he believes, they are "neoconservative" and *anti*modern.

As an old-fashioned German intellectual, Habermas (perhaps the most influential sociological theorist of the 1970s and 1980s) has valiantly tried to hold the fort for what he rather too preciously has described as "old European human dignity" (1975, 143). Unlike Vaneigem (1994, 68), Habermas prefers not to believe that "the Communards went down fighting so that you too could qualify for a Caribbean cruise." Yet according to Bauman (1987), Habermas is the classic "intellectual-as-legislator" who wants to develop the correct blueprint for a better society. For Bauman, the problem with people such as Habermas is that they have outlived the world for which they were intended.

Nonetheless, for the following reasons we must take Theodor Adorno's heir seriously:

1. More than any other theorist, Habermas has helped sociologists grasp both the achievements and the limitations of classical theories of modernity (specifically, Marx's and Weber's).
2. Although, like Baudrillard, Habermas realizes that sociology in its current form (i.e., modernity's self-understanding) has deadended, he believes that, like modernity, this worthy project can still be resuscitated.
3. Because he has attempted a critical reconstruction of Marx, Weber, and Parsons against the backdrop of late modernity, Habermas is well situated to offer an alternative (should one exist) to the postmodernist New Critique of Reason he has condemned so emphatically. As mentioned earlier, Habermas (1983) believes that the rational completion of "the project of modernity" must involve not merely the improvement and refinement of instrumental and technical practices but also the advancement of humankind's moral and spiritual capacities.

A Theory of Communicative Action

In the early 1980s, Habermas incorporated elements from Parsonsian structural functionalism into his analysis of crisis regulation in advanced capitalism. In these works he drew on Parsons's argument that the main feature of societal modernization is the functional differentiation of social institutions.

According to Parsons, functional differentiation and specialization take place in terms of four dimensions—*a*daptation, *g*oal orientation, *i*ntegration, and the *l*atency function of pattern maintenance. (These are known as the AGIL dimensions.) At the level of the social system, the economic subsystem is adaptive, the political subsystem is goal oriented, and the societal community is integrative. The fiduciary subsystem is concerned with pattern maintenance or with the latent function of establishing the ultimate grounds for meaning (see Figure 2.1). In a modern society none of these four subsystems is wholly autonomous; like organs in a body, each depends on inputs from all the other subsystems.

In premodern civilizations the subsystems are only partially differentiated, if at all. Premodern market relations, for instance, are not economically differentiated; rather, they are embedded in a naturelike lifeworld of customary, taken-for-granted obligation, and trading and moneylending are strictly curtailed and circumscribed by custom. In a similar fashion, the premodern political order is not differentiated from the system that distributes status. The polity is accordingly embedded in the societal community, and power cannot be separated from prestige

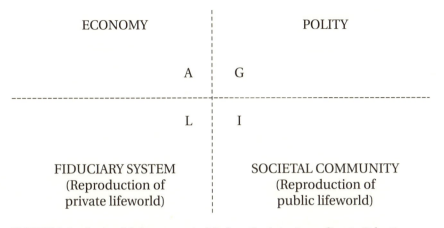

FIGURE 2.1   Societal Subsystems in Modern Society, According to Talcott
Parsons

Note: The terms in parentheses are Habermas's, not Parsons's.

or social honor. By contrast, law in modern, constitutional societies is
differentiated from political domination and (in principle at least) is not
reducible to mere power plays.

In modern highly differentiated society the problems of exchange
among the economy, polity, societal community, and fiduciary subsystems become increasingly complex. Realizing this, Parsons (1969)
turned his attention to the "media of exchange" among such subsystems. In his terms, the economy generates *money;* the polity, *power;* the
societal community, *influence;* and the fiduciary subsystem, *value commitment* (see Figure 2.2).[8] For Habermas (1984, 275), "'influence' can be
more or less translated as 'prestige' or 'reputation'"; "'value-commit-
ment' as 'moral authority.'"

In the modern world, the economy and the polity organize strategic
action: They help "steer" or manage the social system instrumentally
through the use of media that are objective and impersonal. By contrast,
the lifeworld of meaning, commitment, and expression is, as we have
seen, "society" that is grounded intersubjectively or communicatively.
Reconciling Habermas with Parsons, we thus have

1. A system that orchestrates instrumental or purposive-rational
    action, which is subdivided into (A) the economy, where action
    is mediated by *money;* and (G) the polity, including the state,
    where action is mediated by *power.*

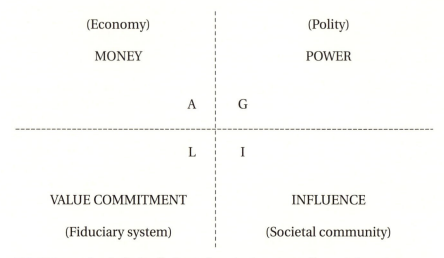

FIGURE 2.2   Symbolic Media in Modern Society, According to Talcott Parsons

2. A lifeworld of communicative interaction containing (I) the societal community, or public lifeworld, generating *normative expectations;* and (L) the fiduciary subsystem, or private lifeworld, generating *moral authority.*[9]

Unlike Parsons, who assumed that modern societies maintained a happy balance among the media of money, power, prestige, and moral authority, Habermas recognizes that modern capitalist societies (1) one-sidedly develop purposive-rational orientations, (2) reduce steering decisions to mere technical criteria, and (3) deny the lifeworld the relative autonomy it must realize if it is to maintain some kind of integrity. As a result, the major tectonic fracture in modern societies is between a weakly developed and increasingly deformed lifeworld of communicative interaction that cannot develop according to its own internal dynamics and a well-developed system of control and manipulation that uses money and power to reproduce structures of domination within the social system.

Habermas and Postmodernity

Habermas helps show how postmodernization is linked with (1) a confluence or dedifferentiation of public and private lifeworlds and (2) a further colonization of the lifeworld, chiefly by money. Whereas dedifferentiation (i.e., the fusion of a code of personal morality with the demands that others make of us) represents a qualitative break from the modern, the colonization of the lifeworld, culminating in the commodified aestheticization of lifestyle, involves an acceleration of tendencies that have been in existence for more than two centuries.

The Dedifferentiation of Public and Private Lifeworlds. Notwithstanding the accusations of some of his critics, Habermas has never claimed that the lifeworld can be made transparently self-reflective. Instead, he acknowledges that the lifeworld is always prereflexive to some extent: It "stands behind the back of each participant" supporting the whole "process of communication" (Habermas in Honneth, Knödler-Bunte, and Widmann 1981, 16; Habermas 1984, 334–337). The lifeworld thus provides a historically located culturally contextual resource of meaning that supplies the historical grist for the philosophical mill of critical self-reflection. Yet if we try to dissect the lifeworld or "take it up piece by piece," it "dissolves and disappears before our eyes" (Habermas in Honneth et al. 1981, 16). How, then, could we make the lifeworld more reasonable—more critically self-reflective—without destroying it in the very process?

One historic solution has been the enhanced differentiation of public and private life spheres in the action domain of the individual subject. The public lifeworld or public sphere (*Öffentlichkeit*) can be defined as that which establishes "loyalty" or generalized expectations about actors' duties and obligations to the societal community taken as a whole (Habermas 1984, 274ff). The public lifeworld accordingly locates and institutionalizes the "internalization of individual and collective identities and solidarities" (such as those of national identity) that are overarching in some sense (Schluchter 1981, 34). In contrast, the private lifeworld (which historically was located in the domestic or familial sphere) defines the moral grounds that enable the individuated actor to develop a sense of "personal integrity" (Habermas 1984, 274ff). The morally self-critical individual is thus enabled to define "core notions of justice and equity" that transcend (1) the influence of immediate solidarities (e.g., friends at high school, comrades in a combat unit, colleagues at work) and (2) the "system" demands of money and power (Schluchter 1981, 37ff).

In sum, the differentiation of public and private life spheres allows individuals to exercise individuated "moral leadership" (personal integrity) and to produce "authoritative admonitions" and "justifications for obligations" that transcend self-interest or particularistic solidarities (Habermas 1987b, 274). Once public and private life spheres are differentiated, individuals discover the courage of their own convictions; they are given access to superordinate moral standards that allow them to challenge the influence of the group and occasionally to resist the demands of money and power.

A key point to grasp here is that "core notions of justice and equity" do not well up from "within" the person. Because they *create* the individual, they do not reflect the mysterious working of a "true self" that the individual self-produced. Early modern philosophers such as Kant explained the presence of moral reason by assuming that it was implanted by God. Bracketing this intriguing possibility, I wish to suggest that individuated moral reason emerges from the aforementioned differentiation of public and private lifeworlds (a structural process that individuals themselves cannot control).[10] Once such differentiation occurs, a societal community can supply a publicly mediated ethical apparatus that can be used by diverse sets of individuals. As Wolfgang Schluchter (1981, 36) has pointed out, such a differentiation provides the subject with quasi-transcendental ethical meanings (determined by the public lifeworld) that can be used selectively and freely by the individual.[11] One consequence of a differentiation between private and public lifeworlds is that although morally committed individuals can be (and often are) good citizens, they do not have to obey public authority unthinkingly. They grasp, for instance, that, depending on the circumstances, patriotism can be either a virtue and a social good or (more likely in the present) a sign of moral retardation.

As we see in more detail later, postmodernity is indeed associated with a dedifferentiation or fusion of public and private life spheres, which has the effect of collapsing what used to be specific to each. Once this dedifferentiation has occurred, the transcendent sense of humanity, the ethical sense of commitment to a well-defined societal community (e.g., the nation), and the sense of personal moral integrity all begin to disappear. For those who consequently lose their bearings, the cultural "fixes" offered by evangelical Christianity or the various kinds of postmodern "support" groups will prove an irresistible attraction.

The "Colonization" of the Lifeworld.   According to Habermas, one of the constitutive features of modernization is that system imperatives constantly attempt to "colonize" the lifeworld. Money and power, in other words, distort communicative interaction, and social action concentrates so much on the technical, instrumentalist exigencies associated with the economy and with power plays that a lifeworld that is supposed to develop according to its own principles begins to wither on the vine. For Habermas (1987b, 392–392), the "new politics" (i.e., the "new social movements" [NSMs]) of the post-1968 period dealing with "the quality of life, equal rights, individual self-realization, participation and human rights" are a reactive response to the problems caused by such "internal colonization."

In brief, Habermas (1984, 183) believes that modern administration and the modern capitalist economy have expanded "at the expense of other domains of life that are structurally disposed to moral-practical and expressive forms of rationality." If this has indeed occurred, then the progressive and rational "completion of the project of modernity" (which requires, as it were, a vigorous movement of "decolonization") can move forward only when humans understand that the enhancement of system imperatives and the refinement of the lifeworld are *both* important for the development of human potential; technological developments (such as TV or computers) are not merely instrumental advances but can also improve modes of communicative interaction (1987a, 322); and the "rationalization" of the lifeworld means making it more just, not making it more effectively instrumentalist. Making the lifeworld more just necessitates the increased reflexivity of culture, the enhancement of critical consciousness, the development of autonomous (free) will formation, and the heightened (moral) individuation of subjects.

A concrete example of how the lifeworld has been colonized would perhaps help clarify matters. Let us briefly examine how television in this country has become an instrument that enables money to pervert the public sphere. One illustration is Cable Network News (CNN).

Network TV programs are typically aimed at the largest possible aggregate of viewers in order to optimize the use and value of airtime. As a result, the form and content of programming are structured by the need to mediate a profitable relationship between the viewing audience and the corporations that pay for the attention TV reliably delivers. The head of U.S. Steel once explained that the business of his corporation was not (as many assumed) to produce steel but to produce steel profitably.[12] By the same token, the purpose of television is not to entertain but to entertain profitably. Simply put, if a program sells, it's right, and the more it sells, the better it is. In these terms, television today (like everything else) is structured in terms of its realization as value (Jhally 1990).

Of course, CNN purports to operate journalistically. Yet its operations are even more penetrated by the logic of commodity exchange than are those of the networks that overtly specialize in entertainment. CNN uses state-of-the-art technology to realize value much more efficiently than its competitors. In addition, it has a flexible workforce and gets a highly competitive return on capital investment, much of which is in use around the clock. In addition, CNN successfully reduces "the news" to a set of images that can be franchised quickly and cheaply. By providing "round-the-clock" news, CNN has successfully eliminated the old, slow, daily cycle of news. Whereas the readers of daily newspapers get news every twenty-four hours, CNN subjects its viewers to instant updates and perpetual half-hour newsprograms that speed up the news cycle 4800 percent. Because the network *wants* to be thought of as a "hi-tech" news-gathering organization that "covers the globe," CNN does not so much provide substance and content as seek to sell the spectacle-commodity at a competitive rate of speed. CNN has accordingly managed to change the definition of news from "something that is reported and maybe even discussed" to "something shown live on worldwide TV." In essence, CNN has turned commodity journalism into a form where "news" becomes those commodified images and sound bites that can be digested most easily and circulated most rapidly.[13]

According to Habermas (1989b), the emergence of modern journalism in the eighteenth century was a critically important "evolutionary advance" because it helped develop a public sphere within which collective deliberation and critical self-reflection could take place. Modern newspapers provided a public record of events ("All the News That's Fit to Print," as the *New York Times* still promises) that allowed a societal community to locate itself by reference to collectively shared historical knowledge. In short, the development of a modern "public" arose with, and was structured by, the exigencies of written debate, which was facilitated by the technological development of print media. Notwithstanding the inverted reasoning of the U.S. Bill of Rights (see Marx 1970, 47ff), the modern, public sphere thus *preceded,* rather than followed, the development of the modern individual.

From Habermas's perspective, however, McOperations such as CNN, or McNewspapers such as *USA Today,* do not constitute much of an advance. If anything, they are a step backward. Even though CNN has technical facilities that were undreamed of a generation ago, the network does not use technology to improve journalism or develop a public lifeworld of informed and involved citizens. Instead, like any other media outlet, it optimizes instrumental effectiveness. The fact that CNN pretends to be primarily a news-gathering business and has some well-intentioned and intelligent people working for it is quite incidental to the central determining fact, which is that its operations are mediated by money in pursuit of profit.

The Limitation of Habermas's Modernist Critique

One obvious difficulty with Habermas's position is that what the lifeworld would look like if it were given a free hand to develop autonomously "according to its own dynamic" is not very clear. We know what a world that is dominated by money and power looks like because we see it when we get out of bed every morning, but the more "balanced" world that Habermas advocates is much more difficult to comprehend. Nevertheless, even if he has not shown us how to escape our current predicament, Habermas has, I think, drawn attention to what it entails.

Habermas's critical understanding of the tensions and contradictions of late modernity can help us understand why the culture of postmodernism has flowed through certain channels and dominated certain sites. Because modernity has "uncoupled" steering subsystems from the lifeworld (i.e., allowed money and power to operate as they will), contemporary subjects are confronted with massively impersonal steering media that appear to be immune from rational recall. The effect of all this is to demoralize the subject and to encourage the continuing proliferation of nonrational modes of behavior divorced from any kind of moral scrutiny.

In some ways Habermas's description of our predicament complements Baudrillard's picture of "postmodern society" and also serves to validate some poststructuralist claims. For instance, Habermas (1984, 44ff) points out—correctly, I think—that pre- (and presumably post-) modern worldviews largely result from the subject's inability to separate signifier from referent. If so, we can begin to understand why contemporary subjects find it so difficult to experience the kind of social and cultural objectifications that modern, rationalized, differentiated culture once helped generate.

If Habermas's observations are correct—and if, as previously suggested, postmodernity is associated with dedifferentiation—we should not be surprised that Durkheim's picture of the individual as something "distanced" from society makes considerably less sense now than it did three generations ago. Moreover, we can note something of a contradiction in Habermas's sociology. On the one hand, Habermas acknowledges that modernity must stabilize itself on the basis of the many divisions it has wrought. On the other, he accepts that many of the differentiating tendencies of modernity are stalled and are perhaps reversible. Habermas earnestly believes that "the project of modernity" can be jump-started one day, but on the basis of present trajectories there seems little basis for optimism.

Unlike Baudrillard, however, Habermas does help us understand something of what postmodernity involves and why it arose. He does not reduce his writings to description of unmediated cultural processes that appear to have a dynamic all their own. Yet because he cannot identify a revolutionary subject capable of opposing what he effectively decries, Habermas is unfortunately unable to suggest a practical solution to the "deformations" he so effectively describes.

Marx: Modernity as a "Mirror of Production"

As the postwar period drew to an end (and with it all hope of a proletarian revolution in the West), Marxism underwent an ironic metamorphosis, becoming, in the humanities and social sciences at least, a "major theoretical orientation." Yet Marxism's institutionalization in the academy did not stem from radical protest or from meaningful political struggle. Rather, it occurred because U.S. scholars used institutional authority to turn Marxism itself into a "classical" mode of inquiry. At a time when modernism was turned into a propaganda weapon against the "first workers' state," Marxism, too, began to be emptied of its older, subversive power. Once it became part of the accepted canon, Marxism's politically incorrect side was quickly abandoned. Among other things, this included Marxism-Leninism, the idea that politics should serve oppressed workers, not the privileged, and the particularly annoying insistence that the world needs changing more than it needs new kinds of theory.

In the 1940s and 1950s, introductory sociology texts in this country ignored Marx entirely or dismissed him and his sentiments in a few words. By the late 1970s, however, Marx was safely interred in the mausoleum of social thought, and American college professors were explaining to increasingly disoriented adolescents that he was, in fact, one of only two or three Great Thinkers who had helped us develop a critical understanding of what was now described as our "modern" condition. So in a strange turn of events, Marxist ideas gained a new lease on life as the emancipatory possibilities of the world Marx described were themselves blocked off—perhaps irretrievably. For Thomas Docherty (1993, 319), it seems as if the whole debate on postmodernism actually "stems from within the discourse of Marxism itself." But the "Marxism" that is part of this debate has become a description of something that did not happen; it marks an event that failed to occur. As Adorno (1973, 8) once noted, a philosophy that once seemed obsolete lives on because the moment to realize it was missed.

An Ironic Reversal

Marxism is not a positivistic science. To the extent that it claims to generate "objective laws" of history (as Soviet cadres used to claim), it relieves its followers of the obligation to think and becomes entirely sterile. Marx's own work constantly shuttled backward and forward between lofty philosophical principles and detailed observations, and many critics have noted an irresolvable tension in Marx's observations. On the one hand, Marx wanted to contribute to what he believed was the long-term project of humanity: a collective effort to learn from history and humanize the world. On the other, he planned to develop quite a specific, concrete, and empirical analysis of capitalism in its extant (nineteenth-century) form.

An acknowledgment of these two different kinds of orientations can help us separate what is dead from what is alive in historical materialism. What seems dead is Marx's vision of a future controlled by those who have realized modernity's emancipatory promises. What is still alive is (1) Marx's analysis of the circuit of capital, which is more determining than ever, and, more controversially, (2) Marx's claim that social domination is always at root a form of *class* domination. The shift from modernity to postmodernity is, I believe, an incremental shift from relatively concrete modes of class domination to something more abstract. Under postmodernity, class relations subdivide humans as well as societies; they create individuals who are both beneficiaries and victims of an exceedingly well-organized system of global exploitation.

As we now can see, what is finished in Marxism is what was most believed 150 years ago (by non-Marxists, too): the ardent faith that Humanity is a Universal Actor unable *not* to learn from history, the certain knowledge that although the path ahead will be difficult and the way bloody, Humanity will ultimately find its way forward. What is symmetrically most plausible today is what was *least* accepted 150 years ago (even by Marx): the fact that capital is not so much a progressive instrument as a blind, purposeless force destined to subvert, corrupt, and cynically degrade what high modernity most valued.

Marxism's Embeddedness in Modern (Classical) Political Economy

In *The Mirror of Production* (written long before Baudrillard became a darling of the American postmodern Left), Baudrillard (1975) claimed that Marx's categories of analysis were themselves mirrored by structures Marx claimed to have surpassed. Baudrillard points out in this work that Marxism reflected modernity *accurately*—not so much because Marxist theory is objective, ahistorical, or transcendental but because it is implicated in modernity by being a part of it.

Like other nineteenth-century models of political economy, classical Marxism treated the individual at core as an instrumental and rational entity. Thus, it unconsciously imported the metaphysical and psychologistic bases of an enlightened modernity into what was meant to be a transcendent (timeless) methodology of critical self-reflection. In essence, Marx took it for granted that the unyielding substratum of "human nature" determines a similarly unyielding, ahistoric, and fixed behavior that pivots on labor. Marx accordingly assumed (quite wrongly) that what sutures us to the world is the incorrigible requirement that we define ourselves through *production.*

Although Marx (1978, 226) did recognize that "all production is appropriation of nature on the part of an individual within and through a specific form of society," he nonetheless treated *the reproduction of the conditions of production* as fundamental to social life. Marx reached this conclusion because of his dubious philosophical anthropology: He just took it for granted that what made us most human was useful production, not, for example, wasteful expenditure. For Marx (1967a, 183–184), production "is human action with a view to the production of use-values, appropriation of natural substances to human requirements; it is the necessary condition for effecting exchange of matter between man and nature; it is the everlasting Nature-imposed condition of human existence, and therefore is independent of every social phase of that existence, or rather, is common to every such phase." As Marx (1978, 236) unambiguously asserted: "Production predominates not only over itself, in the antithetical definition of production, but over the other moments as well. The process always returns to production to begin anew. That exchange and consumption cannot be predominant is self-evident."[14]

Baudrillard (1975, 21–33; 1989), then, was on firm ground when he suggested that, like the other political economists of the modern era, Marx could not step outside a naturalistic and productivist narrative in order to justify what he had made internal to it. Marxist political economy is indeed a "mirror *of production*"; it was not itself immune to the fate that tends to befall "all critical concepts as soon as they claim any kind of explanatory power beyond the historical context that produced them" (Norris 1990, 170). Marxism, in short, is no exception to the rule enunciated by Foucault and others after 1968: It is a mistake to expect knowledge to legislate for any culture other than the one that produced it in the first place.

Marx and the Dialogue of Postmodernism

Marxism mistakenly assumed that Humanity would accumulate historical knowledge and (ultimately) develop the kind of individual envisioned by the Enlightenment. This has not yet occurred and seems less likely to occur year by year. What should we make of the fact that the "higher" type of individual envisioned by Enlightenment philosophers has not yet emerged? According to the poststructuralists, modernity was established on premises that were not only flawed but also oppressive. These antimoderns claimed that the human animal was intrinsically ill-equipped to develop the kind of world that modern intellectuals most wanted to see.

A counterview is presented by the "skeptical postmodernists" who are described in the following chapter. These assert what is in any case difficult to deny: There is nothing inevitable or preordained about the future. "History" is not mysterious; it is merely what humans have made for themselves.

Although both the affirmative postmodernists and the skeptical postmodernists are, in a sense, products of the 1960s, their involvement in, and memory of, that decade are quite different. For the affirmativists, the 1960s were a pivotal era between an older period of restricted opportunity and the current one, which, they believe, offers people like them more options, greater freedoms, and new and exciting possibilities. Like Baudrillard and Vaneigem, however, the skeptics tend to see the 1960s as the last period in which it was still possible to have hope.[15] Affirmativists and skeptics together explain the ambivalence of those intellectuals touched by postmodernism: What some valorize as "breakthrough," others stigmatize as "pathology" (Pfeil 1986, 127).

3 Postmodern Identity and Postmodern Political Mobilization

Affirmative Versus Skeptical Postmodernists

Affirmative postmodernists (or affirmativists) can be subdivided into "New Age" postmodernists or political activists (the "new postmodern liberals"). For the most part, New Agers are not "open to political action" (Rosenau 1992, 152). Arguing "that nothing 'out there' can be changed and that only personal transformation is worthwhile and fulfilling" (152–153), they favor circle dancing, drumming, t'ai chi, yoga, crystal massage, numerology, chanting, clowning, color healing, and so forth.

Unlike modern leftists, the new postmodern liberals are self-consciously "post-proletarian, post-industrial, post-socialist, post-Marxist, and post-distributional" (Luke 1989, 135). They accordingly show little interest in the labor movement, which, together with most other movements rooted in the past, they tend to dismiss as objectionably Stalinist, centralist, authoritarian, homophobic, patriarchal, ethnocentric, sexist, and heterosexist. Among other things, the affirmative postmodernists "raise consciousness," advance the politics of identity, and work with (or on) groups deemed marginal, vulnerable, or victimized. In short, they prefer "a politics of lifestyle" to a more generalized and "emancipatory" "politics of life chances" (Giddens 1991, 214). The postmodern liberals nonetheless maintain important career-boosting ties with the new social movements and the new academic programs.

The postmodern affirmativists are particularly interested in issues of gender and sexuality (see, for instance, Seidman and Nicholson 1995). Because sexuality is often regarded as "the ultimate postmodern discourse,"[1] queer theory and other postmodern forms of expression are plumbed in the attempt to replace "liberal moralism's" outmoded "binary logic of . . . vacillation" with "identities" that are "fluid, open to resignification and recontextualization" (Hennessy 1995, 272; Seidman

1994b). According to Martine Rothblatt (1995), it is time for the lifeworld to stop inflexibly "dividing humanity" into one of just two genders. Pursuing this same line of thought, Kate Bornstein—a male "transsexual lesbian whose female lover is becoming a man"—advocates not merely a subdivision of gender but a logic of mutilation. As s/he (1994, 3) coyly confesses: "Both my identity and fashion are based on collage. You know—a little bit from here, a little bit from there? Sort of a cut-and-paste thing."[2]

Unlike the affirmativists, who live quite happily amid the train wreck of modernity, skeptical postmodernists (or skeptics) are gloomily post-civilizational.[3] Unlike the affirmativists, the skeptics do not see how a politics of lifestyle can possibly avoid recuperation. Not surprisingly, the (mostly male) skeptics bemoan the fate of what Arthur Kroker, Marilouise Kroker, and David Cook (1989, 180) call "the old male cock." "Postmodernism," the Krokers and Cook (180) fear, will replace this once insistent digit with a drooping, wilted, "postmodern penis" signifying "sickness, disease and waste."

Whereas the affirmativists (who are disproportionately female, well educated, and white) exist both inside and outside the American system of higher education, the skeptics are largely confined within the academy—the familiar refuge of choice for all who have failed to accommodate themselves to existing social and economic relations. Viewing punk as probably the last intellectually coherent youth movement, the skeptics do not trust (or like) anyone under thirty. As far as they are concerned, postmodernism is "fragmentation, disintegration, malaise, meaninglessness, a vagueness or even absence of moral parameters and social chaos" (Rosenau 1992, 15). The skeptics, in short, resemble Robert Solomon's (1990, 284–285) observation that postmodernists are "a legion of disgruntled academics . . . who see in the accusations of postmodernism an expression of their own frustration and disappointment."

The skeptical postmodernists are paralyzed by a poignant conjunction of events. On the one hand, they can recognize that the creative destructiveness of capital exceeds even that which Karl Marx and Friedrich Engels (1974) described in *The Communist Manifesto*. On the other hand, the skeptical postmodernists believe that "Marxism is over" (Aronson 1995, 40–67). Yet as they can see, if Marxism *is* over, this is not because the evils Marxism opposes have vanished but because it no longer seems possible to hope for the kind of total social transformation that Marx and the Enlightenment once promised. As Ronald Aronson (1995, 41–42) put it in his touching "farewell" to Marx: Marxism may still be with us as theory, as critique, or as ideology, but it "no longer exists in the peculiar way it itself always claimed as decisive": as a *"project of analysis from capitalism to socialism."*

Unable to adjust to this sad turn of events, the skeptics look back with nostalgia and with bitterness on the squandering of the postwar dream. Many of them have concluded that contemporary western societies are no improvement on the miserable state of affairs that existed before the great "antifascist" struggle of the early 1940s. As far as they are concerned, the rise of the New Right in Britain and America, the abandonment of socialism in France, the reemergence of fascism in Italy, the annexation of eastern Europe by capital, the abandonment of unselfish collectivism in China, and the rise of anarchic criminality and civil war in the territories of the former Soviet Union have erased not merely the gains but also the historical memory of more than a century of working-class struggle and social-democratic gain.

In essence, the skeptics are mourning the end of what Bauman (1993, 128) has called the "'gardener' role" for intellectuals: the belief that intellectuals can mold the "pliability of human nature" in terms of the universal interest of humanity. As Bauman (128) points out: "From at least the seventeenth century, and well into the twentieth, the writing elite of Western Europe and its footholds on other continents considered its own way of life as a radical break in universal history" and took itself "as the reference point for the interpretation of the telos of history." Yet as he (1988, 220) crisply observes, "Nobody but the most rabid of diehards" still believes today "that the western mode of life . . . has more than a sporting chance of ever becoming universal." Given this, we can understand the anger, frustration, and grief of the skeptical postmodernists. As disappointed "Hegelian Marxists," they are unable to accept that culture is irredeemably "pluralistic," "not as a temporary state on the way to the true synthesis in communist society but as a permanent fate of mankind" (Münch 1994, 16).

"Post-Marxism" and the New Social Movements

Like most capitalist democracies in the 1960s, the United States was faced with significant outbreaks of domestic opposition. During the decade, organized protest drew in hundreds of thousands of young people who had expected something more from postwar affluence than the opportunity to risk death or dismemberment in a futile attempt to crush a Third World movement of national liberation.

Mass opposition to state policies largely disappeared with Richard Nixon's fraudulent "Vietnamization" of the war in Southeast Asia. But by 1974, U.S. political authorities were faced with a serious crisis of legitimation. In April 1975, a Lou Harris poll found that from 1966 to 1975 "confidence in the military . . . had dropped from 62 percent to 29 percent, in business from 55 percent to 18 percent, in both President and

Congress from 42 percent to 13 percent" (Zinn 1980, 544–545). According to a report prepared for the Trilateral Commission, the main problem facing the "private sector's Establishment," as the report nicely phrased it, was that "the democratic surge of the 1960's" had undermined people's willingness "to obey those whom they had previously considered superior to themselves in age, rank, status, expertise, character, or talents" (quoted in Zinn 1980, 547). In the words of this influential study (see Crozier et al., 1975), the real threat to America was a disturbing "excess of democracy" that had come to threaten existing forms of political domination (quoted in Zinn 1980, 548).

However, many of these "disturbing" trends turned out to be greatly exaggerated. Fortified in 1976 by the election of the Trilateralists' candidate, Jimmy Carter, most leftists abandoned militancy and the politics of confrontation and instead turned to local, more issue-oriented politicking. A watershed of sorts occurred in 1975 when several activists formed the Conference on Alternative State and Local Public Policies. This brought radicals together on an annual basis to discuss how they could agitate for change within the system. By the 1980s, only a few "fringe" leftist organizations were still insisting that nothing in America could change fundamentally until business and politics were transformed as a whole.

Postmodern Radical Democracy?

In 1985 the "post-" (and ex-) Marxists Ernesto Laclau and Chantal Mouffe published an influential work, *Hegemony and Socialist Strategy,* that addressed the new emphasis on decentralized and diversified forms of resistance. This text aimed to show how the "new social movements" and the new styles of affirmativist politicking could operate in a "post-Marxist" era. As Mouffe (1988, 32–33) explained, *Hegemony and Socialist Strategy* "pursues the 'unfulfilled project of modernity,' but, unlike Habermas, we believe that there is no longer a role to be played in this project by the epistemological perspective of the Enlightenment."

The "radical democracy" that Mouffe and Laclau favor does not see "the development of postmodern philosophy as a threat" but welcomes it "as an indispensable instrument in the accomplishment of its goals" (Mouffe 1988, 44). Rather than emphasize class or structure, "radical democracy" prefers to focus on "the existence of different forms of rationality" controlled by multiple discourses and multiple subject-positions (Laclau and Mouffe 1985, 38). According to Laclau (1993, 343), "postmodern freedom" means the reconciliation of the "dissolution of the myth of foundations" with the "historical validity" of numerous open-ended political projects. "Humankind, having always bowed to external forces—God, Nature, the necessary laws of History—can now at the threshold of postmodernity, consider itself for the first time the creator and constructor of its own history" (341).

A major problem with *Hegemony and Socialist Strategy*, however, was that it did not offer much of a yardstick against which the "progressiveness" of politics might be measured. If a radical democratic politics is not founded on the universalization of human interests (as Marx would expect), or based on an ethical a priori (as Habermas and other Marxist humanists would require), an "antifoundational framework" is likely to lead merely to the dispersal of struggle among a thousand competing and incommensurable political factions.

"Old" Versus "New" Social Movements

In the 1980s and 1990s, Laclau's and Mouffe's version of postmodern radical democracy has been pursued most vigorously by the affirmativist new social movements. In America, these focus on, among other things, women's rights, minority issues, environmental and green issues, vegetarianism, New Age philosophies, AIDS activism, child abuse, animal rights, nonsmokers' rights, and gay, lesbian, and transgender rights. The "unifying practice" of these movements (insofar as they have one) is "a rejection of European enlightenment and its attending parables of development and progress, in favor of a faith in the multiplicity of civilizations and cultural nationalisms" (McIntyre 1995, 456–457).

Whereas "old" (mostly workers') movements were located "within the polity" and were for the most part "formal" and "hierarchical" in organization (Scott 1990, 19), the new social movements (NSMs) are not class based (Offe 1985b; Inglehart 1990b) and do not claim to speak for the working class as a whole (Heller and Feher 1989; Cohen 1985). The NSMs eschew the old Leninist tactic of trying to subsume politics under a single focus (Kitchelt 1990; Müller-Rommel 1990). Because they do not claim "to handle all the public needs of their constituents" or try to seize control of public authority (Calhoun 1993a, 407, 398), the NSMs tend to blur the traditional distinction between a "social movement" and an "interest group" (Scott 1990, 26). Expressing "concerns that are more cultural than economic," and relying on new "knowledges" developed by new kinds of knowledge specialists (Seidman 1994), they aim to change "norms and values rather than productive and distributive relations" (Eyerman 1994, 707; Habermas 1981b). Their goal, in other words, "is the mobilization of civil society, not the seizure of power" (Feher and Heller 1983, 37).[4] In short, they seek "changes in values and lifestyle" and favor "direct action" and "cultural innovation" (Scott 1990, 19). Centered on "life politics," or the politics of lifestyle, the NSMs help collapse or dedifferentiate what used to be the familiar barrier between private and public life spheres.

Whereas "old" social movements followed a generalized emancipatory program that attempted to "shed the shackles of the past" and eliminate hierarchical structures of domination (Giddens 1991, 211), the NSMs take quite a different tack. Some, such as OUTRAGE or ACTUP, are relatively spontaneous and disorganized; others, such as GASP (Groups Against Smoking Pollution) or NAAFA (the National Association to Advance Fat Acceptance), ultimately become quite well organized. Although the NSMs try to get access to public resources, they are not revolutionary in outlook. Indeed, as they develop organizationally, they are more likely to cooperate with the state.

Instead of responding to the kinds of grievances and coalitions that emerge from within the domain of production, the NSMs rely either on "network" and "grassroots" modes of organization or on mass media to organize not classes but "status blocs" (Turner 1988). And because people can join and disengage from these blocs "as the political context and their personal circumstances change" (Dalton and Kuechler 1990, 12), the ensuing "political communities" do not express a "living" "cultural tradition" that developed "in an unplanned nature-like manner" within the lifeworld (Habermas 1975, 70). On the contrary, such imaginary communities (e.g., the "gay and lesbian community," the "black community") are manufactured and contrived, populated by people who have little in common except the illusion of being together.[5]

Because the most important features of NSM activity (e.g., "direct action," "cultural innovation," attention to the "grass roots," and the politicization of everyday life) are not compatible with bureaucratic regulation or formal organization, the more routinized NSMs (such as the National Organization for Women) tend either to fragment into more spontaneous organizations or lose their identity. Yet precisely because formal organization (i.e., bureaucracy) is resistant to NSM mobilization, one consequence of the rise of the NSMs is the attempt by managerial elites to make such formal organization more congenial to the culture of affirmative postmodernism.

Some commentators have suggested that the NSMs are not historically unique. According to Craig Calhoun (1993a), for instance, NSMs concerned with "temperance, nationalism, craft struggle, communitarianism, abolitionism, free-thinking, and camp-meeting religion" can be found as far back as the early nineteenth century, and Sidney Tarrow (1989) has plausibly suggested that many of the traits that are supposedly unique to NSMs apply to all kinds of social movements in their early stages. Yet the movements to which Calhoun refers emphasized the need for "inner regeneration," not life politics. Moreover, the NSMs are not like *any* social movement in its initial phases. What characterizes a "new" social movement is not its newness as a movement, or the relative spontaneity of its members' orientations, but the emphasis on particularistic lifestyle and agenda, the politicization of everyday life as the purpose of the movement, and the deference shown to the cultural entrepreneurs and professionals who help define what should be felt and experienced.

By the end of the 1980s, many of the programs favored by NSM leaders were institutionalized in the American university—usually under the banner of "multiculturalism" or "diversity." Yet rather than develop theory that was holistic, synthetic, or integrative in approach, these new academic programs (NAPs) tended to produce knowledge that was decentered, pluralistic, and flexible. By the 1980s, the NAPs had become postmodernism's port of entry into the American system of higher education.

The New Academic Programs: The Culturally Diverse Campus

Reflecting on some of the changes within the humanities and social sciences over the preceding couple of decades, Steven Seidman (1994, 2)— a self-declared affirmative postmodernist—has observed that "postmodern themes" are "especially visible in the realm of knowledge." As he points out, "Disciplinary boundaries are blurring and new interdisciplinary, hybrid knowledges such as feminism, lesbian and gay studies, ethnic studies, urban studies and cultural studies are moving into the center of the human studies" (2).[6] According to Seidman (1991, 136, 141):

> Postmodernism . . . sees the disciplines as implicated in heterogeneous struggles around gender, race, sexuality, the body, and the mind to shape humanity. . . . Those who appeal to the agency of women or homosexuals or African-Americans intend to become part of the clamor of voices and interests struggling to shape a system of identity, normative order and power. Discourses that use categories such as woman, man, gay, black American, and white American need to be seen as social forces embodying the will to shape a gender, racial and sexual order.

Seidman claims that the NAPs are "interdisciplinary." Yet even though the NAPs develop cross-cutting professional affiliations and break down existing versions of institutional authority, they eschew generalizable critical theory, and they fail to synthesize the findings of established disciplines. Rather, they tend to ignore established research traditions altogether, preferring instead to develop increasingly specialized ways of "seeing," each privileged in its own "special" way. Such a project is unlikely to create much closure or consensus among intellectuals. As Seidman (1994a, 327) admits, "Knowledge in an age of postmodernity will be permanently contested, not because truth surfaces only, and rarely, in the heat of battle, but because knowledge has come to be inseparable from power and is no longer assumed to be beneficent."

In a short confessional piece written as an introduction to a jointly edited work on identity politics, Seidman explains why he stopped being a Marxist and became a postmodernist. This piece is worth discussing briefly because it successfully typifies the intersection between affirmative postmodernism and the NAPs. Seidman (1995, 3) tells us that after the rise of neoconservatism and the New Right during the 1980s he "once again, felt like a stranger in America." He subsequently underwent psychoanalysis and discovered that his "self or 'subject'" was "de-centered" and "populated by multiple, often conflicted identities." Once he decided to out himself as a gay person, Seidman (4; emphasis supplied) began to think about science's role in "servicing" "a heterosexist society" and concluded that "*science*" (not politically organized groups) "denied me a range of legal and civil rights." Postmodernism's main attraction for Seidman is that he (4–5) thinks it can unite "people of color, sexual rebels, Third World gays, working-class gays, butches and fems" in "a new celebration of multiple, composite identities" and "a queer politics of difference" that could remake "bodies and everyday life."

Instead of suggesting that science can be misused and that we need to learn how to use empirical knowledge more appropriately, Seidman insists that modern science is something that must be *overcome*. This task, he asserts, can be accomplished by the aforementioned splintered identity groups, which actually have little or nothing in common—including (and perhaps especially) their sexual practices. How did he reach such a bizarre conclusion? Well, for Seidman (4; emphasis supplied), "coming out had for me far-reaching *epistemological* consequences." His new sexual identity, in other words, did not so much give him a new and more satisfying "private" existence as reason enough for a new politics and a "postmodern" research agenda at a major public university.

Managing Diversity

In June 1995, the National Conference on Race and Ethnicity in Continuing Education was organized by the University of Oklahoma. The Organizing Brochure (OB) for this conference nicely illustrates the kinds of issues the NAPs address. It also shows the intersection among bureaucrats, administrators, and academics organized and legitimated by the NAPs.

The conference in question brought together "senior administrative officers" from colleges and universities; "directors and staff members from offices of affirmative action"; "equal opportunity and minority affairs officers"; "professional staff from student-support services"; "professionals in virtually all activity and service areas of the culturally diverse campus"; "student leaders"; "representatives of state and national institutes, agencies, commissions, associations, and foundations"; and "representatives of community-based agencies and organizations" (OB, 2). Registration fees were $345 ("partial attendance" fees not accepted). Single occupancy at The Eldorado ("the first hotel in northern New Mexico to be awarded the prestigious AAA Four-Diamond rating") started at $130 a night, plus tax (OB, 33).

Among other topics, workshops were devoted to "Planning and Implementing Campus-Based Institutes for the Healing of Racism," "Responding Effectively to Bias Incidents on Campus," "Sexual Harassment on Campus," "Teaching About African-American–Asian-American Relations," "Campus Physical Environments: Promoting or Preventing the Celebration of Cultural Diversity," "Developing a Diversity Training Program for Staff," "Offensive University Mascots," and "How Our Social Identities Affect Our Work in the Multicultural Classroom." "Critical Dialogue Sessions" focused on such issues as "Turning Your Multiple Social Identities into Working Assets in the Multicultural Classroom"; "Implementing a Campuswide, Coordinated Response to Bias Incidents on Campus"; "Exploring the Need to Establish a National Organization for the Minority Affairs Profession"; and showing lesbian, gay, and bisexual students how to cope "with double and triple jeopardy from the intersection of Race/Ethnicity, Gender, and Sexual Orientation" (OB, 5). Sessions that were reserved for "persons at the rank of dean or higher" (presumably to safeguard important administrative secrets) included "Diversity and Total Quality Management (TQM): Establishing a Paradigm to Measure Effectiveness and Excellence" and "Senior-Level Strategies for Implementing Diversity Initiatives on Campus."

Political Correctness?

Some critics have complained that the NAPs try to enforce a stultifying and repressive kind of "political correctness." Yet if this were their only or major contribution to the academy, there would be little that was "new" about them. Since their inception, most American colleges and universities have claimed to provide an authorized "liberal education" for their students, and for well over a century classes in civics, literature, philosophy, and the humanities in this country have promised to create a more fully rounded, more complete human being. Nevertheless, there is one major difference between the humanities class that flourished at the beginning of this century and the classes organized by the NAPs. In 1900 liberal arts courses helped the members of a privileged elite internalize *national* culture; such courses tried to show how the members of this privileged group should play a part in society as a whole. By contrast, the NAPs are geared to particular factions in society that are offered a new and improved version of manufactured group identity.

NAP leaders usually claim that NAP knowledge cannot be generally or universally understood. Men, in other words, are congenitally incapable of grasping the true value of women's studies (they just don't get it). In a similar fashion, whites cannot access many of the truths released in black studies courses because they will never know what it is like to live as a black person in a white-dominated society. The effect of all this is to ghettoize even further those who claim to suffer from their marginality—an ironic result that most academics seem too demoralized to notice. In short, the NAPs teach that particularistic interests are more important than general principles. And by showing that justice is a *special*, rather than a generalizable, quality, NAP classes have become an important and (as we shall see) particularly useful kind of ideological practice.

The NSMs, the NAPs, and Postmodernism: A Preliminary Analysis

During the 1980s, the postmodernist and poststructuralist attack on received tradition and on the more classical schools of thought meshed quite nicely with the NAPs and with the insularity and narrow self-interest of the affirmative NSMs. One thing that can be said in support of tradition or in favor of classicism, however, is that these orientations do at least enable the individual to transcend the limitations of personal or group experience, isolated, as these must be, within particular time-space coordinates. The NSMs, however, form "communities of like-minded people" (Dalton and Kuechler 1990, 12) eager to participate in particularized modes of "consciousness-raising" and willing to base a sense of identity on the celebration of their own insularity. If the NSMs and the NAPs do not reach the constituency for which they are intended (e.g., women, Chicanos, working-class "butches," those at a loss to know what to do with their "multiple social identities"), the message in question can always be adjusted. In the final analysis, the ability to create flexible new group solidarities and identities will take precedence over everything else.

Because of a primary emphasis on communicative, not analytical, skills, both the NSMs and the NAPs lack a historical-transcendental perspective. Not only do they exhibit a kind of "depthlessness," one of postmodernism's basic features, according to Jameson (1984b, 58), but they also encourage their followers to live in a perpetual present. Adherents are therefore unable to develop the tragic or heroic conception of selfhood that was recaptured from the ancients at the beginning of the nineteenth century and was made such an integral part of cultural modernism. Moreover, although the NSMs and NAPs have successfully politicized lifestyle options, they have also encouraged the decline of traditional or taken-for-granted lifeworlds and sanctioned a high degree of political abstinence within the public lifeworld taken as a whole.

As we have seen, the NSMs and the NAPs claim to be more radical than the "old" social movements and academic programs. Yet a modern philosopher such as Georg W.F. Hegel would have grasped immediately that one cannot, in Seidman's terms, "shape humanity" by putting a new linguistic sheen on existing patterns of social and economic relationships. Because our knowledge of the world is never conceptually innocent, categories such as "woman," "man," "gay," "black American," and "white American" (see Seidman 1991, 141) are not virginal or guiltless; they have jettisoned neither the albatross of their history nor the guilt of their past associations.

For the most part, the NSMs and NAPs have succeeded only in dedifferentiating the political-communicative public lifeworld from the inner-transcendent private lifeworld. Once "morality" becomes the exclusive property of artificially contrived and particularistic solidarities, subjects are trapped within a "personal experience" that is neither structurally contextualized nor historically located. By helping to eliminate a publicly mediated ethical apparatus through which localized or personalized orientations might be scrutinized and challenged, the "liberal" NSMs and NAPs operate quite coercively.

What Caused the Rise of the NSMs and NAPs?

Seidman believes that the NSMs and NAPs are driven by "progressive" postmodern intellectuals (like him). Yet according to Ron Eyerman (1994), the NSMs are less an expression of postmodernism than an outcome of postmodernity. Eyerman believes they the NSMs are largely the consequence of (1) the increased importance of mass media and (2) the explosion of the knowledge industry. This latter development, Eyerman (708ff) suggests, is itself linked with "a shift toward knowledge-based, capital-intensive production," which requires a workforce that is more educated and more flexibly employed.

Eyerman (1994, 709) points out that the NSMs are "shaped by the mass media in several ways . . . [for] to be noticed by the media is to gain legitimacy and the ability to influence policy as well as the public at large" (see also Gitlin 1980). As a result, formal procedures of democracy and a politics of administration become increasingly irrelevant. In 1968 student and leftist factions were among the first to turn this new state of affairs to their advantage. Today, however, not only has the New Right learned from the

1960s, but it has also benefited greatly from the centralization and concentration of media ownership. By the early 1990s, the populist, demagogic attacks on "feminazis," "wacko environmentalists," "queers," "quota queens," and other assorted freaks and misfits had increased dramatically. This campaign paid dividends in 1994 when two out of three white males voted for a Republican Party that largely succeeded in portraying overtaxed, underrepresented, put-upon "middle Americans" as the real victims of the out-of-control "McGovernicks" in office.

Eyerman (1994, 708) also emphasizes that "in recent years the links between education and production have become more pronounced and rationalized through various forms of manpower planning." Inflexible "Organization Man" anticipated lifetime employment with an employer that wanted to routinize behavior and make employees interchangeable. But as the American corporation downsizes, downbenefits, and decentralizes, old methods of hierarchical control have to be replaced with the more flexible management of human resources (see, e.g., Thomas 1991).

Who (or What) Is Served by the NSMs and NAPs?

The NSMs and NAPs are particularly susceptible to the machinations of business and the state. There are, I think, two main reasons for this. First, affirmativists tend to belong to relatively weakly organized, or weakly bounded, professional groups that are unable to give practitioners the kind of autonomy and legitimacy enjoyed by more strongly organized professional groups (e.g., lawyers, doctors, architects). Second, affirmativists are relatively "decommodified" (Offe 1985b), meaning they possess cultural credentials (or cultural capital) rather than financial or economic resources. Whereas financial or monetary capital can be invested or liquidated by private individuals without organizational or group support, cultural or symbolic resources (i.e., claims to expertise) usually cannot be "cashed in" without access to organizational structures or professional groups. It probably is safe to assume that NSM and NAP leaders are about as interested in money as anyone else. However, their access to this useful medium is largely determined by their ability to perform cultural services for those who command administrative resources.

The Intersection Between the NSMs and the NAPs

The NSMs and NAPs are both postmodern in a number of ways:

- They are not interested in trying to complete the large-scale "project of modernity."

- They have abandoned "total" emancipatory outlooks such as Marxism.
- They reject the absolute authority of the intellectual-as-legislator.
- Although they politicize beliefs, values, and expression, they do not try to expand or to strengthen civic culture or the public sphere. Instead, they undermine the integrity of the private lifeworld and the "inner" autonomy of the individual.
- They endorse special-purpose groups and show little interest in helping to shape an inclusive movement of political renewal.
- They suggest that the diversity, splintering, and fragmentation of the lifeworld are good in themselves.
- They emphasize culture over structure, status blocs over class membership, cultural credentials over class consciousness.
- Although they are knowledge based, they see "knowledge" as relativistic and as irredeemably pluralistic.
- They recognize that those who define what knowledge is help determine how power is to be exercised.
- They sever the connection between political legitimacy and generalizable values, relying instead on mass media and other new technologies of communication.
- They are geared to consumption and lifestyle, not work or production.
- They never challenge the state head-on, but they do attempt to gain access to the resources it controls.

Postmodernism and the Christian New Right

There are certain intriguing parallels between the NSMs and the Christian New Right (or the "New Fundamentalists," as I call them). First, both are shaped and reproduced by mass media and the state. Second, both helped dedifferentiate public and private life spheres. Third, both aim to develop more flexible (and more useful) identities. Fourth, both show little interest in developing public policy except as this affects their particularistic interests. Fifth, both simulate the "communities" they claim to repair.

If the NSMs and the NAPs represent "a postmodernism of the left," the New Fundamentalists exhibit "a postmodernism of the right."[7] The NSMs and the NAPs have been encouraged and even sponsored by the Clinton administration and by other more liberal government agencies. In turn, the Christian New Right has attempted to form what might be described as an "ideological state apparatus" (Althusser 1971) that could justify and help implement the programs of the Republican Right.

Religious Fragmentation: The Rise of
New Fundamentalists and New Evangelicals

Since the 1950s, the number of Americans who are members of, or who identify with, mainstream Protestant and Jewish religious organizations has declined significantly (Bellah 1990; Anthony and Robbins 1990). At the same time, membership in fundamentalist or Pentecostal organizations not directly tied to established Protestant churches has grown rapidly. Examples of fundamentalist religious organizations include the Moral Majority and Liberty Foundation founded by Jerry Falwell and, more recently, the Christian Coalition founded by Pat Robertson in 1989 and led by Executive Director Ralph Reed and the Promise Keepers, led by football coach Bill McCartney.[8] Because of the rise of such organizations, the "old boundaries" separating "religion, morality, and politics" have become ambiguous and more uncertain (Wuthnow 1988, 207). According to Robert Wuthnow (266), the widening division between more established churches and the newer fundamentalist sects has created "two versions of American civil religion—one conservative, one liberal." "Old" liberal clerics support a separation of church and state, are less dogmatic in outlook, and believe that matters of conscience and salvation are best left to the individual or church in question. "Conservative" fundamentalists, in contrast, are dogmatic about basic values, which they regard as authoritatively fixed or otherwise given.

In emphasizing the verbal inerrancy of the Bible and the need for adult Christians to be "born again," fundamentalist Christianity rejects many of the secularizing and differentiating tendencies of modern societies. But it does not so much sanction a traditional order as provide an effective coping mechanism for those overwhelmed by the complexities of contemporary existence. As Giddens (1991, 142) has suggested, fundamentalism's appeal to fin-de-millennium Americans is that it promises to provide clear-cut answers and directions for a (postmodern) "multiple-option world" that appears to have "abandoned final authorities."

The "New Evangelicals" (e.g., Pat Robertson, Jerry Falwell, Jimmy Swaggert, Oral Roberts, Robert Schuller, Rex Humbard, Bob Jones, Bill McCartney, plus a host of lesser-known personalities) are a subset of the New Fundamentalists. Whereas "old" evangelicals operated small churches and conducted old-fashioned revivalist camp meetings, the New Evangelicals rely on the latest technologies in mass marketing and mass-mediated communication (Wuthnow 1988, 197ff). These include religious TV stations, computerized mailing lists, rapid-response networks, and monthly strategy updates that can be beamed by satellite to hundreds of meeting sites around the country. The activities of the New

Evangelicals accelerated after 1980. In 1972 there were about 350 "Christian" radio stations in this country, but by 1994 this number had risen to nearly 1,600. Today, about one in three Americans listens to "Christian radio," watches "Christian TV," or attends an evangelical or fundamentalist church—and the numbers appear to be rising. From 1988 to 1994, the number of fundamentalist Christians increased from 19 to 25 percent of U.S. voters.

New Fundamental "Conservatives" Versus Old "Modern" Liberals

As noted earlier, Weber (1958) suggested that the religiosity of many early modern Protestant sects promoted the routinization of a sense of personal or "autonomous" conscience. New Fundamentalists, however, are more "other directed" and group oriented. Many old liberal clerics encouraged a differentiation of private and public life spheres, but the New Fundamentalists are not so inclined. Indeed, by reducing "old-time" religious proselytizing to the exigencies of mass-mediated communication, the New Evangelicals refuse even to recognize the "inner-directed" believer addressed by the early modern Protestant sects. As a result, like the "liberal" NSMs that the New Fundamentalists claim to oppose, the Christian New Right has actually helped dismantle the very "inner" resources Weber believed were causally implicated in the birth of modernity. In so doing, the Christian New Right has undermined the functional significance of the "knowing" or "individual" subject, thereby advancing the post- or antimodern tendencies described by Lyotard, Jameson, and Foucault.

An ideal-typical contrast between a New Fundamentalist such as Jerry Falwell and an old-style liberal Protestant cleric such as William Ellery Channing (1780–1842), the founder of the American Unitarian Association, highlights some of the main differences between postmodern and early modern forms of redemption. Channing—a neo-Kantian and (like Marx) a product of German Enlightenment—was a major influence on Weber (see Marianne Weber 1975, 88) and strongly influenced Weber's famous thesis on the relationship between the Protestant ethic and the spirit of capitalism. Channing believed that the relationship between the individual and matters of ultimate concern should be strongly individuated. Like Kant—probably the greatest philosopher of the modern era—Channing recognized that morality that is enforced, compelled, or legislated would serve only to negate the application of the free will that makes private conscience meaningful in the first place. Jerry Falwell, however, disagrees. Like other New (and "old") Fundamentalists, he believes that morality is far too important to be left to the individual. In his words: "Someone often asks—can morality be legislated? The answer is yes. All civilized societies are governed by the legislation of morality" (quoted in Wuthnow 1988, 208).[9]

For Channing and other early modern Protestants such as Kant, individuals were obligated to take an individuated responsibility for themselves. In the final analysis, they would, after all, be judged according to the use they had made of the innate conscience that God had implanted in them as part of his plan to make us all masters of our moral careers. Like Kant and Weber, Channing acknowledged that the world is hopelessly complex, contradictory, and corrupt. The demands of the public and private lifeworlds can never be reconciled; no one, for instance, can serve the state without compromising his or her moral integrity, and no individual can adequately serve both God and Mammon. Nonetheless, for Channing, not all states and not all statesmen are equally bad. Some political systems are even worth defending. Like Thomas Jefferson, Channing believed that the best kind of political community is guided by a constitution that facilitates the development of the type of individual who can act morally.

On the face of it, the New Fundamentalists attach so much importance to "morality" that it seems almost perverse to accuse them of neglecting it. Yet from a critical, Kantian, or modern perspective, the Christian New Right is uninterested in moral reason. For Channing and for Weber, values are good not because they can be resolved scientifically (they cannot), but because they require individuals to give a reasoned or at least formally consistent account of *personalized* vocation and commitment. By contrast, the New Fundamentalists maintain that having "values" does not mean individuals must give an account of themselves. On the contrary, it means that Christians have a banner to flap in the face of anyone old-fashioned enough to ask them to justify themselves.

Mobilizing Support from the "Third Sector"

In constitutionally governed capitalist democracies, it is commonplace for political leaders to tap the value commitments located in what Wuthnow (1989, 5) calls the voluntary "Third Sector" of society. This sector "consists of those activities and organizations that are not subsumed within the formal bureaucratic apparatus of government . . . and are not governed by the supply-demand-price mechanism or the profit incentives of the economic sector" (6). The Third Sector is hence a residual category that contains what is left of the lifeworld when the demands of capital and the state have had their say. Liberal sociologists such as Parsons (1967, 308) largely took it for granted that action in the Third Sector enjoyed a certain autonomy from money and power. By contrast, neo-

Marxists are more inclined to believe that the supposedly free and voluntary activity in the Third Sector is shaped by the strategic media of money and power. Yet if the voluntary wellspring of the Third Sector is drying up—if political subjects are increasingly less able to exercise moral reason—political leaders would consequently be faced with what Habermas (1975, 71ff) calls "legitimation deficits." In other words, political leaders would search in vain for the deeply felt value commitments that could help sanction the vigorous use of political authority. This could have quite serious consequences, for, as Weber emphasized, monocratic bureaucracy and legal authority can never supply all the resources needed by the modern state.

Luckily, however, the New Right is more interested in *producing* (and subsequently policing), not in responding to, supposedly "private" and voluntary commitments. Hence, instead of promoting voluntary associations, self-reliance, or religion indiscriminately,[10] the New Right favors special-purpose religious organizations only. The Reagan administration, for instance, did not place Louis Farrakhan and the Nation of Islam on quite the same pedestal as Jerry Falwell or Jim and Tami Bakker. By the same token, the priests who advocated "liberation theology" in Central America (and who were subsequently targeted by U.S.-trained death squads) were not treated quite as deferentially as the Holy Father in Rome.

I noted previously that the rise of the NSMs is in part attributable to state expansion and intervention into what used to be regarded as "private domains" (Eyerman 1994, 708). In a similar fashion, special-purpose religious groups such as the Moral Majority did not just respond to but were actually "*founded* . . . in direct response to new initiatives by the state" (Wuthnow 1988, 317; emphasis added). Let us look at this in a little more detail.

Reagan and the New Evangelicals

Unlike President Jimmy Carter, a lay preacher and earnest "born-again" Christian, Ronald Reagan was not a regular churchgoer and had never shown much interest in "fundamentalist values" (or in Christianity, come to that) before entering politics. This did not seem to bother evangelicals, however, who focused on the Reagan administration's promise to support their particularistic agenda. At the 1980 Republican National Convention, "Reagan strategists met with Christian Right leaders to determine what contribution they could make to the 'community of shared values' that the candidate hoped to make the basis of the first partisan realignment in 50 years" (Guth 1983, 37). "Both GOP strategists and Christian Right leaders were impressed by poll data which suggested . . .

that only 55% of all evangelicals were registered to vote. . . . Even more . . . tantalizing was Robert Teeter's poll result which showed that 30% of all nonvoters attended church services at least three times a week" (37).

Reagan's 1980 endorsement of Christian fundamentalism helped him sweep the South and garner votes from the dwindling number of "Yellow-dog Democrats": southern voters who habitually supported the Democratic Party. This was something of a coup for the Republican Right, for evangelical Christianity appeals mostly to the poorly educated, the elderly, and the socially disadvantaged—categories of people, in other words, who have not traditionally turned out to support Republican presidential candidates. Yet according to pollster Lou Harris (1980), the Christian New Right put Reagan in the White House.

Reagan's success consolidated the Republican Right's hold on the South and marked the completion of a successful southern strategy first engineered by Richard Nixon in 1968. By 1994 the majority of white southerners was supporting Republican candidates who were disproportionately "conservative," even as Republicans. Yet although both Nixon and Bush successfully played the race card, correctly identifying it as *the* wedge issue that would split the southern Democratic vote, Reagan depended more on evangelical Christianity than race to court white southern voters. This strategy was such a success that by 1988 the allegiance of evangelicals to the Republicans was as strong as that of blacks to the Democratic Party—that is, overwhelming (Hadden 1990, 467).[11] In 1992, 42 percent of the delegates at the 1992 Republican National Convention were evangelicals, and 62 percent of "white born-again Protestants" voted for George Bush (an Episcopalian) against two Southern Baptists, Bill Clinton and Al Gore (Blumenthal 1994, 34).

The relationship between evangelicals and the Republican Right has recently grown even stronger. The Christian Coalition, for instance, based its mailing list on the nearly 2 million names generated by Pat Robertson in his 1992 run for the presidency. Unlike the Moral Majority, the Christian Coalition is more overtly political: "It runs training seminars for political cadres, at which participants are taught the rudiments of taking control of local Republican organizations from the bottom up" (Blumenthal 1994, 36).

Over the past fifteen years, the leaders of the Republican Party have been eager and willing to use the power of office to side with one faction over another in the ongoing and increasingly divisive dispute about "values." The New Evangelicals, for their part, seized the opportunity to develop new kinds of moral entrepreneurship. The relationship was symbiotic. On the one hand, evangelical Christian organizations formulated and helped reinforce the value commitments that New Right candidates used to enhance their electability. On the other hand, once they were elected, these candidates used the power of office to bolster the economic fortunes of the supposedly "private" organizations that had supported them in the first instance.[12]

The Leftist Project of Modernity and the Rise of the New Right

The terms *left-winger* and *right-winger* stem from the French Legislative Assembly of 1791. Whereas the original right-wingers believed that the modernizing tendencies of the revolution had gone far enough, the left-wingers (who sat to the left of the Assembly) argued that the revolution was as yet unfinished. This pattern of political alignment has been replicated in most modern, formally democratic societies. On one side sit the leftists (e.g., Marxists and socialists), who want to hasten the pace of modernization or who believe that the "project of modernity" is not yet accomplished. On the other side are the rightists (e.g., Christian Democrats and other conservative parties). Although the conservatives accept the inevitability of the spread of purposive rationality into all spheres of life, they nonetheless argue that the pace of change should be steady and that it would be a mistake to discard all of the institutions, customs, or traditions that are rooted in the premodern era. From this we can make a most important observation: During the modern era, it was the rightists, not the leftists, who cut against the grain of taken-for-granted trajectories of social development. As a result, most of the interesting debates about public policy over the past two centuries have involved disputes among various factions within the Left. These debates have not for the most part centered on the official disagreement between institutionalized parties of the Left and Right.

The Politicizing Traits of Modernity

From the vantage point of the Left, the modern state advances the "project of modernity" by *politicizing* (which process should not be confused with the process of expanding government or bureaucracy). Politicization refers to the expansion of the scope of public authority and to ways in which such authority can be made more accountable. In essence, it involves either (1) extending or universalizing the full rights of citizenship to new categories of persons (women, blacks, nonproperty owners, gays, etc.) or (2) broadening the domain or scope of public decision-making and civic responsibility so that work, the environment, social security, education, community, and even the family are subjected to a public scrutiny that becomes progressively more reasonable, that is, more self-reflective, more accountable to itself.[13] Among other things, politicization leads to a strengthening and widening of the public sphere and to an inevitable diminution of the kind of economic domination that comes from the private ownership of property and to increased organizational control of "free-market" mechanisms by bureaucratic and administrative structures that use their authority to seek liberty and justice for all.

By the beginning of the twentieth century, most liberal democracies had universalized citizenship rights for nearly all adults living within the territory controlled by the state (thereby realizing, in formal terms at least, the promise of liberal democracy). Hence, during the latter part of the twentieth century, the axis of politicization-depoliticization began to refer more to the issue of making such authority increasingly accountable and less to the task of expanding the scope of public authority.

Leftist Modernizers and Public Authority

Leftist modernizers favored the expansion of public authority because they equated this "progressive" development with the diminution of what they saw as inherently backward and undesirable "naturelike" (i.e., taken-for-granted) social relations. These modernizers believed that modernity's dynamic inexorably moved us toward a greater state of public accountability; they accordingly concluded that modernity would not so much destroy individuality as recreate it in a new (more self-reflective) form.

All leftist modernizers believe that premodern societal communities are unreflectively reproduced, and this assumption transcends the significant differences that otherwise divide them. Whereas Marxist-Leninists assert that dominant classes will never permit the general will to be expressed, let alone realized, without violent insurrection and class war, "democratic socialists" and Social Democratic parties believe that the self-reflective political community can be institutionalized within the constitutional setup afforded by capitalist democracies. In contrast to this, John Maynard Keynes's (1883–1946) even more centrist "new [modern] liberalism" advocated the use of public authority to control and direct "economic forces in the interests of social justice and social stability" (Keynes 1932, 334). Instead of relying on the market, Keynes charged the state with the task of providing a viable and superior nonrevolutionary alternative to the model of revolutionary socialism. From the 1930s to the 1970s, his policies strongly influenced political elites in many western societies—including, most notably, those in Britain and the

United States (see Chapter 4). In stark contrast to the leftist programs just described, the program of the New Right—which to some extent has now been adopted both by Republicans and Democrats—is a *radical* attempt to challenge and derail the project of modernity: the idea that the dynamic of modernization inexorably leads to the kind of political community wherein private individuals act in accord with universal interest.

Lifeworld-System Exchanges

Old leftist modernizers and the New Right promote quite different exchanges among the lifeworld, on the one hand, and system (i.e., polity and the economy) on the other. In ideal-typical terms, these can be described as follows:

1. Leftist modernizers are positive about the enhancement of public authority and skeptical about market relations. Government is good if it defends public accountability and helps structure or even dismantle market relations. Voluntary associations are good if they serve to enhance public authority by mediating between the individual and the state; they are bad if they are socially divisive.

2. The New Right is negative about the enhancement of public authority and positive about developing and freeing *labor* markets (not necessarily the commodity or goods markets). Government is good if it dismantles public accountability (as opposed to state power) and serves capital's newfound mobility. Voluntary associations are good if they help the state abandon some of its public service responsibilities or if they promote labor discipline; they are bad if they oppose the state or provide a basis of opposition to the enhanced marketability of labor.

What the New Right emphatically rejects is not the state per se but the model of the *progressive* state as defined by Hegel: the idea of the state as "the actuality of the Ethical Idea—the Ethical Spirit, as the Substantial Will, revealed, lucid to itself, which thinks and knows itself, and which carries out what it knows in so far as it knows it could" (quoted in Findlay 1962, 326).[14] Old conservatives typically took the position that sentiments such as Hegel's were handsome but "impractical," given "human nature" or some such obstacle. New Rightists, in contrast, reject what they refuse to acknowledge was a valid or worthwhile project in the first place. Set against the long-standing presuppositions of modernity, their stance is not so much ultraconservative as ultra*radical.*

Reversing the (Leftist) Project of Modernity

In seeking to reverse the leftist project of modernity, the New Right relies on the ideology of the market not so much to promote a "pure" market society as to reverse politicizing trends that conservatives had previously believed were irreversible.[15] This policy was vividly personified in Margaret Thatcher, the doyen of the New Right in this and other countries.

Before Thatcher's 1979–1990 administration, British Conservative prime ministers were surprisingly willing to take it for granted that forms of public authority, once institutionalized, could never unilaterally be reversed by a political faction of the Right.[16] In this sense, Thatcher's feisty declaration that all Conservative administrations in Britain (prior to her own, of course) had been incorrigibly defeatist had more than a grain of truth to it (see Thatcher 1993, 3–15). Thatcher shrewdly saw that she, and not her fossilized opponents, was the radical and would-be revolutionary. She pointed out that although her party had claimed since the 1940s to oppose a "centralizing, managerial, bureaucratic, interventionist style of government," it had in actuality "merely pitched camp in the long march to the left. It never tried seriously to reverse it." "The result of this style of accommodationist politics . . . was that post-war politics became a 'socialist ratchet'—Labour moved Britain toward more statism; the Tories stood pat; and the next Labour government moved the country a little further left. The Tories loosened the corset of socialism; they never removed it" (6–7).

Thatcher was never charitable about the leaders of the Labour Party, but she was particularly vitriolic about the men who had formed the Conservative administration before her own. In her memoirs she accuses "Ted Heath's Government" (which served from 1970 to 1974) of proposing and almost implementing "the most radical form of socialism ever contemplated by an elected British Government" (Thatcher 1993, 7). As she sees it, such "socialism" included "the joint oversight of economic policy by a tripartite body representing the Trade Union Congress, the Confederation of British Industry and the Government" (7). What saved the British people from this "corporatist and socialist abomination," Thatcher writes, was the predictable boneheadedness of union leaders who were incapable of recognizing "that their 'class enemy' was prepared to surrender without a fight" (7).

Thatcher, then, did manage to grasp what her dull-witted opponents had missed: that the "ratchet" of modernization, left to its own devices, would inexorably strengthen the fortunes of the Left. It was understandable, then, that she mauled those who claimed that the Conservatives should manage the "orderly process of decline," as one aging mandarin put it to her, much to his regret. Thatcher was a woman who knew what she wanted. She wanted to smash the hegemony of the leftist modernizers.

Postmodern Conservatism

As noted earlier, New Evangelical leaders manage to be antimodern in outlook but quite up-to-date in method. Even though they invariably portray themselves and their movement as "conservative"—an appellation that, for some bizarre reason, tends to be uncritically accepted— there is nothing intrinsically "conservative" about the attempt to replace long-established and mainstream religious churches with consumeroriented, mass-mediated, antimodern sects.

There is, in fact, something deeply Orwellian about the New Right's expropriation of the label "conservative." For one thing, the New Right cannot function without new technologies and the new forms of mass-mediated solicitation. For another, New Right leaders (e.g., Reagan, Quayle, Newt Gingrich, Reed) rely on wholly *manufactured* pasts—such as the one Dusenberry created for the 1984 "Morning in America" commercials. This, in turn, was based on nothing more "traditional" or "conservative" than the popular Pepsi ads that featured a black man who had turned himself into a white woman.

Like the New Fundamentalists, traditional (i.e., "old") religious authorities (e.g., the infamous Ayatollah Ruhollah Khomeini) are dogmatic and inflexible about values. Nevertheless, "old" fundamentalists do not typically attempt to reduce thirteen centuries of scholarship to eight-second McSoundBites. The ayatollah did distribute cassettes of his sermons from exile, but he did not measure religious truth by the size of his mailing lists, nor did he measure the value of his message by the number of cable subscribers his operation could generate. A brief glance at his features and a quick comparison between the uncompromising story written there and the banal narrative painted all over Tami Bakker's face would dramatize most of the distinctions that need to be grasped between "old" and "new" fundamentalists. Some western critics have suggested that traditional fundamentalists are sexist, bigoted, and ignorant old fools. Even so, unlike the New Evangelicals, these "old fools" do seem able to reserve something of themselves that is not completely absorbed and refracted by the medium in which they operate.

Most followers of the Christian New Right are quite incapable of grasping that, as in a Hollywood western, their past is being simulated for them. They do not see that in a postmodern era audience ratings and the commodification of their attention have become the ultimate touchstone of "conservative" appeal. Those who lack historical memory or knowledge are condemned to live in a perpetual present, and many New Evangelicals (most of whom are quite ignorant of the rich tradition of religion) have become the living embodiment of such a fate. Unlike old fundamentalists (Hasidic Jews or the Amish, for instance), the Christian New Right is not burdened by the past. But why should it be? Freed from the anchors and constraints of history, and faithfully gathered together before the glow of the TV, the New Fundamentalists nihilistically await a simulation of the God that modernity expunged. On some deep level they seem to grasp that God's *non*existence has now irretrievably been settled.

Like Reagan, the "televangelists" market their product on TV as one more commodity that must vie for attention. They "play to the media, fill large auditoriums, and speak the words that [seem] most relevant at the moment" (Wuthnow 1989, 180), relying on techniques that work just as effectively to move costume jewelry on the Home Shopping Network.[17] By depending on technology to address isolated individuals in their living rooms, the New Evangelicals help reinforce the belief that religion has become just another commodified "leisure" activity, ensuring that "every individual can pretty much tailor his or her . . . views to personal taste" (115–116). This attitude reinforces the common perception that "personal philosophies," subjective morality, or a particular conception of history can be purchased in much the same way that one would select a new bedroom suite. As religious consumers channel-surf through the nearly four hundred religious television stations that fill the ether, the question most likely to be foremost in their minds is "What's on offer today—for me?"

Postmodernism and the End of "Civil Religion"

By encouraging, fostering, promoting, and sponsoring the New Fundamentalism, the Christian New Right is not, as Wuthnow implies, developing a new kind of "civil religion." Such a religion attempts to sanctify the nation as a whole by associating the institutions, history, and normative practices of the state with matters of ultimate or divine significance (Bellah 1967). Thus, America is deemed to have its own holy day (the Fourth of July), its holy texts (the Declaration of Independence, the Bill of Rights), its holy sites (Arlington Cemetery, the Lincoln Memorial), and so on. During presidential inaugurations and on other auspicious occasions, citizens are invited to address not the God of the Jews, or the God to whom Farrakhan allegedly prays, but the God of the Americans, who (we are asked to believe) has a special relationship to this his most favored nation. Civil religion thus functions to provide political legitimacy for the institutions of the state and for its appointed or elected officials. It helps consolidate value commitments that all citizens can share.

Because of old-fashioned (modern) constitutional requirements about the differentiation of religious principle and political organization, civil religion is the only religion that the U.S. state can legally promote. It is not surprising, then, that the chief executive of the American Republic has often gone to great lengths to develop, dramatize, and explain the connection of his administration to the Moral Progress of the Nation. Yet because the New Right employs special-purpose religious organizations to reach and to manipulate factionalized groups, it uses religion to depoliticize—and, in a sense, to trash—what civil religion once sanctioned. The ultrapatriots of the New Right have no interest whatsoever in trying to represent the integral unity of one nation-state under God if by such an outmoded concept we mean "*one* people," "*one* nation," "with liberty and justice for *all.*"

The New Right in Britain: A Point of Comparison

During her term in office, Thatcher asserted that far too much time had already been spent on meaningless abstractions such as the "collective good." Like Reagan, she claimed to be a strong supporter of individualism. Thatcher made it perfectly clear that as far as she was concerned, the "societal community" was a mischievous invention of leftist modernizers, in whose disreputable company she would have placed Vladimir I. Lenin and Talcott Parsons, John Maynard Keynes and Mao Zedong. As she once explained to her countrypeople: "Society does not exist. Only individuals and families exist."

In the 1980s, the British Conservative Party placed little emphasis on the nurturance of the public sphere. Yet whereas the New Right in America used the New Fundamentalism to buttress its political program, the Thatcherites in Britain made little use of religious rhetoric because Britain is a far more secularized country than the United States and few Britons are antimodern (or unsophisticated enough) to take evangelical Christianity very seriously.[18] Thatcher consequently had a harder time of it than Reagan. Whereas the Reagan administration received the "moral" backing of religious leaders who were able to deliver a sizable flock, Thatcher had no equivalent Judas goats on whom to rely.

During the 1980s, some of the most effective opposition to Prime Minister Thatcher came not from the official socialist opposition but from the bishops of the established Church of England, which puts the monarch, as sovereign, at its head. At the beginning of this century, the Church of England had been described somewhat caustically—if not perhaps inaccurately—as the "Tory Party at prayer." Yet during Thatcher's term of office, some church leaders went so far as to question the morality of government policy. Unlike the Christian New Right in this country, Anglican leaders in the United Kingdom quaintly seemed to believe that they had some kind of obligation to speak out on behalf of the larger societal community. They apparently failed to grasp that in a postmodern era they were supposed to act as just another special-purpose group.

From crimson seats in the House of Lords, some of her majesty's bishops declared that Thatcher's policies were divisive and ethically indefensible. Worse still, a report solicited by the Archbishop of Canterbury concluded in 1985 that "the impoverished minority" in Britain was "increasingly cut off from the mainstream of our national life" and blamed the Thatcher administration for helping to reproduce this sorry state of affairs (quoted in Riddell 1991, 149).[19] Thatcher's reaction to all of this was un-Christian, and she launched a vituperative attack on the Lords Spiritual—none of whom can be appointed without the approval of the Prime Minister's Office and some of whom, much to her rage, Thatcher had managed to select herself.

Postmodern Versus Modern Conservatism

In 1984 Richard Wirthlin ("Adman of the Year" and chief strategist of the Ronald Reagan presidential campaign) helped Reagan win office on the basis of a massive and highly sophisticated research effort that had but one question in mind: What will the voters buy, and what will turn them off? Although the Reagan administration was not alone in its dependence on market researchers and pollsters, it is something of an irony that the main defender of received conservative wisdom was the most dependent on market research and state-of-the-art PR. Even some members of the Reagan administration had some reservations about what was going on. As Leslie Janka, a deputy White House press secretary, acknowledged in hindsight: "The whole thing [from the beginning] was PR"; the Reagan administration "was a PR outfit that became President and took over the country" (quoted in Hertsgaard 1988, 6).

Americans now live in a universe where flux and change are more salient than ever, where Beavis and Butthead reflect the aspirations and achievements of a whole generation (ironically, of course), and where most people's attention span lasts not much longer than the period between TV commercials (twelve minutes). In such a context—if anyone is still paying any attention—the invocation of tradition, "basic values," custom, or the past is an exceedingly ticklish business. It is hardly surprising, then, that the hyperreality of the new conservatism must so inventively liberate itself from all meaningful grounds of reference. Unlike the postmodern "conservatives" of the New Right, "old"—or more accurately—*modern*-conservative politicians (such as Winston Churchill) attempted to reconcile the present with a more traditional lifeworld that was to some extent still a part of living memory. By contrast, New Right leaders view the historical past as an annoying and irrelevant nuisance. As far as they and their followers are concerned, every day is a fresh beginning and a new start; for them (even as dusk falls) it will always be morning in America.

Old (i.e., modern) conservative intellectuals—such as poet T. S. Eliot or critic F. R. Leavis—hoped for continuity in a lifeworld that they recognized had been ruptured. They did not flee from historical knowledge—what Debord (1991, 15) calls "the memorable, the totality of events whose consequences would be lastingly apparent"—but tried to show how history could make itself felt in the present. Like Johann Goethe, Eliot (1975, 38) recognized that tradition in the modern age can no longer "be inherited" but must be obtained "by great labour." It involves "the historical sense . . . and the historical sense involves a perception, not only of the pastness of the past, but of its [continuing] presence." Whereas the postmodern conservatives rely on others to define their contrived identities, their artificial "traditions," their "homespun truths," their "basic values," and their manufactured "pasts," Eliot (1975, 38) painfully attempted to construe a "sense of the timeless . . . and of the timeless and the temporal together." In this way only, Eliot believed, could the modern intellectual become "conscious of his place in time, or his own contemporaneity" (38). Unlike a feudal intellectual, and unlike a contemporary postmodernist, the modernist Eliot saw that subjects could apprehend this "timeless" only by grappling with what modernity had wrought. In contrast, postmodern New Rightists can embrace only the banalities of the immediate. Overloaded by complexity, and routed by forces they cannot even begin to understand, they have agreed to abolish what is for them unbearable: the *sense* of history, the hope of locating oneself in a world where nothing can be trusted and where nothing stays the same for very long.

It hardly needs saying, but there is, of course, nothing authentically "traditional" about the "traditional values" of the New Fundamentalists. Traditional values exist in traditional communities only—in those that manage to function without shopping malls, cable TV, superbowl Sundays, or "I Love America" rallies. In reality, few American "conservatives" could cope with a traditional environment, and reactionary though some of them might be, only a tiny minority of them sincerely believe that sexually maturing males should be castrated, blasphemers stoned, and superfluous girl infants put out to die. In essence, what the Christian New Right would like to see is not the kind of person who would feel at home in the fourteenth century but a creature who is unable to question (or, preferably, even to notice) the abandonment of the modern experiment in representative democracy.

More than two decades ago, Habermas (1975, 122) speculated that "the steering imperatives of highly complex societies could necessitate disconnecting the formation of motives from norms capable of justification" (see also 125). If this happened, he warned, "legitimation problems" would "cease to exist" because it would no longer be necessary to reconcile public policy with matters of private conscience. In this context, the spectacle of *what* the Christian New Right believes is of less importance than *how* it believes. What New Rightists seek is the kind of uncoupling Habermas most feared.

The Christian New Right

We can summarize the intersection of interests between the New Fundamentalists and the New Right as follows. First, the New Fundamentalists use value-laden terminology to help cover the retreat from civic or public accountability favored by the New Right. Although this ideology was taken seriously by only a minority of Americans, this fraction helped tilt the balance of political power in the 1980s. The New Fundamentalists attack the intrinsic value of a public sphere and also undermine the very basis for reasoned opposition to public authority. As a result, the lifeworld of a sector of the American population that was always marginalized becomes even more vulnerable to the mediation of naturelike authority.

Second, the New Fundamentalists aggressively defend the most dynamic and destructive forces that modernity unleashed: capital and the market (on the face of it, a peculiar thing for "conservatives" to do). According to TV preacher Pat Robertson (1982, 151), "Free enterprise is the economic system most nearly meeting humanity's God-given need for freedom," and in Jerry Falwell's terms, "God is in favor of freedom, property ownership, competition, diligence, work and acquisition. All of this is taught in the Word of God in both the Old and New Testaments" (quoted in Wuthnow 1988, 249). In short, the Christian New Right plays a comprador role in supporting business interests that (so it turned out) favor economic domination.

Third, the New Right uses the power and authority of the state to provide legislative and fiscal support for the New Fundamentalists. Christian New Right leaders, for instance, are typically sponsored by the GOP, which featured Pat Robertson and Pat Buchanan as keynote speakers at the 1992 national convention. The Reagan administration used its resources to further the interests of this particular faction. In 1984, for example, the Office of Policy Information at the White House put out a glossy document that endorsed school prayer, a "hot button" issue for the New Fundamentalists. This was "packaged patriotically: Alongside the seal of the President of the United States, emblazoned in red and printed in large uppercase letters were the words 'Issue Alert'" (Johnson 1991, 211). In office, New Right leaders have given evangelical entrepreneurs a free hand to develop, cultivate, and profit from whatever congregations they can produce. The administrative resources of the state have also been used to promote and support the New Evangelicalism. The Federal Communications Commission and the Internal Revenue Service, for instance, were both used by the Reagan administration to protect the profits of the televangelists, whose broadcasts received "public service" status.

New Social Movements and the Christian New Right

As we have seen, the New Fundamentalists define their morality as something fixed and predetermined. As far as they are concerned, a person who does not uphold certain rigidly defined normative expectations has no morality. In contrast, the NSMs are a lot more flexible. Many absurdly advocate the relativity or "equal worth" of the values expressed by all groups (an argument in response to which most of the members of these groups would take violent exception). Yet even though NSM members abjure broad narratives of purpose and destiny and retreat to particular identities, they still maintain that a sense of moral purpose—or, more accurately, a particular sense of solidarity—can emerge from diversified, fragmented, praxis-oriented social movements.

To the extent that the NSMs, the NAPs, the New Right, and the New Fundamentalists reject the narrative of modern progress, they are all postmodern. Only the New Right and the New Fundamentalists creatively manage to be both post- and antimodern. In alternative "liberal/progressive" and "conservative/reactionary" formats, both the NSMs and the New Fundamentalism attempt to cope with the "multiple-option world" without "final authorities" mentioned earlier by Giddens. Yet from the vantage point of modernity, the NSMs are about as "progressive" as the New Fundamentalists (and the New Right) are "conservative."

In sum, the Christian New Right and the NSMs have the following traits in common:

- Both reject the ethical narrative of *public* responsibility that the modern state helped institutionalize.

- Both lack the kind of transcendent or historic perspective that can serve to construct a project of collective purpose.
- Both favor a decentralized politics of coercion over a centralized politics of legitimation.
- Both rely on "imagined communities" that can be shaped by new cultural specialists or mass-mediated technologies.
- Both see the state and public authority largely as entities that control resources that can be cannibalized by effectively organized movements.
- Both are shaped and promoted by the state, whose increasingly fragmented and eviscerated legitimacy they help prop up.
- Neither effectively addresses the "colonization of the lifeworld"— that is, the reorganization of modes of communicative interaction by the media of money and power. In essence, both seek to create the kind of plastic and flexible personality system that is compatible with the new requirements of business and the state.

Today, the rules of the game have shifted. On one side we have anti-moderns, such as the leaders of the Christian New Right, who want to reverse (or forget about) many of the processes unleashed by modernization. As far as they are concerned, most culture since the Enlightenment has been a mistake. On the other side we have the latter-day postmodern liberals who have replaced the old leftist hope of universal emancipation with the endless proliferation of postmodern sects, each one stridently insisting that its own particularistic agenda is just as "progressive" as anyone else's. Like everyone else today, most intellectuals are overwhelmed. They withdraw in despair or retreat into various kinds of careerist-oriented, hyperdiversified, special-purpose organizations.

Global Capital Flows

I return to a discussion of motivation and meaning in the final two chapters of this book. Next, however, I examine the "immense flows of capital, money, goods, services, people, information, technologies, policies, ideas, images and regulations" that Scott Lash and John Urry (1994, 280) have equated with the postmodern condition. Focusing attention on what is *structuring* such flows, I suggest that many of the processes described thus far (e.g., postmodern consumer capitalism, the rise of postmodern liberal affirmativism, the emergence of the New Right, the decentering and splintering of the self-conscious subject) are not so much local events as local political and culture responses to a global reorganization of capital flows. In this regard, both the postmodern liberals and the New Right in the United States are trying to adapt to some very real transformations in the world. Such changes have affected class relations, spatially reorganized the division of labor, undermined the autonomy of the nation-state, compelled the individual to reorient him- or herself, and, perhaps, driven the last nail into the coffin of modern aspirations and dreams.

4 Postmodernity as a "Regime of Accumulation"?: From Fordism to "Flexible Accumulation"

In 1988 the editorial board of *Marxism Today*—the theoretical journal of the Communist Party of Great Britain (CPGB) and at the time one of the liveliest and most influential periodicals in the United Kingdom—decided to tackle postmodernism. The debate that followed (which was called the "New Times" project) aimed to address "the future of the Left . . . from a position rooted in an analysis of present and emergent tendencies in our society" (Jacques and Hall 1989, 11). As *Marxism Today* explained to its readers:

> The world has changed, not just incrementally but qualitatively. . . . Britain and other advanced capitalist societies are increasingly characterized by diversity, differentiation, and fragmentation, rather than homogeneity, standardisation, and the economies and organisations of scale which characterized modern mass society. . . . Many of the features of this new world have been long in the making and are best seen in areas apparently removed from what the left has traditionally thought of as "the point of production." (11–12)

According to Martin Jacques and Stuart Hall—instigators of the New Times project and coeditors of *Marxism Today*—"post-Fordist" modes of regulation in Britain were replacing older, "Fordist" systems of industrial mass production. By "post-Fordism," Jacques and Hall (1989, 11–12) meant

1. A shift to new "information technologies"
2. An emergence of "a more flexible, specialised and decentralised" labor force, together with a "decline of the old manufacturing base" and the growth of "'sunrise,' computer-based, hi-tech industries"

3. A "contracting-out, of functions and services hitherto provided 'in house' on a corporate basis"
4. A "leading role of consumption" and a "greater emphasis on choice and product differentiation, on marketing, packaging and design, on the 'targeting' of consumers by lifestyle, taste and culture"
5. A "decline in the proportion of the skilled, male, manual working class and the corresponding rise of the service and white-collar class"
6. More "flexi-time and part-time working, coupled with the 'feminisation' and 'ethnicisation' of the workforce"
7. A "new international division of labor" and "an economy dominated by the multinationals"
8. A "'globalisation' of the new financial markets"
9. An "emergence of new patterns of social divisions—especially those between 'public' and 'private' sectors and between the two-thirds who have rising expectations and the 'new poor' and underclasses of the one-third that is left behind"

Although the New Times project did perhaps raise the level of discussion among political activists in the United Kingdom, it split, rather than revitalized, the CPGB. On one side of the subsequent divide the affirmativist New Timers described the "orthodox" faction still in charge of the party organization as dinosaurs unable to adapt to a changing world. The "dinosaurs" responded, in turn, that *Marxism Today* had been hijacked by Left yuppies eager to sacrifice a long history of working-class struggle on the altar of pomo trendiness and contemporary pop appeal.[1] Faced with such rancor, and confronted with the collapse of "actually existing socialism," the CPGB decided that the best thing to do under the circumstances was to abolish itself. *Marxism Today* survived for a couple of years, but it, too, folded in 1991.

Fordism-Keynesianism

Julie Graham (1992, 397) has recently noted that "the story of post-Fordism is on its way to becoming the preeminent narrative of capitalist development, at least on the left, in the English-speaking world." According to Graham (397), "The concept of post-Fordism has become a zone of rough consensus" among nearly all theorists participating in the debate about the economic transformations of postmodernity (see, for instance, Harvey 1989a, 121–200; Mathews 1989; Gilbert, Burrows, and Pollert 1992; Crook et al. 1992, 178ff; Amin 1994). Yet as Graham (1991, 54–55) cautions, this perspective has contributed rather too tidily to "a

unified vision of a grand cultural realignment, in which modern industrial society (Fordism), theoretical representations of that society (Marxism), and the cultural matrix that nurtured both (modernism) are simultaneously swept aside. From this perspective, post-Marxism is a
necessary accompaniment of a postmodern, post-Fordist society, an inevitable concomitant of social change."

Like Graham, I think it is wrong to develop (rather ironically in this instance) a sweeping narrative about postmodernization that makes
Fordism equal to modernity and postmodernity equal to flexibility and
that claims, moreover, that Fordism and flexibility are discrete, discontinuous conditions. I also think that it is premature to jettison Marxist
theory as an outdated (modern) perspective that has nothing to say
about our current postmodern condition. Marx's philosophy of the subject might be dated—wrongheaded, even—but the same cannot be said
of Marx's description of the long-term effects of capitalism's "circuit"
and "turnover."

In the sections that follow, I discuss the transition from Fordism to
flexibility with an eye to explaining some of the economic processes associated with postmodernization. But I also maintain that both Fordism
and flexibility are opportunistic responses to crisis tendencies in capitalism. In this regard at least, they have something in common.

Fordism's Beginnings

Henry Ford (1863–1947) was not the first capitalist to use the assembly
line to enforce continuous-flow production, but he was the first to rely
on this new technology to mass-produce a standardized, complex product for an aggregate consumer. Trying to extract the highest possible rate
of return from *fixed* capital, Ford used automation to fuse his workers
into "an organic whole, a genuinely collective labourer, in which the productive contribution of each individual and group was dependent on
the contribution of every other" (Clarke 1992, 19).

Ford believed that American values, Christianity, and a proper deference toward institutional authority would create the kind of subject
most suited to the new methods of work. Unfortunately for Ford, most
of his employees lacked such desirable qualities. Many, in fact, were
barely literate immigrants motivated by little other than the need to get
their hands on the next pay packet. To solve this problem, Ford set up
schools, churches, and what he called the "Sociological Department" to
monitor his employees and their families.

Ford thus attempted to impose a much more ambitious kind of labor
control than that implemented a decade earlier by Frederick Winslow
Taylor (1856–1915), the founder of the "scientific management of labor"

(Taylor 1911).[2] Taylor had relied on time-and-motion studies to study how the precise movements of mobile laborers could be regulated most effectively. Neglecting the problem of motivations—what later was called the study of "human relations"—Taylor treated his laborers as "trained gorillas." Although the "gorillas" in question were forced to complete jobs as efficiently as possible, what they did when they left the workshop was up to them.

Fordism was first analyzed by Antonio Gramsci (1891–1937), one of the founders of the Italian Communist Party. According to Gramsci (1971, 286), Fordism (or "Americanism," as he called it) was a "new order" and a new form of hegemony—a "psycho-physical adaptation to the new industrial structure"—that enabled capital to mold "internal" or human resources that had not previously been fully exploited. Comparing the highly developed Ford factories with the antiquated and even traditional modes of production that still prevailed in Europe, Gramsci noted that Fordism appealed to all modernizers (liberal, communist, and fascist) who were trying to create a "new type of man suited to the new type of work and productive process" (286). As Gramsci (303) emphasized, "Fordist" employment did not just require the worker to "maintain, renew and, if possible, increase his muscular-nervous efficiency"; it also specified that the employee "spend his extra money 'rationally.'"

In the 1920s and 1930s, few of Ford's employees could afford Ford products. Yet insofar as Fordism promoted the development of an "economic culture" marked by a "commitment to scale" and the consumption of the "standard product" (Murray 1989, 41), this ideology obviously encouraged mass consumption. In the immediate postwar period, Fordist principles began to transform both material and nonmaterial culture. Fordist cities (e.g., Detroit 1955) were agglomeratist in nature, they were shaped by large-scale production, and they physically reflected the effects of standardized and industrialized methods of construction and planning. In the Fordist city, families were increasingly nuclearized, and industrial and residential zones were imposed on, and ultimately erased, more traditional sociocultural milieus (Esser and Hirsch 1994, 79).

Fordism's Significance

The term *Fordism* no longer just refers to the methods of labor control initially developed by Ford. Instead, Fordism is now widely used to describe the mode of regulation of a whole society. In this latter sense, Fordism reached an apogee of development in the immediate postwar period. Its essential characteristic was that it attempted to match pro-

TABLE 4.1   U.S. and U.K. Manufacturing Activity, 1972–1993

Employment, Earnings, and Productivity		1972	1976	1980	1984	1988	1990	1993[a]
Employment	U.S.:	101.8	99.9	109.0	100.9	101.1	99.2	93.0
(1987 = 100)	U.K.:	154.3	149.7	133.9	105.0	101.1	104.8	89.4
Real earnings	U.S.	100.0	99.4	93.5	97.5	100.0	96.7	102.6
per employee	U.K.:	73.2	78.6	83.8	91.0	102.9	104.8	109.5
(1987 = 100)								
Real output	U.S.:	59.5	72.6	81.6	91.4	100.0[b]	n.a.	n.a.
per employee	U.K.:	n.a.	n.a.	n.a.	n.a.	n.a.	n.a.	n.a.
(1987 = 100)								
Earnings as	U.S.:	45.3	41.7	40.9	39.1	36.0	35.6	35.7
percentage of	U.K.:	51.3	48.3	48.8	43.8	40.4	42.0	43.5
value added								

[a]Estimate. U.K.: 1992
[b]1987.
SOURCE: World Bank (1994, 668–689, 692–693; 1995b, 700–701, 704–705).

ductivity improvements in "core" industries with commensurate wage increases for the workers who had helped implement such improvements.[3] By recycling increasing amounts of wage-money through an expanding circuit of production that required, in turn, rising demand for massified goods, Fordism created an ascending spiral of prosperity.

From 1946 to about 1965, wages in the United States, the United Kingdom, Japan, the Federal Republic of Germany, Italy, and France kept pace with increases in productivity. During this period, living standards for workers increased dramatically. Between 1950 and 1972, for instance, median family income in the United States tripled. By the end of the 1970s, however, the virtuous circle of increased productivity and increased purchasing power had been broken—perhaps forever. From 1972 to 1988, U.S. manufacturing productivity *increased* 67 percent, while earnings in the manufacturing sector as a percentage of value added *fell* by 21.5 percent (see Table 4.1). In 1986 American manufacturers paid out nearly $22 million less each hour in wages than they had in 1973 (Harrison and Bluestone 1988, 115). More compelling evidence that the Fordist mode of regulation had come to an end could hardly be imagined.

Fordism, during its heyday, appeared benign to many—not just because it depended on the expansion of consumer markets but also because it compared so well to the conditions that had prevailed before the New Deal and World War II. We should remember, however, that a more fully developed consumerism strengthens the relative power of *capital*, not labor. There are two main reasons for this phenomenon. First, the advancement of capitalist commodity production increases the separation of workers from their means of production.[4] By purchasing new kinds of commodities, workers help advance the material conditions of their own dependency. Second, the expansion of commodity markets makes the domestic workforce more mobile and more dependent on commodity goods (hence more likely to devote its energies to capitalist commodity production in the first place). Many of the mass-produced durables Fordism ultimately sold back to the workforce (e.g., processed food, automobiles, washing machines, refrigerators) freed not workers but time, which was subsequently used to increase not leisure but the amount of labor time available for profitable production.

Keynesianism

Fordism depended on Keynesian policies to regulate and to maintain "aggregate demand" at a sufficiently high level.[5] According to Harvey (1989a, 135), Fordism was "a total way of life" that required "Keynesian economic management," as well as "welfare statism" and "control over wage relations."

Nineteenth-century and neoclassical economic theory assumed that the price of labor would naturally fall to the point at which all able-bodied workers would be employed. It accordingly assumed that market mechanisms alone would serve to sustain economies from which everyone could benefit. Yet as John Maynard Keynes (1883–1946) showed in the 1930s, under certain conditions a market economy can achieve stable equilibrium *and* permanent high unemployment. Keynes thus demonstrated that free-market capitalism would not necessarily promote affluence in all circumstances, let alone guarantee continuous growth.

Keynes showed that economic growth and full employment could be sustained if central banks lowered interest rates to the point where as much new capital investment would be generated as was required to absorb the savings that would occur under the conditions of full employment. Arguing that government spending and public works expenditure could reflate an economy, Keynes additionally advocated an increase in public spending and collective consumption as a solution to some of the apparently intractable problems of the Great Depression. Keynesianism hence required public authorities to pursue policies that increased the social wage and invited compromise and cooperation between business and labor.[6] During President Franklin Roosevelt's New Deal, it seemed for a while as if the state had temporarily sided with organized labor in its struggle against capital. In the 1930s, for instance, many U.S. workers were daily greeted by banners that informed them, "Your President Wants You to Join a Union." The use of public authority to force class compromise, however, was strongly resisted by some dominant interests. As Harvey (1989a, 128) points out, "It took the shock of savage depression and the near-collapse of capitalism . . . to push capitalist societies to some new conception of how state powers should be conceived of and deployed."

From the 1940s to the 1970s, both the U.S. and British governments relied on Keynesian policies to steer their economies. In the 1980s, however, Keynesianism was largely abandoned by the Reagan and Thatcher administrations, both of which turned to monetarism instead. Monetarists claim they can control inflation, but they do not promise to deliver economic growth. The substitution of monetarist for Keynesian doctrines thereby signals an important shift in public policy; among other things, it indicates that the state has abandoned earlier commitments to full employment and rising affluence for the "aggregate" domestic worker.

A Second Industrial Divide?

Michael Piore and Charles Sabel (1984, 189–191) attempt to account for Fordism's demise by claiming that capitalist societies went through a technologically driven "second industrial divide" during the 1970s and early 1980s that was as important in its effects as the first Industrial Revolution. The "first industrial divide" of the late 1700s and early 1800s created mass-production technologies, fixed product lines, vertical integration (among suppliers, producers, wholesalers, and retailers), a detailed division of labor, and hierarchical chains of command. The first divide replaced older craft systems that turned out "a wide and constantly changing assortment of goods for large but constantly shifting markets" (5). By contrast, the second industrial divide created "flexible specialization"—that is, "a strategy of permanent innovation . . . based on flexible multi-use equipment, skilled workers . . . and a revival of craft forms of production that were emarginated at the first industrial divide" (17).

According to Piore and Sabel, Fordist systems of mass production had reached a point of *cultural* exhaustion by the early 1970s. By this time, the fragmentation and volatility of consumer demand, together with the increasing value placed on customization, had begun to create insoluble problems for standardized production. In a similar fashion, Scott Lash and John Urry (1987, 199–200) suggest that flexible, post-Fordist methods of production were largely a response to changes in taste, as well as an adaptation to new technologies and the availability of cheaper labor in the newly industrializing countries (NICs) of Southeast Asia.

TABLE 4.2   Average Annual Percentage Increase in Industrial Production in Some Major Developed Societies

Nation	1960–1970	1970–1980	1980–1990
United States	4.9	3.3	2.6
Japan	15.9	4.1	3.9
West Germany	1.8	5.2	2.3
France	6.0	3.0	1.0
Italy	7.3	3.3	1.3
United Kingdom	2.9	1.1	1.8

Note: Except for the United States, the production data for 1990 are based on the first half of that year.

SOURCE: "Globalization, Part 2" (1992).

For Piore and Sabel, the transition from Fordist production to post-Fordist flexible accumulation benefits workers overall. They (1984, 305) claim, for instance, that "flexible specialization" not only responds to human need but can also create a craft-based "yeoman democracy" that promotes "a republic of small holders." As they (306) plausibly assert, "The ideal of yeoman democracy . . . is most likely to catalyze American efforts to . . . win the consensus that is needed for a national shift to flexible specialization."

Whereas Piore and Sabel identify technological innovation and changing cultural expectations as the main factors contributing to Fordism's demise, Harvey (1989a, 194) is "tempted to see the flexibility achieved in production, labour markets, and consumption more as an outcome of the search for financial solutions to the crisis-tendencies of capitalism, rather than the other way round." But Harvey (142), too, argues that Fordism's ultimate problem was that it was wedded to "fixed capital investments" that "precluded much flexibility of design and presumed stable growth in invariant consumer markets." What is clear, however, is that by the 1960s aggregate demand for mass-produced goods was leveling off and that by the early 1970s western capital was faced with a significant profit squeeze (Mandel 1978; Gershuny and Pahl 1979). Rather than help optimize economic growth, Fordism had begun to create intractable rigidities in "labour markets, labour allocation, and in labour contracts" (Harvey 1989a, 142).

The End of a "Golden Age?"

After 1973 the rate of industrial growth in the capitalist "homelands" began to slow dramatically (see Table 4.2). From 1950 to 1973, industrialized nations had averaged a 3.6 percent mean annual increase in their gross domestic product (GDP). From 1973 to 1989, however, growth slowed to less than 2 percent (World Bank 1991, 14). This slowdown suggests that by the end of the postwar period (circa 1968) Fordism had exhausted its ability to promote an acceptable rate of accumulation.[7]

The deep and alarming recession of 1973–1974 was perhaps the first indication that what Stephen Marglin and Juliet Schor (1990) have termed capitalism's "Golden Age" was coming to an end. Yet profits had begun to peak much earlier—in Western Europe in 1960, in the United States in 1966, and in Japan in 1970 (Glyn, Hughes, Lipietz, and Singh 1990, 77). After the mid-1960s, "the share of corporate profit in GDP fell sharply across the whole developed world" (Harrison and Bluestone 1990, 363), and manufacturing profits in the G-7 nations dropped from a robust 25 percent in 1965 to a barely adequate 12 percent in 1980.[8] According to the Organization for Economic Cooperation and Development (OECD),[9] the corporate rate of return between 1965 and 1976 fell by 37 percent in Britain, 16 percent in the FRG and Canada, and by 12 percent in Japan (O'Connor 1987, 21). It is not surprising, then, that in 1974 Keith Joseph (the "father of Thatcherism") complained that British industry was in danger "of bleeding to death from loss of profits" (quoted in Gamble and Walton 1976, 196).[10]

In the United States, the United Kingdom, the FRG, Japan, France, and Italy, however, the profit crunch was most severe in the manufacturing sector of the economy; it far outstripped the fall in the rate of profit overall (Glyn et al. 1990, 52; Harrison and Bluestone 1990). During the 1980s, while the rate of return for U.S. *non*financial businesses fell to less than 5 percent, the financial sector experienced extraordinarily high rates of return. The consequences were predictable. From 1973 to 1993, manufacturing employment in the capital-starved "Rustbelt" fell by more than 33 percent in Illinois and by 44 percent in New York and New Jersey. In the United Kingdom, industrial employment decreased overall by nearly 33 percent between 1974 and 1989 (Therborn 1995, 71). Yet the British financial, insurance, banking, media, entertainment, and leisure sectors flourished—particularly in the affluent southeast. By the end of the 1980s, London had become largely irrelevant as an industrial or manufacturing center. At the same time, however, the London currency trade had become "sixty-nine times larger than [Britain's] trade in products and services" (125).

By 1994 only 68 (13.6 percent) of the people identified by one source as the "500 richest individuals in Britain" were associated—even in the vaguest sense of the term—with the "production" of anything at all (see Table 4.3), and the number of wealthy "captains of industry" was falling year by year. Traditionalists, however, will be relieved to learn that of the "richest 500 individuals in Britain," 90 were members of the landed aristocracy.[11] By the end of the twentieth century, the ratio of the wealthiest

TABLE 4.3   The Source of Wealth of Britain's Richest Five Hundred Individuals, 1994

Source of Wealth	% of Richest Individuals
Manufacturing, industry, textiles, furniture, chemical production	13.6
Land	13.2
Entertainment and leisure	13.2
Finance, insurance, banking, business services	11.2
Retailing	8.2
Property	8.0
Media and publishing	7.6
Food, beverages, and tobacco	6.4
Construction	6.0
Transportation	2.8
Pharmaceuticals / chemicals	2.0
Bequest	1.8
Other	6.0

SOURCE: Calculated from "Britain's Richest 500," *Sunday Times*, April 10, 1994.

industrialists to the wealthiest landed aristocrats in Britain returned to about what it had been two centuries before.

Post-Fordism

In producing a "mobilization of the spectacle" (Harvey 1994, 372), post-Fordism creates new, flexible opportunities for consumption. It aims to sell leisure, play, distraction, anywhere at any time (ideally without limit). The post-Fordist city (e.g., Las Vegas 1995) specializes in the aestheticization of commodities and in the commodification of aesthetics. It is also likely to specialize in financial functions (e.g., London, New York, Hong Kong)—that is, the "production of debt and fictitious capital" (Harvey 1989a, 331). Catering to the decentered, fragmented, "flexible" subject, and created in the image of what Robert Reich, Bill Clinton's labor secretary, called the "symbolic analysts," the post-Fordist city is not a site for production but a space for consumption, contemplation, and enjoyment. The *source* of a great deal of postmodern culture, it also appears to be *dominated* by culture. Appearances, however, can be deceptive.

Flexible Accumulation

Post-Fordist flexible accumulation (or flexible production) is characterized by a "time-space compression" (Harvey 1989a, 147) that deterritorializes business and disperses production and services throughout the globe. Digitized information, for example, allows production and exchange to occur virtually instantaneously, thereby "speeding up the overall accumulation process by collapsing time and space during one of its distinct parts" (Schoonmaker 1994, 183). Flexible accumulation is also greatly dependent on the internationalization and enhanced mobility of financial capital. As Harvey (1989a, 306, 347) points out, this internationalization and enhanced mobility significantly increase the importance of "sheer money power as a means of domination," replacing "direct control over the means of production and wage labour in the classic sense."

Flexible accumulation could not have occurred without the development of new communications technology. Satellites make global communication almost instantaneous; microwave transmissions create multiple, parallel, and highly flexible phone links; and fiber-optic technology allows nearly two thousand simultaneous digital signals (e.g., telephone conversations or computer transmissions) to be sent through a wire as thin as a human hair. Because the costs associated with storing and moving information have dropped considerably in recent years, the distinction between office (work) and home (leisure) has started to disappear. In a twenty-four-hour global economy, laptop, modem, cellular phone, and fax guarantee that the virtual office is everywhere and always on line.

Flexible production involves a new spatial articulation of the diverse activities of line workers, subcontractors, distributors, and suppliers. While automated production and declining numbers of skilled workers are concentrated at the center of a globalized system of production, a low-paid, unskilled workforce is increasingly dispersed at the periphery. Thousands of U.S. firms now operate abroad in order to take advantage of cheaper foreign labor. "In 1965, total direct U.S. investment abroad . . . was less than $50 billion. It took only 10 years to reach $124 billion. And in the next five, it surpassed $213 billion" (Harrison and Bluestone 1988, 26). American firms are increasingly "outsourcing" much of their production in order to obtain "cheaper foreign parts" for goods with "a U.S. label" (26). Outsourcing illustrates another important feature of flexible production—the various components of a single product are often manufactured all over the world. Cargo containers and jumbo jets move manufactured goods cheaply and quickly. This gives capital new flexibility because assembly of a complex product, such as an automobile, no longer occurs at one particular place.

The new information technologies are changing the spatial distribution not just of manual blue-collar work but also of technical and scientific work. Du Pont, for instance, recently moved some of its R&D facilities from the United States to Shanghai—largely because Chinese technical specialists work for less than 10 percent of the salaries paid to American employees. Moreover, the top 5 percent of Chinese-trained scientists and engineers are more highly trained in technical skills and better prepared for useful employment than are their median-level American counterparts. In 1994 Information Handling Services, which indexes technical and engineering data and had sales of $257 million in 1995, outsourced many of its jobs to Madras, India. The positions of relatively highly paid, well-qualified employees at the company's base in Denver were eliminated, and the tasks these people performed were transferred to Asia.

Since about 1982, the OECD (1986) has embraced flexible accumulation with enthusiasm. Even nominally leftist governments have recently dropped their opposition to flexibility—including the French Socialist Party, which initially opposed flexible hiring practices but subsequently embraced them (Howell 1992, 79). As a result, it is probably safe to predict that many future workers will be "flexibly" employed, whether they like it or not.

Flexible specialization results from flexible production (Sabel 1994, 140ff) and refers to the dismantling of the detailed division of labor implemented by Fordist production. The detailed division of labor forces workers to iterate minute tasks that are meaningless in themselves but that produce a complex product once these motions are joined collectively. Because the Fordist system imposed a manufacturing division of labor that broke down "the process involved in the making of the product into manifold operations performed by different workers" (Braverman 1974, 72), that system subdivided humans. By contrast, "flexible" specialization requires workers to assume multiple roles, and to this extent at least, it appears less inhuman.

Piore and Sabel (1984, 213–216) cite *la Terza Italia* (the Third Italy)— Emilia-Romagna, Friuli–Venezia Giulia, Marche, Trentino–Alto Adige, Tuscany, Umbria, and Veneto—as the best example of a region where flexible specialization prevails. When Southeast Asian countries began to undercut the European textile industry in the 1960s, the Third Italy abandoned mass production and started to specialize in high-quality, relatively high-cost fashion and design. Factories became more capital intensive, and the workforce was given more scope in deciding how work was to be accomplished. By relying on outsourcers and subcontractors, whose inputs could be flexibly adjusted, workshops became more autonomous and were able to respond more rapidly to specific orders. As Allen Scott (1988) notes, the Third Italy escaped much of the "deindustrialization" that many industrial regions of the world experienced after the early 1970s. From 1971 to 1981, "when industrial employment in the rest of Italy expanded by only 4.3% (with a decline of

2.2% in the region of the Industrial Triangle [i.e., Genoa-Milan-Turin]), it increased in the Third Italy by as much as 19.7%" (45). By 1981 "the Third Italy accounted for as much as 37.3% of the nation's total employment in manufacturing" (45).

Flexible specialization is typically associated with artisan and design-intensive industries, but it can also promote the more labor-intensive ethnic and immigrant "sweatshops" that produce fashionwear in Paris, New York, or Los Angeles, as well as "high-technology industrial sectors with significant R&D inputs" such as those in Baden-Württenburg, Germany; Sakaki, Japan; Silicon Valley, California; Route 128 in Boston; Boulder, Colorado; Austin, Texas; Cambridge, United Kingdom; and La Cité Scientifique outside Paris (Scott 1988).

According to Piore and Sabel (1984), *flexible firms* specialize in flexible production. They serve "niche" markets and, unlike the Fordist factory, can quickly adjust to changes in fashions. The flexible firm uses "just-in-time" (JIT) methods of inventory control, benefits from above-average turnover, and is geared to a fragmented, highly diversified set of consumers. Because JIT enables tasks to be done when they are needed, and not before, "in just the amount required to meet desired output levels," it "is a pull rather than a push system" (Sayer and Walker 1992, 170–171). JIT requires a more flexibly specialized workforce whose members are willing to transfer roles and adjust tasks in order to make sure that production lines run at the speed required for job completion.

Flexible firms are not governed by aggregate demand, and they do not churn out interchangeable products for homogenized, aggregate consumers.[12] Many flexible firms specialize in business, financial, and personal services, such as those performed by tax advisors, travel agents, counselors, or even fast-food servers. Whereas Fordist firms rely on economies of scale in order to justify high levels of fixed capital investment, the flexible firm uses "economies of scope" to produce a wider range of commodities for a more diverse group of consumers (Crook et al. 1992, 179). It is thus likely to rely on new programmable technology, such as computer-integrated manufacturing and computer-aided industry, as a means of effectively taking advantage of craft and small-batch production.

As we have seen, Fordism developed a dual labor market that separated the more productive, better disciplined, higher-paid "core" workers from those who were less productive, less compliant, and less well paid. By contrast, the flexible firm of the 1990s develops new kinds of labor market segmentation (see Table 4.4). Whereas a "core group" of primary workers provides "functional flexibility," or multiskilling (i.e., flexible specialization), a "first peripheral group" within a secondary labor market provides numerical flexibility. The members of this first periph-

TABLE 4.4   The Flexible Firm

Conjunctural Causes	*Outcomes*
Weak trade unions	Primary labor group
Unemployment	Functional flexibility
	(variability of tasks)

FLEXIBLE
⇨ EMPLOYMENT ⇨
PRACTICES

	Secondary labor group
	Numerical flexibility
	First peripheral group
	Short-term workers
Greater competitive pressure	Second peripheral group
	Part-timers
Greater vitality and uncertainty	Temporary workers
	Casual workers
Technological change	
	Distancing, i.e., subcontracting
	Pay flexibility

SOURCE: Atkinson and Meager (1986).

eral group include clerical, secretarial, and lesser-skilled manual workers who experience high turnover rates and "natural" wastage. A "second peripheral group" provides even greater numerical flexibility and includes part-time workers and workers on short-term contracts, such as public subsidy trainees.[13] Additional flexibility is added by subcontractors, who reduce labor costs, and by variations in pay, which are tied to performance and job productivity. Subcontracting, or distancing, spreads risk and helps to eliminate the dysfunctional consequences of overcapitalization and the rigidity that can result from vertical integration. Flexible firms therefore "enjoy the organizational advantages of vertical integration without the financial obligations" (Sayer and Walker 1992, 176). Pay flexibility provides the "carrot and stick" that enable employers to implement all of these features (Atkinson and Meager 1986).

Fordist firms retained a permanent staff of salaried, fully benefited personnel and maintained a relatively permanent workforce of production workers who "clocked in" on a daily basis. By contrast, flexible firms rely on a spatially dispersed network of workers, many of whom maintain very weak ties with the parent firm. Benetton, the Italian fashionware company, for instance, does not even own its own stores: "The full cost of setting up shop must be borne by the operator although s/he must operate within the rules of Benetton's shop organization, that is, no backroom stockholding, a particular interior design and selling only Benetton products" (Lash and Urry 1994, 177). Benetton's production facilities employ only about fifteen hundred workers, whose efforts are complemented by two hundred subcontractors, each employing thirty to fifty workers. Commenting on such trends, *The Economist* (June 11, 1994, 74) has remarked on the difficulty of trying to decide whether firms such as Benetton or Nike are "big" or "small": "Judged in terms of their core workers, both firms are small local operations; judged in terms of contract workers, however, they are sprawling multinationals. Indeed, organizations such as this are not so much single entities as fluid networks, adding value by co-ordinating activities across geographical and corporate boundaries. In other words, the best firms are both 'big' and 'small,' depending on what they are doing."

Nike (annual sales $4 billion in 1994) "subcontracts 100 per cent of its goods production, employing 9,000 people directly in design, product development, marketing, distribution, data processing and sales and administration. Labor-intensive manufacturing tasks are performed by a workforce of 75,000 at the subcontractors' facilities in developing countries" (*World Investment Report* [*WIR*] 1994, 193). Twenty years ago, these subcontractors were situated in Japan, the United States, and the United Kingdom, but now they are located in China, South Korea, Malaysia, Taiwan, and Thailand (*WIR* 1994, 193). Nike's business methods are not that unusual: Most of the clothing sold in major stores in the West is produced in factories that employ ten or fewer workers (Lash and Urry 1994, 177).

Although subcontractors are often wholly dependent on parent companies, they do not, of course, receive a share of the profits proportionate to the value they add. The example of Japan helps makes the point: The major manufacturing Japanese companies and the financial *keiretsu* such as Sumitomo, Mitsui, and Mitsubishi use subcontractors largely to reduce the price of labor, as well as to make it more flexible. According to the Japanese Ministry of Trade and Industry, "The average Japanese auto maker had 171 first-layer, 4,700 second-layer and 31,600 third-layer part makers. Many of the third layer are 'crowded backyard workshops' where families turn out small stampings on floor presses ten hours a day, six to seven days a week" (Lash and Urry 1994, 73). Lifetime employment does not exist in the subcontract sector, and pay is up to 40 percent less (Sayer and Walker 1992, 176). In dominant Japanese manufacturing companies, "the increasing use of subcontractors . . . typically account for a third of total costs," while labor absorbs only 5 percent of total costs (*The Economist* June 11, 1994, 64).

American companies are playing catch-up—some quite successfully. At the end of the 1980s, Chrysler procured "fully 70 percent of the value of its final products from outside suppliers" (Harrison and Bluestone 1988, 48), and Compaq, the Houston-based firm that became the world's biggest personal computer maker in 1994, has managed to cut direct labor costs for some of its products to an astonishing 2 percent (*The Economist* July 2, 1994, 59). Even a classically Fordist entity such as IBM (whose chief executive officer received $12.6 million in salary alone in 1994) is now in the process of abandoning job security and adopting more flexible patterns of employment. IBM eliminated sixty thousand jobs in 1994 alone. The following newspaper report conveys the flavor of recent improvements:

> In New Jersey, the company shut six branch offices and housed the 50% who survived the cull under one roof, where everyone is visible all the time. . . . [The] new district office . . . is divided into 350 bare work stations with just a telephone, a computer jack and a black plastic in-tray. . . . Nothing is allowed to be left overnight because every day somebody new is assigned to each desk. . . . Jobs for life are vanishing and now that a laptop computer can become a traveling office the symbol of a desk-as-home is dead. (Greig 1994, 22)

Companies such as Compaq (which in the United States are still the exception rather than the rule) have significantly undermined the opportunities for worker organization and resistance to capital. The workforce in the flexible firm is often virtually invisible, even to itself. Yet although the direct labor costs of the flexible firm are very low, the flexible firm has not, of course, *abolished* labor in some sense, let alone ceased to exploit it. Rather, the flexible firm has fragmented labor, cheapened it, outsourced it, and controlled it far more effectively than before.

Explaining the Transition

Some theorists—of which Piore and Sabel are the best example—have used the idea of "flexibility" as a way of *describing* some of the features associated with "postmodernization" without actually having to explain what is driving this process. Post-Fordism, we are told, is an "inevitable" outcome of "technology" and indicates that consumers are more demanding and more in control of their lives than ever before. The problem with such assertions is that they assume technology is applied in some socially unmediated way and that postmodern consumer capitalism will inevitably promote more freedom and greater autonomy for the subject.

By merely opposing "industrial" to "postindustrial" societies, and "mass production" to "flexible production," Piore and Sabel fail to acknowledge (1) that industrialization is currently responsible for some of the highest rates of growth in our "postindustrial" world and (2) that flexibility has always been an important (perhaps the major) part of capitalism. Moreover, while Fordist enterprises such as Burger Chef go from strength to strength, many "flexible" firms such as Benetton often struggle to stay afloat.[14] Perhaps the most "flexible" workers in the world are subcontractees, but few of these find it as easy to make money as Fortune 500 companies. Another difficulty associated with the claim that Fordism belongs to the past is the fact that the Japanese model of development, while highly flexible, is neither neatly Fordist nor post-Fordist in nature. Keynesianism, moreover, has not exactly disappeared in "post-Fordist" societies. As Adam Tickell and Jamie Peck (1994, 295–296) have emphasized, Reagan's and Thatcher's economic programs centered on a "repackaged version of regional Keynesianism (coupled with regressive income redistribution)" that used state defense spending to boost rapid growth in California and New England in the United States and in the "M4 corridor" in England.

An additional problem that stems from reliance on a dualistic opposition between Fordism and flexibility is that even those theorists who have taken a more critical view of post-Fordism have tended to turn Fordism, by comparison, into a lost social democratic paradise. Harvey (1989a, 126–127; emphasis added), for instance, claims that Ford had a "vision" and an "explicit recognition of, among other things, "a new kind of rationalized, modernist, and populist *democratic society."* But Ford was not a liberal or social democrat. On the contrary, he was racist, anti-Semitic, and thoroughly undemocratic in orientation. He strongly opposed Roosevelt's New Deal and managed to keep the United Auto Workers out of his factories until 1941.[15] Moreover, Ford did not introduce the much-hyped "Five-Dollar Day" so that his employees could purchase Ford automobiles. Rather, as Gramsci (1971, 279–318) points out, Ford's workers were offered this rate in order to get them to implement a new method of production.[16] The "Five-Dollar Day" was in any case quickly abandoned during the economic downturn of the 1920s.[17]

The worst feature of the Fordism-to-flexibility model, however, is the attempt to associate post-Fordism (the condition) with post-Marxism (the theoretical approach). Yet an analysis of the causes of increased flexibility is not beyond the scope of historical materialism.

Regulation Theory

If we want to *explain* the shift from Fordism to post-Fordism, we must turn to the Marxist-inspired regulation approach, pioneered by Michael Aglietta (1979), Alain Lipietz (1987), and Robert Boyer (1986).[18] Regulation theory looks at "the changing forms and mechanisms (institutions, networks, procedures, modes of calculation, and norms) in and through which the expanded reproduction of capital as a social relation is secured" (Jessop 1990a, 154). It tries to show how capital uses both economic and "extraeconomic" conditions to institutionalize "modes of regulation" (particular customs and practices) and "regimes of accumulation" (relatively stable and long-lasting sets of practices) to "secure the expanded reproduction of capital" (Jessop 1990b, 309).

Many theorists of postmodernity (e.g., Crook et al. 1992) have used the concepts of Fordism and post-Fordism to describe postmodernization. Yet these theorists tend to ignore the fact that these terms initially were developed by a Marxist school to explain the emergence of crisis-aversive strategies in capitalist societies. Concepts, of course, can be used by anyone for any reason (postmodernism, after all, is supposedly a democracy of signs), but it is somewhat ironic in this instance that insights developed by neo-Marxists are now employed by theorists of postmodernity to equate postmodernization with post-Fordism and post-Fordism with post-Marxism.

Regulation theorists (or regulationists) believe that "capitalism is always mediated through historically specific institutional forms, regulatory institutions and norms of conduct" (Jessop 1990b, 309). Capital cannot therefore author or reproduce its own circuit, for there are no automatic mechanisms (economic or otherwise) that could guarantee stable accumulation. Profit optimization, in other words, always requires the right configuration of economic strategies, values, motivations, organizational structures, political settlements, and public initiatives; "conceptualizing and describing these is the special domain of regulation theory" (Jessop 1990a, 177). Unlike Hegelian Marxists, regulationists do not claim that there is something inexorable or preordained about history. As Lipietz (1987, 15) observes, particular "modes of regulation are *chance discoveries* made in the course of human struggles and if they are for a while successful it is only because they are able to ensure a certain regularity and a certain permanence in social reproduction."

Like Marx, regulationists view class struggle as integral to capitalism. But they see classes as fluid and shifting entities fashioned and consolidated not just by "economic" factors but also by organizational power, culture, and the state. Classes, in this sense, do not just precede regulatory practices but are also created and sustained by them. Regulationists, taking their cue from Marx, believe that social change occurs "when emergent rigidities and new social conflicts escape normalization and so create zones of instability (where emerging antagonisms can no longer be mediated by structural forms) and bases of rupture (where strains have become so intense that institutions function perversely, transmitting rather than absorbing tensions)" (Jessop 1990a, 172–173).

Among other things, regulation theory helps reveal some of the deficiencies of the models of "advanced" or "state" capitalism that were developed in the 1970s by James O'Connor (1973), Jürgen Habermas (1975), Ernest Mandel (1978), Göran Therborn (1978), and Nicos Poulantzas (1978). With the benefit of hindsight, we now can recognize that many of these neo-Marxists attributed positive features or "normalities" to advanced capitalist societies that these societies could never realistically have hoped to sustain. Many of these theorists did not anticipate that within a few short years welfare statism would begin to be dismantled. They blithely assumed that dominant elites in developed economies had some kind of commitment to internationally competitive manufacturing sectors, and they also failed to anticipate the abandonment of policies that sought full employment and rising living standards for the bottom four-fifths of the populations.

Regimes of Accumulation

For the regulationists, a "regime of accumulation" is "a macroeconomically coherent phase of capitalist development" (Tickell and Peck 1992, 192) that opportunistically emerges within a matrix of class struggle. What solidifies such a regime is its ability to achieve a relatively "long-term stabilization of the allocation of social production between consumption and accumulation" (Lipietz 1987, 14). A regime of accumulation thus articulates the underlying "conditions of production" and "the transformation of the conditions of the reproduction of wage-labour . . . within a national economic and social formation, and between the social and economic formation under consideration and its 'outside world'" (14). A regime of accumulation helps, in short, to institutionalize a particular mode of class domination, and it reproduces wage earners in an appropriate form—with the right attitudes, the right skills, the right values, and the right spending habits (Lipietz 1986, 19).

Regulationists claim that four major regimes of accumulation have existed since the beginning of the eighteenth century. They are as follows:[19]

1. *Extensive accumulation,* which replaces traditional social relations with extensive market relations. In this regime, accumulation occurs as capitalism develops new industrial products and expands into new areas—mostly in Europe and North America; wages are negotiated by individual firms; markets are preeminent; and the state is largely noninterventionist.
2. *Intensive Taylorist accumulation,* which applies the techniques of the scientific management of labor to the workplace. In this

regime, profitability is threatened by insufficient levels of consumer spending power, which threatens to shrink to the point where it would fail to return the value of productive capital. The main contradiction of the whole system is that higher wages cannot be negotiated within the framework of existing (largely private) relations of production. The end of this period is marked by the Great Depression of the 1930s, which caused a 60 percent fall in international trade and massive unemployment in developed economies.

3. *Intensive accumulation with mass consumption* (i.e., Fordism), which is marked by significant increases in productivity and wages. In this regime, the most successful corporations tend to rely heavily on economies of scale, meaning that "bigness" is an advantage. Monopoly capitalism is secured;[20] hence prices can to a certain extent be maintained regardless of demand. Collective wage bargaining within economic sectors is institutionalized. "Core" industries are based on manufacturing, and each industry is responsible for its own R&D and for the financing of its operations. The corporatist state reaches a zenith of development, which is solidified and boosted by the war mobilization of the major capitalist powers in the late 1930s and early 1940s. Keynesian planning controls cyclical ups and downs and regulates consumption. Welfare statism appears to be irreversibly established, and organized labor is given a "social wage" (i.e., public benefits and public subsidies of various kinds) that supplements waged income and helps legitimate the enhanced powers of the state. Labor is domestically segmented between workers who are well organized and well paid, on the one hand, and workers who are poorly paid and badly organized, on the other. Capital becomes increasingly vulnerable to interruptions at the point of consumption.

4. *Post-Fordism,* which organizes a regime of "flexible accumulation"; spatially reorganizes labor and productive facilities; develops new "core" industries based on information, communication, finance, tourism, and leisure; ends collective wage bargaining and eliminates "corporatist" settlements between big business and organized labor; produces an increasingly segmented labor force, with a greater emphasis on temporary, part-time, and casual workers; and favors design-intensive, high-technology financial and personal services.

As well as accounting for historical variation, regulation theory also attempts to explain the diverse regimes of accumulation that inhabit particular time-space locations within a globalized (i.e., internally differentiated) world economy. Within such a system, different mixes of money and power, applied in different locations, have created diverse structures of accumulation. These include "blocked Fordism" (Britain), "flex-Fordism," (West Germany), "state Fordism" (France), "delayed Fordism" (Spain, Italy), and "peripheral Fordism" (South Korea, Brazil, Mexico).

Primitive Taylorism—what Lipietz (1987, 76) aptly calls "bloody Taylorization"—is prominent in Southeast Asia. The term refers to the transfer of "branch circuits" of the circuit of production "to states with high rates of exploitation (in terms of wages, length of the working day and labour intensity)" (74). Although the jobs that are transferred are labor intensive, "fragmented, and repetitive," they are not, strictly speaking, Fordist because they are not connected by any "automatic machine system" (74), and they do not need to match productivity improvements with real increases in wages.

Flexibility's Impact on Labor

Some theorists (most obviously Piore and Sabel) have suggested that flexible specialization has reversed many of the processes by which labor was degraded in the past. In opposition, the regulationists argue that the whole point of flexibility is to weaken the possibilities of worker resistance in the face of intensified exploitation. According to Anna Pollert (1988, 72), "The language of 'flexibility' reveals itself as the language of social integration in the 1980s [and the 1990s]: how to live with insecurity and unemployment and learn to love it." But flexibility has not just created insecurity and underemployment; it has also reduced aggregate levels of pay—even in the much-celebrated Third Italy (Murray 1987). As we have seen, aggregate labor earnings in this country have fallen by more than 20 percent since 1972.

From 1945 to 1973, nearly 25 percent of new jobs in the United States were created at a high pay scale. From 1979 to 1986, however, the proportion fell to 14 percent, and it has slipped since (Braun 1991, 168ff; Harrison and Bluestone 1986, 1988, 21–52; Aronowitz and DiFazio 1994, 93ff). A significant part of this fall in wages was caused by the reduction of higher-paid, exporting- and importing-competitive jobs in the manufacturing sectors of the old Fordist centers (Harrison and Bluestone 1988; Thurow 1987). Median *household* income in the United States began a slow decline in the late 1980s and fell every year from 1989 to 1995 (Mishel, Bernstein, and Schmitt 1996). This decline suggests that the overall slide in U.S. wages is no longer being slowed by further increases in the number of working wives.

In Britain not only has the official unemployment rate soared from less than 3 percent in the 1960s to more than 10 percent in the early 1990s, but also the proportion of full-time jobs has fallen dramatically. A recent study conducted by the University of Durham in England found that while 173,941 new part-time jobs were added in the last three months of 1994, 74,120 full-time jobs disappeared. According to the study, the net gain of 99,825 jobs was entirely part time (Routledge 1995b). In 1979 nearly 15 million men were employed full time in Britain. By 1995 this figure had fallen to 9.5 million, with 5.5 million women also in full-time work (Routledge 1995b). Because most of the new (part-time) jobs in Britain are taken by women, the workforce is becoming more feminized as well as more flexible and more part time. By 1996, for the first time ever, more women than men in Britain had some kind of paid job. According to some estimates, more than 1 million men who are not retired, who are not sick or disabled, and who are of working age are "missing" from the unemployment rolls in the United States. These men apparently are unable to find work at all or are unwilling to take jobs that pay less than they think they are worth.

One of flexibility's main features, then, is its tendency to feminize the workforce, as well as to rely more heavily on ethnic or immigrant enclaves of cheap labor in the First World.[21] First World feminists have usually equated the commodification of women's labor with women's (and society's) "progress" overall.[22] However, the relation between female employment and female "empowerment" is rather more complicated than that suggested by this simple equation. Within the global system of production, many firms and multinationals prefer to hire women because this enables them to take advantage of, not dismantle, existing gender inequalities. For instance, the *maquiladora* factories just across the U.S.-Mexican border are almost exclusively staffed by women, who are seen by their (mostly male) American bosses as more docile, more obedient, and more nimble than their male counterparts. Females in other parts of the world are often deemed to have similarly desirable qualities. As one Malaysian investment brochure expresses it: "Oriental women are world famous for their manual dexterity. They have small hands, and they work quickly and very carefully. Who could be better qualified by both nature and tradition to contribute to the efficiency of an assembly-line? . . . Wage rates in Malaysia are amongst the lowest in the region, and women workers can be employed for about $1.50 a day" (quoted in Lipietz 1987, 75).

According to the *World Investment Report* (1994, 202), "Women have provided TNCs [transnational corporations] . . . with the flexibility they seek: cost-cutting initiatives, undertaken by TNCs, such as part-time work or adaptable working hours, have evoked favorable responses among female workers." Somewhat inconsistently, however, *WIR* (203) also reports that "in export-processing zones [in the NICs] in which around 80 per cent of the labor force comprises women from the age of sixteen, working conditions are often poor and hazardous to health . . . production is often speeded up, working hours are 25 per cent longer than elsewhere and wages are lower (between 20 and 50 per cent lower) than those of men working in the same zones."

Flexibility as a Resource for Capital

Flexibility leads to the production of a much wider and more varied range of commodities, to a fragmented but more flexible workforce, to less vertical and more lateral communication, and—according to Piore and Sabel, at least—to new forms of localized, decentralized, and demo-cratic forms of labor organization and participation. We must remember, however, that flexibility means *flexibility for capital, not for labor.* The "flexible" worker may, in fact, be tied more closely to particular firms than was the Fordist worker, whose limited skills were easily transferable among industries. Flexibility reduces job security, feminizes the workforce, increasingly "ethnicizes" labor pools, and creates higher rates of unemployment, underemployment, temporary employment, and part-time employment. Flexibility relaxes the legal constraints on worker exploitation, deflates the value of labor, and makes the wage system more liquid and more variable. It additionally permits business to shed some of the responsibilities it had earlier accrued.

The latter development is particularly important. As flexible patterns of employment are introduced, employers can jettison the costs of health care, housing, child care, recreation, leisure, and so forth. To the extent that these lost benefits can be recouped, they have to be made up from personal income or financed by increased levels of public spending (not very likely in the current political climate). In an increasingly "flexible" world, the state must cope with demands from taxpayers that their burden be lightened and must also deal with unrealistic expectations that entitlement payments will compensate workers for their increasingly devalued labor contracts. The subsequent squeeze, of course, is inevitably portrayed as a quasi-political "budgetary problem" of the public sector, not as an inevitable consequence of heightened exploitation.

The "solution" to this crisis is generically described by the Republicrats in America as lower taxes, shrinking public services, and a decline in the number of people permitted to feed at the public trough (though not, of course, the removal of those who sup hardest and stay longest). Such measures are politically "bankable" with a suitably prepared electorate, many elements of which are ignorant enough to believe that "handouts" to the truly needy take up more than a tiny and inconsequential part of the federal budget. Although these measures can temporarily alleviate some symptoms of "fiscal crisis," they fail in the long run to address, let alone resolve, the structural problems responsible for such crisis in the first place. As these are caused by globalizing trends, they largely are beyond the scope of national governments.

To comprehend more fully how and why flexible accumulation has produced, in Harvey's words, a "time-space compression," we must turn to Marx's (1967b, 23–350) analysis of the formal and invariant mechanisms associated with capital's circulation and turnover. Whereas regimes of accumulation and modes of regulation are historical and temporary, the formal properties of capital's circuit are invariant. In this regard, the circuit of capital describes *continuities* between modern and postmodern systems of domination. It thus describes what is essential to processes of capitalist accumulation.

5 The Globalizing World Economy, the Compression of Time, and the Spatial Reorganization of Social Domination

Marx (1967b, 23–152; 1964–1972) defined capitalism as a formally rational and instrumentally effective system of accumulation that recycles value through three distinct phases: "financial," "productive," and "commercial" (see Figure 5.1). During this circuit, capital assumes distinct functions in three different types of markets: (1) it collects and consolidates credit in the *financial* market, (2) it purchases inputs and organizes production through the *labor* market, and (3) it realizes the augmented value that results from the profitable sale of commodities in the *commodity* or goods market. As mentioned earlier, the highest levels of marketability are always likely to be found in the labor market. Centralization in the financial markets and economic domination in the commodity markets—what Weber (1978, 943) defined as the power of property and property relations—reduce marketability in these latter domains of economic activity. As part of a circuit that must be continuously reproduced, money, in turn, signifies (1) *financial capital,*[1] which normally purchases the means of production, including labor power; (2) *productive capital,* which organizes the inputs of this production so as to create a commodified output "of more value than that of the elements entering into its production"; and (3) *commodity capital,* which enables the capitalist to become a seller of commodities and recoup invested value and profit (Marx 1967b, 23ff).

Like a blind man feeling the different parts of an elephant, economic specialists tend to see capitalism from different perspectives. Bankers, for instance, view capitalism in terms of the circuit of finance capital. They focus on assets, and they tend to regard capital as a circuit of self-expanding value that is interrupted by the slow, risky, and often tedious process of production (Marx 1967b, 57ff). In contrast, commercial sales-

119

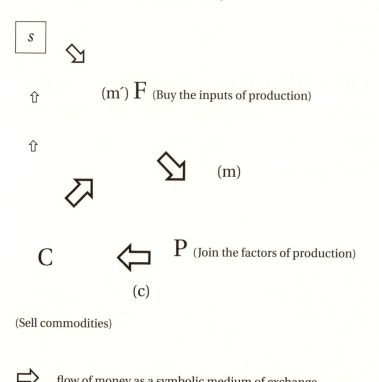

(m′) F (Buy the inputs of production)

(m)

C

P (Join the factors of production)

(c)

(Sell commodities)

⇨ flow of money as a symbolic medium of exchange

Function of Money

F = Financial (Money) capital
1. Consolidates business credit.

P = Productive capital
2. Purchases labor power, means of production, and raw materials.

C = Commodity capital
3. Realizes augmented value as merchandise.

s = surplus

FIGURE 5.1 The Circuit of Capital in Its Monetary Form, According to Marx

people and advertisers act as if selling were the beginning and the end of business activity. Industrialists, however, believe profitable production is at the heart of capitalism.

Marx himself believed that capitalist accumulation is determined chiefly by the circuit of productive capital rather than by the circuit of financial or commodity capital. According to Marx (1967b, 35), productive capital is used to turn every "enterprise engaged in commodity production" into "an enterprise exploiting labour-power." As a result:

1. Workers are made part of a rationalized system of production, meaning that labor power is commodified and labor marketability is optimized.
2. Workers are separated from their own means of production or livelihood and turned into producers of commodities.
3. All commodity production is turned into capitalist commodity production, and all workers become dependent on the sale of commodities.

Capitalism's financial system operates to facilitate the recycling (and augmentation) of value, represented by Marx as $M \Rightarrow C \Rightarrow M'$, where M = financial capital, C = productive capital, and M' = the value that is recouped after commodities have been sold (see Figure 5.1). According to Marx (1967b, 26), financial capital turns "money-functions into functions of [productive] capital" by playing "the definite role . . . in the movement of capital" through time and space. As Marx (28) emphasized: "It makes no difference to [financial capital] into what sort of commodities it is transformed. It is the universal equivalent of all commodities."

Financial capital "presupposes the existence of a class of wage-labourers on a social scale" and "reproduces to an ever increasing extent the class of wage-labourers, into whom it transfers its vast majority of direct producers" (Marx 1967b, 32). The function of financial capital (and the full mobility of capital) is not in these terms realized until the outer limits of the expansion of capital as a social relation have been reached. Although in the West most social relations are adapted to capitalist commodity production, this has not occurred to such an extent in NICs such as China. As a result, capital promotes uneven development throughout the world system, as it always has in the past.

Figure 5.1 describes the circuit of capital in the most abstract (and elementary) form only. Yet it helps define what is, at base, definitive about capitalism. We can see from the above, for instance, that capitalism should not be identified with "industrialism" per se. Capitalism and industrialism came together in the modern era not because there is some *necessary* association between them but because industrialization and proletarianization were at the time best suited to the needs of capitalist accumulation.

In Harvey's (1989a, 107) terms, "the circulation of capital restlessly and perpetually seeking new ways to garner profits" is the "single unitary principle" that serves to reproduce what seems on the surface to be "the revolutionary upheaval, fragmentation, and perpetual insecurity" of capitalist societies. Figure 5.1, then, is as applicable to Viacom or to the Disney Corporation as it was earlier to smokestack Victorian enterprises. All capitalist enterprises purchase inputs (including muscle and brain power) in order to produce commodities (e.g., cars, symbolic resources, or carnival rides) that are subsequently sold at a profit. Capitalism, in short, is a system that recycles abstracted, quantified (contentless) value in the service of accumulation. It is blissfully indifferent about *what* is recycled—and therein lies the secret of its profound nihilism.

Financial Capital and Postmodern Culture

Over the past two or three decades, the internationalization of financial capital helped productive capital attain much higher rates of mobility.[2] But during the same time period, new and highly speculative financial markets emerged that often had little or nothing to do with production. Over the past quarter century, financial markets helped create a new spatial division of labor, together with a globalized system of production and distribution. But these markets also developed new "fast" instruments, such as "derivatives," by which money often appeared to give birth to itself.

Many of the surface characteristics of postmodern culture stem from the increased functionality of finance capital in various parts of the world. In facilitating productive capital's mobility, and in organizing a new spatial division of labor, financial capital has globally transformed the meaning of place. And by developing new apparently autoprofitable instruments, financial capital has at the same time effectively compressed time.

The Global Movement of Capital

During the 1980s, financial capital was globalized in two senses. First, existing national financial markets (the market in stocks, bonds, and government securities transactions) were liberalized. This was achieved by governments (1) eliminating most restrictions on cross-border financial flows; (2) allowing transnational participation in the key financial markets (e.g., the flotation of foreign firms on the London and Tokyo Stock Markets in 1986 and 1987); (3) introducing new financial instruments (e.g., the floating rate note, currency and interest-rate swaps); and (4) removing domestic price and quantity restrictions (e.g., the 1981 repeal of the Glass-Steagal Act of 1933, which had previously prevented U.S. banks from underwriting foreign securities).

Second, international finance was increasingly securitized throughout the 1980s. This led to a decrease in the amount of credit raised in the bank loan market and an increase in the amount of money raised in the securities market (Folkerts-Landau 1989, 188ff; see also Lash and Urry 1994, 18–22). As a consequence, the secondary market for securities (e.g., Eurobonds) grew significantly, assets that had not previously been marketed as securities (e.g., household mortgages) began to be offered as tradable assets, and a new market took off in zero-sum futures and options contracts (e.g., derivatives contracts and currency futures).

Beginning in the 1970s, several western countries—of which Britain is perhaps the best example—increasingly began to specialize in internationalized financial services. By the mid-1980s, the burgeoning international financial markets had begun to dwarf the market in merchandise. In 1985, for instance, the London Eurodollar market (the major clearinghouse for international borrowing and lending) had "a volume at least 25 times that of world trade" (Drucker 1986, 782). In the 1960s, "the volume of international banking had equaled about 1 percent of the gross domestic product of the combined market economies of the world. . . . By the mid-1980s, however, [this had] reached 20 per cent of the GDP of the world's market economies" ("Globalization, Part 1" 1992, 2).

The deregulation of financial markets in the 1980s, together with the improvements in the rate at which information could be processed and transmitted, helped make U.S.-based global financial transactions more profitable than U.S. merchandise and service transactions (Allen 1989, 267). It is not surprising, then, that in the 1980s financial markets expanded much more rapidly than the markets for merchandise and services. During the decade, many western societies (most notably Britain) became increasingly dependent on "invisible" earnings—those from specialized transnational services in commerce and finance and from holdings of property and enterprises abroad. By the beginning of the 1990s, these earnings exceeded 50 percent of total U.K. earnings, which did to some extent compensate for the loss of income caused by the decline in manufactured exports.[3] The returns were often spectacular. In 1993 the internationally based investment bank Goldman Sachs reported profits of $2.6 billion. Each of the 161 partners received $5 million as an annual bonus, on top of the usual salaries, benefits, and expenses.

The Globalization of Production and Consumption

The increasing internationalization of financial capital during the 1980s enabled productive capital to become effectively globalized in its reach and operation. Moreover, as Morgan Guaranty Trust noted at the time, by contributing "to the effective integration of financial markets globally," the "financial innovations" of the 1970s and 1980s "helped overwhelm and marginalize [the] traditional and regulatory segmentation of national markets" (quoted in "Globalization, Part 2" 1992, 4).[4] As a result, the old Fordist "territorial coincidence of mass production and mass consumption" was broken, and an "untrammeled competition in the search for new outlets for capital" was unleashed (Van der Pijl 1984, xviii).

By the 1990s, many major U.S. corporations were "American" in name only. Colgate-Palmolive Company, for instance, continues to sell many supermarket brands that are usually seen as "American," but fewer than 17 percent of the corporation's employees are U.S. residents. Moreover, by 1996 nearly 75 percent of Colgate's annual sales came from outside the United States. In the 1970s, Colgate's performance was less than stellar. Stock bought for $1,000 in 1970 sold for only $969 in 1980 (Moskowitz, Katz, and Levering 1980, 202). Colgate cut its domestic workforce from 21,800 in 1980 to 6,410 in 1996. From 1980 to 1996, the corporation's profits soared 374 percent and the stock price increased 287 percent, from $0.65 a share in 1980 to $1.54 a share in 1996 (Bartlett and Steele 1996, 35A).

The "Uncoupling" of the Financial and Productive Circuits of Capital

During the 1980s, banking and financial systems not only were internationalized but also achieved "a degree of autonomy from real production unprecedented in capitalism's history" (Harvey 1989a, 194). According to Drucker (1986, 781), the "symbol economy" of "capital movements, exchange rates and credit flows" had by the mid-1980s increasingly come to operate independently of what he rather archaically calls "the 'real' economy—the flow of goods and services." Drucker (783) suggests that "in the world economy of today the 'real' economy of goods and services and the 'symbol' economy of money, credit and capital are no longer tightly bound to each other; they are, indeed, moving further and further apart" (see also Sweezy 1994, 2). Coming from quite a different direction, Baudrillard notes the same phenomenon. As he (1993b, 21–22) expresses it: "Purged of finalities and the *affects* of production, money becomes speculative. [It] is transformed from a referential sign into its structural form—the 'floating' signifier's own logic. . . . Money can thus be reproduced according to a simple play of transfers and writings, according to an incessant splitting and increase of its own abstract substance."

In recent years, the "uncoupling" that Drucker describes has increasingly been facilitated by the rise of financial markets that promote speculative financial ventures that are increasingly divorced from production. These offer mostly institutional investors the opportunity to participate in fast zero-sum games where cumulative winnings always equal cumulative losses. Let us look at a couple of examples:

Derivatives. America's largest investment banks (including Goldman Sachs, J. P. Morgan, Morgan Stanley, Merrill Lynch, Kidder Peabody, and Paine Webber) each spend about $1 billion a year just to purchase and run software that gives them (they hope) a marginal advantage in the $35 trillion market in "derivatives": financial instruments whose values depend on, or are derived from, some underlying financial asset, such as stocks, bonds, currencies, or commodities. Derivatives help manage, manipulate, and spread risk, protecting the managers of assets from the volatility of currencies, interest rates, or commodity prices. A derivatives contract typically permits certain swaps or options, giving the parties involved the right but not the obligation to buy over a certain period of time. When derivatives trade, value is husbanded, hedged, shared, swapped, lost, and gained, but never added.

Under certain conditions, derivatives do expand capitalist commodity production and are therefore not entirely speculative. By underwriting some of the assets of a company that pays capital costs in Singapore dollars but sells in U.S. dollars, a derivatives contract could support production that might otherwise fail to materialize. Yet the so-called over-the-counter derivatives, which are not traded at organized exchanges, are merchandised not so much as aids to production but as apparently autoprofitable financial instruments that can magically make more money out of some money (i.e., $M \Rightarrow M' \Rightarrow M''$) without having to go to the trouble of turning financial capital into productive capital. Although these instruments have netted billions of dollars for major banks, they have also cost many of the clients whose particular interests they supposedly protected large sums of money. Proctor and Gamble, Glaxo (the British pharmaceuticals firm), and Metallgesellschaft AG, for instance, have recently admitted losses of hundreds of millions of dollars from derivatives (Alexander 1994, 4; Lipin 1994, A3). Bad derivative speculations were also blamed for Orange County's bankruptcy in southern California in 1994. According to the *Wall Street Journal* (December 8, 1994, A10), eighteen Ohio municipalities had declared losses of $14 million by 1994, the "Louisiana state pension fund estimated its losses at about $50 million[, and] City College in Chicago is seeking to recover $96 million, virtually its entire investment portfolio."

To attain a marginal advantage from a derivatives contract, banks pay derivatives specialists as much as $1 or $2 million a year to develop and to apply the formulas that are used to write such contracts. In this context, *knowledge,* not labor, becomes the key to profitability. Not only is such knowledge "produced in order to be sold," but it also "ceases to be an end in itself"—that is, "it loses its 'use-value'" (Lyotard 1984, 4).

The Foreign-Exchange Markets. During the 1980s, foreign-exchange transactions were about "12 times the worldwide trade in goods and services" (Drucker 1986, 782). Today, daily net turnover on the foreign-exchange market is "about $900 billion, only $50 billion or so less than the total foreign-currency reserves of all IMF [International Monetary Fund] members" (*The Economist* [U.K. edition] August 15, 1992, 54). From April 1989 to August 1992, this market grew by more than one-third (54). As a result, centralized or national banks become increasingly irrelevant. A market that trades nearly $1 trillion in foreign currencies daily will not be much affected by the few billion dollars that the Federal Reserve Bank can drop in a twenty-four-hour period. Even if the Fed wants to defend the value of the U.S. dollar against, say, a rising yen or deutschmark, the leverage it can apply is extremely limited.

For those who know what they are doing, who know how to *valorize* knowledge (see Lyotard 1984), the profits in the currency markets can be very lucrative. Citicorp, for example, makes about $500 million a year from the foreign-exchange market, and the London-based Barclays bank made $400 million profits in 1991 alone (*The Economist* [U.K. edition] August 15, 1992, 54). Foreign-exchange dealing is even more speculative than the derivatives market. As one business publication observed: "Only a fraction of the turnover . . . seems to reflect customers' foreign-exchange needs. Less than 5% relates to underlying trade flows, the demands of companies that buy and sell abroad or those of globetrotting individuals. . . . Most . . . is the dealing that banks and investment banks mainly do among themselves" (54).

The good news, however, is that small investors can now join in. One currency fund (Guinness Flight Global Asset Management) solicits would-be investors with the claim that "since its launch in May 1980 our Managed Currency Fund has produced a return of 662% in Sterling terms" (*The Economist* [U.K. edition] November 27, 1993, 13) and that $10,000 invested in this fund in 1980 would have returned $76,247 in 1993 (a better return than the equities market). As the managers of this fund explain: "Unlike equities, where all markets can decline simultaneously, a fall in one currency will be accompanied by a rise in another. To take advantage of this and produce outstanding returns requires skill in training and judgement. . . . Our funds offer the opportunity for greater potential gains than those available from single currency funds and they provide a lower risk alternative to global equity and bond funds" (13).

In the 1860s, Marx laboriously unraveled the "secret" of *productive* capital: the process whereby money was magically used to make more money (M $\Rightarrow$ C $\Rightarrow$ M´). According to Marx, the surplus thus extracted was sweated out of the worker's hide. Today, however, we can see an even more magical process: that of financial parthenogenesis, where fast-moving money apparently gives birth to itself without anyone having to get involved in the slow, messy, and inconvenient business of productive labor. Some postmodernists (e.g., Kroker and Kroker 1988) have suggested that whereas sex once required material organs and bodies, postmodern cybersex involves "teledildonics" (Rheingold 1991) or sex without bodies, "without secretions," and without any mess. If we resort to analogy, what we see in this kind of speculation similarly appears to have divorced itself from anything gross, earthly, or material.

New "Spatial Fixes"

David Harvey (1989a, 185) has suggested that the economic crisis that faced capital at the end of the Fordist era can "to some degree be interpreted . . . as a running out of" the kinds of spatial and temporal displacements that had "theretofore helped resolve overaccumulation problems since the 1940s." He (1989a, 194) suggests that the internationalization of financial capital in recent years not only has facilitated much of capital's "geographical and temporal flexibility" but has also provided new "fixes" or new profit-making opportunities that help offset capitalism's crisis tendencies.

If free-floating financial speculation provides a new, fast, temporal "fix" for capital, the ability of power and organizational rationality to channel money to particular locations represents new spatial fixes. As Marx would have anticipated, the "sheer power" of money continues to compress time and space in the service of capital accumulation. Nonetheless, as Weber would have predicted, legal authority and organizational resources still structure and augment this power.[5] Global capital flows no longer just allow rich capitalist societies to reorganize poor undeveloped economies exclusively in the former's interest. Capital, instead, reorganizes and internally differentiates all the territories over which it holds sway. Instead of separating, say, a rich America from a poor China, capital now brings the itinerant laborers of Asia to the New World cities. Capital also situates ethnicized, poverty-stricken East Palo Alto (the 1992 "murder capital of America") next door to Palo Alto—one of the richest and costliest cities in America, home to Stanford University and Hewlett-Packard's new corporate campus. On the other side of a continent, capital surrounds poverty-stricken, destitute Bridgeport, Connecticut, with a sea of affluence and conspicuous consumption.

Consumption and Production in
the Developed Economies

In discussing spatial arrangements such as those just described, geographer Harvey (1989a, 295) points out that flexibly constituted "corporatist forms of governance" must endeavor to sell the "qualities of place in the midst of the increasing abstractions of space":

> If capitalists become increasingly sensitive to the spatially differentiated qualities of which the world's geography is controlled, then it is possible for the peoples and powers that command those spaces to alter them in such a way as to be more rather than less attractive to highly mobile capital. Local ruling elites can, for example, implement strategies of local labour control, of skill enhancement, or infrastructural provision, of tax policy, state regulation, and so on, in order to attract development within their particular space.

One way in which such development can be secured is through the construction of reservations for postmodern consumer capitalism. Local and state governments have played a major role in helping to create serially produced and managed spaces for consumption, such as New York's South Street Seaport, Liverpool's Albert Dock, Sydney's Darling Harbour, Boston's Quincy Market, Atlanta's Peach Tree Center, London's Covent Garden, or Baltimore's Harbor Place—not to mention the thousands of shopping malls that have sprung up since the 1960s in various localities all over America.

In addition to creating spaces for consumption, however, decentralized "corporatist forms of governance" (Harvey 1989a, 295) must also compete for internationalized flows of productive capital. The state of Alabama, for instance, recently offered Mercedes-Benz "an incentive package amounting to $253 million, almost matching the size of the investment ($300 million)" (*WIR* 1994, 51). Nearly half of this publicly financed package was earmarked for a training center for Mercedes-Benz's workers—this in a state that has some of the most abysmal schools in a nation with one of the worst public school systems in the developed world. Forty-six out of fifty states in this country offer training programs or other inducements to TNCs. Direct loans, for instance, are offered by Georgia, Illinois, Louisiana, Massachusetts, New Jersey, South Carolina, Texas, and West Virginia; and state tax exemptions and credits are provided by Arizona, Georgia, Illinois, Louisiana, Massachusetts, New Jersey, South Carolina, Tennessee, Texas, and West Virginia. Following the lead taken by NICs such as the People's Republic of China, public officials have also set up "foreign trade zones" in New Jersey, Oregon, and Texas (*WIR* 1994, 51).

In a dramatic turnaround from previous years, foreign direct investment (FDI) into the United States increased significantly in 1993, and during that year America overtook China as the biggest recipient of foreign investment in the world. In part, this was because labor costs are significantly lower in the United States than in Japan or western Europe, but it also reflects the fact that America is still the biggest consumer market in the world.[6] In 1995 the World Economic Forum found that the United States had the highest levels of productivity anywhere (measured in terms of the interaction between technological investment and labor costs). Thanks to the reduction of the industrial workforce that had taken place in recent years (or, to use Marxist jargon, the increase in the rate at which absolute surplus value was extracted), some American manufacturing companies were once again able to compete quite successfully against high-wage European and Japanese firms.

Even though globalization has created new forms of development in some localities in this country (mostly in the "right-to-work," low-tax Sunbelt), other (mostly Rustbelt) communities have largely been abandoned. In Camden, New Jersey, for instance—a thriving blue-collar town with a population of 3 million in 1950—per capita income had fallen to $5,700 by 1985, and by 1990, 60 percent of its residents were (like Mercedes-Benz) on public assistance (Lazare 1991). Unlike Mercedes-Benz, however—or unlike Chrysler, come to that—the problems of cities such as Camden, which is situated in one of the wealthiest states in the wealthiest country on earth, are made incalculably more difficult by the fiscal policies of the federal government, which, as part of the overall effort to cut the social wage, has significantly reduced funding for cities over the last couple of decades. The fate of thousands of once-prosperous municipalities such as Camden and Bridgeport is determined by the intersection between financial capital and power. In a localized context, the organizational and coercive strategies of fragmented and decentralized loci of power innovatively structure and channel capital flows, shaping and directing capital's impact on space. In Camden and Bridgeport residents were never given much of a chance to assert control over the place in which they were trapped.

As the old industrial centers in the West were increasingly abandoned in the 1970s, new capital flows shaped the structure and the culture of new "world cities," such as Hong Kong, Shenzhen, Bangalore, and Seoul, all of which began to contain internally differentiated spaces that microcosmically replicated the extremes of the world system taken as a whole. No one, for instance, who has viewed the bizarre juxtaposition of consumerist and new industrialist imagery set against a backdrop of squalid poverty in places such as Shanghai, Jakarta, Manila, Bombay, or Bangkok can possibly doubt the symbolic power of capital to penetrate, differentiate, and reorganize the nooks and crannies of territories once discarded as unworthy of attention. Shaped by similar forces, Los Angeles—the "second city" of the richest nation on earth—had become, by the 1990s, the "Capital of the Third World" (Rieff 1991).

For Lyotard (1984, 76), the epitome of the postmodern lifestyle is "eclecticism": the chance to eat "McDonald's food for lunch and local cuisine for dinner," the opportunity to "wear Paris perfume in Tokyo and 'retro' clothes in Hong Kong." He could have added that a "postmodern lifestyle" also allows one to tour a Salvadoran slum in Los Angeles in the morning and shop at Harvey Nichols in Shanghai that same evening (surrounded by people whose per capita income in 1994 had risen to eighty-seven cents a day).

Production in the Newly Industrializing Countries

The countries that have received the highest level of FDI over the last twenty-five years or so (Brazil in the 1970s, for instance, and China in the 1990s) have tended to be those where dominant groups can use bureaucratic, organizational, and political resources to consolidate themselves as an exploitative class. The organization of work in Brazil in the 1970s and in China today reflects a strategy that combines many of Fordism's advantages (e.g., the rationalization of production, the centralization of management functions) with the elimination of what capital is likely to regard as disadvantages (e.g., organized labor, the generalized belief that a rising tide should lift all boats).

According to *WIR* (1994, 98), "FDI flows into developing countries grew rapidly in the 1990s." Although the "fastest growth . . . occurred in China," other "main recipients" were "Asian countries with rapidly growing economies and a well-trained, relatively low-paid labor force" (98). Over the past few years, capital "has been flowing to low- and middle-income countries at record levels. These flows are estimated to have totaled $175 billion in 1994, more than four times the 1989 figure of $42 billion" (World Bank 1995a, 61). By 1993 fifty thousand foreign affiliates with a total stock of $61 billion were operating in China alone (*WIR* 1994, 68). They employed 6 million Chinese—a workforce in excess of that employed domestically by the forty biggest U.S. corporations. In 1993 FDI in China accounted for around 10 percent of gross national investment and as much as 40 to 50 percent in the coastal "free-trade" zones that are fully reorganized in terms of capitalist commodity production (68).

By the beginning of the 1990s, China had achieved the kind of growth rate (nearly 13 percent of GDP per annum) that would have seriously frightened governing elites in the West if they had seen anything even approaching it in their own nations. According to *WIR* (1994, 109), "China's outstanding performance in international trade over the past 15 years . . . has been, to a considerable extent, facilitated and prompted by FDI."[7] Some of the credit, however, must go to the Chinese Communist Party (CCP), which in the early 1980s decided it could safely abandon socialism without abandoning power. Like the military dictatorship that ruled in Brazil during the 1970s, what the CCP has to offer is not money-capital but primitive Taylorism, methodically reproduced by power and by working conditions that were outlawed by the English bourgeois Parliament in the 1830s. Since about 1981, the CCP has delivered a seemingly endless supply of cheap and reliable labor to businessmen and -women who will never have to worry about, let alone pay for, the long-term effects of exploitation, rampant corruption, out-of-control inflation, social dislocation, and cultural degradation.[8]

Like the PRC, the four "tiger" economies in Asia (South Korea, Taiwan, Singapore, and Hong Kong) have all drawn their strength from highly authoritarian and highly organized political regimes. In Lee Kuan Yew's Singapore, for instance—described by one business journalist (Pilger 1995) as "the first Stalinist state in corporate form"—freedom of the press is denied, religious leaders are forbidden to mention social issues, labor organizations are banned, and citizens' rights are strictly curtailed in the interests of national security. In South Korea, which has probably imprisoned more labor representatives than any other country on earth, and where the possession of certain books is regarded as a serious crime, corporate state power is used to reproduce the economic domination of the major business conglomerates, or *chaebols*, whose rule is consolidated by arranged marriages among the ruling families.[9] Sales of the top thirty *chaebols* in South Korea generate about three-quarters of the country's GNP, and in 1993 the combined receipts of the four biggest *chaebols* alone (Samsung, Hyundai, Daewoo, and Lucky Goldstar) "accounted for almost a third of all the sales of South Korean companies" (*The Economist* June 11, 1994, 71). Not surprisingly, CCP leaders view the four tigers, not a "decadent" America, as a picture of what they would like to accomplish in the plantations they run.

The "People's Republic" possesses some of its own *chaebols:* business conglomerates that are equivalent in size and maybe even in sales to major western corporations. According to one source, the People's Liberation Army (PLA) is "reckoned to own 20,000 companies. The army's annual profits are thought to amount to something like $5 billion, putting it on a par with big American multinationals such as Ford or Exxon" (*The Economist* June 11, 1994, 23). Many of the powerful leaders of the PLA—grizzled generals who are the survivors of fifty years of armed struggle—are dollar millionaires with a vested interest in the survival of the system founded by Deng Xiaoping. Before long, these plutocrats will be ready to flex their muscles, and they will not necessarily be doing it through the market.

At the end of the twentieth century, those who cannot resist the globalization of money power, who have limited access to organizational resources, and who have only their labor to sell are caught in a truly desperate position. The dollar-a-day laborers in the New Economic Zones, planned, policed, and maintained by the Chinese state, who work indirectly seven days a week for American corporations such as Toys 'R Us (whose chief executive officer, Charles Lazarus, received $60.03 million in 1987 [Braun 1991, 11]), compete "freely" with about 700 or 800 million other people in Southeast Asia alone who would like to take their place. These laborers are unable to use their locale, their nation, their ethnicity, their traditions, their culture, their nonexistent unions, or anything else for that matter to escape the brutality and degradation of the capitalist commodity-labor market. Similarly, the 46 million children who toil in nineteen countries to make goods for the U.S. market are unlikely to regard the "new world order" with much enthusiasm. In contrast, the chief beneficiaries of class domination in Southeast Asia—including the children of high party officials who drive around Beijing, Shanghai, and Shenzhen in their Mercedes and Lexus cars with the kind of spending power about which ordinary Americans can only dream—are so far removed from market relations that they would not recognize one if it came up to them and smacked them in the face.

Compared to what exists in China, Indonesia, Thailand, Malaysia, Pakistan, and Bangladesh, the relatively benign Fordist forms of corporatism that prevailed in the West from the 1940s to the 1970s are starting to look like something from another era, if not from another planet. State/civil society combinations are now so hyperdiversifed and so spatially distanced in the service of capital that it is impossible to believe in one generic emancipatory model that could fit all circumstances. Perhaps, then, it is time to rethink the old truism that capital accumulation or economic growth is best suited to (modern) liberal bourgeois democratic forms—an old and increasingly tired canard that is still warmed over, dressed up, and trotted out occasionally by western intellectuals.

As long as Japanese and western business classes continue to finance the CCP's comprador role (which, considering what is at stake, is not much in doubt), access to the bureaucratic authority of the state in China equals money. Meanwhile, access to global free-market competition (for those who cannot avoid it) equals poverty. In this sense, *both* China and the United States exemplify a defining principle of the new world order: socialism for the rich and powerful, competitive market capitalism for everyone else. Instead of ineffectually (and rather irrelevantly) trying to liberate labor from the market, the laboring masses might thus be better off trying to liberate socialism from capital.

The End of History?

Many of the "postmodern" developments described in this chapter—flexible accumulation; the decline of the nation-state; financial speculation (or "casino capitalism"); the rise of new, more flexible forms of governance; the apparent uncoupling of financial and productive systems; the increased use of money to reorganize and differentiate space across vast distances—can be reconciled with the Marxist paradigm of explanation without seriously jeopardizing the latter. In a sense, these processes can be described as "business as usual."

The difficulty, however, is that, like the "bourgeois ideologues" whom Marx opposed, he took it for granted that the liberal forms he associated with capitalist democracy were uniquely adapted to the present age. And although Marx acknowledged that the formally democratic procedures of liberal capitalism were a kind of pseudo democracy that created formal "political" but not real "human" emancipation, he never doubted that these emancipatory reforms were a step in the right direction and that the story of their overcoming and transcendence was immanent in the history that the proletariat was writing about itself. If postmodernity today really can be distinguished from modernity, it probably is because of the collapse of all hope in this project.

And yet . . . at the end of the twentieth century we see a revolutionizing of the forces of production in China; rising and insupportable indebtedness in the Third World; dramatically increasing levels of inequality just about everywhere; rebellious insurrections on America's southern flank; the absolute degradation of living standards in the territories of the former Soviet Union; general strikes and persistent labor unrest in Argentina, Korea, Bulgaria, and Albania; and the proletarianization of hundreds of millions of new workers throughout the world. Perhaps history has not come to an end, after all!

Marx never assumed, of course, that class conflict would always be sustained in its Victorian form. Although he did manage to persuade himself that the struggle between the nineteenth-century proletariat and bourgeoisie would be the ultimate class battle, Marx viewed class struggle as a dynamic and emergent process: an ongoing war on many fronts and in many theaters. Just as subordinate classes are themselves constituted by their opposition to the system of oppression they oppose, so, too, will particular modes of regulation reflect the different kinds of struggle, resistance, and accommodation existing among opposing factions at particular points in time and space. Marx always made a point of emphasizing that capital has a long and proud history of aggressively undermining the "normalities" it once helped institutionalize. Why should the future be any different?

6 Postmodernity and Flexible Stratification: Is Class Still Material?

The compression of time and the differentiation of space described in the preceding chapter seem to have disoriented social theorists, as well as postmodernists. Many sociologists have failed to recognize that whereas western societies have placed proportionately less emphasis on industrial production since the 1960s, the same is not true of the NICs. If we examine capital's now *globalized* circuit, we would be hard pressed to conclude that industrialization, production, and proletarianization are things of the past. Admittedly intense levels of wasteful consumption at various sites in the world are just as important today for capital's globalized circuit as is the reproduction of the conditions of production in Jakarta and Ciudad Juárez. It does not follow from this, however, that we are in some sense at the "end of production" or that humanity has entered—or is about to enter—a new age where knowledge, information, culture, leisure, and democracy have (at last) become the real conditions of life.

Yet we wouldn't necessarily know this from reading what most intellectuals have to say about the subject. While Baudrillard (1989) announces "the end of production," the impressively banal John Naisbitt and Patricia Aburdene (1990) proclaim the arrival of a new information age, where well-educated Americans push pixels around on their TV monitors, live where they want, choose work that is increasingly fulfilling, and happily organize their own conditions of employment. Sociologists such as Scott Lash and John Urry (1987) report the end of *organized* capitalism, a trend somewhat at odds with the picture given in the preceding chapter. According to Lash and Urry (1994, 10–11): "Disorganized capitalism disorganizes everything. Nothing is fixed, given or certain, while everything rests upon much greater knowledge and information, on institutionalized reflexivity." Other sociologists even claim that organized class relations have dissolved (see, for instance, Gorz 1982; Crook et al. 1992, 125; Lash and Urry 1987; Lash and Friedman 1991; Laclau 1993). According to Crook, Pakulski, and Waters (1992, 115, 116), "post-modernization" means that "the capitalist class is . . . displaced (or at least absorbed)" by "fluid and shifting" relations. Not only has the "traditional capitalist class" vanished from sight, but also, we are told, the very "class system" itself has been "deconstructed" (113). As far as Crook et al. are concerned, structured relations of class exploitation are withering away.[1] This finding, I suspect, could seriously startle quite a few people around the globe.

In this chapter, I critically evaluate the following two claims made either by theorists of postmodernity or by those who have contributed in some way to the discussion about postmodernity: (1) that we are at or near "the end of production," a historical condition usually associated with the disappearance of the proletariat, and (2) that class systems in the West either have disappeared or have changed so dramatically since the end of the Fordist period that Marxist theories of stratification have little or no relevance today.

The End of Production?

The industrial proletariat in most of the developed economies has recently experienced a relative decline in its numbers. We should interpret this trend cautiously, however. For one thing, there are far more industrial workers alive today than ever before. And as Paul Kellogg (1987, 109–110) has noted, even during the worldwide recession of 1977–1982 "the industrial working class in the 36 leading industrial countries (in terms of numbers of employed workers in the industrial sector) . . . increased its numbers from 173 to 183 million." From 1960 to 1983, the number of industrial workers actually increased in the United States, Canada, Japan, France, and Italy. The absolute fall in the number of industrial workers in most of the developed capitalist economies after the 1960s was fairly small (except in Britain, which had 9 million industrial workers in the early 1960s but only 5 million two decades later). Since the 1950s, however, except in Japan and Italy, the *proportion* of industrial workers in the workforce overall has fallen sharply for most developed economies.

Although manufacturing employment in the United States and United Kingdom has fallen over the last two decades, this is not true of NICs such as China, Turkey, Brazil, India, Thailand, Malaysia, Indonesia, and South Korea (see Table 6.1). The 12.8 percent growth in GDP in China during 1992, for instance, was "brought on largely by a 20 per cent increase in industrial production" (United Nations 1993, 51), and this growth rate was sustained both in 1993 and in 1994 (Qu 1994, 8; see also

TABLE 6.1 Industrial Growth in "Emerging Market Economies" and in Four Leading OECD Nations

| | Percentage Change in Growth | | | | | |
| | Gross National Product | | | Industrial Production | | |
Nation	Mean Annual Increase, 1986–1991	1992–1993[a]	1993–1994[b]	Mean Annual Increase, 1986–1991	1992–1993[a]	1993–1994[b]
China	+8.9	+12.0	+12.7	+21.2	+20.8	+20.5
Hong Kong	+6.6[c]	+5.0[c]	+5.6	n.a.	n.a.	n.a.
India	+5.9	+4.4	+4.2	+6.8	+2.0	−0.9
Indonesia	+7.2	+6.6	+7.0	+8.7	+5.2	+18.2
Malaysia	+10.8	+8.3	+8.4	+14.0	+9.0	+10.6
Philippines	+2.1	+0.1	+3.8	+4.2	−0.1	+0.8
Singapore	+10.7	+5.0	+11.0	+11.9	+4.9	+11.9
Rep. Korea	+12.1	+4.7	+9.1	+13.8	+3.2	+1.8
Taiwan	n.a.	n.a.	+6.1	n.a.	n.a.	+6.3
Thailand	+13.4	+7.7	+7.8	+19.6	+9.3	+10.7
Argentina	nil	+10.0	+4.5	−2.4	+9.1	+5.4
Brazil	nil	+1.6	+5.7	−1.3	−8.7	+7.4
Chile	+8.9	+10.8	+4.5	+6.1	+9.7	+9.8
Mexico	+3.9	+2.9	+0.5	+3.5	+2.6	+1.2
Venezuela	+3.7	+6.6	−2.4	+4.7	+17.2	n.a.
Greece	+1.3	+1.6	+0.7	+1.1	nil	+5.7
Israel	+5.5	+7.0	+9.3	n.a.	n.a.	+7.1
Portugal	+5.3	+1.3	−1.4	n.a.	n.a.	+3.8
S. Africa	+2.2	−2.3	+3.2	+0.6	−1.6	+2.1
Turkey	+5.1	+6.1	+3.5	+5.3	+6.8	−13.6
Czech Rep.	−3.2[d]	n.a.	+3.5	−14.7[d]	n.a.	+4.6
Hungary	−0.8	−11.3	+1.0	−14.2	−9.2	+11.7
Poland	−2.2	−1.8	+4.3	−3.0	+2.9	+20.5
Russia	−2.0[e]	−19.0	−19.1	−2.2[e]	−16.3	−29.0
United States	+2.0	+2.4	n.a.	n.a.	n.a.	n.a.
Britain	+1.8	+0.6	n.a.	n.a.	n.a.	n.a.
Japan	+5.3	+1.5	n.a.	+8.3	n.a.	n.a.
Germany[f]	+4.1	+1.0	n.a.	+2.2[g]	n.a.	n.a.

Note: "Emerging market economies" as defined by *The Economist*.

[a]Estimate.

[b]*The Economist* (July 23, 1994, 102).

[c]Gross domestic product.

[d]Czechoslovakia.

[e]The Soviet Union. The Soviet economy collapsed after 1989.

[f]Includes the former GDR after 1990.

[g]1986–1990.

SOURCE: Calculated from World Bank (1993, 1994); and *The Economist*.

TABLE 6.2   Mean Annual Contribution to GDP Growth in Industry and
Services for Selected Countries and Trading Blocs, 1972–1988

Economic Unit	Industry	Services
Japan	1.85%	2.46%
U.S.[a]	0.71%	2.05%
All OECD countries[b]	0.78%	2.1%
East Asia[c]	3.29%	2.8%
Latin America and Caribbean	1.5%	1.86%

[a]1972–1987.

[b]The U.S., Canada, Japan, the European Community countries, Austria, Iceland, Sweden, Switzerland, Turkey, 1972–1987.

[c]China, Fiji, Indonesia, Republic of Korea, Malaysia, Mongolia, Papua New Guinea, Philippines, Solomon Islands, Thailand, Tonga, Vanuata, Western Samoa.

SOURCE: Calculated from World Bank (1992, 36–37).

Bowles and Dong 1994). In the OECD nations, the service sector contributed almost three times as much to growth during the period from 1972 to 1988 than did the shrinking industrial sector (see Table 6.2). Yet this relationship was reversed throughout much of Southeast Asia. Growth there was driven by the industrial development, first, of Japan, which had almost a 50 percent absolute increase in industrial employment from 1960 to 1983 (Kellogg 1987, 106); second, in the 1960s and 1970s, of Hong Kong, Taiwan, Singapore, and South Korea; and, third, in the 1980s and 1990s, of Malaysia, China, Indonesia, Thailand, and Vietnam. What these statistics indicate is that since the 1960s the proletariat has increased in size and has been redistributed.

Although these trends are important, we should not, however, overemphasize the significance of the *size* of the proletariat. Marx, for instance, attributed a special role to this class not because it was (or ever could be) a majority class but because it was supposedly a "universal" class, capable of representing the interests of humanity as a whole. In fact, the proletariat has always constituted a minority of the workforce. U.S. manufacturing employment, for instance, was never higher than about 27 percent of the employed workforce, and total U.S. employment in industry (i.e., manufacturing plus mining and utilities) never exceeded about 37 percent of all paid workers (Sayer and Walker 1992, 105). The decline in the absolute numbers of a relatively well-organized working class nonetheless has had a significant effect on national culture and on political structures within the nation-state. But what has had the greatest overall impact in the developed capitalist economies is not so much the absolute fall in the numbers of industrial workers (which, as we have seen, has been minor in most nations) as the weakening or dismantling of the political structures through which organized labor historically expressed itself. This latter process has come about largely through deindustrialization, not deproletarianization (Bluestone and Harrison 1982). The difference is as follows: If deproletarianization sheds production, then deindustrialization *sheds labor.*

With the exception of Japan, all of the developed capitalist economies have experienced significant deindustrialization since 1970—particularly Britain and the United States. Bob Rowthorn and Andrew Glyn (1990, 218) have calculated that: "If industrial employment [in the OECD] had continued to rise at the pre-1973 rate," it would have reached "129 million people in 1985 instead of 104 million." Yet as financial capital became increasingly internationalized during the 1980s, it was, of course, inevitable that many industrial jobs would move from high-wage to low-wage regions. Capital in the past often "took the coolie to the job." But why bring the "coolie" to the job when we can now take the job to the "coolie"? Taking the job to the "coolie," however, is only one side of capital's newfound mobility. The other, as we are beginning to see, is bringing the Third World to the First World—a process that creates enclaves of superexploited workers in most American cities.

In 1964, 25.8 percent of the workforce in the United States was employed in manufacturing. By 1982 this number had fallen to 19.6 percent, and in 1992 it had dropped to about 18 percent. This is a significant decline. However, the share of GDP produced by the manufacturing sector in the same period did not fall at the same rate. In 1964 this sector produced 28.8 percent of GDP; in 1982, 22.8 percent; and in 1992, about 23 percent (Callinicos 1989, 123; *International Financial Statistics Yearbook* 1994). By and large, then, the United States and the United Kingdom are "postindustrial" only in the sense that they have shed labor, not production (see Table 4.1). Put somewhat differently, we can say that it is the American workforce, not the American economy, that is being deindustrialized. What has happened in this country over the past twenty-five years is that the moderate decline in the proportion of value that manufacturing has added to GDP has been far exceeded by the fall in the numbers of manufacturing workers. As mentioned earlier, this improvement in productivity occurred at a time of falling or stable wages. This would not have been possible under a Fordist regime of accumulation because, as we have seen, Fordism matches productivity improvements with wage increases. Yet from 1972 to 1987, during a period when manufacturing productivity improved nearly 70 percent, real wages for manufacturing workers declined (see Table 4.1).

During the 1980s, much of the lost employment in U.S. manufacturing was made up with relatively low-paying jobs in service and leisure sectors of the economy (Harrison and Bluestone 1988, 121–128). Ac-

TABLE 6.3   Percentage of Full-Time Year-Round Workers with Low Earnings in the United States, 1979–1993

Worker Age	1979	1984	1989	1993
18–24 years old	23	33	34	41
25–34 years old	9	12	13	16

Note: Low earnings are defined as $13,483 in 1993 constant dollars.
SOURCE: U.S. Census Bureau.

cording to the Congressional Office of Technology Assessment, only 60 percent of the workers who were displaced during 1979–1984 found new jobs, and nearly 50 percent of these had to accept pay cuts (cited in Noble 1986, A1). One recent study has shown that wages earned by redundant workers in their new jobs who had been helped under the 1974 Trade Adjustment Assistance Program fell 25 percent from a median wage of $425 a week before redundancy to a median wage in the new jobs of $320 (Bartlett and Steele 1996, 41A). Entrants to the U.S. labor market now start at a lower level of real income and progress more slowly than did their fathers in the 1950s or 1960s.[2]

In recent years, these trends have become even more pronounced. According to one study, real wages between 1989 and 1993 fell a further 7.8 percent for all workers with high school diplomas (Mishel and Bernstein 1994). During the same period, wages for new workers with college degrees dropped 6.1 percent. According to the U.S. Census Bureau, the proportion of young workers with "low earnings" (less than $13,483 in constant 1993 dollars) has nearly doubled since the late 1970s (see Table 6.3). By 1994 more than 14 million Americans who worked full time earned wages below the officially designated poverty level for a family of four. This represents a 50 percent increase since 1970.

Weekly aggregate income in this country fell by 16 percent from 1973 to 1987. But over the same period, the income of the wealthiest one-fifth of U.S. families actually rose by 14.1 percent. During the 1980s, the mean income of the top 1 percent of U.S. earners rose by about 75 percent (Harrison and Bluestone 1990, 353; MacEwan 1991, 86; Greenstein and Barancik 1990; Bartlett and Steele 1996, 33A).

Postindustrialism

In "postindustrial societies," professionals, scientists, technicians, and cultural experts supposedly gain power and influence at the expense of those who own economic resources (Touraine 1969; Bell 1973, 1990; Giddens 1990; Bourdieu 1984, 1990; Kellner and Heuberger 1992). For

Harvard sociologist Daniel Bell (1973, 212), "The post-industrial society, it is clear, is a knowledge society in a double sense: first the sources of innovation are increasingly derivative from research and development . . . second, the weight of the society—measured by a larger proportion of Gross National Product and a larger share of employment—is increasingly in the knowledge field." Twenty-five years ago, Bell (374) claimed that "the major class of the emerging new [postindustrial] society is primarily a professional class, based on knowledge rather than property." Although his use of "class" here is, to say the least, eccentric, Bell wanted to emphasize that social inequality in developed nations such as the United States increasingly reflected differential access to "knowledge" and to "expertise" rather than to ownership or control of the means of production. As far as Bell (374) was concerned, this shift meant that old-fashioned (Marxist) class struggle in the developed economies had now been replaced by competition over "who manages the political order."

In the early 1970s, Bell predicted that economic growth and job creation in postindustrial society would increasingly occur in the tertiary, or "service," sector of the economy, and this does indeed seem to be a very real trend in many developed economies. By the 1950s, for instance, most U.S. workers were categorized as "service workers," and, as Bell had forecast, their numbers were increasing. Today, the Census Bureau and the Labor Department classify about 72 percent of the working population as "white-collar" or "service" workers. In 1945 less than 50 percent of the workforce was so defined. We must be cautious, however, about taking such official categorizations at face value. For one thing, the increase in the count of service workers over the last thirty or forty years partly reflects changes in how the state has changed job classifications (see Braverman 1974, 434ff). For another, many "service" jobs are integrally or partially connected with production (Callinicos 1989, 121–127). A postindustrial society does not, in fact, lessen its dependence on manufacturing and industry, even internally. On the contrary, it can—and often does—contain vital industrial and manufacturing sectors that are still growing.

In 1973 Bell noted that U.S. corporations were increasingly earning their income from operations abroad, but he did not at the time attribute much importance to this trend. Rather, he predicted that in the future U.S. corporations would place less stress on the narrow pursuit of profit and put more emphasis on what Bell described as "sociologizing" functions: those having to do with the training and retaining of a knowledge-based, well-educated, scientific or professional workforce. According to Bell (79), this was bound to happen because the "knowledge societies" of the future would be those in which "the scientist, the professional, the *technicien,* and the technocrat will play a predominant role in the political life of the society." In "the last thirty years," Bell (288) claimed, "the corporation has been moving steadily, for almost all its employees, towards . . . *sociologizing* . . . [the workforce]." For Bell, a relatively beneficent "socialism" had already pretty much arrived in the United States by 1973. In the future, he predicted, Americans could sit back and contentedly anticipate a future where "all workers are guaranteed life-time jobs," and where "the satisfaction of the workforce becomes the primary levy on resources" (288). In support of these cheery projections, Bell (288–289) remarked that "one has only to note, in the rising percentage of 'fringe benefit costs,' the index of that shift [to the "sociologizing" end of the scale]—vacations, disability pay, health insurance, supplementary unemployment benefits, pensions, and the like."

As we can see, if Bell was right to predict a fall in the number of blue-collar workers in America and a rise in the number of credentialed or "knowledged" workers, he was wrong to associate these trends with rising incomes. Perhaps the "socialist" Bell might at least have toyed with the possibility that advances in knowledge might be used to empower chiefly business and the state, not just everyone indiscriminately.

Daniel Bell (1973) equated the emergence of the tertiary sector in his "information society" with the rise of what he called the "knowledge class"—"the scientist, the *technicien,* the professional." Has domination by a "knowledge class" now become preeminent? To answer this question, we first must look at where knowledge or information is concentrated and how it is likely to be used.

Unlike Bell (and unlike most postmodernists), Weber emphasized that if a "knowledge class" were to emerge in the future, it probably would become dominant through its control of bureaucracy. As Weber (1978, 225; emphasis supplied) observed: "Bureaucratic administration means fundamentally *domination through knowledge.* . . . Bureaucratic organizations . . . have the tendency to increase their power still further by the knowledge growing out of experience in the service."

If bureaucracy organizes information and amplifies knowledge in the service of formal rationality and administrative domination, then capital promotes knowledge that enhances accumulation. A capitalist "knowledge society" will thus seek to monitor workers by means of electronic devices, and it will also rely on "reengineering" processes to eliminate hidden and wasteful benefits to employees. Seeking to cheapen the inputs of business, a capitalist knowledge society will create "virtual universities" that will allow virtual students to earn credits in cyberspace without anyone having to pick up the tab for a library, real-life professors, student services, or even a campus. By the same token, a capitalist knowledge society makes consumers scan their own groceries (fewer cashiers), book their own flight tickets (fewer travel agents), and pay their bills with a PC, a modem, and a personal access number (fewer bank tellers). And while a capitalist knowledge society allows the executives at BigBurger Headquarters to monitor the number of fries sold worldwide, it does not, of course, require the "assistant manager" working the pictures on the cash register to subtract or carry the numbers involved in simple arithmetic.

Notwithstanding all the breathless excitement and "gee-whiz" talk about the hi-tech workplace and America's critical need for highly trained information workers, most jobs in the growing tertiary (service) sector of the developed economies turn out to be relatively unskilled (see Kumar 1978, 211–219; 1995, 23–27). According to the U.S. Bureau of Labor Statistics, although between 1986 and 2000 there will be openings for "64,000 new paralegal personnel, 56,000 data-processing equipment repairers, 24,000 peripheral data-processing equipment operators, and a quarter-of-a-million computer systems analysts," during the same period there will also be a need for "2.5 million new workers in restaurants, bars and fast-food outlets, more than half a million new employees in hotels and motels, and almost 400,000 additional workers in department stores" (cited in Harrison and Bluestone 1988, 71–72).

In 1993 the McKinsey Global Institute conducted a comparative study of U.S., German, and Japanese industrial performance. According to this comprehensive survey, Japanese productivity in automobiles and machine tools was well ahead of productivity in the United States and Germany. But perhaps the most surprising part of the study was the finding that when Japanese producers attained higher levels of productivity, their need for skilled labor *fell*. In these instances, flexible production and flexible specialization successfully *deskilled* or "dumbed-down" the workforce, institutionalizing, in a new "flexible" form, a process that Harry Braverman (1974, 425) described twenty-five years ago: "The more science is incorporated into the labor process, the less the worker understands of the process; the more sophisticated an intellectual product the machine becomes, the less control and comprehension of the machine the worker has."

It would help here if we distinguished between "skill" and "expertise." Skill reflects the amount of knowledge and ability required to perform certain tasks; expertise reflects a process of social labeling. Increases in skill can be matched with perceived increases in expertise (and vice versa), but we cannot assume that the two qualities run in tandem. Belief in the reality of a knowledge-based or information society stems largely from confusion about the significance of "creeping credentialism" (Collins 1979). Credentialism upgrades supervisory workers and develops new forms of "professionalism" that make people "expert" without requiring them to develop new practical skills.[3] Over the last twenty or thirty years, for instance, many U.S. employers have insisted on a college degree merely because well over 1 million graduates are produced every year. As a result, a college degree does not so much qualify the graduate for a good job as represent a hurdle that must be jumped before a person can gain access to the pool of people who will compete for jobs that offer more than an opportunity for casual labor.

In the developed economies, many supposedly "knowledge-intensive" workers actually perform jobs that are less skilled than those of "lo-tech" manufacturing workers a generation ago. These jobs, moreover, are almost certainly less knowledge intensive than the all-round practical knowledge of many eighteenth- or nineteenth-century agricultural workers.[4] It would be quite wrong, in any case, to conclude that the development of highly specialized forms of information is necessarily associated with a rise in knowledge among the population as a whole. Because the "information societies" in which we live develop *sectoral*, not general, knowledge, rather than all of us knowing more, in the future more of us will know less. In post-Fordist societies, knowledge will chiefly be used to create a "cost-effective division of labour, a fragmentation of the production process, integrated control of all facets of production, and optimum use of the management structure of centralized decentralization" (Hamelink 1986, 137).

Just as Marx himself could not escape the naturalistic and productivist narrative of his day, so, too, it seems, many postmodernists cannot escape postmodernism's own account of itself. As Robert Goldman and Steven Papson (1994, 250) have suggested, postmodern theorists "so intently foreground the simulations . . . that they miss the exploitation and inequality that make possible a public space devoted to glorifying, and reproducing, commodity sign values." Perhaps, then, the "truth of postmodernism" must be seen upside down, as if through a camera obscura, as a historical life process that pushes production "to the inner recesses of our consciousness," while making "consumption," "desire," and knowledge "overwhelming presences in our lives" (225).

Does Class Still Matter?

In opposition to Crook et al., I do not believe that structured or organized relations of class domination are disappearing. And even though I do acknowledge that classes have become far more fragmented than before, and that class relations are more complex, abstract, and spatially distanced than ever, I also think that the *inability* to recognize systematized exploitation in the world is strongly associated with the widespread misconception that postmodernity is far too dizzying to be grasped as a whole. Unlike Crook and colleagues (1992, 35), I do not believe that postmodernity means that the "power of the large-scale social phenomena of modernity, including states, monopolistic economic organizations . . . is attenuated as cultural currents propagate and sweep the globe." Similarly, I cannot accept that under postmodernization "action is *divorced* from underlying material constraints (or rather these constraints disappear) and enters the voluntaristic realm of taste, choice and preference" (35; emphasis supplied).

Crook et al. (1992, 222) correctly observe that the traditional working class in the West has fragmented, and they also point out quite correctly that inequalities in postmodern consumer societies have begun "to be structurated by patterns of consumption rather than production." Even so, can we seriously believe that class domination has simply gone away? What about the global context? If we examine the admittedly abstracted social relations—and they are now *social* relations—among, say, a partner in Goldman Sachs who cleared $8 million in 1993; a thirty-nine-year-old laid-off worker in Yorkshire, England, who will never work again; and a factory worker in Thailand who makes $37 a month for working a sixty-eight-hour week, can we reasonably conclude that "material constraints" and structured domination are of nothing in the lives of these people? Is it reasonable to conclude that all social difference within the global system of capital can be explained merely in terms of "the voluntaristic realm of taste, choice and preference?"

But can Marx be of much assistance in helping us explain domination today? As the regulationists would be the first to acknowledge, we no longer live in the kind of world that Marx described in *Capital*. America might be a divided society, but the divisions are fine-grained and multidimensional. There is no longer a neat division between a property-owning class, on the one hand, and a militant, well-organized proletariat, on the other. Rather, in the developed economies at least, class relations subdivide humans, as well as society.[5] This means that we are all at different times and at various locations both beneficiaries and victims of a well-organized, detailed system of exploitation. It also means that "class identity" (in the Marxist sense of the term) becomes increasingly problematic and "class mobilization" increasingly unlikely.

Let us examine what Marx and Weber might have to offer in the way of interpreting postmodernity. First, however, let me take a stab at representing what an irascible old Victorian gentleman might want to say on his own account:

KARL MARX (irritably): What Engels and I described in *The Communist Manifesto* as "naked, shameless, direct, brutal, exploitation" is now spatially and culturally distanced; first, by capital taking jobs to the Third World; second, by capital bringing a largely invisible Third World to parts of the First World. Political and legal attacks on increasingly desperate First World immigrants sustain Third World conditions in First World, working-class ghettos. Internal colonialization in the United States and in other developed economies— such as the creation of an American (or French) Third World in what used to be the metropolitan center—inevitably fosters programs designed to manage, contain, and, in some cases, reproduce racial divisions.

Below the oppressed Third World workers who live in the First World we find an underclass thrown off when the most repulsive forms of work were taken away from it and given to workers in the Third World. The social degeneration of this passively rotting mass helps justify the reactionary policies of dominant classes, which no longer believe they need be burdened by the abstracted political liberties introduced by the old bourgeoisie, whose death knell the twentieth century long since rang.

Although the more privileged First World workers neither own nor manage surplus value, the dominant position of finance capitalists in the world system and the technical introduction of new methods of storing, transmitting, and exchanging dead value help make such workers the partial beneficiaries of a new international division of labor. Some of the surpluses they produce, for instance, are invested "on their behalf" in locations where the rate of exploitation is highest. Because First World workers occupy a contradictory social location, they are effectively immobilized by the very forces that created them. Abandoned and afraid, fragmented and cynical, they have long since lost their identity as a self-consciously *revolutionary* class. In the Third World, however, class consciousness among the superexploited proletariat is on the rise.

But capital does not live only on labor. Overseeing the whole rotten system in the First World are legions of "symbolic analysts" and intellectuals who serve to manage and to obscure the real conditions of production. These parasitical and impossibly bloated creatures feed on living labor time; their loathsome secretions, which are fed to the young, include "multiculturalism," "postindustrialism," "postmodernism," the "end of production," and the "end of history."

With reference to the major shifts in regimes and modes of regulation described earlier, let us now briefly consider how Weber as well as Marx might have theorized such transformations. Associating class formation with "interests involved in the existence of the market," Weber (1978, 927–928) took it for granted that a displacement or weakening of market relations necessarily lessens the influence of class. The problem with this assumption, however, is that it precludes consideration of how class domination is reproduced by nonmarket variables in regimes other than those of "extensive accumulation" (Wolff 1995). As we have seen, class relations in Fordist or "advanced" capitalist formations are sustained by organizational rationality and the legal authority of the state, as well as by "market situation."

Weber (1978, 82) recognized that the enhancement of "marketability"—"the degree of regularity with which an object tends to be an object of [free] exchange on the market"—and the spread of capitalism were not the self-same process.[6] He (1958, 13) nonetheless assumed that the highly differentiated *economic* rationalization of life first institutionalized in the West by regimes of extensive accumulation represented "a line of development having *universal* significance and value." As a result, he concluded (incorrectly, it seems) that the nestling of market relations within capitalism in early modern capitalist societies was a universal process that would come to characterize every society.

Marx, however, emphasized that market relations became structurally determining in the early modern period only after the bourgeoisie had managed to establish itself as a dominant class. As he (1978, 715) noted, the proletariat "became sellers of themselves only *after* they had been robbed of all their own means of production and of all the guarantees of existence afforded by the old feudal arrangements." From this perspective, the market could normalize class relations only after "the property order has shed its political form and been converted into a relation of production that [legitimates] itself" in the "political anonymization of [bourgeois] class rule" (Habermas 1975, 22). Political theorist Crawford Brough Macpherson (1965, 11) once described the relation between markets and modern forms of liberal, parliamentary representative democracy rather well: Liberal (capitalist) democracy "did not abandon its fundamental nature . . . by admitting the mass of the people into the competitive party system." On the contrary, "it simply opened the competitive political system to all the individuals who had [already] been created by the competitive market economy" (11).

In short, whereas Weber viewed early modern extensive accumulation as apolitical and instrumental (and unavoidable), Marx saw it as a historically specific and temporary instrument of class domination. Unlike Weber, Marx did not believe that the reduction of social relations to the formal principles of market rationality was the inevitable outcome of a mysterious, disembodied process of rationalization that had managed to impose itself over the heads of real historical actors. Marx (1978; 1967a, 713–716) thus did not believe that the class relations of the modern era had developed just by "chance in the market" or had arrived merely through the impersonal mechanisms of "competitive price struggle." Although he certainly would have agreed with Weber that the autonomy given to markets during the early modern period enabled the bourgeoisie to destroy traditional society by promoting an economically differentiated rationality, he could have cited Weber's own comparative and historical research to make the point that bourgeois societies were in a sense anomalous. Most ruling classes had quashed free markets, not given them free rein. The bourgeoisie in this regard were the exception, not the rule.

Marx defined class relations as the product of a social division of labor in which a minority of people (the dominant class) commandeers the surplus labor of an exploited majority. He saw class relations as property relations, and he defined "property" not as a possession but as a social relation. A "property right" gives to persons who can make others believe they are entitled to the "right" in question the exclusive use of a scarce resource. Unlike Weber, Marx saw markets as derivations: They tend to conceal the real social relations of exploitation occurring beneath the surface.

What Marx saw as invariant about class domination is that it is a social process transferring surplus from those who have produced it to others who derive some advantage or benefit from it. *How* this transfer occurs is a matter for empirical and historical investigation, but when it occurs, we can talk about a "class" relation. Such a relation can be fairly concrete (e.g., the worker produces for the factory owner in the mill town) or relatively abstract (e.g., the worker in Shenzhen, China, indirectly helps produce dividends for a French woman holding Wal-Mart stock).

Because class relations can subdivide humans as well as societies, they do not merely separate groups that are wholly exploitative from groups that are wholly nonexploitative. On the contrary, class relations typically organize extremely complex social relations among groups and individuals whereby quite different media (e.g., money, power, expertise, value commitments) can help sustain an overarching system of class domination that perpetuates or widens existing structures of inequality. The existence of such a system necessarily presupposes the existence of some systematized mechanism for extracting value, but it does not follow from this that such a mechanism must involve the creation or reproduction of increasingly well-organized, self-conscious classes. Class exploitation is not predicated on class identity.

A mode of class domination (which can combine markets, power, ideology, etc., in any regulatory combination) generates particular and historically variable class relations (property relations). These describe the relations between slaves and slave owners in the ancient world, but they also refer to the relations between factory workers in China and the billionaire members of Deng Xiaoping's family. By the same token, the abstract relation that exists, say, between a merchant banker in London and a millworker in Bangladesh, whose work is organized by the bank's capital, is also a property or class relation. In short, different modes of class domination (made up, for instance, of different "mixes" of market forces, organizational power, professional authority, traditional authority, legal authority) can generate quite different kinds of class relations.

In the United States, a new dominant class seems to be emerging; it comprises an alliance between a "technological aristocracy" and corporate executives whose compensation is increasingly tied to corporate share price (Head 1996, 50). The technological aristocracy applies "reengineering" techniques to create a more flexible workforce that can work with JIT components that are easy to assemble. The corporate managerial elite, for its part, downsizes and downbenefits the workforce and manages the new relations of production that in recent years have transferred massive amounts of wealth from average wage earners to the holders of capital assets.

The foregoing discussion suggests that Marx, rather than Weber, is of the greatest assistance in helping us theorize the quite complex regulatory changes that have occurred throughout the twentieth century. Although historical materialism insists that no capitalist society can exist without a formally free *labor* market (i.e., without the "free" exchange of labor for a wage), it is quite capable of recognizing that Fordism, for instance, imposed a mode of class domination that institutionalized market-*replacing* and market-*aversive*, as well as market-affirming, regulatory modes.

In *The Communist Manifesto* (1848), Marx and Engels (1974) equated the capitalist regime of accumulation with little other than the naked, brutal form of exploitation sustained by the "cash nexus" (i.e., by the market), but three decades later Marx (1967c, 436) acknowledged the increasingly important role played by managers who were remunerated according to the contribution they could make to the overall process of accumulation. Marx described such managers as "officers" for the ruling class. They occupied a *stratum*, the members of which had in common a functional dependence on what at the time were still the actual owners of the means of production (380–387). As Marx (386) sardonically commented, "It is quite proper to compel the wage-labourer to produce his own wages and also the wages of supervision, as compensation for the labour of ruling and supervising him."

I believe, however, that classical Marxism must be supplemented when it comes to the assumption that class domination is restricted to ownership of (or control over) the means of *production*. As we have already seen, the expansion of capital as a social relation depends increasingly on the reproduction of patterns of consumption, as well as on the reproduction of the conditions of production. Among other things, this suggests that class domination now requires a larger army, or stratum, of intermediaries than ever before. Some of these intermediaries nourish and help reproduce "postmodern consumer capitalism" (see Chapter 9), while others perform ancillary services that specialize in liberal postmodern affirmativist versions of motivation and legitimation (see Chapter 8).

Crook et al. (1992) are not wholly wrong, then, when they emphasize that capitalism is now "structurated" by "patterns of consumption." However, they *are* wrong to imply that such patterns have somehow replaced those associated with production. The act of shopping has not yet become infrastructural. Production and consumption both remain an integral part of the circulation of capital, albeit within spaces that are globally differentiated.

Social Domination in the "Postmodern" West

Let us now review how *others* have theorized "postmodern" forms of stratification. I find much of the literature on this topic tangled and confused. There are, nonetheless, nuggets worth extracting. Theorists who have discussed the emergence of "postmodern" stratification have tended to claim that Marx's "ruling class" has been *replaced* by a so-called service or knowledge class and that the operations of this class cannot be reconciled with Marxist or neo-Marxist theory. For these theorists, Marx is still important, if only in the sense that "postmodernity" has finally put his ideas to rest.

Most theorists of postmodernity use the idea of the emergence of a service class to buttress their claims that postmodernity has somehow dissolved organized, persistent, identifiable mechanisms of class oppression. Unfortunately, however, the concept of the service class is used so vaguely and inconsistently by Nicholas Abercrombie and Urry (1983); Bell (1973); John Goldthorpe (1980, 1982); Lash and Urry (1987); Urry (1989); and Crook, Pakulski, and Waters (1992), among others, that it turns out to be all but useless.[7]

The Rise of the Service Class?

The notion of a service or knowledge class goes back a long way. (As we have seen, its significance was anticipated both by Marx and Weber, albeit in different ways.) One of the first descriptions of the service class is given by James Burnham in his influential book *The Managerial Revolution* (1941). In an argument that develops a position first stated by Marx, Burnham points out that by the end of the first third of the twentieth century accumulation had increasingly become the responsibility of managers and technical experts, not the *owners* of production. More recently, other social theorists (e.g., Renner 1978; Mills 1951; Goldthorpe 1982; Crook et al. 1992, 111–118) have claimed that managerial bureaucrats and business administrators are now, as they put it, members of a new "service class."[8]

In the most general terms, the service class is usually defined as something made up of well-educated, credentialed professionals, administrators, managers, and public service employees (and in this sense it obviously subsumes Bell's knowledge class). In Karl Renner's (1978) original formulation, the service class included (1) Burnham's managers of industry, (2) social service workers, and (3) state bureaucrats (see also Crook et al. 1992, 112). In short, the service class encompasses high-ranking personnel who serve capital in an administrative or a professional capacity. Even though this class does not include low-ranking white-collar workers (e.g., petty clerical staff) or nonfarm, nonindustrial service workers (e.g., college kids flipping hamburgers), it does include rather a wide array of occupations—"including, for example, corporate CEOs and senior state officials on one hand and laboratory technicians, librarians and direct supervisors on the other" (116).

According to Lash and Urry (1987), the service class is the new *dominant* class in developed capitalist economies and comprises those workers who control the "ownership" and use of cultural, intellectual, and knowledge-based resources within formal organizations (see also Abercrombie and Urry 1983; Lash 1990). As Lash and Urry (1987) observe, the expertise of the members of the service class can be applied only *after* these individuals have gained access to the resources of organizational bureaucracy. From this perspective, the service class contains groups that combine control of knowledge and information with access to bureaucratic authority. This is an interesting insight because it raises the possibility that certain strata gain access to the media of expertise and power by showing that they can use these media to articulate capital and labor.

Crook et al. (1992) pursue quite a different line of inquiry, however. They claim that the service class resulted from the "emergence of egalitarian citizenship" in the middle of the twentieth century (119). Hence, the emergence of the service class signals the *end* of class struggle between capitalists and the industrial working class. Following Thomas Humphrey Marshall (1973), who defined "citizenship rights" rather inclusively, Crook and colleagues (1992, 119) suggest that the full establishment of such rights was only established by about 1960: "As the working class took control of, or at least began to influence, the state so that it became transformed into a welfare state, workers placed themselves in a new position in the system of inequality. They no longer struggled to take control of the production system. Rather, the working class established itself as a client of the state engaged in distributional competition with employers." The service class is thus concerned primarily with managing and reproducing a highly flexible, highly decentralized political order. As Crook et al. (115) point out, the members of the service class "cannot [themselves] appropriate surplus value," accumulate ownership of capital resources, or directly "expropriate the labour of others." Consequently, they are "rather more like workers than like capitalists" (115).

The concept of the service class is obviously far too fragmented and too disorganized to be a "class-for-itself" in the Marxist sense of the term—that is, a class with an "identity of interests," a sense of "community," a "national bond," a common "culture," or a common purpose of political organization. According to Crook et al. (1992, 115), the emergence of the service class signifies a phase shift from traditional (Marxist) class struggle between capital and wage labor to a *highly fluid,* more flexible, and more Weberian competition among many differentiated social and cultural factions that compete for "control of political authority in organizations." The nub of Crook et al.'s (222) argument hence seems to be that as "the working class fragments," the "capitalist class is displaced by a service class." Like Lash and Urry (1987), Crook, Pakulski, and Waters (1992) link postmodernization to the breakup of modern class systems. This dissolution reflects increased differentiation on multiple dimensions of inequality and leads to a greater emphasis on cultural or knowledge-based distinctions. Although these are undeniably real trends, most, if not all, of them have already been noted—by Bell (1973), for instance, who failed to note anything "postmodern" about them at the time.

Like Abercrombie and Urry (1983) and Lash and Urry (1987), Crook, Pakulski, and Waters point out that the activities of cultural or knowledge elites in large bureaucratic organizations have created new and highly complex "work and market situations." In this context

> class boundaries are no longer determined by structurally given divisions of interest but by the ability of such groupings to effect closure against outsiders and thus to maximize the quality of their working conditions and their capacity to extract rewards from the labour market. So classes are currently defined by shared work and market situations rather than by a com-

mon relationship to property ownership. The class structures of late capitalism are altogether more Weberian than Marxist in flavor. (116)

Having reached this conclusion, however, Crook and colleagues (1992, 116ff) then suggest that the service class is neither a dominant class in the Marxist sense nor probably a "class" at all in the Weberian sense. As they point out, the service class is not a *Marxist* dominant class because it does not own the means of production, nor does it expropriate labor. Moreover, it is not a *Weberian* class because it does not "constitute a closed set of homogeneous and market situations" (116).

On the one hand, Crook, Pakulski, and Waters (1992) argue that the service class was promoted by the corporatist welfare state in the 1940s and 1950s; on the other, they link it to postmodernization. Their extremely convoluted argument appears to rest on the claim that postmodernization is an unintended consequence of the promotion of the service class. As they see it, this service class is a fragile, temporary, highly differentiated, and highly disorganized class/occupational category, a "way-station" in a "process of social change, confined to the end stage of organized capitalism" (117). According to Crook et al., the rise of this highly flexible "class" reflects the end of late capitalism *and* the growth of "fluid and shifting" relations of power (i.e., postmodernization).[9]

Crook et al.'s discussion of the service class is important because they valiantly try to make something of the concept. At the end of the day, however, they merely illustrate the uselessness of a concept that ultimately appears to deconstruct itself. Because the idea of the service class is so confusing, I suggest we abandon the concept altogether, but without neglecting the issues that gave rise to its use. The term clearly refers to different kinds of people engaged in quite diverse activities. It also suggests many different kinds of exchanges among the state, classes, professional groups, administrators, cultural experts, and so forth. What the foregoing brief discussion does suggest, however, is that relatively well-defined and bounded class identity is breaking down. In this regard, we must grant Crook et al. and other theorists of postmodernity their point that organized, well-integrated, self-conscious classes appear to be disintegrating in the West and that this process has been under way for several decades. As mentioned earlier, class domination is now highly abstracted, multidimensional, and global in its reach and scope.

The Rise of a "New Class"?

According to Mike Featherstone (1988, 200–201), if we wish to understand postmodernism, we "should focus upon the actual cultural practices and changing power balances of those groups engaged in the production, classification, circulation and consumption of postmodern cultural goods." He defines those responsible for such goods as "cultural intermediaries" (1991, 43–47; see also Bourdieu 1984). For Featherstone (1988, 211, 206), such intermediaries are members of a new middle class, or "new petite bourgeoisie," "who rapidly circulate information between formerly sealed-off areas of culture."

These remarks are both promising and confused. They are promising in that Featherstone makes the much-needed connection between postmodern culture and the interests of certain groups. They are confused in that Featherstone (1991, 35–36, 43ff, 57, 62–63) fails to distinguish adequately between a new class that sells "postmodern cultural goods" and value-oriented experts. The problem here is that he conflates quite different media of exchange. Value-oriented knowledge and culture elites, for instance, do not typically establish themselves on the basis of their ability to *merchandise* commodities. The value and significance of what they do are otherwise determined.

Like those theorists who have emphasized the importance of the service class, New Class theorists tend to emphasize the significance of the state in class formation. Lash and Urry (1987), N. Albertsen (1988), and Hans-Georg Betz (1992) have all argued that the New Class has a class interest in the expansion of state-administered social welfarist policies. In support of such policies, New Class members will receive either direct public benefits or employment and a salary for performing "public services." According to Betz (102), the New Class represents "the core support group of social democracy, organized capitalism and the welfare state." He (94) suggests that "the rise of postmodernism can fruitfully be explained in terms of a competitive struggle [involving the state] between various substrata within the new middle class over the definition of culture." "The cultural and social specialists" are hence "core promoters of postmodern culture" (101). They have a "class interest in the expansion of government" because this "new class possesses little financial but large amounts of cultural capital, which its members consider undervalued by the market" (101; see also McAdams 1987). "By institutionalizing its values and political preferences via the state whose resources it controls, the new class has created a power base which allows it to pursue its interests in conflict with other classes" (Betz 1992, 104).

Betz's (1992) and McAdams's (1987) emphases on the New Class's interest in expanding governmental programs is promising, but it seems to suggest a knowledge-elite ⟺ state exchange, not a class ⟺ state exchange. Like Featherstone, Betz and McAdams conflate the idea of a class with the concept of a cultural or professional group. If the New Class "pursues its interests" by "institutionalizing its values," as Betz

(1992, 104) claims, it is hard to see how it is a "class" (controlling economic resources), as opposed to a group of professional or experts (controlling cultural resources). It would, I believe, be more appropriate to see Betz's New Class as a culturally defined group comprising *professional* groups or other experts whose "expertise" is actually sanctioned or supported by capital or the state as recompense for services rendered.

Nonetheless, Betz's claim that postmodernity is linked with the emergence of new "social and cultural specialists" who trade cultural resources is highly insightful.[10] The state, for its part, could use *its* organizational resources, including its fiscal resources, to supplement or pay the salary of these "specialists." One hundred fifty years ago, Marx claimed that the legal universalism of the state was a fiction that concealed the material interests of the bourgeoisie. What Betz is suggesting, however, is more complex and, in the present context, far more interesting. He is hypothesizing that the state enters into some kind of exchange with parasitical (but rapidly multiplying) social and cultural retainers whereby both its interests and the interests of these various "substrata" are satisfied.

Sorting the Tangle

Let us now try to eliminate some of the confusion that others have introduced. Notwithstanding the vagueness of the concept, Crook et al.'s and Renner's "service class" is not a class at all—either in the Marxist or in the Weberian sense. Although the set of all occupational positions held by members of the so-called service class can give the holders of these positions power over others, the service class cannot by definition exercise dominance as a *class*. From Weber's perspective, members of both the service class and New Class appear to be professionals or experts. Hence, they are *culturally,* not economically, privileged. From Marx's perspective (which at least has the virtue of consistency), the service class is not a class at all but an organized stratum. In Marxist terms, the existence, nonexistence, growth, or disappearance of administrative strata can tell us nothing in itself about the expansion or diminution of capitalist class domination.

The tendency to conflate classes with professional groups seems to be a feature of many discussions about postmodernity. In an article that to some extent complements the arguments put forward by Betz (1992) and McAdams (1987), James Davison Hunter and Tracy Fessenden (1992, 163) claim, for instance, that a New Class of cultural advocates is at the center of the great increase in "moral entrepreneurship taking place in America in recent decades." Hunter and Fessenden (163) argue that "in the last half of the twentieth century" such moral entrepreneurship has become "a measurable sector of the information economy." They do not adequately explain, however, how or why a "class" would engage in "moral entrepreneurship"—that is, help reorganize or implement *value commitments.*

Crook et al. develop a position that they claim is more Weberian than Marxist, but they tend to muddle distinctions that would have been of significance to Weber. As we have seen, Crook and colleagues (1992, 116) claim that postmodern *class* boundaries are determined mostly "by the ability of such groupings to effect closure against outsiders." Weber (1978, 43–46, 341–343), however, would have pointed out that status occupational groups try to effect such closure in order to shelter their members from the unpleasant effects of markets, commodity relations, and bureaucracy. Although the impact of the market or the impact of commodity relations usually cannot be avoided entirely, professional authority is typically used to mitigate their undesirable effects. Law professors, for instance, earn higher salaries than their colleagues in other disciplines not because they are objectively more "expert" than chemists or mathematicians but because the American Bar Association will not accredit universities unless they pay a premium to law faculty.

To attain the kind of closure mentioned previously, occupational status groups must use real or contrived cultural and status distinctions to protect themselves from the more direct or "naked" forms of economic exploitation that are based on the cash nexus. In this context, groups effect closure against outsiders not so much to extract rewards from the labor market, as Crook et al. (1992) suggest, but to *avoid* being dependent on bureaucratic authority or large-scale, well-organized, commercial interests that will use the commodity-labor market to deflate wages. Neither in the Weberian nor the Marxist sense, however, is this kind of activity a *class* activity. What Crook, Pakulski, and Waters are describing is a strategy of professionalization.

Theorists of postmodernity (such as Crook et al. 1992; Lash and Urry 1987; Urry 1989) are right to stress that contemporary occupational structures are extremely differentiated and fragmented along multiple fissures that have nothing to do with the traditional classes of industrial capitalism. Given this, however, we must examine how status differentiation occurs as a first step toward trying to determine whether there is any structural order in this apparent chaos and disunity. If we can comprehend how knowledge-based or information-based occupational groups are established, we can then turn to an analysis of the relationship between these groups, on the one hand, and state power or bureaucratic authority, on the other. We should ask, for instance, how the organizational resources of bureaucracy are exchanged for the cultural resources of specialists. Can the medium of money alone achieve such an exchange? Frankly, I doubt it.

The Role of the State

If the state is a player in any of the exchanges just described, we should ask to whom or to what does rational state administration answer. Can we accept, as Crook et al. (1992, 118) claim, that the inclusion of members of the working class "in wider societal structures of citizenship" is so well developed and successful that the state has become little other than a neutral arbiter of social conflict? Or, as Marx would have anticipated, is the power of the state (in the famous "final analysis") used to reproduce an overarching system of class domination? As I have already suggested, this system is now globalized. But what does this suggest about the changing nature of the state? Can we, in short, see postmodernization as a shift away from the hegemony of the nation-state and toward a political system where power and formal organization are increasingly channeled by globalizing processes? If so, how would this affect expert groups in the West? How could "motivations" or legitimations be functionally adapted in such a context? It is to such questions that I turn in the following chapter.

7 Reorganized Capitalism: New Processes of Power and Motivation

Citing flexible accumulation, some theorists of postmodernity have claimed that in a parallel political and organizational development the corporatist structures of the past have been replaced by a new kind of "disorganized capitalism" (Offe 1985a; Lash and Urry 1987). If "organized capitalism" is the Fordist regime of intensive accumulation plus corporatist structures of national administration, the *end* of organized capitalism means post-Fordism, together with the end of collective bargaining, class-based politics, and the "old" social movements. Urry (1989, 101) has suggested that disorganized capitalism means in essence that "the 'class struggle'" no longer contains "a dynamic sufficient *in itself* to transform modern societies in a socialist direction." Maybe so—but capital, I believe, still embodies a dynamic sufficient in itself to explain postmodernity.

In this chapter, I first discuss the political structures associated with the Fordist period. My argument is that capitalism today is not so much disorganized as *reorganized*. In this regard, the bipartisan support that currently exists for many of the policies of the New Right can be regarded as an adaptation to the internationalization of trade, FDI, and finance that has occurred since the beginning of the 1980s.

Corporatism

Corporatist political structures are the result of a temporary accommodation between capital and a relatively well-organized working class. Hence, the corporatist state is "deeply implicated in (rather than standing above) class conflict" (Jessop 1990b, 112). In the most general terms, corporatism can be defined as "a system of interest representations" in which "constituent units" such as labor or business organizations are "recognized or licensed (if not created) by the state and granted a deliberate representational monopoly within their respective categories in exchange for observing certain controls on their selection of leaders and articulation of demands and supports" (Schmitter 1979, 13).

Unlike some European societies, the United States never realized "a fully evolved societal corporatism" (Weiner 1987, 250). We can view President Franklin Roosevelt's first term (1933–1937), however, as the highwater mark of corporatist tendencies in this country. Among other things, the New Deal created social security, the National Recovery Administration, the National Labor Relations Act, the National Labor Relations Board, the Fair Labor Standards Act, the Public Works Administration, the Civilian Conservation Corps, the Farm Credit Administration, the Civil Works Administration (which employed 4 million people), and the Housing Authority. All of these public agencies were created to help mediate or administer the relation between capital and labor and to deal with the economic crisis of the 1930s.

In *Legitimation Crisis* (published in Germany in 1973), Habermas (1975) asked why so many "advanced" capitalist societies adopted corporatist mechanisms of conflict management during the second third of the twentieth century. Habermas did not at the time address postmodernity, nor did he discuss the globalization of capital (itself an interesting reflection of how things have changed in the last twenty-five years). Although dated, *Legitimation Crisis* provides an impressively inclusive account of the "crisis tendencies" of late capitalism. Under the circumstances, it is not, then, surprising that Habermas's work has become "a focal point for debates about whether a full-scale phase shift [to postmodernity] is currently under way" (Crook et al. 1992, 27).

According to Habermas (1975, 27), corporatism was a contemporary adaptation to the "fundamental contradiction" of all class societies, which is that "individuals and groups" must "repeatedly confront one another with claims and intentions that are, in the long run, incompatible." Because capital itself can only exacerbate, not solve, this conflict, the corporatist state is compelled to adopt a policy of "reactive crisis-management." Among other things, this requires administrative apparatuses to coopt and manage organized labor, regulate the economic cycle, and utilize "excess accumulated capital" (34). Once the price of labor is no longer exclusively set by the market but negotiated "quasi-politically" among organizations "to which the state has delegated legitimate power" (57), the crisis tendencies of capitalism shift "from the economic to the administrative system" (68).

By contrast, relations of production in early modern regimes of extensive accumulation were viewed largely as "an unplanned, nature-like [*naturwüchsig*] movement of economic development" (Habermas 1975, 23). Because differentiated market relations appear untouched by power relations, they do not need to be legitimated in the political arena. The corporatist state, however, replaces market functions with "quasi-political" and legal institutions. Because these transparently are the result of an increasingly *politicized* process, subordinate groups are given both the means and, increasingly, a reason to challenge the rule of dominant classes.

To block such a political challenge and keep latent what Habermas sees as the "fundamental contradiction" of class society, the corporatist state must *depoliticize* public authority, while expanding its domain of operations. The corporatist state does this by turning what might otherwise be democratically shaped inputs from below into administrative techniques that can be imposed from above (Habermas 1975, 68; see also Negt and Kluge 1973; Offe 1972; Weiner 1981, 155ff). In other words, the state replaces potentially unmanageable class conflict with (1) bureaucratic regulation (e.g., the National Labor Relations Board) and (2) legal authority (e.g., the Fair Labor Standards Act, 1937). This renders administrative decisions largely independent of the specific motives of citizens (Habermas 1975, 70). We should not forget, however, that the "lever for the pacification of class antagonisms" in "organized" capitalist democracies "continues to be the neutralization of the conflict inherent in the status of the wage laborer" (Habermas 1989a, 55).

Public officials within the corporatist state are thus compelled to dance a very complex minuet with labor and citizen groups (Offe 1984). Depending on particular circumstances, such groups sometimes have to be solicited and even encouraged to mobilize in predetermined ways; at other times their demands must be blocked or endlessly deferred. In short, the corporatist state both politicizes and depoliticizes. It politicizes by

- Enlarging the scope of public authority
- Placing greater reliance on planning decisions that invite input and cooperation from below
- Publicly inviting the warring factions in civil society to formulate their grievances prior to trying to resolve them[1]
- Promoting the need for consensus based on compromise
- Encouraging a public debate about issues of national importance
- Replacing apolitical "free-market" relations among individuals with bureaucratic and rational-legal control of the goods, capital, and labor markets—as in the 1947 settlement between General Motors and the United Auto Workers, which defined the terms of "industrial peace" in auto plants for the next twenty-five years (Wallerstein 1982, 12)

The corporatist state depoliticizes by

- *Bureaucratizing*—that is, turning contestable political issues into administrative procedures to be resolved by formal organizations directly or indirectly controlled by public officials.
- *Juridifying*—that is, reconstituting political actors as fictional legal persons whose fate can be adjudicated by legal experts loosely controlled by the state. Legal authority thus replaces collective (political) actors with entities that are effectively "immobilized before the law" (Bumiller 1988, 116).

As can be seen from the foregoing, "advanced capitalist" social formations are inherently—although not self-evidently—contradictory in orientation. For instance, modern capitalist democracies must one-sidedly further the particularistic interests of dominant groups, while trying to show that generalizable interests prevail. Modern capitalist democracies also develop their power by expanding a domain of authority that must be legitimated in terms of public interest. But this strengthens the hand of those who want to protest the state's one-sided defense of the particularistic interests of capital.

What all this boils down to is that liberal corporatist states are held hostage to their ability to produce inputs of legitimation from below. As a result, they unsurprisingly tend to favor a "process that elicits generalized motives" or "diffuse mass loyalty" but does not actually encourage a high level of "participation" in the political process (Habermas 1975, 36). We can say, in sum, that the governing elites of "organized" modern democracies or "advanced" capitalist societies depoliticize defensively in response to demands that threaten to overburden the resources of the state.

Breaking the corporatist mold, the New Right attempts to uncouple political rule from the requirement that the state legitimate its actions in terms of an appeal to public interest. In this regard, what is specifically anti- or postmodern about the New Right is that it refuses to accept that the expansion of state power necessitates a parallel expansion of publicly accountable authority. The ideological thrust of the New Right is hence the attempt to diminish public discourse and reduce the level of expectation vis-à-vis public policy. Yet as we have seen, this is not just a "philosophical" position, for such policies are intended to have a material effect: to implement new crisis-aversive regulatory modes. For instance, Margaret Thatcher's success as a political leader was due in part to the fact that she did seem to have some kind of handle on what was actually going on in the world. By contrast, the nominally "socialist" Labour Party, which made up the official political opposition in Britain throughout the 1980s, was content (1) to oppose Thatcherism, (2) to oppose what was happening in the world, and (3) to oppose the abandonment of Fordist and neo-Keynesian policies. Frankly, this did not amount to much of a program.

New Right programs in this country have been spearheaded by the Republican Right, but it would be wrong to tie their fate to the domination of any particular party or faction. While some "moderate" Republicans have resisted some New Right policies, many Democrats have enthusiastically embraced them. The official "candidate of the Left" in 1992 and 1996, Bill Clinton, has strongly defended capital's increased mobility and has shown no interest in using the power of office to shape, strengthen, and then mobilize "old" social movements. In many ways it could be argued that the "pragmatist" Bill Clinton is far more useful to the New Right than is Newt Gingrich. To a very large extent, Clinton is to the right of Nixon, just as Tony Blair, the leader of "New Labour" in Britain, is to the right of Ted Heath, who was Conservative prime minister from 1970 to 1974. President Nixon, let us recall, was the chief executive who once declared, "We are all Keynesians now."

Politically Reorganized Capitalism

Marx (1967a, 566ff) viewed the state largely as an entity that would intercede to sustain the circuit of production if and only if this circuit could not be sustained by the "sheer force of economic relations" (a reasonable assumption to make from the vantage point of the mid-nineteenth century). By contrast, the regulationists, as we have seen, point out that the state is not just "a committee for managing the common affairs of the whole bourgeoisie," as Marx and Engels (1974, 61) expressed it in *The Communist Manifesto,* but rather a relatively autonomous power that can normalize social relations that extend beyond the market and "well beyond the wage relation" (Jessop 1990a, 198). Regulationists, moreover, emphasize that contemporary economies are increasingly affected by external linkages with other societies. As a result, it is no longer possible to conceptualize modes of production exclusively as national units of organization.

The modern state was classically defined—most notably by Weber (1978)—as a regulative entity that uses rationalized (bureaucratized) means of administration backed up by the threat of coercion to seek legitimate authority over activities within the territories it controls. Yet the increased liquidity of finance capital has undermined the ability of nation-states to exercise some kind of political or even administrative control over their own "internal" affairs.[2] After the beginning of the 1980s, all national states—even the most powerful—were compelled to accept, as *The Economist* (June 11, 1994, 17) put it at the time, that "international [financial] markets had grown too powerful for any national government to oppose them successfully." Once financial capital is internationalized, national exchange rates will inevitably remain unstable and unpredictable as long as particular countries continue to adopt different monetary policies. As David Marquand (1989, 206) points out:

> The Keynesian revolution of the 1940s was designed to make the nation state master in its own economic house: to give national governments a battery of regulatory mechanisms which would enable them to maintain full employment in the face of the recessionary forces of the sort that baffled the governments of the 1920s and 1930s. . . . Keynes' fundamental insight that the level of employment depended upon the level of demand may still be true in principle, but it is no longer possible for a medium-sized nation state to put that insight to work in the real world, unless it can persuade other medium-sized nation states to do the same.

Some theorists have plausibly suggested that postmodernization is associated with "a general shift away from corporatist centralism and towards a more decentralized and fragmented minimal state" (Crook et al. 1992, 103). Yet as one recent contributor to the *New Left Review* writing about the "new global economy" recently concluded, "The role of the state has grown substantially since the early 1970s; state policies have become increasingly decisive on the international front, not more futile" (Gordon 1988, 63). These apparently contradictory stances, however, can be reconciled once we realize that whereas Crook et al. are describing the demise of the modern nation-state, David Gordon is referring to the emergence of political strategies that respond to, *and are shaped by,* globalization. In the first case, the nation-state plays a primary and waning role in shaping interstate relationships; in the second, a more decentralized form of authority administers and supervises the arrangements that are most accommodating to the globalizing world system. As mentioned earlier, power still endeavors to sell the "qualities of place in the midst of the increasing abstractions of space" (Harvey 1989a, 295). As a result, the contradictions felt by many within contemporary political spaces (expertly probed by political entrepreneurs such as Pat Buchanan) no longer reflect the hopeless attempt to reconcile generalized public needs with particularistic business interests. Rather, the contradiction facing contemporary political elites now pivots on the (typically unexpressed) requirement that public authority be used to manage the supranational and highly mobile interests of capital on behalf of a constituency that is largely tied to place.

As Harvey (1989a, 170) emphasizes, nation-states today are "called upon to regulate the activities of corporate capital in the national interest at the same time as [they are] forced, also in the national interest, to create a 'good business climate,'"—that is, to induce "trans-national and global finance capital, and to deter (by means other than exchange controls) capital flight to greener and more profitable pastures." This intractable contradiction helps explains why Thatcher in Britain and François Mitterrand in France were both so eager to endorse the "end-of-production" thesis and embrace the tendencies associated with "New Times." By the same token, the inability of contemporary western political elites to acknowledge the aforementioned contradiction explains their unwillingness to confront what used to be regarded as "real" problems—including those of falling living standards, industrial decline, joblessness, alienation, rising lawlessness, increasing levels of inequality, and out-of-control deficit spending.

The corporatist states of the past helped organize a regime of intensive accumulation that depended on public resources and public authority to defend nationally prominent industries. As a result, the deterioration of such industries was regarded as prima facie evidence of economic failure *and* as something that could threaten political legitimacy.[3] What was different about the Thatcher and Reagan administrations, however, was that by promoting flexibility, rather than industrial development, they successfully severed the old corporatist tie between political legitimacy and the stewardship of the economy. The pinstriped members of the Thatcher administration liked to portray themselves as responsible, sober, and Victorian in outlook. But unlike the far more conservative leaders of the Labour Party, Thatcher's cabinet made no effort to pretend that capitalism *had* to be linked to the production of anything useful at all—like jobs, for instance. Unlike the "old" socialists, who appeared to believe that the British economy should produce useful products and useful services, the Tories answered chiefly to the needs of financiers and rentiers and actively promoted the "uncoupling" of financial from productive capital. Highly attuned to temporal "fixes," the leading lights of Thatcher's administration showed little interest in the slow and arduous process of creating real wealth. As Nigel Lawson, Thatcher's chancellor of the Exchequer, proudly emphasized, "It makes no difference [to us] whether a pound is earned from making and selling a product or buying and selling Deutschmarks" (quoted in MacShane 1993, 20). But it made a lot of difference to other people—most obviously those whose lives were wrecked by speculation, deindustrialization, and social anomie.

During the 1980s, opportunity structures in Britain began to reflect what Thatcher had helped wrought. While employment in the public industries and in the capital-starved manufacturing sector was widely spurned, jobs in the "City," London's financial enclave, took on a new cachet. Not surprisingly, between 1983 and 1987 "demand for places in accountancy rose by over a half [in British colleges and universities], with applications for economics and management studies up by a third. By contrast, demand for places in mechanical engineering and computer studies fell" (Riddell 1991, 77). Should we be surprised, then, that in this context Baudrillard's (1993b, 9ff) claim that "we are at the end of production" resonated so strongly with intellectuals (including the New Timers associated with the Communist Party of Great Britain)? According to Baudrillard, "Production, the commodity form, labour power, equivalence and surplus-value, which together formed the outline of a quantitative, material and measurable configuration, are now things of the past" (9). Although perversely wide of the mark, Baudrillard's thesis could nonetheless have served as a motif for the subjective experience of many Britons.

During the 1980s, Thatcher's policies were quite popular with many business leaders. A decade later, however, some were having second thoughts. One of these was John Banhan, director-general of the Confederation of British Industry from 1987 to 1992. Noting that Britain had still "accounted for about a fifth of the combined exports of the world's major manufacturing countries" as recently as "the mid-1950s," Banhan (1994b, 8) belatedly criticized the Thatcher administration for acting on the assumption that "manufacturing was of no special importance, provided the deficit in visible trade could be financed through borrowing, investment from overseas and the surplus on the so-called invisible account that includes financial and other services and tourism." As Banhan observes, anyone who disagreed with Thatcher "was simply dismissed by the economic policy establishment, the media and the government as a reluctant refugee from the failures of the corporate state era" (8).

Banhan (1994a) now appears to believes that it probably would have been better if the Thatcher administration had not declared war on the country's organized workforce. As he points out, there were alternatives—although there was little chance of discussing them at the time. During the 1980s, neither the German nor the Japanese government found it necessary to decimate its own industrial sector. By 1987 West German manufacturing was generating more than twice the value of the British sector ($347 billion in the FRG, compared with $169 billion in the United Kingdom [*International Financial Statistics Yearbook* 1994]). Yet as recently as the early 1960s, Britain had employed more industrial workers as a percentage of its comparably sized workforce than the FRG (Kellogg 1987, 105).

Is the State "Shrinking"?

Observing the undoubtedly shrinking sphere of public discourse, many theorists of postmodernity have made the mistake of concluding that the state, too, is shrinking. According to Crook, Pakulski, and Waters (1992, 79), for instance, "The scope of state power and responsibility" has now "started to diminish." As they (103) see it, postmodernization reflects the "growing realization that the state cannot make people free, safe or equal just as it cannot make people beautiful or happy." In other words, "the 'nanny state' has aged . . . her breasts are drying up and she shows some early signs of schlerosis. Her performance is suffering and there are suggestions of relieving her of some of her duties" (79). Like Crook et al., Urry (1989, 101) observes that most people today do finally understand that there are limits to what the state can do politically. On closer examination, however, these "limits" turn out to be what the state cannot be expected to do anymore for health care, public education, cities, job creation, and the public at large, not necessarily what it cannot do for capital or for itself. In short, even though the capitalist state is now quite willing to abandon some of the public and corporatist obligations it assumed earlier, it shows considerably less interest in relinquishing power.

Crook et al.'s observations about the shrinking state are seriously out of kilter—first, because the capitalist state was never exactly motivated by the need to succor the needy and, second, because there is, in any case, little objective evidence that western states "shrank" in power or size during the 1980s. The number of lobbyists in Washington, D.C., did not fall during the decade (Flammang, Gordon, Luke, and Smorsten 1990), nor did the number of civil servants in Britain (*The Economist* July 16, 1994, 48). Under Reagan, the U.S. federal budget nearly doubled from $591 billion in 1980 to $1,183 in 1988; during this period public spending as a proportion of national income actually rose. By 1996 the federal government was paying $240 billion a year in interest payments alone on the deficits created by the Reagan and Bush administrations. In Britain, government expenditure increased from £68.5 billion ($137 billion) in 1979 to £190.7 billion ($381.4 billion) in 1990 (World Bank 1994, 624–625). As a proportion of GDP, public-sector spending in the United Kingdom did not fall as much as a single percentage point from 1979 (the year in which Thatcher assumed power) to 1993 (*The Economist* July 2, 1994, 89).

Instead of lessening the hold of what Louis Althusser (1971, 143ff) called "the repressive state apparatuses," the Thatcher administration created a new "Disciplinary State" (Middlemas 1983) that mobilized the police and army to break the power of organized labor. The bureaucratic apparatuses of the Department of Education were used to enhance the centralized control of education, and Thatcher's successor, John Major, introduced a new crime bill that ended centuries-old civil liberties. When Londoners democratically elected a Greater London Council that vigorously opposed Thatcher's policies, she solved this particular problem by abolishing this local authority and by selling its imposing riverside building to the Japanese, who turned it into a luxury hotel for foreign tourists.

In the United States, the "war on drugs" was used as cover for the virtual abandonment of civil liberties in many areas of life. By the mid-1990s, the costs of processing and incarcerating prisoners had become so high in many states that public spending on education and other social services had to be sharply curtailed.

Deregulation and Privatization

According to Crook et al. (1992, 99), the "deregulation" and "privatisation" policies of the Reagan and Thatcher administrations show that the "postmodern" state is abandoning "corporatist etatism" and substituting "the 'invisible hand' of the market" for "the 'visible hand' of politics." Yet although efforts at "deregulation," such as the 289,000-page federal telecom bill passed during Clinton's first term, might have created a level playing field for giants such as Compaq, IBM, and Microsoft, they have done little or nothing to reduce the power of property.

Even though the New Right undeniably supports free *labor* markets (i.e., it favors wage earners freely participating in a global race to the bottom), its commitment to the competitive marketing of goods is not quite as emphatic. While adapting policies to the needs of dominant global interests, the New Right abandons small business operators and increasingly defends the economic domination imposed by TNCs.[4] Unlike the old conservatives, the New Right has little interest in preserving the sanctity of place. Thatcher's "deregulation" of retail trade, for instance, put tens of thousands of shopkeepers out of business and consolidated the hold of a few giant grocery chains. As a result, many British market towns lost their identity and their centuries-old vitality.

Deregulation and privatization have thus often *reduced* marketability or market competition. The deregulation of the media by the Reagan administration, for instance, did not create a sphere of free competition among the purveyors of information. Among other things, the Reagan-appointed Federal Communications Commission ended the "Fairness Doctrine," which had mandated the airing of alternative viewpoints and discouraged the concentration of media resources, including the multiple ownership of newspapers, magazines, and TV stations (Schiller

1989).[5] During the 1980s, the profits of TV stations soared and numerous takeovers occurred. Capital Cities Communication acquired ABC, General Electric (the nation's biggest "defense supplier") took over NBC (the second largest network), and the Loews Corporation assumed control of CBS (Johnson 1991, 142). By 1996 what *The Nation* (June 3, 1996, 23–26) called "The National Entertainment State" had been reduced to four major divisions:

1. General Electric (the biggest corporation in America), comprising the NBC network, numerous cable stations, and other properties
2. Time Warner, comprising Time Warner Entertainment; Turner Broadcasting; CNN; Warner Brothers; HBO; numerous magazines such as *Time, Fortune,* and *Life;* numerous publishing houses such as Little, Brown and Time-Life; numerous other cable channels; numerous production services such as World Championship Wrestling; and other properties.
3. Disney Corporation/Capital Cities, comprising the ABC network; several TV stations in major urban areas that together reached 25 percent of American households; numerous cable stations such as the Disney Channel, ESPN, and the Lifetime Network; numerous magazines; numerous newspapers such as the *Kansas City Star* and the *Fort Worth Star-Telegram;* numerous retail stores; sports teams; theme parks; record companies; motion picture companies; and other properties.
4. Westinghouse Corporation (one of America's biggest defense contractors), comprising the CBS network; the CBS radio network; numerous cable stations such as TNN and the Nashville Network; satellite distribution companies; and, of course, Westinghouse's nuclear power and nuclear engineering divisions.

As Douglas Gomery (1989, 98) has observed, one consequence of media concentration is that "a book can be published by [Rupert Murdoch's] Harper and Row subsidiary, be serialized in his numerous magazines or newspapers, produced as a mini series or movie by his Twentieth Century Fox studio, shown on his Fox television network, [and] promoted by his movie/television magazines *Premiere* and *TV Guide*" (see also Schiller 1989, 78ff; Aksoy and Robins 1992; Kellner 1990, 63–67). Although the *effects* of such concentration are conventionally described as "postmodern," the cause of such postmodern culture is, of course, economic domination.

The privatization programs of the Thatcher administration liquidated the social assets of publicly run industries with little regard to their fair market value. Electrical utilities were sold to corporate investors for about 30 percent of the value these utilities realized when they were subsequently resold for a quick profit. Yet if privatization robbed the public of socially owned assets, top-ranking managers gained much from the "reforms." The salary for the CEO of newly privatized British Gas, for example, increased 76 percent during 1994 alone. In 1995 the seventy-seven leading directors of privatized electricity in England and Wales awarded themselves more than £72 million ($112 million) in share options (Routledge 1995a). Wage increases were just as spectacular. Before privatization the mean annual emolument for the director of a regional utility companies was $44,000. After privatization it was $175,140. One utility company (Norweb) managed to raise the salaries for its directors 1600 percent (Routledge 1995a).

Other beneficiaries of privatization in the United Kingdom were several of the politicians who had initiated the "reform" in the first place. Lord Tebbit, for instance—a former trade and industry secretary—joined the board of British Telecom, which he had privatized while in office. Norman Fowler is a director of the National Freight Consortium, which he privatized while he was transport secretary. Lord Wakeham, who was energy secretary from 1989 to 1992, is paid £25,000 ($39,000) a year by Evelyn de Rothschild, who helped Wakeham privatize utility companies when Wakeham was a member of the government. Lord Young, who used to be trade and industry secretary, now earns nearly £1 million ($1.52 million) as chairman of Cable and Wireless, to which he granted operating licenses before he left office (see Chittendon and Oldfield, 1995).

Instead of using the power of office to "shrink" the state and subsequently undercut the effectiveness of their administrations, the Thatcher and Reagan governments used state apparatuses to attack an institutionalized network of reciprocal obligation that had been in place for several decades. Although neither Thatcher nor Reagan reduced the power or fiscal authority of the state, they did cut its public obligations, justifying this policy by attacking what they characterized as the tired old "liberal" or "socialist" programs of a bygone era. As Reagan put it, in one of his much-rehearsed one-liners: "Government is not the solution to our problem. Government *is* the problem" (quoted in Alexander 1989, 47). In a similar fashion, Nigel Lawson, Thatcher's chancellor of the Exchequer, declared that the problem facing the British people was not so much that the "management of the prevailing consensus was inefficient" but that the "consensus" in question was "intrinsically flawed" (quoted in Riddell 1991, 6). Both in the United States and Britain, the main losers in the new "consensus" were working people and those most dependent on social services; the main winners were the corporate elite and the public officials who were in a position to trade public assets and public authority for personal gain.

Globalization and the New Politics of Domination

The (postcorporatist) political program of the New Right in Britain and the United States has centered on (1) the use of state apparatuses to devalue the price of labor and (2) the effort to reduce social spending. Although both Thatcher and Reagan tended to mouth the same ideology, the political strategies they adopted differed because the particular needs of dominant interests in their respective nations were not identical.

The Devaluation of Labor: The United Kingdom

Thatcher could be a breast-beating patriot when the need arose, but she exhibited no sense of loyalty whatsoever either toward British industry or toward British working-class communities. Her industrial policy had two main strands to it. First, her administration wanted to reduce the number of publicly funded or state-supported industries. Inevitably this would lead to job losses and to a shrinkage of the industrial sector. Second, her administration wanted to see an improvement in productivity. This was to be achieved through an elimination of surplus or inefficient workers and an increase in the output of those remaining. In pursuit of these goals, Thatcher's government declared war on the "dictatorial" union bosses who had saddled British employers with insupportably high labor costs. The Employment Acts of 1980 and 1982 significantly reduced the unions' freedom to bargain collectively and banned "sympathy" strikes or coordinated strike action among different unions. In addition, although strikers could no longer sue employers for unfair dismissal, unions could now be sued for damages resulting from trade disputes (Coates 1994, 121–123; Marsh 1992).

Thatcher, of course, was not personally responsible for flexible accumulation, but her administration did encourage it as something that would inevitably depreciate the value of domestic labor. From 1980 to 1988, the earnings of British manufacturing workers as a percentage of value added fell by 16.6 percent (see Table 4.1). Her Conservative administration openly encouraged capital flight and deregulated the financial markets, so that this could be accomplished more easily. As a result, the United Kingdom became "the world's largest outward investor" (*WIR* 1994, xvii) from 1985 to 1989, serving as the source of more capital outflows than any other country—including the United States. These outflows exacerbated the effects of industrial decline. By the end of the 1980s, Britain had ceased to be competitive, let alone dominant, in global manufacturing. It seems probable that in 2000 more Korean than British cars will be sold to Britons in their own country.

Trends such as these are usually portrayed as unavoidable.[6] However, there was nothing inevitable about the high rate of loss of manufacturing jobs in Britain (or in the United States, come to that) during the 1980s. Although no administration could have ignored the appeal of flexible accumulation, the dependence on monetarism and the dogmatic insistence that free (labor) markets would solve all problems were *political* responses to a changing world. The loss of relatively well-paying blue-collar jobs in the United Kingdom and the United States over the past twenty years cannot be explained merely as a consequence of competition from low-wage countries. These losses occurred because of increasing competition from low-wage countries *plus* the willingness of governing elites to use the power of the state to enhance capital's mobility and labor's marketability. By the 1980s, labor in West Germany had become much more expensive than labor in Britain,[7] so if low-wage countries were solely responsible for job losses in the older industrial centers, job shrinkage should have occurred at a much greater rate in West Germany than it did in the United Kingdom. Yet during the 1980s, Britain shed industrial jobs at a much higher rate than the FRG. According to John Banhan, this happened because British manufacturing was deprived of the kind of state support enjoyed by West German and Japanese industry. Britain, as a consequence, lost about 20 percent of its manufacturing capacity in the first three years of Thatcher's administration alone—a much greater rate of destruction than that inflicted by the Luftwaffe during the blitz.

In many ways, Thatcher's government produced the worst of all possible combinations. On the one hand, it significantly reduced public responsibility for national economic well-being (the central goal of the New Right everywhere). Yet largely because of the extensive rioting that occurred throughout England in 1981, her administration left the safety net of social benefits (including indefinite unemployment benefits, housing benefits, and free medical care) largely untouched. As a result, what can hardly be called "an industrial reserve army" is now reproduced as so much social detritus. Although some redundant workers have been reemployed at lower wages, most are left with little else to do than draw their beer money and cultivate the increasingly hostile modes of behavior in which they are encouraged to specialize. By the 1990s, the official unemployment rate for young males in many of the officially "depressed areas" exceeded 60 percent. As a result, the crime rate skyrocketed. Although violent crimes are far lower in Britain than in the

United States, the rate of property crimes (e.g., burglary, robbery, auto theft) now exceeds that of many cities in the United States.

During the 1980s, and *against* the wishes of the majority of the electorate,[8] Thatcher's government implemented one of the most radical programs of social change ever seen in Britain. Although certainly not responsible for long-term industrial decline (which probably began in the 1880s), the Thatcher administration viewed retrenchment in the industrial sector as a political solution, not as a political problem. Besides creating unprecedented levels of social dislocation, the subsequent crash seriously aggravated Britain's persistent balance-of-payments problem, forcing the government to resort to deficit spending.[9] Nonetheless, Thatcherism cannot be judged a failure in terms of the goals that it set for itself. By 1997 wages in Britain were among the lowest in the European Community, the power of the unions had been broken, and, perhaps most significantly, the opposition Labour Party had promised not to reverse the New Right gains of the 1980s.

The Reduction in Social Spending: The United States

Because the Thatcherites correctly understood that none of their other programs could be realized until the power of the unions had been broken, organized labor (or "the enemy within," as Thatcher put it) provided the first target of the attack in the United Kingdom (see Thatcher 1993, 92–121, 264–280, 339–378). By contrast, the Republican Right spent less time waging war on a labor force that had been unable to mount an effective political challenge to anything for more than fifty years. Instead, the Right focused its attention on the social wage—particularly on means-tested social insurance programs and, to a lesser extent, on programs that invested in human capital.

The "social wage" is not earned by individual workers in the labor or commodity markets but is planned and consumed collectively. It reflects (1) "social consumption outlays" and (2) payments for "human capital" (O'Connor 1973). *Social consumption outlays* include payments for collective consumption, such as "goods and services consumed collectively by the working class" (124). Because these payments create new opportunities for private businesses, they serve capital, as well as labor. In this country, collective consumption has supported transportation networks, urban development projects, "Section Eight" Assistance, public housing, home mortgage guarantees, mass transit subsidies, some child care and recreational facilities, and some hospital facilities.

Social consumption outlays also include "social insurance against economic insecurity" (O'Connor 1973, 124). The state uses these payments to produce long-term commitments. Like collective consumption outlays, social insurance schemes are well suited to class compromise. Some social insurance payments are means-tested—Aid to Families with Dependent Children (AFDC); Supplemental Security Income; Earned Income Tax Credit (EITC); the Women, Infants, and Children Program (WIC); the food stamp program; the school lunch program and other nutrition programs. Others are contributory—social security, Medicare, workers' compensation, unemployment insurance, public employees retirement.

Human capital payments are designed to improve worker productivity. They typically involve social investment in education or in various kinds of job training (O'Connor 1973, 101ff). Federally supervised human capital payments include Pell grants to students, guaranteed student loans, and the Head Start program.

The social wage benefits business as well as labor by making the working class "more and more dependent on capital and ultimately on the state" (O'Connor 1973, 211) and by circulating public funds through private businesses. "Social spending," in short (i.e., all of the payments just described), helps organize and cheapen the inputs of production and provides inputs of legitimacy for the state.[10] It is *not*, of course, designed to give handouts to the needy and undeserving. Rather, social spending largely involves transfer payments among working people (see Foster 1988).

During capitalism's "Golden Age" (1946–1965), the state used social spending as "a powerful countercyclical tool, producing deficits during recessionary periods and (at least in theory) surpluses during boom times" (Pierson 1994, 3). Such spending thus developed "social-welfare programs [that] served to partially offset important market failures" and additionally introduced "health care, housing, and a modicum of economic security," all of which produced motivations conducive to the proper conduct of business (3). In periods of growth, social spending additionally offset the private sector's tendency to underinvest in its own workforce.

Yet compared to most western European social democracies, the level of social spending in the United States has always been meager. As a result, the social wage in this country (particularly noncontributory insurance support) has functioned largely to reduce the cost inputs to businesses that employ marginal or low-wage workers. Food stamps, WIC payments, free school lunches, subsidized housing, EITC, child support credits, and so on have accordingly enabled many U.S. employers to pay *less* than a living wage. There is a certain irony to this. Marx always assumed that private employers would at least have the decency to pay commodity labor the wages it needed to reproduce itself. He thus took it for granted (wrongly, it seems) that private capitalists, not the public at large, would pay the real cost of production. By the end of the postwar period, however, it was public, not private, money that was increasingly supporting low earners, whose existence (as Marx had earlier predicted) had long since become insupportable through free markets.

Today, those close to, or earning, the minimum wage (nearly one-quarter of the workforce) cannot *earn* their way out of poverty, no matter how hard they try. In 1992, for instance, a head of household working full time and earning the minimum wage grossed $7,438, which is one-half the poverty-level wage for a family of four. This indicates how important social subsidies are (or perhaps were) to many working people. Until recently, about one-half of the income of the bottom one-fifth of the *working* U.S. population came through public subsidies (Piven and Cloward 1982, 15). We can see, then, that for many working Americans public subsidies such as the food stamp program have made the difference between earning a subpoverty wage and receiving a near-poverty income.

As mentioned earlier, meager social consumption outlays in this country have effectively subsidized low-wage businesses. As a result, cuts in such payments do not have the effect of forcing people into the labor market. Rather, because social consumption outlays to individuals tend to be means-tested, they tend to encourage low earners to work less. This is, in fact, what happened during Reagan's first term. As several economists have pointed out, the welfare cuts imposed by the Reagan administration tended to be self-negating because they "fell most heavily on one group, the so-called working poor, made up primarily of female heads of household and their children living on a combination of earned income and welfare" (Nathan and Doolittle 1984, 28). The net effect of the reductions was to increase the number of families *with a working head* who were "lopped from the AFDC rolls" (28). Once the level of income that recipients could earn and *still* qualify for Medicaid, food stamps, and housing subsidies support was lowered, many marginal earners were given an incentive not to work (or to work less). This unintended consequence would have been mitigated if wages had been high and rising (as they were from 1946 to 1965) because the people thus affected would have had alternatives in the marketplace to minimal levels of public subsidies. But the failure of Reagan's "supply-side reforms" to create "trickle-down" wealth for those at the bottom of the heap actually increased the number of people who qualified for means-tested payments—even after the criteria had been toughened.[11]

Once this conundrum is understood, the "welfare reforms" of the 1990s begin to make some sense. Unlike Fordism, flexible accumulation does not rely much on the use of public money to cheapen the inputs of production. Moreover, flexibility relies less on inputs of legitimation, largely because the structures that would facilitate dangerous protest from below have already been removed. A cut in the social wage can be a problem for inflexible Fordist producers, but it does not present much of a threat to mobile TNCs. Flexibility is a problem for employers if and only if they are compelled to increase their employees' wages to compensate for lost unearned income. They might have to do this if workers are well organized or if they have access to even minimal levels of social insurance (e.g., AFDC). Managers would not have to do this (1) if workers have few or no social insurance programs on which they could fall back (i.e., no alternative to subpoverty wages if they were lucky enough to get them)[12] or (2) if employers could find either domestic or nondomestic workers willing to take subpoverty wages as the best option available to them.

In short, the current attack on levels of social spending that happened to be functional for capital in the past is not on the face of it an inherently irrational strategy. At the time of this writing, there is little or no political opposition to this trend, which is invariably portrayed as "inevitable" in some sense. But given the increased globalization of labor and capital flows, why, after all, should TNCs inflexibly be tied to human resources at one particular location when such assets can be reproduced elsewhere at lower cost? Why pay for social consumption outlays intended to reduce the costs of labor *at home* when capital's newfound mobility means that labor that is tied to place has no particular significance? Why bother to develop social insurance schemes that are designed to promote labor discipline in this country when the global market in labor achieves the same end far more efficiently all by itself? Why offer "earned taxed credits" to workers receiving poverty wages if these workers now recognize that to accept such wages is not the worst that can happen to them? Why invest in human capital in the United States when "American" corporations increasingly prefer to employ workers in the Third World? And what, in any case, is the point of using public spending to "regulate the trade cycle" or utilize "excess accumulated capital" when the means to achieve such goals are largely beyond the scope of the nation-state?

We should not forget, however, that the New Right has no intention of cutting public spending per se. (After all, these people are not nineteenth-century neoliberals.) What the New Right rejects is "wasteful" spending on the kind of social insurance and social investment programs that will no longer return either the amount of value or the degree of legitimacy that could justify such expenditure in the first place.[13] Subsidies for business and support for economic domination are something else entirely. More than $150 billion of public money will continue to be given annually on a "cost-plus" basis to General Dynamics, General

Electric, Lockheed-Martin, McDonnell Douglas, United Technologies, Hughes Aircraft, Boeing, Westinghouse, IBM, AT&T, and others (Huff and Johnson 1993, 314; see also Gansler 1988).[14] Deals such as the one offered to Northrop Grumman, which was given $30 billion by Congress to build B-2 bombers that the U.S. Air Force claims it does not need, are unlikely to become a thing of the past. Major agribusinesses probably will still be able to depend on public subsidies of $25 billion a year, two-thirds of which is spent on just three thousand operations (Huff and Johnson 1993, 314; see also Paarlberg 1988).

In sum, the fiscal cuts that the New Right seeks to impose are no more driven or *caused* by ideology or "values" than were the Fordist programs of the past. Rather, they are a measured response to the needs of the constituency actually represented by the U.S. Congress. We can rather easily discover who that constituency is by examining how legislation is produced. In the meantime, all the froth and blather about "conservative principles," "fundamentals," "ideals," "traditional values," and "a return to basics" reflects a political unconscious that is structured in terms of what *cannot* be thought or discussed: namely, that in a world changing at a frightening rate of speed, capital's circuit must still be sustained and defended at any (human) cost.

The Economic Program of the New Right

We can now identify the main causes of the economic policies pursued by the New Right. During the middle third of this century, the capitalist state assumed increased planning responsibilities and guaranteed labor a minimal social wage. As a result, it secured labor peace but also incurred the obligation to find the necessary fiscal resources. Over time, the public sector suffered from fiscal crisis or a shortfall of receipts over expenditure. This led to an institutionalized public-sector borrowing requirement that became unmanageable after the economic downturn of the 1970s.

As capital became more mobile after 1975, the division of labor became increasingly internationalized, and many of the more labor-intensive manufacturing and industrial jobs moved to countries such as Brazil, Mexico, Taiwan, South Korea, and China. This internationalization of manufacturing, together with the globalization of capital flows, devalued labor in the West and lessened the ability of nation-states to regulate their domestic economies through the demand and exchange-rate management that had prevailed from the 1940s to the 1970s (Glyn et al. 1990, 87–88; Marquand 1989; Held 1989). By the 1980s, it was doubtful whether *national* governments could have imposed workable corporatist solutions even if they had wanted to, and in this sense at least, Thatcher's rejection of the "discredited" programs of the past was not entirely without foundation.

After the 1960s, class membership in developed western societies became less homogeneous, partly because labor markets were deliberately segmented. New forms of credentialism, some of which were intended to have particular effects, additionally created new kinds of occupational specialists who did not, of course, possess any "class consciousness" in the Marxist sense of the term. The production and consumption of commodities, the financing of this cycle of production, and the organizational management of the whole process of accumulation were abstracted, globalized, and differentiated to an unprecedented extent. Labor organizations that had developed over the previous century, and that had learned to live quite happily with Fordism-Keynesianism, were unable or unwilling to adjust to these changes and suffered as a result.

If the Reagan and Thatcher administrations were unable to drive a stake through the heart of what in the popular imagination was "the welfare state," they nonetheless succeeded in using the power of the state to redistribute income upward. During the 1980s, income inequality sharply increased both in Britain and the United States (Karoly 1989; Harrison and Bluestone 1986, 1988; Marglin and Schor 1990; Thurow 1987; Braun 1991, 137–198). As Paul Pierson (1994, 4–5) has emphasized, "Public policy played an important role in this process" (see also Department of Social Security 1990, 1993; U.S. House of Representatives 1990).

The welfare cuts—and, of greater importance, the changes in the tax law implemented by the Reagan administration—rewarded the one-fifth of the population that gave Reagan active support and, by 1995, also saved American corporations about $250 billion in taxes per year. Although taxes for the top 25 percent of the population dropped significantly during the 1980s, the tax burden of the bottom 50 percent of the population actually increased (Oliver and Shapiro 1990; Hoover 1987). During Reagan's first term, while low-income families lost about $23 billion in income and federal benefits, high-income families gained more than $35 billion (Davis 1986). In Britain the Thatcher administration used financial deregulation, abolition of the corporatist wage councils, and changes in the tax code to create the highest levels of inequality seen in Britain since the Great Depression.

In Britain the poorest 10 percent of families with children were in real terms £40 ($62) worse off a month in 1994 than they had been in 1979. Meanwhile, the richest 10 percent of families were £1,000 ($1,540) better off a month than they had been fifteen years earlier.[15] Between 1979 and 1987 in Britain, "living standards increased by just 1 percent . . . for the poorest fifth of the population, compared with a gain of 30 percent for the richest fifth" (Riddell 1991, 234; see also Department of Social Security 1993). According to the OECD, the "earnings dispersion" during the 1980s created in Britain "the sharpest growth in poverty that any OECD nation has experienced since 1950, with a quarter of the EC's poor now to be found in Britain" (MacShane 1993, 20).

Although commenting about Thatcher's policies in Britain, Michael Rustin (1989b, 310) could just as easily have been writing about "Reaganomics" when he noted that "the tax policies of the national state have massively reallocated incomes from poor to rich. The aim is nothing less than the restratification of British society, in which a minority . . . enriches itself in power by the use of the distributive and disciplinary power of the state. . . . It seems an odd time to be debating the obsolescence of class, or the irrelevance of central state power to class interests."

The End of Modern Politics?

In the final two chapters of this book, I examine the functions that the "new professionals" and the New Class perform for the state and for capital. But, first, we should look at some of the crisis tendencies of late modernity, which I believe are largely responsible for the rise of these new cultural and economic elites.

Habermas and the Crises of Advanced Capitalist Societies

In *Legitimation Crisis*, Habermas (1975) suggests that "advanced" or corporatist social formations experienced two kinds of crisis:

1. *Rationality Crisis:* a crisis of "output," which occurs when "the administrative system" of the state "does not succeed in reconciling and fulfilling the imperatives received from the economic system" (46). A "rationality deficit" in public administration means that "the state apparatus cannot . . . adequately steer the economic system" (47).
2. *Legitimation Crisis:* a crisis of "input," which occurs when "the legitimizing system does not succeed in maintaining the requisite level of mass loyalty" (46). "A legitimation deficit means that it is not possible by administrative means to maintain or establish effective normative structures to the extent required" (47). Such crisis "can be avoided in the long run only if the latent class structures of advanced-capitalist societies are transformed *or* if the pressure for legitimation to which the administrative system is subject can be removed" (93; emphasis supplied).

Rationality crisis is caused by the demand overload experienced by the corporatist Fordist state, which is expected to organize "more-and-more-socialized production" (61). The state is consequently expected to bear "the infrastructural costs directly related to production (transportation and communication systems, scientific-technical progress, vocational training)," "social consumption" outlays, "social welfare" payments, and the overall costs of "environmental strain" (Habermas 1975, 61). As we have seen, such public responsibilities tend to politicize relations of production.

In response to such politicization—what Michael Crozier, Samuel Huntington, and Joji Watanuki (1975) call the "crisis" or "excess" of democracy—"advanced" capitalist societies increasingly separate the "instrumental functions of administration" (e.g., formal law, bureaucracy) "from expressive symbols that release [a] readiness to follow" (Habermas 1975, 70). The capitalist state benefits from this separation by attaining some relief from democratic inputs that threaten its domination; the problem, however, is that "readiness to follow" among the masses becomes increasingly hard to manipulate.

Baudrillard (1983a), of course, has suggested that the contemporary masses can no longer be reached, let alone manipulated, because they can no longer be addressed as social individuals. In any case, a "postmodern" solution to the problems engendered by the exhausted strategy of politicization/depoliticization would be to have those specialists and intermediaries responsible for promoting postmodern culture produce versions of privatism that would be functional for a post-Fordist, post-corporatist, postmodern world.[16]

In discussing the "cultural and social specialists" who are "the core promoters of postmodern culture," Betz (1992, 97) suggests that we distinguish between the "carriers of new values and a new politics" and the "producers, transmitters and consumers of postmodern culture." Such a distinction would yield *new professionals* (or new cultural specialists) who develop "values" and "a new politics" (see Chapter 8) and *a New Class* (or new cultural intermediaries) that operates within a commercial sphere to sell culture as lifestyle (see Chapter 9).

Let us briefly review what would be "new" about such specialists and such intermediaries. More than twenty years ago, Habermas (1975, 75) defined *vocational privatism* as a "family orientation with developed interests in consumption and leisure on the one hand, and in a career orientation suitable to status competition on the other. Such privatism corresponds to the structures of educational and occupational systems that are regulated by competition through achievement." Yet if vocational privatism used to be rooted in closed occupational status groups, "pro-

TABLE 7.1   Modern/Postmodern Versions of Privatism

	Civil Privatism	*Vocational Privatism*
Modern	Based on familial or personal property ownership	Centered on professional occupational status, regulated by achievement within closed collegially organized groups
Postmodern	Increasingly includes sumptuary consumption, i.e., the purchase of commodified semiotic privileges marking cultural distinctions	Includes the attempt to promote hyperdiversified value commitments and the ability to create new forms of expertise and cultural capital

fessionalism" today tends to have a much more flexible and diversified meaning (see Table 7.1).

The ethic of vocational privatism in modern societies (i.e., the idea of professional service to the community) was based on generalizable interests that supposedly reflected what was right for the community as a whole. Today, however, the new professionals are more particularistic and fragmented in outlook. Their opportunity structures are adjusted by the state's ability to manipulate and configure "private" occupational structures and professional status markets that are "regulated by competition through achievement" in "the educational and occupational systems" (Habermas 1975, 75).[17] Marxist theory would predict that the new professionals will be rewarded for helping to channel NSM activity in ways that are nonthreatening to, or preferably supportive of, existing modes of class domination. We can anticipate that the careerist strategies of the new professionals would not cut against the logic of legal persons in the marketplace, nor would they threaten economic domination or directly challenge the bureaucratic authority of the state. Here we can test some of the more extravagant claims made by Crook et al. and Lash and Urry. What extrinsically structures the internal status markets of these new professionals? According to Crook, Pakulski, and Waters (1992, 116), there are no bounds. All is flux, fluidity, and decomposition.

Habermas (1975, 37) defined *civil privatism* as "political abstinence combined with an orientation to career, leisure, and consumption." Emphasizing "money, leisure time and security," it compensates for the "low-input" involvement of citizenry in political decisionmaking (75). Two decades ago, Habermas (73) suggested that because civil privatism chiefly promotes leisure and consumption, it encourages individuals to trade diminished "meaning" for greater spending power. Today, however, it is probably more accurate to say that those who participate in the spectacle-commodity economy are not so much "trading away" a politically meaningful existence as participating in a process whereby the "self-made man" is replaced by a "flexible" entity capable of making itself "not just once but repeatedly" (Goldman and Papson 1994, 243). The New Class helps produce postmodern culture not by promoting "a single authoritative interpretation of a text," but by encouraging "a multiplicity of interpretations" leading "to an *alleged* cultural pluralism" (Goldman and Papson 1994, 238; emphasis supplied). Like financial specialists, the New Class endeavors to provide new temporal "fixes" for capital by developing an intensified competition that causes "the rate of circulation of sign-values to accelerate" (230).

Habermas in the Shadow of the Silent Majorities

Another way of describing the activities of the new specialists and intermediaries is to see them as groups that to some extent deal with what Habermas (1975, 75–91) called "motivation crisis." Such crisis, which Habermas (1982, 281) later acknowledged was "a parallel case to legitimation crisis," occurs when there is "a discrepancy between the need for motives declared by the state, the educational system and the occupational system on the one hand and the motivation supplied by the sociocultural system on the other" (1975, 75). Motivation crises occur when the masses are insufficiently diverted, that is, when they are not offered the "consumable values" or status opportunities that could compensate them for the political meaning they have lost.

We can note here an intriguing and generally overlooked convergence between Habermas and Baudrillard. Baudrillard (1983a, 10, 37) would suggest that "motivation crisis," as Habermas defines it, is no longer possible because as "the masses" are no longer "permeable to action and to discourse," they no longer present a threat to a system of domination (which, in any case, according to Baudrillard, has ceased to exist). As Baudrillard (22) sees it, the masses "are no longer (a) *subject* (especially not to—or of—history), hence they can no longer be spoken for, articulated, represented, nor pass through the political 'mirror stage' and the cycle of imaginary identifications. One sees what strength results from this: no longer being (a) subject, *they can no longer be alienated*—neither in their own language (they have none), nor in any other that would pretend to speak for them."

The main difference between Habermas and Baudrillard can thus be summarized as follows. Habermas believes that capital and the state are still trying to cope with the fallout from the unresolved economic/political/organizational/motivational crises of late modernity. Baudrillard, however, believes that the need for legitimation no longer exists, for "politics" now depends on a strategy of seduction ("a mastery of the symbolic universe"), not on a strategy of power (which to some extent must address something "real," something outside itself) (quoted in Kellner 1989, 145).[18] In Baudrillard's view of things, postmodern artifacts such as Reagan, Quayle, or Oprah Winfrey merely simulate a "public" into which their followers are drawn. In contrast to this simulated reference group, old-fashioned "modern" politicians (e.g., Roosevelt or Truman) to some extent responded to "real" voluntary (Third Sector) activities that provided a relatively autonomous resource for political mobilization.

With regard to the differences sketched here, I side with Habermas. I do not accept the proposition that the state is powerless to manipulate internal constituencies and that its efforts to leverage subjects will inevitably be neutralized by the perfect indifference of the mass. I assume, then, that the "postmodern state" is reacting to *real crises* of motivation and legitimation that pose *real threats* to class domination. Nonetheless, Baudrillard's vision of postmodern America is at least an emerging possibility. It certainly does seem to capture some contemporary features of American popular culture. But Baudrillard's perspective is seriously limited, for he refuses to examine how the real manifestations he describes are generated by capital and power. He merely takes for granted what he sees on the surface, which is another way of saying he is not a critical theorist.

The End of the Need for Legitimation?

I suggested earlier that the "postmodern" New Fundamentalists sought to uncouple the formation of political motives from norms capable of justification. This can be described as the *radical* solution to the "problem of legitimation," for if this solution were to occur, "legitimation problems per se would cease to exist" (Habermas 1975, 122). A *less* radical solution would be to rely on the fragmentation, diversification, and disorientation afforded by current modes of postmodern civil and vocational privatism.

Habermas (1975, 122) suggests that if motivation deficits were to be entirely eliminated (which, according to Baudrillard, has already occurred), "individuation" would have to be detached from "effective socialization." It is as yet unclear whether this radical postmodern option could materialize. If it did, however, Baudrillard's (and perhaps Foucault's) vision of the present would be a reality. In Habermas's terms, the "autonomous ego-organization" of the historic "bourgeois individual" would be transposed in such a way that the social system could be reproduced without the intercession of autonomously motivated individuals. As a result:

1. Complex societies would no longer be held together normatively, and "system integration, treated from a steering perspective, [becomes completely] independent of a social integration accessible from life-world perspectives" (131).
2. Subjects would recognize that the world must now be understood as "contingent," "infinitely open," and "ontically indeterminate" (132).[19]
3. In the political management of the state, decision processes would become autonomous "vis-à-vis the input of generalized motivations, values and interests" (132).
4. The "political system [would] no longer derive its identity from the society" (132). In such a context, as Baudrillard (1983a, 5) has put it, "there is no longer any social signified to give force to a political signifier."
5. The "problem of a rational organization of society in conjunction with formation of motives through norms that admit of truth [would have] lost its object" (Habermas 1975, 133).

8 The New Professionals: Changes in Authority and Formal Organization

This chapter focuses on the new professionals: the "postmodern" "cultural and social specialists" who serve as the "carriers of new values and a new politics" (Betz 1992, 97) and help elaborate what Anthony Giddens (1991, 9) has called the "reflexive project of the self." We can define these professionals as well-educated, credentialed, cultural specialists or experts who tend to work with, or for, bureaucratic organizations and who regard the state as an entity controlling resources for which they can compete. By contrast, the "old" professionals (e.g., physicians, lawyers, architects) typically did not work for large organizations,[1] did not regard the state as a major benefactor, and did not equate their expertise with social activism.

Suggesting that the new professionals are "the major carrier . . . of the postmodern consciousness,"[2] Bernice Martin (1992, 129) argues that "postmodern" applications of functional rationality now apply Weber's "rule of the experts" to "culture and everyday life." Whereas "the old professions sought only to rationalize (in Weber's sense of the world) *limited* areas of human life," the "life-style engineering" of many of the new specialists is "potentially *without limits*" (Kellner and Berger 1992, 4). The "fluidity" of "these new professions," in other words, tends to lead to a "built-in imperialism": "Each one is a budding, potentially all-embracing empire" (4) eager to address problems that range from eating disorders to postearthquake stress, from "sexual inadequacy" to "sexual addiction." By contrast, "the old professions were modest, conservative nation-states, contentedly cultivating the rose gardens within their clearly marked borders" (4).

Whereas the identity of old professionals was based on membership in a closed occupational status group, the identity of the new professionals tends to be flexible, dynamic, multidimensional, and uncertain.

As one new specialist explains, she is "a woman, a teacher, a daughter, a mother, a feminist (should I add a heterosexual, a Jew, an immigrant, middle class, an only child, a mother of sons?), within the institutions of patriarchy, of motherhood, of literary studies, of feminist studies, of the university in the United States (should I add of marriage, of divorce, of the Ivy League, of Comparative Literature and French Studies, of the development of Women's Studies?)" (Hirsch 1989, 17).

The contribution that the new professionals make in producing postmodern culture is discussed later. First, however, we should examine the dynamics of professional occupational groups. This will enable us to understand how the new specialists can maneuver in larger organizational and political settings.

When professional organizations were first instituted in the early nineteenth century, they tried "to establish status closure and to resist control by bureaucratic, state and commercial interests," especially in "academica, law and medicine" (Waters 1989, 969). "Collegiality" denies outsiders access to a professional status group and the right to earn a living until credentials have been vetted and approved from *within* the group. "Prestige" is a function of the social honor associated with belonging to an exclusive group. The more exclusive the group is, the greater is the honor and the higher is the degree of professional authority. Strong collegiate organizations do not need, and will not tolerate, significant levels of outside influence or interference. In this regard, professionals operate differently from other workers. Mere "wage slaves," for instance, cannot escape the market, and petty clerical staff are usually at the mercy of the hierarchical organizations they serve. Yet because of collegial ties, new professionals can to some extent insulate themselves both from the market and from the effects of legal or economic domination.

In an "exclusively collegiate organization," "the authority of a group of professional colleagues is undivided by bureaucracy" (Waters 1989, 961). Such organizations, however, are rare or nonexistent. In the real world, "collegial formations" tend to "coexist with bureaucratic formations in organizations" (969). Such a formation can be defined as "predominately collegial" if "the internal authority of the college over members is undivided" and only "its external authority is mediated by bureaucracy" (961). In predominately collegial formations a professional occupational group uses one kind of medium (knowledge or expertise) to organize members' activities internally and another to organize exchanges across the boundaries of the collegial group (e.g., money or power). Professional groups are *not*, of course, classes in any sense of the term, but the members of such groups can (and typically do) *serve* a class, class domination, or the state. Weberian theory is best equipped to comprehend the internal mechanisms of status differentiation. Marxist theory is more likely to explain why such groups might proliferate and how they might serve the state.

The iron law of the marketplace is—and always has been—"if it sells, it's right," but the members of occupational status groups are unmoved by such vulgar dicta. What professionals nourish and cherish are not forms of commercial expertise (the ability to make the sale) but the *cultural* goods that are "historically and collectively produced" (Gouldner 1979, 19). And just as ordinary investors want to increase the capital they hold (real estate, stock, bonds), so, too, professionals and intelligentsia have a vested interest in developing *their* "cultural capital" (knowledge, education, credentials). Although the "capital resources" of the new professionals produce authority, not economic power, they also have the "latent function" of increasing "the incomes and social control of those possessing it" (22). Cultural capital, in other words, can easily be converted into economic capital (money), and, contrariwise, money can be turned into "symbolic capital" or prestige (Bourdieu 1977)—which is what occurs when a university awards an honorary degree to a wealthy donor. Given that the new professionals depend on symbolic resources for their livelihood, it is not, then, surprising that although they are vociferously egalitarian with regard to "old" privileges (such as those bestowed by inherited wealth), they are strikingly inegalitarian with regard to the democratizing or sharing out of the capital resources *they* "own" or manage (Gouldner 1979, 20).

The Activities of the New Professionals

Nearly a century ago, Weber (1946) emphasized that scientific or professional expertise should be guided by a sense of "vocation." This, he believed, would enable the expert to serve both "God" and Science, self and others. Weber emphasized that a professional career required exclusive forms of collegiate organizations (and, very often, private wealth, too). By contrast, the post-Protestant new cultural specialists do not belong to exclusively collegiate organizations. For one thing, their authority tends to be mediated by bureaucracy; for another, new specialists such as the postmodern humanities teacher, the "human relations" consultant, or the multicultural therapist must partially "sell" the client on the idea of expertise. As we have seen, modern, "liberal" societies sought to politicize the relation between political authorities and citizen groups. By contrast, the new specialists practice a far more decentralized method of control: They tend to politicize the relationship between themselves and their clients.

Among other things, the new professionals run the NAPs, work for the Equal Employment and Opportunity Commission (EEOC) or for the Civil Rights Division of the Justice Department, advocate and advance "cultural diversity," counsel drug users and various kinds of "survivors," locate "sexual abuse" and "sexual harassment," "deprogram" those who have spent too long in religious communities (this one would have puzzled Weber), advise on health matters, administer "total quality management" and "human development" programs, develop "excellence" in corporate America, empower those who feel powerless, help those who feel helpless, work with public-interest groups, counsel those made redundant by "sunset industries," and in general perform the numerous advisory and regulative functions of capital and of the state that are associated with the proper use of "human resources." In essence, the new professionals specialize in penetrating and administering domains of feeling and experience not previously exposed to the probing of "expert" knowledge. They accordingly take full advantage of the dedifferentiation or implosion of public and private lifeworlds described earlier.

The Reflexive Project of the Self

According to Giddens (1991, 214), the new professionals play a major role in influencing "life politics." Such a politics, he claims, rests on the reflexive project of the self and is an inevitable consequence of the breakup of old hierarchies and "the fixities of tradition and culture." As Giddens (215) explains:

> Self-identity today is a reflexive achievement. The narrative of self-identity has to be shaped, altered and reflexively sustained in relation to rapidly changing circumstances of social life, on a local and global scale. The individual must integrate information deriving from a diversity of mediated experiences with local involvements in such a way as to connect future projects with past experiences in a reasonably coherent fashion. Only if the person is able to develop an inner authenticity—a framework of basic trust by means of which the lifespan can be understood as a unity against the backdrop of shifting social events—can this be attained.

Unfortunately, if Giddens is right (which he probably is), the reflexive project of the self is less likely to establish "inner authenticity" than to perpetuate serial and discontinuous strategies, all of which promise authenticity anew, because life politics does not encourage inner-transcendent closure. On the contrary, postmodern politicking tends to produce a rapidly increasing proliferation of cultural options, all of which additionally elaborate the "reflexive" project of the self. Even so, life politics is not completely beyond the reach of organizational, political, or economic domination. Rather, the growing significance of such politics reflects the current ability of power and organizational domination to invade and reshape the now colonized "personal" lifeworld.

Exchanges Between the New Professionals and Other Organized Groups

As we have seen, Betz (1992, 100ff) has claimed that "the transmitters of postmodern values" need access to the bureaucratic resources of the state in order to establish themselves as professionals. Studies conducted by Hanspeter Kriesi in the Netherlands have in turn indicated what the new professionals can do for the state. Kriesi (1988, 1989) shows that NSMs in Holland receive much of their support and leadership from socially active young professionals, and the same relationship has been posited in this country by Russell Dalton and Manfred Kuechler (1990) and Steven Seidman (1994a, 234–280). Henrick Kreutz and Gerhard Fröhlich (1986) have shown that two-thirds of those engaged in "alternative projects" in West Germany were university graduates. The majority came from the social sciences or humanities. Like Kreutz and Fröhlich, Hans-Georg Betz (1989) has discovered that the greatest support for NSMs in Germany come from the younger social and cultural specialists who concentrate on teaching, social services, and other primarily cultural occupations. This suggests that the new kinds of professionals that Featherstone and Betz have tacitly linked with postmodernity could help mediate between state bureaucracy and formal organization, on the one hand, and the NSMs, on the other.

When professionals sell their expertise *directly* to clients, expertise trades for money in the marketplace. Yet the relations between professionals and their clients or students in formal organizations must be mediated by bureaucracy. Professionals cannot control the means of organizational domination (i.e., bureaucracy), and they do not monopolize financial resources. Nonetheless, they can trade the value commitments they produce as outputs from their clients for fees or a salary. But to generate such outputs, they have to rely on the influence they can bring to bear plus their right to be recognized as authorized experts who are entitled to credential and label others (see Figure 8.1). For instance, when a college professor gives a student an "A" for "excellent" work, certain social realities are created. By doling out scarce—or perhaps, in this instance, inflated—symbolic credits, the credentialer in question (the college professor) can motivate the student to develop stronger commitments to an institutionalized opportunity structure that may or may not serve this subject's real interests.[3]

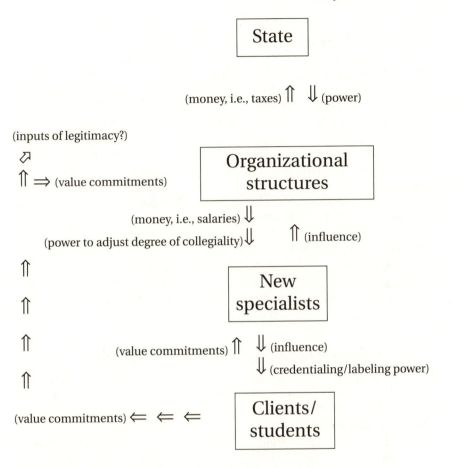

FIGURE 8.1   Exchange Media Involving the New Specialists

Formal organizations exercise leverage on professionals and dictate the scope of their activity by controlling, or even by creating, the collegially managed spaces within which the specialists flourish. Bureaucracy, in other words, gives compliant and appropriately credentialed cultural retainers opportunities to exchange their service functions for a salary and the right to enjoy collegial, rather than hierarchical, forms of supervision. Because the newer kinds of "professionalization" tend to take place along a continuum (from weak to strong collegial authority, from low to high penetration by bureaucracy), the amount of autonomy permitted can be calibrated and adjusted with a certain degree of organizational precision. As a result, the cultural or symbolic capital that is created is not just a personal benefit for the individual or a group benefit for the status occupational group. It is also a flexible resource for bureaucracy and the state.[4]

We now can see why many of the new professionals have a vested interest in the expansion of government. Unlike technical or business elites in the private sector, these specialists tend to favor administrative support for their activities—in part because they expect the state to support and help legitimate the capital they possess. They tend, in other words, to believe that government should "provide suitably genteel employment and suitably middle-class wages" to "highly educated men and women [chiefly themselves, of course] . . . whose skills the market does not value" (McAdams 1987, 27). As a result, they often *welcome* efforts to coopt their activities by enlarging the spaces in which they can operate. The new professionals do not, of course, support the organizational and bureaucratic resources of state apparatuses because they have voted for the government or because they support democracy in some trivial sense. (In fact, they are quite likely to reject the government of the day.) Rather, they have a vested interest in ensuring the viability and security of a banking system in which they have deposited the only capital they are ever likely to possess.

Postmodern Organizational Rationality

Several commentators have suggested that postmodern organizational forms are relatively commonplace in advanced capitalist societies (see Lash and Urry 1987; Whitley 1990; Offe 1985a; Clegg 1990; Wilmott 1992; Carter and Jackson 1990; Cooper and Burrell 1988; Power 1990). According to one theorist, "postmodern organizations" create "de-demarcated and multi-skilled jobs" and replace vertical authority with more horizontal relationships that emphasize subcontracting and networking (Clegg 1990, 181ff). Developing the arguments introduced in the previous section, we can say that the emergence of these new organizational forms is to some extent a reflection of the new specialists' needs to expand and protect their cultural capital (Abercrombie and Urry 1983; Lash and Urry 1987; Jacoby 1994a). This emergence also indicates that organizational rationality is adapting to the needs of the flexible firm.

Modern Formal Rationality

Weber (1978, 52) defined modern "formal" organization as "an association with a continuously and rationally operating staff." Such organizations exercise a bureaucratic domination characterized by reliance on technical knowledge and "a spirit of formalistic impersonality . . . without hatred or passion, and hence without affection or enthusiasm" (225). As Weber (975) observed, "Bureaucratization offers . . . the optimum possibility for carrying through the principle of specializing administrative functions according to purely objective considerations"—that is, discharging business "according to *calculable rules* and 'without regard for persons.'" As a result, the *modern* form of bureaucracy "develops the more perfectly, the more it is 'dehumanized,' the more completely it succeeds in eliminating from official business love, hatred, and all purely personal, irrational, and emotional elements which escape calculation. This is appraised as its special virtue by capitalism" (975).

There are two objections that can be leveled against the Weberian conception of formal organization.[5] First, Weber's ideal-typical description of bureaucracy was flawed from the very beginning because it never managed to capture even the prevailing tendencies of modern organizational forms. Formal organizations, for instance, do not inevitably tend toward rigidity and specificity. Rather, they often produce internal areas of spontaneity, informality, and flexibility. As we have seen, Weber claimed that "pure" bureaucracy maximizes calculability, impersonality, ethical neutrality, and cost-effectiveness. Yet as numerous studies have shown, no organization can function efficiently without tempering some of the worst excesses of bureaucratic overregulation (Kanter 1977; Goode 1967; Drucker 1983). Bureaucracies are supposedly rational, procedurally fair, and efficient. At the same time, they are inflexible, unyielding, and self-defeating. In short, whereas Weberian bureaucracies are *efficacious* (i.e., they are instrumentally effective transmission belts for the execution of centralized decisionmaking), they are not, strictly speaking, *efficient*. All bureaucracies to some extent implement the revenge of employees who defend themselves with the maxim "You can make me do this, but you can't make me make any sense."

Second, the nature of white-collar work has changed since Weber's day, which has affected the structure of organizational domination. As Claus Offe (1985a) has pointed out, it is often hard to use formalistic methods of control to monitor the kind of administrative, managerial, and social service work that is expanding under late capitalism—not because suitable techniques of surveillance do not exist, but because it is difficult to measure the "effectiveness" of what service, information, or knowledge workers are supposed to do (think of college professors as an example). In this regard, Offe (138) suggests that the changing nature of work has forced many organizations to become more collegial or professional in order to optimize the effective use of human resources.

Unleashing the "Thunderlizard Evangelist"

The old bourgeoisie did not have to be liked by the people it employed. Yet once ownership of business enterprises was separated from control of them, the issue of how to use managerial authority to produce the right kinds of motivations increasingly came to the fore. In response to such a problem, the Fordist "human relations" movement of the 1940s and 1950s concentrated largely on showing how management could help build a team consensus.

Extending this project, "postmodern" organizations attempt to develop ways in which the "private" or "personal" world of employees can be colonized more effectively and more absolutely. In so doing, they significantly depart from the dependence on formal rationality that Weber described nearly a century ago. "Organization Man" is no longer processed as compliant object. More is required of her. As "management guru" Tom Peters gushes:

> Now is a fantastic time. . . . The nature of products is changing, and it's just fantastic to be in charge of everything. . . . We're going to have to reinvent our country, reinvent our companies, and reinvent our selves and our careers. But that's a challenge that sounds to me like fun, frankly.
>
> And so, my final advice is (a) be weird and figure out how to tap the raging inexorable thunderlizard evangelist which I think resides in the hearts and minds and souls of people in this room. (quoted in Newfield and Strickland 1995, 42)[6]

Most affirmativists seem to believe that the psychological changes associated with Peters' "Excellence" movement reflect the happy shift that will inevitably occur once progressive, enlightened leaders get into positions where they can impose progressive, enlightened ideas on everyone else. According to Hugh Wilmott (1992, 61), for instance, postmodern forms of organization reject "the impersonal 'dehumanizing' effects of machine-like organization" and develop "'progressive' procedures and techniques," including "codes of practice, career planning and 'participative' styles of management." For Wilmott (62), "the key to productivity and performance" in "postmodern" organizations "is to create a culture that fosters commitment by enabling individuals to think and feel that they are autonomous without simultaneously making them feel insecure."

Wilmott (1992, 61; emphasis removed) points out that "it is only with the advent of the 'Excellence' literature [e.g., Peters and Waterman (1982)] that management is urged to become directly and purposefully involved in determining what employees should think, believe or value."

It does not occur to Wilmott that there might be something coercive about postmodern forms of management. As far as he (1992, 58, 66) is concerned, postmodernism just "acknowledges and celebrates the ineliminable presence and potency of chance and play. . . . The discourse of Excellence strives to manufacture, mobilize and manage the playful, ironicizing energies of postmodernism in an effort to revitalize the modernist life of capitalist relations of production" (see also Carter and Jackson 1990; Cooper and Burrell 1988; Power 1990; Deal and Kennedy 1982).

Paul Piccone (1991, 138) has suggested that whereas Weberian bureaucracies are "tightly coupled and linearly-interactive," "postmodern California-style" bureaucracies are "loosely-coupled and complexly-interactive." According to Piccone, "California-style bureaucracies do not really function in the same way as their Prussian-style counterparts. They no longer adhere to formal rationality" (138). Unlike Prussian bureaucracies, California-style bureaucracies achieve their goals by means of "a variety of informal, often contradictory forms, entirely independent of traditional formal rationality" (138). Piccone (140) concludes that the "new California-style bureaucracies . . . are actually chaotic organizations with no viable means seeking to achieve fundamentally contradictory goals, rather than bureaucracies in any traditional sense." In opposition to Piccone, I believe that "Californianization" (or what might be called "de-Prussianization") does not mean a weakening of organizational authority. Rather, it orchestrates more flexible and often more collegial forms of work, which collapse the barrier between the "office" and the "home." As well as increasing the number of hours employees work, flexibility in this context also means a shift from hierarchical control to flexible specialization. As Lash and Urry (1994, 5) have observed, once employees are "freed from the structural rigidity of the Fordist labour process," we should expect to see a shift in modes of organizational domination that encourage such employees to be "increasingly self-monitoring."

Nearly a century ago, Weber predicted that the spread of impersonal, calculable, and instrumentally oriented bureaucracy would impose on life an "iron cage" of objective rationalization from which humans would try to escape, but in vain. According to Weber, the spread of formal rationality would devalue ethical commitment, depersonalize social relations, and place technique and instrumentalism above everything else. However, postmodern forms of organization *appear*, at least, to be rather more user friendly. The superficial appeal of such forms, however, soon dims once one grasps that in a sense they are more manipulative and more invasive than the "pure" type of bureaucracy Weber described earlier.

New Specialists in the New Academic Programs

As knowledge-based research and credentialing agencies, U.S. colleges and universities operate largely as institutions of exclusion that are loosely controlled by the state.[7] Marxists and neo-Marxists should thus have already figured out that the American system of higher education plays a major role in reproducing existing class-based relations of production. Yet as Frank Heuberger (1992, 24) has observed, "Even the more sophisticated Neo-Marxists have not adequately updated their theory to grasp the growing significance in modern society of abstract knowledge and higher education." The American system of higher education is overall quite homogenized. Although there are both "public" and "private" sectors, the distinction between them is highly artificial, and the system as a whole is largely dominated by the public sector.[8]

Within the academy, there is a relatively smooth, collegial articulation of interests between intellectuals and managers, in part because administrators are typically drawn from the ranks of academics. Of course, neither the state nor bureaucracy *dictates* the ideological practices of the cultural specialists. Rather, organizational structures exercise leverage by controlling the purse strings and by creating and sizing the collegially organized spaces within which the new professionals can operate. Within the NAPs, the rewards that the new specialists can receive are not just pegged to "expertise" (i.e., determined by peer review) but are also tied to the ability to create the right kind of motivations or value commitments. Affirmative postmodernism and a commitment to the NSMs, for instance, are obligatory in many of the NAPs and play a significant role in promotion and tenure decisions. Faculty in the humanities and social sciences are not always quite as enthusiastic about affirmative postmodernism as faculty involved in the NAPs, but here, too, significant inroads have been made.

As noted earlier, old-fashioned "enlightenment rationalist fundamentalists" such as Ernest Gellner have complained that the NAPs foster a "*Relativismus über Alles.*" Yet we should not be surprised at this. Weak collegial ties tend to be associated with high levels of support for cognitive relativism. Whereas the members of an exclusively collegiate organization vigorously police disciplinary boundaries, the new specialists tend to be opportunistic scavengers, always trying to expropriate a piece of "expertise" the members of some other group have not guarded jealously enough. The modern university was founded on the rejection of cognitive relativism and on the institutionalization of well-bounded collegiate organizations. Today, however, the autonomy of collegiate organizations in the American system of higher education is increasingly undermined by the incursions of business and money in the natural sciences and by the rise of interdisciplinary programs in the humanities. While money reorganizes science as a mere appendage of business or the state, the supposedly "interdisciplinary" NAPs permit bureaucracy to penetrate and reorganize professional activity more flexibly.

Rather than resist such incursions, many new specialists are eager to help delegitimize the collegiate organization that gave them authority in the first place. In an article aptly entitled "The End of Sociological Theory," affirmative postmodernist Steven Seidman (1991, 131), for instance, claims that sociologists must "renounce . . . the increasingly absurd claim to speak the Truth, to be [*sic*] an epistemologically privileged discourse." As far as Seidman (137) is concerned, when sociological theorists abandon discredited modernist, foundationalist, and totalizing projects, "what they have left is social theory as social narrative." Seidman apparently believes one story is as good as another. His leading article (published in the official theory journal of the American Sociological Association) definitively announces the end of sociological "storytelling" as an authoritative or "privileged" practice.[9] But if this is how sociologists see their profession, how do they expect other people to regard their claims to knowledge?

Sociology

During the first five decades of this century, American sociology was dominated largely by clergymen and by surplus members of the upper class. In the 1960s and 1970s, however, sociology was revitalized by an influx of younger, more leftist, more critical, and more "activist" practitioners. Because it appeared increasingly open to real-world issues such as racism, poverty, and social injustice, the discipline flourished during this period. By the 1970s, sociology had begun to cultivate ties with the NSMs. Although this connection could have encouraged a more critical approach, and could have compelled sociology to focus on generalized issues of social justice, it ultimately had the effect of dispersing and ghettoizing largely idealist and increasingly opportunistic practices. Lacking collegiate exclusivity, and failing to develop much sense of mission or identity, "sociology" today seems to have fragmented and blown away.

The golden age of sociology appears to have occurred at about the same time as the golden age of capitalism, when Parsons announced to a stunned colleague in a related discipline that he and the other members of his team were, as he put it, "about to split the sociological atom" (quoted in Gellner 1992, 43). Sociology now contains a truly impressive number of theoretical, ideological, and methodological orientations. Whereas some sociologists still claim that their discipline should be modeled after the methodology of the natural sciences, others reject this goal entirely. For many practitioners, "sociology" is a flag of convenience. Like the medieval pope who claimed not to believe in God, some sociologists even deny that sociology exists.

Of course, if Baudrillard is right, it is no mystery why sociologists are fleeing their discipline and attempting to colonize new areas of inquiry such as the interdisciplinary NAPs. Yet disciplines such as sociology, which are relatively open to outside influence and extrinsic (noncollegial) modes of control, are particularly likely to contain experts who have no time for the patient labor of scholarly research. Today, there are both "push" and "pull" factors that encourage sociologists to leave their discipline. Even though the benefits that sociology offers diminish year by year, new opportunity structures do emerge. As a result, many practitioners are encouraged to negotiate with power and organizational domination directly.

The NAPs do not have a monopoly in this regard. For instance, the increasingly popular "Criminal Justice" (CJ) programs found in many American universities are not based on exclusively collegiate authority, nor do they claim to have any particular access to privileged knowledge. CJ programs ideologically promote the idea that there is some kind of relation between the repressive activities of the state and "justice" (no mean feat under the circumstances). They additionally produce the next generation of cops and security guards, whose futures at least seem secure. Although the substantive orientation of CJ programs is different from that of the NAPs, the formal procedures governing their operations are basically the same. Like many of the NAPs, CJ programs are funded not to generate knowledge that is independently scrutinized, but to show how highly penetrated collegiate organizations can serve bureaucracy and the state.

Postmodernity and the New Specialists

Most theorists of postmodernity have failed to examine how the NSMs and NAPs are shaped by some of the more decentralized and manipulative tactics of organizational authority and state power. According to Crook et al. (1992, 151), for instance, the NSMs are "uncompromised," value-oriented movements that condemn "bureaucratized institutions and politics." The "stance" of the NSMs, they insist, "makes new movements radical in the socio-cultural (but not necessarily political-programmatic) sense" (151). We should not, however, conclude too quickly that just because the NSMs appear to be "value-laden, anti-centralist," and countercultural (151), they have escaped being shaped by bureaucratic and legal authority.

As long as their expertise is officially sanctioned, the new professionals can help promote or consolidate value commitments that are functional for existing structures of domination. In a Foucauldian mode, such a promotion would suggest that the state is to some extent involved in shaping activity in the supposedly autonomous Third Sector, so that it can subsequently be seen to respond to what it actually helped produce. One consequence would be the wholly desirable result of ensuring that institutionalized authority will be confronted only with inputs from below that are already managed. Another would be that the state can play a major part in creating the "political" issues that can subsequently be cited as justification for enhanced modes of legal and political domination.

These relations are important because they can help us understand how the postnationalist state might exercise some leverage over motivations and solidarities that can no longer be shaped inclusively. As we have seen, postmodernity is largely the consequence of the greater autonomy and globalization of financial capital flows. Given this—and given that the United States now has the greatest capital inflows and outflows in the world—Americans must learn to live with the postcorporatist abandonment of policies of national integration and the increasingly ethnicized production of First and Third World labor pools. In addition, the increasing importance of flexible specialization and the flexible firm makes the cooptation and exploitation of women increasingly salient. We should not thus be surprised that the new professionals have abandoned the role of the "public intellectual" and prefer instead to focus on particularistic issues of race and gender.

But do the new specialists in the vast American system of higher education *critically* examine the material and structural determinants of ethnic and gender exploitation, or do they largely help formulate a reflexive project of lifestyle and life politics that turns out to be quite accommodating to dominant interests? Do "women's studies" programs, for instance, examine how gender distinctions are differentially shaped by undifferentiated domination, or do they cultivate a reflexive project of the self that encourages a classroom full of young women to cultivate the "correct" narrative of self-identity? Do women's studies courses show how the female "manager" in the First World benefits from the superexploitation of female labor in the *maquiladora* factories, or do they encourage college-educated American women to pursue precarious lower- and middle-management positions?

By the same token, does the NAP obsession with "cultural diversity" and "multiculturalism" help American students see how ethnic divisions are increasingly implicated in the extraction of surplus value—both in the Third World and in the Third World ghettos of the First World? Do such students study when and why the *state* thought up the category "minority"? Or is the multiculturalism authorized by the new professionals largely intended to mediate between the "educable" minorities who have gained access to college and the larger needs of business and the state? Do the authorized programs in cultural diversity help us comprehend the dignity of a Guatemalan peasant who has confronted imperialism and U.S.-funded terrorism all her life, or are they more likely to cultivate an appreciation of Kwanzaa—a postmodern "African" holiday that was invented a few years ago by an American academic? How many black studies professors ask why the athletic programs at their schools pluck black kids out of Third World enclaves and employ them in such a way that it is practically impossible for these kids to succeed on First World terms?

Multiculturalism and Diversity as Motivational and Organizational Resources

Multiculturalism in this nation has now become a major industry—not just in the system of higher education but also in the corporate workplace (see, for instance, Ponterotto, Casas, Suazki, and Alexander 1995; Banks 1995). Such efforts are so broadly institutionalized that to oppose them seems perverse. Yet from the vantage point of an "old" leftist such as Piccone (1993, 87), multiculturalism is a form of "collective self-congratulatory idiocy" "cretinizing students with courses in vacuous, highly politicized, victimological disciplines such as Women and Gender Studies, Black Studies or Cultural Studies." In a similar fashion, Paul Gottfried (1993, 107) suggests that multiculturalists "are the agents of monoculturalism, seeking to replace [real] human diversity with an homogenized, victimological and/or consumerist culture."

Within the academy, multiculturalism typically means the expansion of curricula to include the particularistic "needs," "history," or "special concerns" of a group that has been marginalized, such as females, blacks, Native Americans, Chicanos, or gays. Multiculturalism often additionally entails hiring and retaining academics on the basis of ascribed characteristics. Often this means hiring a black to head a black studies program or appointing a woman to run women's studies, but also, and increasingly, it means fragmenting and diversifying, as well as extending and redefining, the criteria used to shape and evaluate academic careers. This process promotes new internal markets for status competition (i.e., even more fragmented claims to expertise). As this process weakens the significance of collegial authority, it flexibly institutionalizes cultural capital that can be more easily controlled managerially. Let us look at an example of this process.

In a recent discussion of the importance of what he calls "Afrocentricity," Molefi Kete Asante (1992, 16) claims that "African American studies ... is not simply the study and teaching about African people, but it is the Afrocentric study of African phenomena." For Seidman (1994a, 255), Asante is leading "a movement towards a postmodern African-Americanism" (a claim that is hard to reconcile with Asante's insistence that there is a core African identity and a core African perspective). Asante (1992, 22) believes that Afrocentrism must reject a "Eurocentric" approach to data. In his terms, "since the Afrocentric perspective is not a racial perspective, but an orientation to data, anyone willing to submit to the rigid discipline of the field might become an Afrocentrist." The norms of this "rigid discipline," however (i.e., what would define "expertise" in this instance), are not specified in any great detail, nor are they well defined by a collegiate organization of Afrocentric practitioners.

The institutionalization of a program of African-American studies obviously represents the successful institutionalization of a new kind of cultural expertise. This is unlikely to occur without organizational connivance, however. We must expect the "expertise" of Afrocentrists, in other words, to be mediated by forces that originate outside the weakly organized college of experts who claim to understand what "Afrocentricism" is all about. Acquiescence in such an arrangement is likely to be a Faustian bargain, for, unlike astronomers or engineers, Afrocentrists tend to be held hostage to their ability to politicize their relations with clients and students in ways that are tractable to organizational power. One way in which this might be done is to tie the new knowledge the Afrocentrist controls to a NSM over which the state needs to exercise leverage. Not to put too fine a point on it, there is probably quite a strong relationship between organized black protest and the professional fate of the Afrocentrist.

Multiculturalism as an Expression of Affirmative Postmodernism

According to Ernest Gellner (1992, 70), "The relativism to which [postmodernism] aspires does not have, and cannot have, any kind of programme, either in politics, or even in inquiry." As Gellner (24, 71) sees it: "Postmodernism as such doesn't matter too much. It is a fad which owes it appeal to its seeming novelty and genuine obscurity, and it will pass soon enough, as such fashions do. But it is a specimen of relativism, and relativism does matter."

Unlike Gellner, however, I think that the politics of postmodernism is fed, not hindered, by the very relativism it helps reproduce. As Aronowitz (1988, 51) has pointed out, what "postmodernists deny is precisely [the] category of impartial competence." In this sense, "competence" and the right to speak are "constituted as a series of exclusions" that must be endlessly corrected (51).

Let me try to illustrate this latter point with reference to the influential, entrepreneurial, and often-cited work *Contingencies of Value*, written by Barbara Hernstein Smith (1988), a professor of English at Duke University and a past president of the Modern Language Association. Smith states her case well, and I think her work typifies the kind of theory associated with the new professionalism. My outline of her argument is intended to draw attention to the general approach and cannot do justice to the complexities of her argument. Although I cannot offer a critique of the work here, I want to point out that *Contingencies of Value*, which is often cited approvingly by affirmative postmodernists, could be used—and, for all I know, *has* been used—to provide an intellectually respectable defense for the reorganization of higher education in ways that would enhance multiculturalism. Smith (1988, 30) argues that "all value [including truth value] is radically contingent, being neither a fixed attribute, an inherent quality, or an objective property of things but, rather, an effect of multiple, continuously changing, and continuously interacting variables." According to Smith, it is not possible to identify anything "absolute," "objective," or "universal" about the way in which objects are individuated and appropriated. "Radical contingency" means that what appears to be objective or absolute is merely the result of "a co-incidence of contingencies among individual subjects" (40).

For Smith (1988, 43), "the literary and aesthetic academy" "develops pedagogic and other acculturative mechanisms directed at maintaining . . . a *sub*population of the community whose members 'appreciate the value' or works of art and literature 'as such.'" Thus, "the endurance of a classic canonical author such as Homer" must be explained not by reference "to the alleged transcultural or universal value of his works but, on the contrary, to the continuity of their circulation in a particular culture" (52–53). Pursuing this line of thought, Smith attacks the traditional axiological theories of David Hume and Kant, which, she believes, ground value in universal features of human nature or universal cognitive apparatuses. She (69ff) concludes that although Hume and Kant proceed "from two traditionally opposed positions," neither is capable of acknowledging, or coming to terms with, the radical contingency of value, which is always rooted in the variability of experience, need, and interest.

The lessons of Smith's book are clear enough. If all value is radically contingent, and if no absolute or universal standards of taste or truth exist, then the models of the university developed, for instance, by Weber, Parsons, or John Newman are more than passé.[10] Smith does not overtly address (a characteristic omission) the question of why there should be a coalition between "progressive" faculty and administrative bureaucrats with regard to contingency, relativity, or cultural diversity. Why should the state or, more specifically, formal organization *promote* multiculturalism within the academy? Is it because bureaucracy and the state are social work agencies that intrinsically favor liberal, humane, and more "caring" programs? Or is it because radical contingency provides the intellectual justification for the splintering of status markets and for a more flexible reorganization of human resources? Or, more to the point, does the institutionalization of radical contingency once and for all put an end to outmoded attempts to develop the kind of "total" critical understanding pursued by dead white males such as Hegel, Marx, or Adorno?

Multiculturalism and Authority

Multiculturalism exists not only within the American system of higher education but also in the shape of "diversity management," which has become an increasingly important component of American business (MacDonald 1993, 22). In the corporate world, multiculturalism today is a million-dollar industry. "Diversity consultants," for instance, can earn $2,500 a day giving "culture audits" and organizing workshops in "sensitivity training." The seven-part "Valuing Diversity" video series made by Griggs Productions costs from $3,000 to $4,500 to purchase and has been sold to "almost 5,000 business, government and educational organizations, including Kellogg Company, Lockheed, MCI, Yale University and the University of California, as well as the U.S. Department of State, Justice, Labor, Transportation, Defense and Energy, among others" (24).[11]

By 1994 at least one federal agency (the Department of Housing and Urban Development) had initiated a personnel policy that required managers and supervisors to "participate as active members of minority, feminist or other cultural organizations" or to "participate in EEOC activities or cultural diversity programs" in order to qualify for an "outstanding" evaluation (cited in Price 1994, A1). In many corporations and public bureaucracies it is standard procedure to make measurable "sensitivity" to the "special needs" of women and minorities a factor in promotion and advancement decisions. Whatever else such tactics may achieve, they allow organizational rationality to breach and to colonize what used to be regarded as private, "inner," or morally *autonomous* domains of feeling and subjectivity. In this sense, imperialism and foreign adventurism are not at an end. There are still citadels to be breached, prisoners to be taken, and foreign soil in which flags can be planted. In *The Communist Manifesto,* Marx and Engels (1974, 64) argued that western capital was using "the cheap prices of its commodities" as the "heavy artillery with which it batters down all Chinese walls" and "forces the undeveloped nations' intensely obstinate hatred of foreigners to capitulate" (64). Today, however, affirmative postmodernism, "Total Quality Management," and the "Excellence" movement provide formal organization with the "artillery" *it* needs to "batter down" residual citadels of resistance. Attempts to oppose such a barrage are doomed from the beginning. Those who get in the way of "enlightened sensitivity" have about the same chance of surviving the ensuing assault as did the Chinese peasants of the 1840s who turned sixteenth-century technology against modern cannons wielded by professionals.

New Disciplinary Mechanisms

The groups addressed by multiculturalism tend to have the following characteristic: Their members tend both to be excluded from what Crook et al. have comprehensively called the "service class" *and* are being recruited into this "class" to a historically unprecedented degree.[12] According to government statistics, resident white males of the United States will constitute only 15 percent of new entrants to the labor force between 1990 and 2000 (U.S. Department of Commerce 1991, 384). During this same period, resident white females will constitute 42 percent of new entrants. According to the Equal Opportunities Commission, in Britain there will be a fall in male employment of 300,000 by the year 2000. At the same time, there will be 500,000 new jobs for women. By 1994 "the percentage of white male professionals and managers working in the United States [had] dropped . . . to 47 percent. The same category of white women [had] jumped . . . to 42 percent" (cited in Campbell 1994, C3). According to Bob Taylor, director of training for the Memphis Race Relations and Diversity Institute, what is "driving diversity training" is demographic change (C3). As one business magazine recently pointed out, this trend will significantly affect corporate America:

> During the rest of the 1990s the number of youngsters entering the workforce each year will be smaller than at any time since the second world war; but two-fifths will be from minorities, mostly Hispanics and blacks. . . . Corporate America is starting to wake up to all this. Last year a group of 45 Fortune 500 executives and university presidents, known as the Business-Higher Education Forum, published a report saying that the country could not ignore the growing isolation of its inner-city minorities. (*The Economist* [U.K. edition] March 30, 1991, 21)

Although the highest levels of business and government are still overwhelmingly dominated by white males, in some regards at least entry-level females are beginning to outperform entry-level males. In Britain the official unemployment rate for males (18 percent) is three times higher than that for females. Although this statistic partly reflects the fact that men are still more likely than women to seek work, it also suggests how superfluous many males have become as producers. In most developed capitalist economies (and in many developing countries, too), the workforce is becoming feminized at an extraordinary rate. A generation from now, the era when the office or the workplace was a bastion of male culture will seem positively antediluvian.

Today as men try to adjust to their plummeting value as spouses, they are simultaneously confronted in the workplace with management strategies that effectively undermine what were once considered "manly" virtues. According to management consultants Faith Popcorn and Lys Marigold (1995), for instance, the new corporate workplace should seek to encourage "FemaleThink"—a form of "clicking," as they describe it, that replaces hierarchical, male-dominated structures with decentered, flexible, and somehow more caring social relationships. As Popcorn and Marigold breezily explain, women are really more useful to corporations because they are more ready to assume multiple roles and because they are used to juggling their schedules. The possibility that the clicking woman fluent in what Popcorn and Marigold call "Popcorn-speak" might be a functional adaptation to flexible forms of domination is not, however, a feature of PopcornThink. Nevertheless, as Popcorn and Marigold make clear, the inflexible "old" male is now more of a liability than an asset to the corporation.

Legal Domination and the Reproduction of Inequality

In recent years, the state has increasingly relied on new legal and bureaucratic specialists (the "new social regulators," as some have called them) to penetrate and reorganize occupational hierarchies in ways that are most accommodating to dominant interests. The best illustration of this trend is the mixed bowl of strategies popularly described as "affirmative action." The New Right favors dismantling some of the older, more liberal programs of cooptation and support because it does not believe that legitimation inputs are as important as they once were. Whether this tactic is "politically correct" remains to be seen. The issue will be resolved in the political, not the academic, arena (if we assume, of course, that "politics" still exists).

Affirmative action is at a crossroads, in part because it is associated with the supposedly discredited "liberal" programs of the past. Nonetheless, precisely because affirmative action has worked so well, the more pragmatic faction within the Republican Party continues to show a great deal of ambivalence toward it. We should not, then, conclude too readily that affirmative action (or something very much like it) has outlived its usefulness. For one thing, as one journalist recently complained, "affirmative action is a policy that is found in so many forms and in so many places that it can't be affected by a single measure" (such as a constitutional amendment) (Knight 1995, G1). For another, it seems doubtful that organizational rationality will simply abandon the leverage such programs afford. To understand the functions affirmative action has played in the past, and to see how it was adapted by the new social regulators, let us briefly examine its history.

Affirmative Action and the New Social Regulators

In 1964 the Civil Rights Act promised to use law to protect minorities from discrimination in public accommodation, the use of public facilities, public education, and employment. The act itself contained nothing that could be used to support race quotas or the hiring of a less qualified black over a more qualified white.

Title VII, Section 603(j) of the act specifically states that no employer shall be required "to grant preferential treatment to any individual or to any group because of the race, color, religion, sex, or national origin of such individual or group on account of an imbalance which may exist with regard to the total number or percentage of persons of any race, color, religion, sex, or national origin." As Senator Hubert Humphrey, one of the 1964 bill's supporters, emphasized at the time, "Title VII prevents discrimination" because "it says that race, religion and national origin are not to be used as the basis for hiring and firing" (quoted in Graham 1990, 198). Yet as Hugh Davis Graham (1990) has shown, the Civil Rights Act of 1964 was administratively subverted by the EEOC and by other state bureaucracies, including the Civil Rights Commission (CRC) and the Office of Federal Contract Compliance (OFCC). By the 1980s, "equal opportunity" meant quotas, "race norming"—introduced not by liberal democrats during the 1960s but by the Reagan administration in its first year of office—and "affirmative action" to legitimate the hiring of "basically qualified" minorities over better-qualified nonminorities.[13] By 1971 the Department of Labor, in which the OFCC is located, was defining affirmative action as a program designed to address the needs of an "affected class" of minorities that were "underutilized" by employers (Code of Federal Regulations 60-2.11).

In 1970 the CRC released a report, entitled *The Federal Civil Rights Enforcement Effort*, that insisted that there had been a "major breakdown" in federal enforcement of civil rights, even though little or no attempt was made to document actual discrimination (Graham 1990, 458). This shift in emphasis provided the new social regulators with new kinds of leverage over management practices. Once the burden of proof is placed on an employer to show that a "good faith" effort has been made to hire members of "underutilized" groups, "the simplest way of behaving to avoid the severe penalties of loss of contracts or heavy costs in back pay ... is simply to meet the goals" (Glazer 1978, 59).

Public institutions of higher education have been particularly affected by proportional hiring quotas, often under the promptings of the Department of Health, Education, and Welfare. Many colleges and universities have some kind of "Target of Opportunity" program that either reserves or even creates positions for blacks or other minorities, and most college teachers in America today have witnessed the often comical lengths to which many affirmative action bureaucrats are willing to go in order to find suitable candidates from a very small pool of applicants.

At the local level, many affirmative action programs have become highly entrepreneurial. Developed by new specialists working closely with the NSMs and NAPs, these programs have little or nothing to do with the original 1964 Civil Rights Act. Northeastern University, for instance, has implemented not protection but preferential hiring and promotion procedures for homosexuals. According to the *Chronicle of Higher Education:* "University officials have yet to finalize their recruitment strategy for gays. But they say it could include sending job announcements to gay organizations and offering incentives to departments to hire gay scholars" (Cage 1994, A13). Such examples are extreme but of incalculable value to "conservative" groups.

From Modern to Postmodern Liberal Strategies

As Graham (1990) has documented, there were two quite distinct phases to the "civil rights era." Phase one, which lasted until 1965, enacted antidiscrimination policy into federal law. During this phase, the state extended the rights of citizenship to new categories of persons who had previously been excluded. During phase two, however, "the problems and politics of implementation produced a shift of administrative and judicial enforcement from a goal of equal treatment to one of equal results" (456). Leftist modernizers won the battle for civil rights with the passage of the 1964 Civil Rights Act, the 1965 Voting Rights Act, and the Fair Housing Act of 1968. During the 1970s, however, the liberal coalition changed tactics: "In the process of implementing the anti-discriminatory commands of Phase I of the civil rights reforms of 1964–65, the EEOC and OFCC, together with their allies in the civil rights coalition and in the agencies and Congress and also increasingly the federal courts, fundamentally transformed the Phase I goal of equal treatment into the Phase II goal of equal results" (457).

Graham (1990, 462) suggests that what I would see as the postmodern "Phase-II shift of civil rights policy appears to have been the unwitting cutting edge of a vast but quiet revolution of the American state itself." He notes that "the deep, national shift . . . away from the consolidation that [had] followed the New Deal and World War II" reflected the emergence of a new kind of "regulatory apparatus that paradoxically combined disaggregation with growth and with even greater intrusiveness" (462). This "new social regulation" (Vogel 1981; Graham 1990, 463–466) emerged during the period 1964–1972 and was responsible for the EEOC (1964), the OFCC (1965), and the Office of Minority Business Enterprise (1969).

The Effects of Affirmative Action Programs

Although affirmative action programs supposedly bring minorities and nonminorities together, this can occur only under the paternalistic supervision of bureaucratic regulation and legal authority. As Piccone (1991, 136) has pointed out, affirmative action in the American system of higher education has the entirely desirable effect of encouraging or even requiring minorities "to internalize only a pathological relation to authority or a particularistic relation to knowledge"; affirmative action programs "sponsor the particularization of universalistic identities and thereby end up socializing students into sharply segregated intellectual ghettoes where they can succeed only by indefinitely perpetuating the kind of social barriers affirmative action was meant to remove." In short, rather than helping to break down the very real divisions in the larger society, affirmative action programs encourage and reinforce ethnic divides. As a result, blacks and whites mingle less today at public colleges and universities than they did twenty years ago. In recent years, some universities have even introduced apartheid-style facilities.[14]

At the end of a period in which affirmative action, race norming, and multiculturalism have flourished, we can see two clear trends emerging. First, fewer people in this country are willing to believe that racial divisions will heal. In answer to a question posed by the Gallup organization in 1993—"Do you think that relations between blacks and whites will always be a problem for the United States, or that a solution will eventually be worked out?"—53 percent of whites said that such relations will always be a problem, compared to 55 percent of blacks (*Gallup Poll Monthly* October 1993, 5). When the same question was put to Americans in 1963, *before* the implementation of affirmative action (and before civil rights legislation), 44 percent of whites and only 26 percent of blacks said they thought race relations would always be a problem in this country.

Second, the economic plight of the majority of blacks who have not prospered in the last two or three decades has worsened relatively.[15] From 1960 to 1980, black unemployment was fairly consistently twice the rate of white unemployment. By 1990, however, black unemployment was nearly three times higher than white unemployment (Hacker 1992). The earning power and wealth of employed blacks have changed hardly at all in comparison to whites over the last thirty years.

Over the last two or three decades, the differences among blacks have considerably widened along class lines. According to the Census Bureau, more blacks were clustered in low-income jobs (less than $10,000 per annum) and high-income jobs (more than $35,000 per annum) in 1990 than in 1970 (using constant dollars and cited in *The Economist* [U.K. edition] March 30, 1991, 22). (The same pattern exists for whites—so in this sense at least some kind of equality *has* been achieved.) As Graham (1990, 453–454) points out: "Since the Civil Rights Act of 1964 ... class divisions among blacks became larger than those among whites. By 1988 the top fifth of white families ranked by income made 8.6 times as much as the bottom fifth, but among blacks the figure was 13.8 times."

Although some members of minority groups have benefited from such programs, one of the effects of such programs, as Jennifer Hochschild (1988, 76) has discovered, was that "twice as many whites attribute the continuing disadvantaged state of blacks to personal faults as to discrimination." Whites, in other words, tend to assume *mistakenly* that because affirmative action programs do effectively "solve" or even overcompensate for problems of unfairness and inequity, any residual inequality between the so-called races is likely to be the fault of the individuals concerned. Kristin Bumiller (1988, 10ff) replicated these findings. According to one Gallup poll conducted in 1993, nearly three-quarters of whites believe that the economic disadvantages of blacks are due not to "discrimination" in some form but to "something else." Perhaps surprisingly, a plurality *of blacks* (49 percent) agree with this conclusion, while 44 percent of blacks continue to cite "discrimination" as the main cause of inequality (*Gallup Poll Monthly* October 1993, 5).

Affirmative action, then, embodies a highly effective ideological practice. As Peter Hadreas (1991, 222) has pointed out, "If blacks are *popularly perceived in toto* to be recipients of Affirmative Action, they will bear the burden of the popular belief that the dismal statistics [of black achievement] are due to their personal failure."[16] One consequence of this perception is that Americans can repress, or push out of consciousness, the rather significant fact that by 1986, 51 percent of black children were living in poverty—the highest rate in fifteen years (Hoover 1987,

257). Although being poor is not in itself an invariably crippling condition, growing up as a poor child in a viciously divided society where marginal groups are effectively separated from the kinds of personal, familial, and material resources that most "middle-class" people take for granted inevitably solidifies existing inequalities.

Although affirmative action has helped some individuals, it has done nothing to eliminate structural discrimination and institutional racism, which are as valuable a resource to capital today as they ever were. Ethnically subordinate groups in the United States have always suffered disproportionately during periods of economic retrenchment, and the past twenty-five years have been no exception in this regard. What *is* different today, however, is that both the United States and the American workplace are becoming less white and less male. As a result, capital and the state have to reconfigure "race" and "gender" because reproducing the white male in the core industries as the centerpiece of a policy designed to create a comprador white male "labor aristocracy" is no longer advantageous. In corporatist, Fordist systems, white males were given privileged positions, and women and "minorities" were deliberately and overtly excluded from the primary sector. Post-Fordism, however, finds it far more effective (and far less costly) to develop decentralized, local, and flexible means of using race and gender as part of the familiar (and wholly unoriginal) "divide, devalue, and rule" strategy. As we have seen, unlike Fordist systems, post-Fordism relies heavily on Third World labor and on Third World labor pools in First World spaces.

Affirmative action programs are popular among the new cultural specialists and the new social regulators because they create opportunities for institutional, organizational, and professional growth during a period of economic retrenchment. The emphasis on cultural diversity, for instance, has the added benefit of encouraging academics to develop their own "expertise" (and hence their cultural capital) by specializing in idealist strategies that preserve, rather than bridge, the gap between thought and activity, theory and practice. Support for affirmative action programs both institutionalizes and helps legitimate the paternalistic intervention of state apparatuses that are chiefly concerned with reproducing and managing, not eradicating, injustice and exploitation. In this sense, it makes little difference whether the factions in control of the state are at the present time expanding, sustaining, or limiting such programs, for such adjustments reflect little other than the outcome of a social experiment designed to test how the costs of authority can be minimized as its effectiveness for a system of class domination is optimized.

As far as the capitalist state is concerned, the main advantage of affirmative action programs is that they give bureaucracy a decentralized and flexible mechanism to address and control tensions and conflicts within a rapidly changing civil society—not, of course, at their point of origin where they might have to be addressed (or, worse still, solved), but in the school, the university, or the workplace, where they can be deflected and managed. Affirmative action bureaucrats both reproduce and justify increasing levels of inequality in an increasingly ethnicized and viciously divided civil society. They promise, in sum, that legal and administrative specialists can both manage and resolve the problems that rational legal authority helped define in the first place.

Postmodernity and the New Class

The Contemporary Economy of Signs

According to Harvey (1989a, 121–200), Fordist economies of mass production reached a crisis point by the end of the 1960s, at which point they began to gag on the endless duplicates of the cheap, standardized goods they so effortlessly spewed forth. As noted earlier, Baudrillard (1975, 143) once claimed that capitalism's "fatal malady" "is not its incapacity to reproduce itself economically and politically, but its incapacity . . . under the sign of economic rationality . . . to reproduce itself *symbolically.*" From Baudrillard's perspective, Fordist mass production prevented culture from developing and extending its own order. But as a Marxist would note, it was no accident that Fordist cultural crisis occurred at a time (the 1960s) when the Fordist regime of accumulation had reached the limits of its own potential.

As it turns out, Homo Economicus abandoned utility and embraced symbolic exchange precisely at the stage when the continued expansion of capital was threatened by capital's own frightening *success* at solving the problems of scarcity. As Debord (1994, 30) pointed out, whereas early capitalism had treated the proletarian as mere tool or worker, "these ideas of the ruling class are revised just as soon as so great an abundance of commodities begins to be produced that a surplus 'collaboration' is required of the workers" (30). Thus, "the *humanity of the commodity* finally attends to the workers' 'leisure and humanity' for the simple reason that political economy *as such* now can—and must—bring these spheres under its sway." As a result, "the totality of human existence falls under the regime of the 'perfected denial of man'" (30).

Marx hoped that once workers realized they could produce their needs by laboring, say, one day a week, they would demand liberation from the system of commodity production and exchange that had enslaved them in the past. Yet as Debord (1994, 18) emphasized, the spectacle-commodity economy is in a sense a more complete form of alienation, for "the absolute denial of life . . . is no longer projected onto the heavens, but finds its place instead within material life itself." The spectacle-commodity economy, in these terms, "is a permanent opium war," for "in the spectacle, the totality of the commodity world is visible in one piece, as the general equivalent of whatever society as a whole can be and do. The spectacle is money for contemplation only [think of Las Vegas as an example], for here the totality of use has already been bartered for the totality of abstract representation. The spectacle is not just the servant of pseudo-use—it is already, in itself, the pseudo-use of life" (30, 33).

Baudrillard, in his most recent writings, seems to miss the connection between Fordist economic crisis and postmodern consumer culture entirely. Yet Baudrillard was not always so idealist or neglectful in orientation. In his early work on the "Political Economy of the Sign," for instance, he (1981, 147) acknowledged that the Marxist "code of political economy" is "the fundamental code of our society." He (118, 114ff) agreed, moreover, that this "code" supports "the fetishized value of the object" and that it is linked to class domination. In his later work, however, the earlier assertion that the circulation of signs might help to reproduce class domination is abandoned. Instead, Baudrillard (1990b, 185) describes the circulation of commodities as a mere "will to spectacle and illusion, opposed to all will for knowledge and power." By the late 1980s, Baudrillard began to view culture and the circulation of signs as dominant. He consequently produced "a vision of society, especially in his later writings, in which signs proliferate and come to determine the course of social development"(Harms and Kellner 1991, 57). As a result, Baudrillard's "postmodern social theory obscures the extent to which 'radical semiurgy,' the proliferation of signs and images, is itself a function of the current stage of capitalist development" (57).

Yet regardless of whether the causes of postmodern consumer capitalism are primarily material (as a Marxist, or Debord, would suggest) or cultural (as Baudrillard and Featherstone believe), it is nonetheless indisputable that the main problem facing capital today is associated with the reproduction of the *demand* for meaning (Baudrillard 1981, 145). No longer content with merely organizing the factors of production, and no longer prepared to let consumption take care of itself, capital now concentrates on new structures of feeling. As the Ford ad of the 1990s explains, "We build excitement." But even though consumerism is an increasingly important component of the circuit of capital, it does not, and cannot, absorb the totality of human material existence. Many sociologists (of which Baudrillard is but one example) tend to assume that there are no ecological constraints on the costly proliferation of consumer capitalism—a system that creates waste as its main product. Capital, however, is still based on production, as well as consumption, and is still driven by the cold desire for profit, not, as Baudrillard (1988b) occasionally implies, by a hot or "orgiastic" desire for the ecstatic, mindless discharge of expenditure. In this regard, historical materialism must serve as a necessary corrective to postmodernism.

From Use Value to Sign Value

In simple capitalist production, the use value of labor is exchanged for the exchange value of the wages that workers must earn in order to purchase the use values cum exchange values that will support them and their families. As we have seen, the capitalist extracts measurable surplus value from this cycle in the form of profits (see Figure 5.1). Today, however, capital increasingly requires commodities to assume not merely the "dual character" of use and exchange value that Marx (1967c, 41–48) described earlier but also the "dual character" of exchange and *sign* value. As a result, the recycling of value through capital's circuit involves the exchange of money for stratified opportunities to engage in symbolic as well as commodity exchange (see Figure 9.1).

"Sign value" is a nonquantified and nonquantifiable measure of prestige and social honor that affords the consumer access to a desired status group. Although it can always be converted into an equivalent exchange value (e.g., one can say that a coveted yacht is worth $5 million), sign value cannot simply be *reduced* to its monetary equivalent, for this would imply that money (a formal measure of quantity) can connote qualitative social prestige in a socially unmediated fashion.

In manufacturing industries, labor creates surplus value as part of a process that is designed to turn commodity capital back into productive capital (see Figure 5.1). As Baudrillard (1981, 115) notes, however, "sumptuary operations" (i.e., the acquisition of sign value) produce a different kind of surplus value: *status* domination. Although this is "linked to economic power," "it does not 'emanate' from it automatically." Rather, "it issues from it through a reworking of value" (115). Status domination hence enables consumers to demonstrate, according to some social rubric, that they are persons of real taste and distinction. Yet as they purchase their intangibles (the "right look," the "right style," etc.), consumers also generate profits for business organizations because they must trade exchange value (their wages) for sign value (the semiotic privileges they are given the freedom to purchase).

The merchandising of primarily *symbolic* goods accelerates the recycling of quantified value as follows. First, unlike goods that primarily have use value (e.g., bread, blankets, baking soda, candles, violins, escalators), the variety and range of "symbolic" goods (e.g., "Old Masters,"

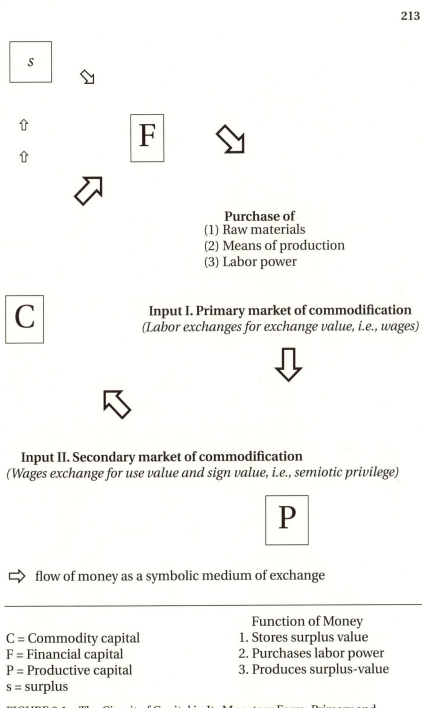

s

F

Purchase of
(1) Raw materials
(2) Means of production
(3) Labor power

C

Input I. Primary market of commodification
(Labor exchanges for exchange value, i.e., wages)

Input II. Secondary market of commodification
(Wages exchange for use value and sign value, i.e., semiotic privilege)

P

⇨ flow of money as a symbolic medium of exchange

	Function of Money
C = Commodity capital	1. Stores surplus value
F = Financial capital	2. Purchases labor power
P = Productive capital	3. Produces surplus-value
s = surplus	

FIGURE 9.1   The Circuit of Capital in Its Monetary Form: Primary and Secondary Markets of Commodification

$180 jeans or a $44,000 brace of shotguns) can be developed indefinitely, thus guaranteeing constantly expanding markets for capital. Second, consumer turnover for cultural goods is likely to be somewhat closer to the time unit deemed optimal by Marx: "the twinkling of an eye." This helps explain why capital responded to the overall fall in the rate of profit at the end of the Fordist period by speeding up the rate of consumption as well as by increasing productivity. It also accounts for the shift in emphasis in the more developed capitalist economies from secondary (industrial) production to tertiary (service) functions. As Harvey (1989a, 156) points out, the "half-life" of a "typical" product (e.g., a washing machine, a refrigerator, an automobile) in the 1940s and 1950s was "from five to seven years." Today, "in certain [economic] sectors (such as textile and clothing industries)" the half-life of a product is less than three years; in "the so-called 'thoughtware' industries (e.g., video games and computer software programs) the half-life is down to less than eighteen months" (156).

Baudrillard (1981, 112–122) uses the example of the "art auction" to illustrate how sign value is created. Needless to say, the value of a coveted piece of art is not entirely added by labor. Moreover, the bidders who compete for ownership of a rare work of art cannot engage in a fully rationalized, fully objectified calculation of the value of the commodity in question. Instead, they follow sumptuary laws, which "act as consumption-regulating devices, prescribing which groups can consume which goods" (Featherstone 1991, 17; Douglas and Isherwood 1980). Baudrillard (1981, 113) points out that the "wasteful" expenditure at the "art auction" makes of consumption something that is "sacrificed, eaten up according to a logic of difference and challenge." As a result, we find in "the agonistic community of peers . . . a competition, a wager, a challenge, a sacrifice, an *aristocratic measure of value*" (113). If "in the economic order, it is the mastery of *accumulation*, of the appropriation of surplus value, which is essential," in "the order of signs (of culture), it is mastery of *expenditure* [i.e., symbolic exchange] that is decisive" (115).

Sumptuary practices do not, of course, lead to the kind of standardized mass consumption characteristic of Fordist modernity. On the contrary, "the concern with fashion, presentation of self, the 'look' on the part of the new wave of urban flâneurs points to a process of cultural differentiation which in many ways is the obverse of the stereotypical images of mass societies in which serried ranks of similarly dressed people are massed together" (Featherstone 1991, 97). Postmodern consumerism thus creates special places or special enclaves—Soho in New York, Queen Street West in Toronto, the Castro District in San Francisco, or the King's Road in Knightsbridge, London, where status groups position themselves through a display of signs. As Featherstone (1991, 13) points out, the "satisfaction" and "status" that derives from such consumption depends "upon displaying and sustaining differences within conditions of inflation"—that is, in conditions where the value of consumption immediately falls as soon as it is widely distributed (think of fashion as an example). It is precisely for this reason that new types of consumption have to be circulated at an ever-increasing rate of speed.

Excursus: Marx and the Cultural Dopes

Marxists are often accused of treating ordinary individuals as "cultural dopes" who are riddled through and through with "false consciousness." According to Baudrillard, for example, the claim that consumer capitalism produces "false needs" is quite absurd. As far as he is concerned, our proclivity for wasteful consumption is neither a reflection of class oppression nor our supposedly "alienated" current state. If anything, it is a throwback to earlier (premodern) states of consumption, involving "potlatch, 'devil's share,' consumption, symbolic exchange," wasteful shows, or excess—in short, various kinds of showing off (Baudrillard 1988b, 11). Like Bataille, Baudrillard argues that it was the parsimonious investor and hoarder in the modern era who was the anomaly, not the "savage" or the postmodern consumer. From Baudrillard's perspective, the postmodern subject has probably returned to "consumption" in the original sense of the term, which means "to destroy, to use up, to waste, to exhaust" (Williams 1976, 68).[1]

Like Baudrillard, several other critics of Marxist theories of culture have also insisted that Marxism assumes people have to be hammered into a state of "false consciousness" before they are ready and willing to consume what capital *needs* them to consume. Mark Gottdiener (1985) and Dick Hebdige (1988) suggest, moreover, that Marxist theories of culture assume that the creation and communication of meaning in contemporary society are monolithically hegemonic. In opposition to this point of view, Gottdiener and Hebdige emphasize that the "culture industry" does not one-sidedly impose meanings on a passive and helpless audience. Gottdiener (1985, 998) argues that "ideological control in modern society can never attain closure and there is a struggle over meanings for cultural objects and events that both the dominant and subordinate groups in society must face." According to Gottdiener (997), advertising and marketing "graft . . . sign values to the apparent use value of commodities in order to sell them on the competitive market." However, consumers continuously modify and change the meaning of these commodities for purposes of self-identification. As Gottdiener points out, subcultures are particularly influential in helping to transform the meaning of fashion or music.

Gottdiener (1985, 998) claims that just as he has shown that consumers adapt and transform the meaning of commodities, his "semiotic approach [has modified] the concept of hegemony as it is conceptualized by many Marxist critics of mass culture." He (981) argues that the "Marxian critique of mass culture" is guilty of "functional reductionism" because it reduces everything to the claim that the masses suffer from "false consciousness" or are terminally "confused." Yet as previously noted, the Marxist view of capitalist "domination" or "hegemony" does *not* imply that the capitalist class deliberately or *instrumentally* controls consciousness. There is not now (nor has there ever been) some kind of simplistic or mechanistic cause-effect relationship between "infrastructural" material factors and "superstructural" modes of consciousness. Because consumption today is so obviously "a social and cultural process involving cultural signs and symbols, not simply . . . an economic utilitarian process" (Bocock 1993, 3), it is quite apparent that the New Class cannot impose meaning on consumption one-sidedly. Rather, it communicatively interacts with those to whom it sells. As Robert Goldman (1992, 226) concludes in his study of advertising: "Ads structure meanings so that they become a means of producing commodity-sign value. To produce sign values, advertisers colonize the sphere of cultural life in their search for meanings which will add value to their product or service. Viewers' interpretive participation is absolutely necessary to the completion of commodity-signs. . . . Consumers produce value, they don't just consume it."

Admittedly, some leftist intellectuals have insisted that *other* people (not themselves, of course) live some kind of vicarious, substitute existence but will readily see the error of their ways once it is pointed out to them how stupid and deluded they really are. These leftists might just as well lecture the fish about the water in which it swims. The whole point about the "colonization of the lifeworld" described earlier is that the reality of commodity relations comes to provide the taken-for-granted basis for communicative interaction in the first place. From this perspective "the world of true needs" has not been subordinated to "the world of false needs." Rather, "the realm of needing" within the spectacle-commodity economy has itself become a "field of communication" that is almost exclusively mediated by commodity relations (Leiss 1978, 18). And as Andrew Sayer and Richard Walker (1992, 106) point out, marketing today demands "an intricate and far-ranging tissue of circulation, which can only be established and maintained through immense social undertakings and constant social attention. . . . One cannot, therefore, think of work as an individual pursuit, or consumption as an individual satisfaction. They are irreducibly social production and social consumption on a scale, and to a depth, never before seen."

The New Class of Cultural Intermediaries

The economic specialists who market postmodern consumer capitalism comprise a New Class of "cultural intermediaries" who "cater for and expand the range of styles and lifestyles available to audiences and consumers" (Featherstone 1990, 18). The New Class reinforces the belief that shopping is not so much "a purely calculative rational economic transaction to maximize utility" but "a leisure-time cultural activity in which people become audiences who move through . . . spectacular imagery" (Featherstone 1991, 103; Fiske 1994). As Jameson (1989, 381) points out, the "cultural practices and values" and "local ideologies" of the New Class merchandisers of signs and services now articulate the "dominant ideological and cultural paradigm for consumer capitalism."

In essence, the cultural intermediaries are paid to help mediate between the cultural needs of consumers and the economic requirements of business. Their task is to aestheticize commodities in new and exciting ways for the "postmodern" consumers, who have become "well-trained experts in the peculiar art of reading the good sex life into toothpaste or deodorant, the pastoral picnic into the bottle of Gallo chablis" (Pfeil 1988, 389). These intermediaries sell to consumers who, like caddis larvae, mix and match what is made available to them, creating their own sense of personal style in order to take possession of the spaces they must occupy.

Although New Class intermediaries are largely apolitical, they tend to be liberal in outlook and to reject "traditional values," including the sanctity of the "traditional" (actually modern) family comprising Mom, Dad, and the two kids. Yet denizens of the New Class are not anticapitalist. If the established (i.e., *modern*) version of repressive "bourgeois culture is in decline, [this is] because it is no longer an adequate stimulus. . . . The conflict between the so-called new class and the old moneyed class rests not on the former's rejection of capitalism per se but on its rejection of the moral order that sustained capitalism at a particular stage in its development" (Hunter and Fessenden 1992, 187).

Most of the new cultural intermediaries work for well-organized and powerful commercial interests. They are employed as advertisers, public relations specialists, fashionware and software designers, entertainers, artists, leisure consultants, market researchers and media strategists, among other occupations. They specialize in developing and extending commodity relations that expand both commodity and symbolic exchange. The latter involves marketing images, lifestyle products, and other symbolic goods that in one form or another attest to "the taste and distinction of the owners" (Bourdieu 1977, 188). Often this means little other than selling signs, and increasing the pace at which signs can be sold, but it also involves repackaging economically useful goods as culturally significant products (Leiss, Kline, and Jhally 1986; Jhally 1990; Harms and Kellner 1991). Unlike the new professionals, the value of what the new intermediaries do is measured almost exclusively by money. Even though their outlook does not greatly differ from that of the advertising men and women of the 1920s, their techniques are far more sophisticated, and the services they perform are increasingly important for capital's circuit. For members of the New Class and for their customers, "Culture has ceased to be, if it ever was, a decorative addendum to the 'hard world' of production and things, the icing on the cake of the material world. The word is now as 'material' as the world" (Jacques and Hall 1989, 119).

New Classers lack traditional or professional support. Living as they do in a world that is mediated almost exclusively by money, they tend to commodify their own selves as well as everything else. They are, as a result, well practiced in the kind of "impression-management" that Erving Goffman (1959) used to describe so well. In this regard, the new intermediaries are completely different from the "old professionals." As we have seen, the "expertise" of the old professional was established by occupational status groups and was "transferable from individual to individual" (Giddens 1991, 18–19, 243). Because the identity of such old professionals was vested in an exclusively collegiate organization, it was like a traditional or ascribed identity—it was relatively stable because it was anchored by a clearly bounded community. By contrast, a self that is vulnerable to the media of money and power is dynamic, calculative, transient, and cynical. For most members of the New Class, life is nothing more than "a bowl of strategies," as Clifford Geertz once said of Goffman.

Compared to the old professionals—or even to self-employed businesspeople—the yuppie workers in public relations, marketing, media, or advertising live in a permanent state of anxiety. Unable to use status group closure to establish a professional identity, they are always at the mercy of changing economic and (within the context of the organization) shifting political realities. For New Classers, the one stable point of reference in a world without bearings is money: a medium that does at least have "a standard value . . . interchangeable across a plurality of contexts" (Giddens 1991, 18; see also Simmel 1978). Yet while giving subjects instrumental leverage, money does not create a sense of rootedness. As Willy Loman observed in *Death of a Salesman:* "For a salesman, there is no rock bottom to the life. He don't put a bolt to a nut, he don't tell you the law or give you medicine. He's a man way out there in the blue, riding on a smile and a shoeshine. And when they start not smiling back—that's an earthquake" (Miller 1987, 138).

For the new white-collar employee, the right suit, the right "look," the right kind of lifestyle, are indispensable if others are to be persuaded that the object in view is a valuable and valued commodity. As one job-hunting manual advises students who wish to compete in the commodity-labor market: You must turn yourself into a commodity—"Think of your resumé as a marketing tool to sell yourself as a product. Your goal is to sell your way into an interview, or to sell yourself to an interviewer" (cited in Calhoun, Light, and Keller 1994, 83).[2]

New Marketing Strategies

In modern societies, production and consumption were, for the most part, gender-specific, repressive, and instrumentalist. By contrast, "postmodern" lifestyles are less gender specific and more permissive.

Consuming Gender

Frank Mort (1989, 165) has pointed out that 1940s- and 1950s-style industrial production involved "a highly gendered" style of life that "heroised the butcho, macho heavy industries and ranked workers in the new service sector as secondary and inferior." Unlike members of the more effete classes, working-class men in the 1940s and 1950s did not waste their time trying to develop themselves as persons of refined taste and culture, nor did they have much inclination (or chance) to be "career oriented." As far as these "old" males were concerned, "real men" did not have crises of identity; they did not care to shop, and they did not pay much attention to the trivia of the "feminized" domestic sphere. In the workplace, they poured molten ore, mined coal, and erected dams, bridges, and towers. In their spare time, they participated in traditional male-only activities.

Today, however, males and females jointly roam the shopping malls of America, and both Mom and Dad happily participate in family-oriented rites of consumerism: "the world of holidays, home interiors and superstores" (Mort 1989, 169). The recent shift in normative expectations about gender-based behavior is often portrayed as some kind of happy shift from "backwards" or "regressive" modes of thought to values and attitudes that are "enlightened" or "progressive" in some unspecified sense. The functional support this value shift provides for the circulation of commodities, however, is hard to miss.

Consuming Lifestyle and Ethnicity

Whereas the Fordist economies of the 1950s were massified, "postmodern" economies, as we have seen, are based more on symbolic exchange and on the purchase of semiotic privilege. Because of this, niche markets for specialty goods in the developed capitalist economies grew much faster during the 1980s than "mass markets for standardized products" (Graham 1992, 397). Rather than being aimed at the aggregate or typical consumer, such markets try to create "differential sign value" by catering to various status groups—providing these real or imagined communities with the symbolic resources they crave.

To map such consumers, the cultural intermediaries splinter or "break down markets by age (youth, young adults, 'gray power'), by household types (dinks [double-income, no kids], single-gender couples, one-parent families), by income, occupation, housing and, increasingly, by locality. They analyze 'lifestyle,' correlating consumption patterns across commodities from food to clothing, and health to holidays" (Murray 1989, 43). "Lifestyle" in such a context does not just reflect *what* people want to consume; it also helps account for how they define themselves as subjects in the first place. These motivations thus become a new resource for capital, which encourages lifestyle groups to locate themselves in the marketplace of signs.

In 1995, for instance, the Travelers Bank began to market its "Rainbow Visa Card" for gay men and lesbians, and the Boston Bank of Commerce introduced its "Unity Visa Card" for African Americans (Hirsch 1995). The Rainbow Card (which allows customers who don't qualify for the maximum $15,000 credit line to apply for the card with a same-sex partner) carries the logo of Fuji Heavy Industries Ltd. and features the tennis star Martina Navratilova as the product's spokesperson. Application forms for the card feature Navratilova as a "champion for our cause" and promise to spend a proportion of the card's profits on organizations such as the National Center for Lesbian Rights and the AIDS Information Network. Unity Card holders are wooed with claims to black solidarity and are charged 16.65 percent on unpaid balances. According to Kevin Cohee, who acquired a majority stake in the Boston Bank of Commerce in 1995, the founders of the Unity card hope to do well. As he explained to the *Wall Street Journal:* "We have no intention of not making a lot of money" (Hirsch 1995, B7).

In 1996 Subaru of North America began to test advertisements for their automobiles that featured homosexual men and women (Suris 1996). Unlike Detroit's Big Three automakers (GM, Ford, and Chrysler), which among them have nearly three-quarters of the U.S. market, Subaru's market is niche oriented, serving a small segment of U.S. consumers who want to purchase four-wheel drive passenger cars. The ads in question show either two women or two men together in front of a Legacy station wagon. The caption reads: "It loves camping, dogs and long-term commitments. Too bad it's only a car."

Major TV networks have also recently tried to create racially defined niche markets, which, once fragmented, become more profitable in the summation of their parts than were the old massified "color-blind" (actually white-oriented) markets in the 1950s. This is a fairly new development, for as recently as 1985–1986 the "15 or the 20 shows most popular among blacks were also top 20 shows among all viewers" (Fahri 1994, 2A). Yet by 1993–1994, "only three programs among the top 20 had 'crossover' appeal among both black and non-black households" (2A). As an executive vice president at CBS, David Poltrack, explains: Before the 1980s the three major networks (NBC, ABC, CBS) had more than 90 percent of the prime-time audience each night (15A). Given this kind of penetration, "niche programming" based on race was uneconomical. But with "cable, independent broadcast stations and home video all eroding the networks' dominance, blacks now constitute a very attractive bloc of viewer" (15A). Even though they have a lower aggregate income, blacks to some extent are *more* attractive than whites because, as Nielsen Media Research has shown, they "watch far more TV than other households. The TV set is in use 10 hours and eight minutes each day in the average black household, compared with six hours and 47 minutes for non-blacks" (15A). The successful attempts of major corporations to reconsolidate "racial identity" as a marketing device is, of course, portrayed by nearly everyone—including most blacks, of course—as a positive and progressive development about which we all should be proud. As Doug Alligood, a vice president for BBDO Worldwide, a major New York ad agency, recently emphasized, the increase in the number of shows aimed at black audiences is "a celebration of diversity, and it's wonderful" (2A).[3]

As these examples suggest, we should not be surprised that many of America's most "devoted multiculturalists" include the sales departments of major corporations (Jacoby 1994b, 125). As a "Director of Multicultural Marketing" at AT&T recently stated to *Time* magazine (with a directness and succinctness few academics could ever hope to match): "Marketing today is part of anthropology" (quoted in Jacoby 1994b, 125). If we turned this executive on her head (as Marx liked to do with Hegel) and made her declare, "Anthropology today is part of marketing," we could make her rather tidily describe what the New Class and its masters, U.S. corporations, truly think about "diversity" and multiculturalism.

A comparison between diverse groups such as the pre- or antimodern Amish or Hasidic Jews, on the one hand and the kind of manufactured groups just defined, on the other, shows quite clearly how much money has helped reconfigure lifestyle or ethnic options. After all, if people find it necessary to define themselves exclusively in terms of commodity relations, this suggests not so much that they are "in touch with themselves" but that their lifeworld is absolutely commodified. Because the Amish and Hasidic Jews succeed in *living* their cultural identity, they do not have to purchase it in a recuperated form. Lost in all of this, as Russell Jacoby (1994b, 123) notes, is the fact that "America's multiple 'cultures' . . . exist within a single consumer society. Professional sports, Hollywood movies, automobiles, designer clothes, name-brand sneakers, television and videos, commercial music and CDs pervade America's multiculturalism. . . . Chicano's, like Chinese-Americans, want to hold good jobs, live in the suburbs, and drive well-engineered cars. This is fine—so does almost everyone—but how do these activities or aspirations compose unique cultures?"

If America *does* have a common culture, it is the worship of consumerism. As Carl Husemoller Nightingale illustrates in *On the Edge,* a powerful study of how poor black children view their world, the lifeworld of such children is fundamentally colonized and rearranged by the larger culture. "From the late 1960s," Nightingale (1993, 10) writes, "mainstream marketers have targeted black inner-city youth for promotional blitzes." As a result, "kids like the ones described in this book have enthusiastically embraced the American consumer culture—hundred-dollar sneakers, sports jackets, gold, and all. . . . The growing number of killings associated with status symbols like sneakers and gold chains only attests to the extent to which mass consumption has, under the desperate circumstances of the inner city, turned into a passion to kill" (10–11).

The Postmodern Reorganization of the Lifeworld

Nineteenth-century "wage slaves" were dominated by what appeared to be a "naturelike" commodity form and by market relations that appeared unassailable. They knew they were enslaved by the market, just as they realized they had to work or starve. In contrast, many contemporary subjects devote a great deal of energy to revivifying or solidifying the commodity relations that have become such an integral part of their social existence. This does not prove that these subjects have escaped the commodity form. Rather, as Debord (1994) pointed out thirty years ago, it suggests that commodification has reconfigured consciousness itself. What threatens turnover today is anything that might encourage alternative (noncommodified) means of self-formation. One illustration of this is the undermining of the "old" modern familial domain, together with the "old" authoritarian father.

In an analysis of popular TV situation comedies, Mark Crispin Miller (1986) has shown how the portrayal of "Dad" changed dramatically from the 1950s to the 1980s. In the 1950s, Dad was still an old-fashioned authority figure who could still say, "No—no" to more pocket money and the freedom to spend it, "no" to TV, "no" to late nights out at the expense of homework. In popular shows of the 1950s such as *The Donna Reed Show, I Love Lucy, Father Knows Best,* and *Leave It to Beaver,* men left home each day for productive careers, while women remained feminized and "domesticated" (Firth-Cozens and West 1991, 195). In the 1960s and 1970s, however, Dad became a "butt": someone who was invariably dumber than the women and children, an anachronistic and ludicrous figure who persistently tried (and, of course, failed) to impose his will on offspring who were invariably cooler than he and more in touch with the all-important, all-consuming exigencies of consumerism.

By the late 1970s, according to Miller (1986, 202), TV's "pseudofeminism" was in full swing, "invariably calculated to stroke the female viewers in some way, presenting a heroine who is untrammeled, plucky, confident, 'assertive,' always in the right, and therefore not to be suppressed by any of the lecherous, pig-eyed males who keep trying to pick her up, slobber on her, rape her, or who succeed in raping her." As females in TV-land became completely self-directing and totally in control of their lives, poor old Dad was finally allowed to rejoin the company of humans—but only after he had shown that he could be educated by those he used to boss around all the time. As Miller (207) puts it: "Certainly, today's good Dad will sometimes have a big maudlin reconciliation scene . . . but this routine effusion is always represented as a sign of healthy weakness on Dad's part. He is casting off his usual masculine reserve and 'getting in touch with his feelings.' Even his moments of unrestrained affection, then, demonstrate that Dad is at his best when *giving in.*"

What the "sensitive," "educated," postmodern Dad is giving in to, however, is the old-fashioned right to exercise some autonomous control over his offspring, not to mention the right of spouses to exercise some control on each other. As mentioned earlier, critical theorists such as Habermas (1984, 274ff) argued that the reproduction of a differentiated private lifeworld located in the domestic or familial sphere helped define the moral grounds that enabled the individuated actor to develop a sense of "personal integrity" that could transcend the "system" demands of money and power. Yet as Miller (1986, 215) notes, "The point of TV comedy is that *there can be no transcendence*": "Such is the meaning of Dad's long humiliation since the fifties. . . . Because he would have stood out as an archaic model of resistance to the regime of advertising, Dad was, through the sixties and seventies, reduced from a complicated lie to a simple joke."

As mentioned earlier, many "conservatives" appear not to like what happens when money and power reorganize the lifeworld. Nevertheless, they seem congenitally incapable of understanding *why* this transformation is occurring. Yet there might be a perfectly good reason that the mass of students at U.S. schools and universities are systematically and persistently mediocre, illiterate, disoriented, unmotivated, and ignorant of most things outside the nexus of commodity relations. There could be an explanation for why so many young people go through sixteen years of continuous education without having to do so much as complete one written assignment. Perhaps it is not merely a chance occurrence that American high school students spend far more time watching television than studying. In *Culture of Complaint*, Robert Hughes (1993, 103) laments that

> in 1991, the majority of American households . . . did not buy one single book. Before long, Americans will think of the time when people sat at home and read books for their own sake, discursively and sometimes even aloud to one another, as a lost era—the way we now see rural quilting-bees in the 1870s. No American university can *assume* that its first-year students are literate in more than a technical sense. . . . It is hard to exaggerate the narrowness of reference, the indifference to reading, the lightly dimpled cultural shallowness of many young products of American TV culture, even the privileged ones.

Hughes blames both left-wing and right-wing "extremists" in America for this sorry state of affairs—thus implying unconvincingly that a reversion toward the mean would solve the problem at hand. According to Hughes, American culture reinforces a worship of "pseudo-history," a "polity obsessed with therapies," a debasement of values, an obsession with "victimhood," a rejection of "quality" in literature and art, and an overall stupidification of just about everyone. Hughes condemns post-structuralism, postmodernism, and many other new-specialist activities. He (1993, 83) describes multiculturalism, for instance, as "a worthless symbolic program, clogged with lumpen-radical jargon." Yet there is little or no analysis in his book—more, perhaps, than one would expect from a New Fundamentalist but not much more. Like most neoconservatives, Hughes can offer no historical or structural explanation for the cultural trends he deplores, the causes of which remain deeply mysterious to him.[4]

Marx was perhaps the first to grasp how totally capitalism would destroy traditional society, and in *The Communist Manifesto* he (1974) described with great prescience how this would occur. One of the ironies of history, however, is that Marx to some extent seems to have underestimated capital's deadly potential not only to transform the forces of production but also to invade, colonize, reshape, and dissolve the prereflexive lifeworld of community. He accordingly overlooked how much capital would come to undermine what used to be the basis for what old-fashionably might be called *human* self-awareness.[5] Industrial societies, with their slow, clumsy, and outmoded emphasis on the production of *goods*, not consumers, now seem about as up-to-date as a computer full of vacuum tubes—yet another artifact to be placed in the museum of our past.

Postmodern Consumer Culture

Postmodern consumers largely take it for granted that they can rely on the market to supply them with a personalized sense of style. In contrast, status in traditional (i.e., premodern, post–hunter-gather) societies was largely acquired at birth and hence seen as "naturelike." Before the end of the nineteenth century, clothes reflected not an acquired sense of style but a fixed status bestowed on rich and poor alike. Status distinctions seemed to mirror natural hierarchies, and they determined the occupational distinctions that were passed down from one generation to another. The mere possession of money could never change such an intractable system of ascribed status. Indeed, it was only as recently as about 1900 that ordinary people began to see that they might go so far as to purchase and display an apparel of personal choice (Caplan and Stowell 1994).

Status Groups and the Spectacle-Commodity Economy

Weber (1978, 305) defined "social status" as "an effective claim to social esteem in terms of positive or negative privileges." According to Weber (936), "All stylization of life either originates in status groups or is at least conserved by them." "Status honor," in these terms, "is normally expressed by the fact that above all else a specific *style of life* is expected from all those who wish to belong to the circle" (932). From Weber's perspective, the monopolistic consociations of status groups in traditional societies effectively impeded the early capitalist money economy because it restricted either the scope or the permissible terms of commercial transactions (638ff). As Weber (307) emphasized, *traditional* "status society lives by conventions, which regulate the style of life, and hence creates economically irrational consumption patterns and fetters the free market through monopolistic appropriations and by curbing the individual's earning power."

In contrast, postmodernization promotes semiotic privilege, new kinds of status groups, and a new status order, the development and refinement of which are dependent on the extension and elaboration of commodity relations. Although Weber did not rule out this eventuality, he seems not to have anticipated it—probably because he mistakenly equated the trajectory of capitalism with the promotion of a differentiated market rationality. Yet postmodern consumer culture effectively conflates "expressive" (culture) and "utilitarian" (economic) activity. The cultural intermediaries, in other words, help consumers make "effective" spending decisions in pursuit of highly diverse and incommensurably different status group identities. New Class merchandising hence collapses the old distinction between instrumentally "rational" economic behavior and "irrational" concern with status. This, I think, would have been seen as retrograde by Weber and by Parsons, both of whom erroneously assumed that modern societies would continue to differentiate between status orientations and activities associated with instrumentally rational, market-oriented decisionmaking.

The New Culture Industry: The End of Art?

More than twenty years ago, Theodor Adorno (1991, 85) declared that the "culture industry intentionally integrates its consumers from above," forcing together "the spheres of high and low art" "to the detriment of both" (see also Adorno and Horkheimer 1972). For Adorno (1991, 85), the virtue of "low art" was that there was "a rebellious resistance inherent within it." By contrast, "high art" did at least address what the Enlightenment had excluded in its emphasis on formal and instrumental rationality: "the claim of sensuous particularity and rational ends" (Bernstein 1991, 5–6). Adorno believed that high art, in these terms, could provide some basis of opposition to the oppressive cultural philistinism of the bourgeoisie. As we have seen, however, high modern art could not sustain its oppositional and critical thrust. By the 1950s, it was absorbed, digested, sponsored, and displayed by corporate America, becoming at this stage just one more commodified sign among many others.

For Adorno, the commercial smoothing out of the difference between high and low art removed the last vestiges of aesthetic resistance to total commodification. As he (1991, 86) expressed it: "The cultural commodities of the industry are governed . . . by the principle of their realization as value, and not by their own specific content and harmonious formation. The entire practice of the culture industry transforms the profit motive naked onto cultural forms. . . . Cultural entities typical of the culture industry are no longer *also* commodities, they are commodities through and through."

The problem with Adorno's analysis, however, is that he assumed capital would always massify and homogenize culture. Moreover, Adorno overemphasized capital's ability to complete its commodification of aesthetic form. During the modern era, "the profit motive" was certainly steadily imposed "onto cultural forms" (TV would be a good example here), and the aspirations of both high and low art were both neutered and massified industrially. However, the "culture industry," as Adorno described it, never quite succeeded in turning *all* cultural forms into "commodities through and through," however hard it tried. Similarly, it has never completely eliminated the distinction between low and high art.

In contrast to the "old" culture industry described by Adorno, the *new* (i.e., postmodern) culture industry does not try to homogenize or massify. Moreover, as we have seen, its special genius is to encourage buyers to participate in the process of creating value. Hence, rather than trying to close the gap between high and low art, the new culture industry concentrates instead on closing the gap between itself and the rest of life (Bernstein 1991, 20ff). But in this sense the obsession with "lifestyle"— that is, the marketing of life as style, "the permeation of these styles into the home," "the pervasiveness of music, the way in which products have become a direct extension of their advertising image"—betokens the full "aestheticization of social reality": the inability of the consumer to perceive any "gap" between what is aestheticized and what is real (20). As Jay Bernstein (21) perceptively notes, the new culture industry today has attained "what a [modernist] avant-garde always wanted: the sublation of difference between art and life." But if art means the ability to aestheticize some kind of *alternative* to particular, or partial, modes of experience, this development "must signal a kind of 'end of art'" (21).

For Bernstein (1991, 20), by the late 1950s the "homogenization of consciousness" had "become counter-productive for the purposes of capital expansion; new needs for new commodities had to be created, and this required the reintroduction of the minimal negativity that had been previously eliminated." In other words, in the 1960s the culture industry abandoned its failed attempts at homogenization and began to sell back to consumers diverse packages of stylized "resistance" or "aesthetic opposition" that might counter the boring mundanities of their sorry existence. Such recuperated "resistance" could not, of course, address real political issues because this would only confuse people and undermine the continuing need to sell. Such "resistance" accordingly had to be jokey, ironic, or cynical—"postmodern," if you like. Yet as Bernstein (22) points out, "Because postmodernist practice alters the empirical world without transforming it, its abstract affirmations belie the despair that sustains it."

Hypercommodification and the Fragmentation of the Self

Postmodern consumer capitalism did not invent the reflexive project of the self, for modern economies also provided an array of resources through which identity could be mediated. As Georg Simmel (1978) emphasized ninety years ago, fashion, for instance, is merchandised as sign value, not purchased as use value (see also Veblen 1979). In Simmel's (1911, 44–45) terms, it is "the best arena for people who lack autonomy and who need support, yet whose self-awareness nevertheless requires that they be recognized as distinct and as particular kinds of being." Attempts to establish a permanent sense of identity on the basis of such sumptuary consumption are, of course, tragic because they are not only futile but also *endlessly* futile.

According to Featherstone (1991, 90–91), the "new petit bourgeois" is a narcissistic pretender whose "search for expression and self-expression," "fascination with identity, presentation and appearance" make this creature "a 'natural' consumer." Yet the boutique bourgeoisie are no more "natural" consumers than eighteenth-century laborers were "natural" factory workers. Postmodern consumer culture is predicated on the separation of consuming subjects from their own means of self-formation.

In early modern society, "civil privatism" meant the consumption of products in one's private time and the individual's ability to develop an enhanced—and often more clearly demarcated—sense of self. Industrial capitalism may have exploited laborers as producers, but it did not seek to separate them from their traditional, customary, and noncommodified means of *private* self-expression. The bourgeoisie may have been the historic class that first let the genie out of the bottle, but "bourgeois identity" was shaped with the *assistance* of commodities, not entirely *through* commodification.[6] By contrast, postmodern "civil privatism" means the absorption of highly flexible, highly diversified, aestheticized processes of commodification within the lifeworld of the subject. It involves the attempt to create the impression that reality itself can be aestheticized.

As personal existence is increasingly aestheticized, the distinction between *what* is represented (the self) and *how* this self is expressed becomes increasingly confused. Early modern patterns of consumption required the individual to routinize personal identity—at least in the sense that the presentation of self had to follow certain norms of consistency. By contrast, postmodern subjects see nothing wrong in assuming incommensurable, disconnected identities at various times and in various places (think of the pop icon Madonna, for instance). There is, in short, no "core" identity or "true self" consistently addressed in, or culti-vated by, postmodern sumptuary practices.

If cultural modernism both facilitated and fragmented the modern cultivation of self, cultural postmodernism disperses and dissolves indi-viduality: people's ability to individuate anchored selves. Note that this is promoted both by New Class activity and by the therapeutic or "car-ing" new specialists who tend to discourage reliance on "inner" re-sources (Hunter and Fessenden 1992). The postmodern undermining of the means of personal autonomy, together with the endless fragmenta-tion of self, makes it all the easier for New Class entrepreneurs to de-velop new services and new forms of commercial expertise. These can then be marketed to those who believe that if you think money can't make you happy, you have not yet learned where to shop.

In the marketplace, hypercommodification is facilitated by a "hyper-rationalization": the development of increasing numbers of highly spe-cialized markets in taste and style that are coherent to their adherents but incoherent to just about everyone else (Crook et al. 1992, 61–68). Youth markets tend to be at the forefront of this kind of postmodern de-velopment (Weinstein 1992; Kaplan 1987). Heavy metal markets, for in-stance, can further be differentiated into "glam" and "thrash" submar-kets that have their own arcane meanings for adherents.

The significance of hyperrationalization is that once forms of expres-sion attain a certain level of fragmentation, they lose all connection to an aesthetic or cultural order that might have its own sense of integrity and become, instead, mere "styles" that can be flexibly dispersed (Crook et al. 1992, 65ff). Easy to assume and easier still to jettison, they are so splintered and hyperdiversified that from the vantage point of the con-sumer they can seem to offer a refreshing alternative to what everyone else is doing. Once decontextualized, the image or sign, moreover, can be *recontextualized* in any way that is useful to the market. The permu-tations are endless: "A television commercial sells cat food by setting the sales pitch to the music of a Mozart aria, Andrew Lloyd Webber writes a hugely successful pastiche of a late Romantic Requiem, the Kronos string quartet plays Hendrix" (37).

In short, the hyperrationalization of the culture industry "solves" what was always a major problem for capitalism: the need, on one hand, to massify culture and absorb all possible sites of resistance and, on the other, the expectation of consumers that they be touched or supplied with something special, something unique. At the same time, however, hyperrationalization will ensure that the meanings that emerge from postmodern sumptuary social relations are not only provisional but also so fragmented that there is no rational basis for making sense of them as a whole. Just as the NSMs and NAPs fragment political motivations so extensively that the idea of "justice" or law can no longer be generalized, so, too, New Class workers fragment the lifeworld so extensively that the images they deploy seem to have arrived from Venus, without context, without history, and without any possible relevance to the totality of life. Yet precisely because of this, as Sut Jhally (1990, 18) has pointed out, "advertisements do not lie to us." Because they depict the "*pseudo*-use of life," they are beyond objectivity. Just as the Great Communicator did not exactly *lie* to us, so, too, New Class merchandisers do not sell people what is demonstrably false.

Industrial capitalism sustained a system of signs that denied or screened the realities of social production. Postmodern consumer culture, in contrast, does not so much hide the social relations of production as promote the social relations of consumption. As Jhally (1990, 51) emphasizes: If "production empties," "advertising fills." At a "secondary level," and in a secondary market of sign values, "the hollow husk of the commodity-form needs to be filled by some kind of meaning, however superficial" (51). The task of the advertising industry is to help fill this gap. Postmodern consumer capitalism consequently *creates* meaning (endlessly); it is not primarily concerned with repressing it. And because consumer capitalism responds to "the denial of freedom," even to "the possibility of freedom," with "the granting of liberties" (Marcuse 1964, 244–245), it instantiates what Herbert Marcuse recognized as a repressive form of tolerance.

The Secondary Market of Commodification

The primary goal of the New Class is to assist consumers in using commodities in the secondary market so as to mediate between their actual existence and their "dreams" or aspirations. New Classers consequently must pay close attention to the "needs" of such consumers. If these consumers transform and subvert the meaning of corporate rock—by inventing punk, for instance—corporations must respond by in turn offering "New Wave" music: a "sanitized" and recuperated version of punk music (Gottdiener 1985, 996). In the same fashion, the music industry can recuperate what originally was a folk art first as "country and western," second as "progressive country" (country and western for yuppies).

Producers hire New Class researchers and advertisers to help them determine and discover what sells.[7] But as we have seen, if individuals revitalize the meaning of what is available to them in commodified form only, they are effectively working on their "own time" for dominant corporations. A young person listening to Indie music might very well decide that the music has a very personal meaning for him or her, that it expresses his or her disenchantment, rebellion, and so forth. Another purchaser might attribute quite a slightly different meaning to the commodity. This kind of variation, however, does not in itself undermine commodity exchange. On the contrary, it strengthens commodity exchange's grip by permitting increasingly fragmented subjects still to internalize the mechanism of commodification.

In a study of "qualitative market researchers" in Britain, Bernice Martin (1992), for instance, discovered that the New Class workers she investigated (mostly female graduates in the social sciences) placed little or no emphasis on controlling or manipulating thought. Rather, they claimed that what they were doing was "democratic"—that is, they helped people decide what they really wanted, within a limited range of options, of course. The producers and merchandisers who employed the young merchandisers Martin studied did not want to know "how many will buy X" rather, they wanted the answer to the question "if I want to sell my low-alcohol beer, my new small car, or my pension scheme to young artisan-class consumers, what images do I need to deploy[?]" (139). According to Martin (137), the researchers she studied were engaged in "the postmodern project . . . [of] reflecting professionally and persistently on the lifeworld of consumers *and* of themselves." Nonetheless, the only way to mediate among these "lifeworlds" was through the elaboration of money relations. The researchers she studied were paid to expand the scope of commodity relations—nothing else.

The "secondary market of commodification" described in Figure 9.2, is not, of course, exclusive to postmodernity, for such markets existed even in the seventeenth and eighteenth centuries (Campbell 1987; McKendrick, Brewer, and Plumb 1982). Postmodern consumer culture, however, creates a new kind of subject: one whose sense of the dialectic between "freedom" and subjectivity, on the one hand (played out within the "secondary market"), and constraint and need, on the other (experienced with the "primary market"), *is itself subsumed by the system of commodification.* Marx old-fashionedly believed that even a denuded lifeworld (and, as we have seen, an unyielding substratum of "human nature") would provide a backdrop against which the reality of worker alienation could be felt. Yet for the subject caught up in the circuit of capital shown in Figure 9.1, there is no longer any benchmark against which the totality of the commodity can be challenged. As mentioned earlier, this is perhaps the best definition of postmodernism.

Postmodern Culture and Critical Theory

Postmodern culture develops and encourages a further elaboration and development of the bricolage of personal style. Yet because postmodern culture erases the distinction between such style and "inner" identity, it does nothing for individualization. Because postmodern subjects are

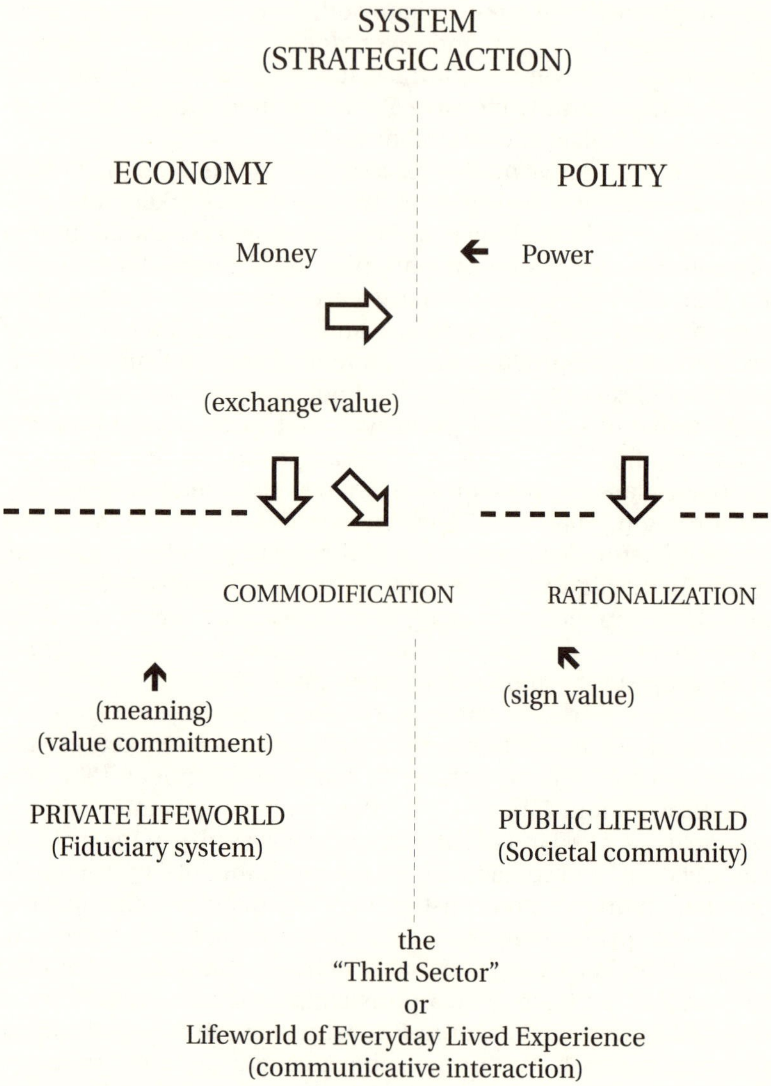

SYSTEM
(STRATEGIC ACTION)

ECONOMY   POLITY

Money   ⬅ Power

⇨

(exchange value)

---------------⇩ ⬃   ------⇩----

COMMODIFICATION   RATIONALIZATION

🡑   🡔
(meaning)   (sign value)
(value commitment)

PRIVATE LIFEWORLD   PUBLIC LIFEWORLD
(Fiduciary system)   (Societal community)

the
"Third Sector"
or
Lifeworld of Everyday Lived Experience
(communicative interaction)

⇨ Colonization of the lifeworld

🡒 Media that provide inputs into the economic system, where information flows in the opposite direction to that provided by money.

FIGURE 9.2   Late Modern or "Postmodern" Colonization of the Lifeworld by Steering Subsystems

evacuated of "inner" being—unable, as Lash and Urry (1994, 133) put it, to oppose "moral-practical categories" to "popular-culture objects"—they exist only to be seduced into the spectacle. Their goal is to have "the most secret facts and thought . . . commuted into spectacle . . . to attain ecstasy in a scene" (Baudrillard 1990b, 185). In short, the substitution of postmodern aesthetic/consumerist orientations for internally validated moral-practical choice does not just replace one kind of orientation for another. It also effectively eliminates the basis for individuation in the first place. But this transition is not *felt* as such by postmodern subjects, who come to redefine "self" as something that is (and always was) based on the aesthetics of choice. Increasingly, however, the "choice" in question becomes indistinguishable from the logic imposed by the circuit of capital. Moreover, the grounds in terms of which the "obscenity of the spectacle" might politically, morally, or aesthetically be challenged and resisted are progressively absorbed.

Even so, it does not follow that critical theory is entirely without scope. Even Baudrillard recognizes that most contemporary individuals are just as mystified by the processes of sumptuary consumption as were those earlier industrial workers dominated by the fetishism of their day. In his terms:

> The sign value cannot admit to its own deductive abstraction any more than exchange value can. . . . Whatever it denies and represses, it will attempt to exorcise and integrate into its own operation: such is the status of the "real," of the referent, which are only the simulacrum of the symbolic, its form reduced and intercepted by the sign. . . . [Thus,] the sign attempts to mislead: it permits itself to appear as totality, to efface the traces of its abstract transcendence and parades about as the reality principle of meaning. (1981, 162)

To put this a little less pretentiously: Under the conditions of consumer capitalism, many people truly believe that they can establish a worthwhile identity on the basis of sumptuary consumption. However, they comprehend neither the mechanism of such identity formation nor the futility of trying to consolidate "inner" identity on such a slippery and elusive foundation. In these terms there is indeed some space left for critical theory. But rather than lecture those who are merely trying to locate themselves in the world in which they were placed, critical theory must encourage subjects to evaluate the consequences of their own cultural practices. In the present context, this means forcing people to contemplate, and preferably be made to pay for, the ecological costs of their behavior.

Because Marxist-*humanists* believe that there is something inherently moral, civilized, or restrained about human beings, they have at least managed to maneuver themselves into a position where they are forced to defend the proposition that humankind's "natural" instincts are benign and that it is capitalism that is "unnatural" and hence wicked. Yet although Marx did believe that humans were perfectible, he never claimed that humans were good in the here and now. Marx's assumptions about the impact of social existence on human potential came straight from Rousseau; Marx took it for granted that imperfect societies would produce imperfect (i.e., mutilated and damaged) human entities. Many of the Marxist-humanists might learn from postmodernism what they should in any case have already figured out by themselves: There is a reason that consumer capitalism is more successful and more popular with many than socialism is. Yet to make such an observation is *not* to justify or endorse commodification or the attempt to aestheticize reality. Rape, plunder, homicide, and aggressive acts of vengeance are quite popular among humans, too, and can be intensely satisfying and personally rewarding, but it does not follow that we should justify or endorse the exercise of such natural liberties. As Sigmund Freud (1962) suggested, perhaps the whole point of civilization is to repress the human animal, not turn it loose.

Were Marx alive today, he would be dismayed not so much by the contemporary subject's involvement with symbolic or cultural goods, or even this creature's overriding concern with status. What challenges the very core of Marxist belief about humanity and the course of history is the successful separation of the postmodern subject from the relatively autonomous resources of a lifeworld that once might have opposed and thereby "humanized" the inhuman structure of commodity production and exchange. Although Marx did foresee the possibility that capital would increasingly penetrate and colonize sociocultural resources—thus invading and extending the more plastic "inner" world of the human subject—he never really grasped how radical this transformation would be. In essence, he never anticipated that this colonization would be so extensive that it would undercut the very being on whose behalf struggle was initiated in the first place—thus making the idea of "emancipation" appear not so much "wrong" as irrelevant. Today, the ideals of "communism" seem not so much dangerous as, well, boring. Why, after all, would anyone even *want* to leave the spectacle and try to make a world without diversions, popular culture, or serial leisure opportunities? It is quite difficult sometimes to remember what all the fuss was once about.

Postmodern System-Lifeworld Exchanges

We are now in a position to characterize some of the "exchanges" among the societal subsystems identified by Parsons and to place these in a "postmodern" context (see Figure 9.2). First, the "colonization of the life-world" that Habermas detected is facilitated and extended by post-modernity. As a result, it becomes increasingly difficult for the private lifeworld to operate according to the kinds of normative principles or value standards that Marx, Habermas, or even Parsons (all moderns) would have recognized as appropriate to the needs or functions of this subsystem.

Figure 9.2 sketches only the most important exchanges among the economy, the polity, and the public and private lifeworlds. It shows the pervasive importance of the media of money and power, both of which dissipate relatively autonomous private and public lifeworlds in order to reproduce a more effectively managed lifeworld in the interests of capital and the state. Postmodern solutions to Habermas's legitimation and motivation crises involve capital's and the state's ability to extend their boundaries into the sociocultural domain *without* creating subsequent legitimation or motivational deficits.

As we have seen, the abandonment of corporatist strategies and wel-fare statism helps alleviate public responsibility for steering the econ-omy, which in any case is increasingly structured by global flows. By ma-nipulating the new specialists, power can channel and check potentially dangerous forms of grassroots mobilizations. To the extent that com-modities increasingly have sign value as well as exchange value, honor and meaning can be *purchased* within the economic domain, which binds individuals even closer to the mechanism of commodity ex-change. As commodification advances, and as a common, shared public lifeworld turns into a million life pools, the subjective domain becomes increasingly self-absorbed and increasingly uncritical. Postmodernity, in short, uses capital and power to reorganize the "inner" world of the subject without subsequently creating the kind of alienated being likely to oppose such colonization. If the modern era helped create contradic-tion, crisis, and opposition, postmodernism helps smooth away what Marx once saw as modernity's fateful dialectic.

10 *Conclusion*

I argued in the preceding pages that postmodern culture is not just a reflection of intellectual feebleness; more specifically, it is an outcome of the restructuring and globalization of capital's circuit, which have significantly impacted political strategies, class organization, and life chances in the West. It is, I believe, possible to talk about *post*modern trends. Nonetheless, many of the features associated with postmodernity are best theorized as reactive and crisis-driven responses to modern phenomena that have been in existence for several generations.

Unlike many other theorists, I have attempted to "periodize" postmodernism by tracing its emergence to the perceived end of the postwar period (circa 1945–1968). As we have seen, the generally diffused belief in the emancipatory narrative of modernity began to evaporate after about 1968. The fall of communism in 1989 marked another important watershed, the significance of which we are only just beginning to grasp.

The end of the USSR and the global restructuring of accumulation were contingently related events. But acting in tandem, they lent support to the idea that many of the processes associated with modernity were in decline. I have identified the following tendencies in support of such a thesis:

- Increasing doubt that modern intellectuals can master or "humanize" the environments through which they are shaped
- The lessening significance of national structures of political and economic regulation
- The breakup of relatively well-organized class systems that in the past provided stable referents for political mobilization
- The abstraction and globalization of capital
- The ascendency of financial capital
- Greater emphasis on the reproduction of the conditions of consumption, as well as on the expansion of the circuit of production
- The creation of spaces for the purchase and display of semiotic privilege

- The reduction of distance between subjects and their symbolic products
- Increasingly frenetic attempts to aestheticize reality in the name of the commodity
- The steady marginalization of liberal democratic forms
- The globalization of class domination and the spatial reorganization of the division of labor
- A speedup of labor and of capital's circuit
- New social movements and new forms of political leadership that stress the virtues of particularistic group identity over generalizable interests
- Reactionary efforts to adapt consciousness and identity to a world that many believe no longer can be grasped as a whole
- New, more flexible forms of expertise and new, more particularistic "knowledges"
- New types of exchanges between the state and elites that promote new versions of privatism
- Power's increasing ability to operate outside objectifying, rationalizing, centralizing, impersonal processes
- The marginalization of subjects capable of reconciling personal integrity with public-mindedness
- Declining faith that humanity progresses by resisting the forces that prevent it from achieving a potential it did not itself define

As we now can begin to recognize, despite the many defects of Stalin's Soviet Union, it was partially, if indirectly, responsible not just for much of the stability of the postwar era but also for American political, military, and economic domination during this period. Moreover, the establishment of the Soviet Union as a major world power in 1945 forced many western nations to implement policies that otherwise would never have been adopted. It was no coincidence, for instance, that in the immediate postwar period the development of welfare statism and social democracy in the capitalist democracies was correlated with proximity to the Soviet bloc—Finland, Austria, West Germany, and Sweden having the most generous systems; the United States, having one of the least.

At the end of the 1980s, few western intellectuals mourned the ignominious end of "the first workers' state." Yet as the Polish émigré Zygmunt Bauman (1992, xxv) noted, "The collapse of communism was the final nail in the coffin of the modern ambitions which drew the horizon of European (or Europe-influenced) history of the last two centuries. That collapse ushered us into an as-yet-unexplored world: a world without a collective utopia, without a conscious alternative to itself." Perhaps surprisingly, this view is shared by Vaclav Havel, who was elected president of Czechoslovakia in 1989. For Havel (1992, A15), a leading anti-Soviet dissident during the 1970s: "The fall of Communism can be regarded as a sign that modern thought—based on the premise that the world is objectively knowable, and that the knowledge so obtained can be absolutely generalized—has come to a final crisis."

Notes

Chapter 1

1. The term *intellectual* does not describe mental abilities or reflect the amount of thinking a person does. It refers to a *social* position based on "knowledge."

2. As Kellner (1989, 78) notes, Baudrillard's "historical sketch of the orders of simulacra [was] heavily influenced by Foucault's archeologies of knowledge in *The Order of Things.*"

3. This example is taken from Bill Moyer's interview with Neil Postman in Moyer's documentary "The Public Mind," shown on PBS in 1990.

4. See, for instance, Woolf's (1955) modernist classic *To the Lighthouse.*

5. This quote was originally from the *Dada Almanach.*

6. Udo Rukser, *Dada Almanach* (1920).

7. Henri Lefebvre, *Les Temps des mépris* (Paris: Stock), 39–40.

8. In this sense, I approach postmodernity as an unreconstructed, unrepentant (and probably nostalgic) modernist, not as a dizzy postmodernist.

9. A "commodity" is something produced for sale through the market for buyers not immediately known. "Commodification" refers to the process whereby everything (and everyone) is increasingly reduced to the status of the commodity—including, for instance, education, health care, sexual satisfaction, honor, and style. A commodity has use value in that it satisfies human need; by definition, this kind of value cannot be quantified. A commodity possesses exchange value when its value can be quantified in monetary terms, i.e., shown to be equivalent, or not equivalent, to other commodities. According to Marx (1967a, 41–48), all commodities have the "dual" character of possessing both use and exchange value.

10. For an illustration, see Goldman and Papson's (1994) study of Reebok commercials.

11. For an English version, see Jean Baudrillard, "The Reality Gulf," *The Guardian,* January 11, 1991. For a critique of Baudrillard's "ludicrous theses on the Gulf War," see Norris (1992, 11–31).

12. Although, at Althusser's behest, Foucault joined the Communist Party in 1950, he resigned in 1953, and his relationship with Marxist philosophy remained ambivalent for the rest of his life. For Foucault's own explanation of why he left the PCF, see (1991, 52ff).

13. Lyotard was also an influential member of the radical Mouvement du 22 Mars, which was allied with the Situationist International.

14. "The Decline and Fall of the Spectacle-Commodity Economy." *Internationale Situationniste,* no. 10 (March 1966).

15. Ibid.

16. "Of Student Poverty, Considered in Its Economic, Political, Psychological, Sexual, and Particularly Intellectual Aspects, and a Modest Proposal for Its Remedy," in *Ten Days That Shook the University* (London: Situationist International), p. 11.

17. In Baudrillard's own words, he was a "pataphysician at twenty—Situationist at thirty—utopian at forty—transversal at fifty—viral and metaleptic at sixty—that's my history" (Baudrillard, *Cool Memories II* [Paris: Galilée, 1990]). Quoted in Best (1994a, 42).

18. See Postman (1986) for numerous examples.

19. The felicitous heading of this section comes from Vaneigem (1962).

20. It is thus not surprising that Reagan so often confused "real life" with some of the film scripts he had acted out in the past. For numerous examples, see Rogin (1987, 1–43).

21. See, for instance, the interview with Michael Deaver on Bill Moyer's 1990 PBS documentary *The Public Mind*. Deaver, who ran the Reagan White House, boasts that his Press Office was able to decide each morning which images would appear on the evening news shows.

22. As Nancy Reagan once explained: "There are not two Ronald Reagans. There is a certain cynicism in politics. You look in back of a statement for what the man really means. But it takes people a while to realize that with Ronnie you don't have to look in back of anything" (quoted in Rogin 1987, 7).

Chapter 2

1. The sociology of Talcott Parsons, which was dominant in America from the late 1940s to the mid–1960s, can be viewed as a third variation. It tried to mediate between Weber and Durkheim, arguing that although the differentiated spheres of social action could never be reconciled in terms of some absolute logic of development, they could nonetheless achieve some kind of equilibrium. For Parsons and his followers, Eisenhower's America was the best illustration of a system that approximated such a happy balance.

2. The fallacy in this argument, as Henri Poincaré once pointed out to Durkheim, is that one cannot derive the normative proposition "Don't eat toadstools!" from the scientific discovery "A toadstool is a poisonous mushroom" (Lukes 1977, 500).

3. Like Foucault a generation later, Bataille used pornography, sexual violence, and other "limit-experiences" to try escaping the strictures of the modern. He also helped found a neopagan secret society. Because this was to be "organized around sacred rituals of death and human sacrifice," Bataille and the other members of his cult "planned to stage an actual 'sacrifice' of their own," going so far as to identify a suitable candidate (Miller 1993, 86–87; see also Richardson 1994, 116). Unhappily for them (if not for the hapless victim), the outbreak of World War II apparently forestalled the "sacrifice" in question.

4. In this sense, Bataille's picture of capital is compatible with Marx's (1971, 87), who described in the *Grundrisse* how, under the sway of capital, "living labour appears as a mere means to realize objectified, dead labour," which subsequently is seen "as having an existence independent of [living labour], as the objectivity of a subject distinct from living labour capacity and standing independently over against it" (Tucker 1978, 252–253).

5. Debord took his life on November 30, 1994. After the breakup of the Situationist International in 1972, he had retired to the countryside, reluctant even to let Gallimard, his publisher, reprint *Society of the Spectacle*.

6. See Baudrillard's interview in Williamson (1986).

7. See Bogard's (1986, 1990, 1992, 1993) effective critiques of the attempts by some U.S. sociologists to make a "postmodern social theory" out of Baudrillard's rejection of the social. Kellner (1994b, 10) describes Gane's "attempt to separate Baudrillard from the discourse of the postmodern" as "futile." Yet Gane (1993, viii) merely wishes to make the point that "Baudrillard's own relationship with postmodernism is hardly positive."

8. In Parsonsian terms, "power," like "money," is a "circulating medium" that has "a generalized capacity to secure the performance of binding obligations by units in a system of collective organization when the obligations are legitimized with reference to their bearing

on collective goals and where in case of recalcitrance there is a presumption of enforcement by negative situational sanctions" (Parsons 1967, 306, 308).

9. Note that aesthetic-expressive orientations rather fall out of the frame here.

10. For Weber (1958), this differentiation was initially triggered by the Puritans' individuated search for salvation.

11. Premodern societies do not contain sufficiently differentiated life spheres for this distinction to become meaningful at the level of the actor.

12. David Roderick, chairman of the board, U.S. Steel. *The Business of America*, California Newsreels.

13. Although "talk shows" abound on CNN, these largely generate empty chatter or produce manufactured and contrived "debates" between studio opponents who function to normalize the officially sanctioned opposition between "liberals" and "conservatives."

14. In light of this quotation, we can see why Marx is commonly portrayed as someone who argued deterministically that humans are produced instrumentally (i.e., out of "necessity") *and* as someone who insisted that humans emerged from a social praxis or history that they had made for themselves. Because in a sense he wanted to have it both ways, it is always possible to quote selectively from Marx's work in support of these two quite contradictory positions.

15. The terms *affirmative* and *skeptical* postmodernist are adopted from Rosenau (1992, 14–17), although the meaning given these concepts has been changed.

Chapter 3

1. See the blurb on the back cover of Simon (1996).

2. See Rothblatt (1995) for additional examples.

3. As Douglas (1986) has pointed out, many mid-nineteenth-century Russian intellectuals turned to nihilism because of their political impotence and because of their sense of hopelessness about the serfs. She draws a telling analogy between these earlier skeptics and the latter-day postmodernists who have lost all hope about the increasingly desperate situation in the Third World.

4. Civil society is the domain of the private individual, wherein social and economic relations are based on contract or free associations among relatively atomized, relatively autonomous actors.

5. For a refreshingly different conception of how liberal affirmativists might actually *confront* the state, see Duggan's (1995) recommendations for the "Sex Wars."

6. In trying to further the kind of project that Seidman envisions, the American NAPs plumb poststructuralist ideas in an often comical attempt to show that the NSMs are well grounded in the latest kind of theory. For affirmativist Halperin (1995), for instance, Foucault was a founder and patron "saint" (Halperin's expression) of American gay and lesbian studies.

7. Solomon (1990, 284–286) has suggested that the attack on "secular humanism" by the Evangelical Right is a barely disguised postmodernism of the right. Having advanced this proposition, however, he fails to develop it.

8. Information supplied by Americans United for Separation of Church and State.

9. "Christians in Government: What the Bible Says" (Pamphlet distributed by Moral Majority, Lynchburg, Virginia, 1981).

10. For instance, the Reagan administration used the FBI and other agencies to spy on those "liberal" religious organizations that opposed the American-backed war against democratic movements in Central America.

11. In 1980 the Moral Majority succeeded in unseating prominent Democratic liberal senators such as George McGovern, Birch Bayh, Gaylord Nelson, John Culver, Warren Mag-

nuson, and Frank Church, chairman of the Senate Foreign Relations Committee, but it also sought to remove recalcitrant GOP candidates. For instance, Representative John Buchanan of Alabama, an ex-Baptist minister and Sunday school teacher, lost his primary because of opposition from the Christian New Right (Johnson 1991, 205). Although the Moral Majority no longer exists, the 1.8 million member Christian Coalition is growing in strength. It claimed to spend $2 million distributing 33 million voter guides to 60,000 churches around the country in 1994 alone and successfully targeted House Speaker Tom Foley and Dan Glickman, chairman of the House Intelligence Committee, for defeat in the 1994 congressional elections.

According to the periodical *Campaigns and Elections*, written for "professionals in politics," the New Christian Right is "dominant" (i.e., "constitutes a working majority on major issues") in Republican Party organizations in eighteen states and exercises "substantial" influence in thirteen others (Persinos 1994, 22).

12. Wuthnow (1989, 51) has pointed out that "the special-purpose [religious] group" did not really come into its own in the United States until the 1980s and that before 1945 few religious organizations had "political influence as their primary goal" (1988, 114). In 1900 major religious denominations had "outnumbered special purpose religious groups . . . by a ratio of about 2 to 1" (112). Yet by the mid–1970s, "special purpose groups outnumbered denominations" (113). After 1960 the number of special-purpose religious groups increased dramatically.

Wuthnow (1989, 51) notes that until fifteen or twenty years ago "persons with religious convictions" who wished to participate in public affairs usually did so as "private individuals" operating within "secular groups" and were typically steered into activities that were "sponsored at the national or regional levels by denominations" or "at the local level by local churches and synagogues."

13. In this context, it should be noted that privatization does not invariably mean depoliticization.

14. Hegel (1967, §257).

15. Among other things, these included labor laws, social security, and the application of Keynesian principles.

16. In Britain the National Health Service and the public ownership of transportation, utilities, and communications were untouched by pre-Thatcherite Conservative administrations.

17. By the 1980s New Evangelicals monopolized 90 percent of the TV broadcast time devoted to religion (Martin 1988). According to one 1987 Nielsen poll, about 60 million Americans tuned into at least one evangelical program weekly, and most of these "were heavy consumers of conventional as well as religious TV" (cited in Calhoun, Light, and Keller 1994, 369).

18. According to Moore (1994), religious life in the United States has always been permeated by the logic of the market. The difference between a nineteenth-century huckster and Jim and Tami Bakker, however, is that the Bakkers were able to use the kind of mass-mediated techniques of salesmanship and persuasion that television and video have made possible.

19. *Faith in the City*, the Report of the Archbishop of Canterbury's Commission on Urban Priority Areas (Church of England, December 1985).

Chapter 4

1. For a critique of the New Timers, see Hirst and Zeitlin (1991) and Rustin (1989a, 1989b).

2. According to the principles of "scientific management," a workplace is fully rationalized when (1) individual laborers are working as fast as possible, (2) only the most physically able workers are employed, (3) the work process is broken down to its smallest parts

(particular movements) and these are recombined as efficiently as possible, and (4) the design of work (an exclusive concern of management) is completely separated from its execution (the domain of labor).

3. "Productivity" is usually defined as the ratio of the real price of goods and services to labor costs.

4. In *capitalist* commodity production, commodities are produced and exchanged as part of a capitalist enterprise. By contrast, workers in "simple commodity production" buy their own means of production, produce commodities, and then exchange them, retaining for themselves the value that is added (Marx 1967c, chap. 10).

5. The overlap between Fordism and Keynesian is not quite as tidy as Harvey makes out. As Hirst and Zeitlin (1991, 9) point out, "Neither West Germany nor Japan followed 'Keynesian' policies in their major periods of postwar expansion, adopting instead orthodox fiscal and monetary policies." And although, like President Nixon, many junior members of the Roosevelt administration (1933–1945) were self-declared Keynesians, President Roosevelt never himself admitted to this title.

6. The social wage comprises benefits to workers that do not accrue to particular individuals by virtue of the wages they earn.

7. For Marx, "accumulation" means growth in the value of fixed and productive capital, the expansion of the capitalist system of production into new areas of the globe, the incorporation of more people into this system of production, and (most important) an intensification of the rate of exploitation overall. In Marxist terms, "exploitation" (e) is defined as the ratio of surplus to necessary labor time ($e = s/v$), where s = surplus labor time or work for the employer's benefit, and v = variable capital or value that is returned to the worker in the form of wages and other remuneration.

8. The G–7 nations are the United States, the United Kingdom, Canada, France, Germany, Italy, and Japan.

9. The OECD comprises Australia, Austria, Belgium, Canada, Denmark, Finland, France, Germany, Greece, Hong Kong, Iceland, Ireland, Italy, Japan, the Republic of Korea, Luxembourg, the Netherlands, New Zealand, Norway, Portugal, Singapore, Spain, Sweden, Switzerland, Taiwan, Turkey, the United Kingdom, and the United States.

10. Interview in the *Financial Times*, August 9, 1974.

11. According to the *Sunday Times* (April 10, 1994, 4–5), which conducted the survey in question, "The 1980s probably threw up more new millionaires than any period in British history. . . . Britain's rich are getting richer; and there are more of them. . . . Five years ago the top 200 were worth £38 ($57) billion between them. Today the top 200 . . . are worth 36% more, or £54.3 ($81) billion. So much for the recession."

Number 303 on the list of the "500 richest" was Mark Thatcher, the son of Margaret Thatcher. As the *Sunday Times* explained with commendable delicacy, "Thatcher . . . is reckoned to have made lucrative commissions on deals he helped secure. . . . His fortune is difficult to pin down as it is shrouded in Swiss secrecy, but £40m ($60m) is reckoned to be accurate" (41).

12. Followers of Piore and Sabel tend to place a great deal of emphasis on computer-integrated manufacturing and computer-aided industry, but the worldwide introduction of these technologies is very limited to date (Mathews 1989a; Fix-Sterz and Lay 1987).

13. In this country the use of temporary workers has generated some innovatory new technology. "Executive temps" in California, for instance, are issued "white stickers to enter their offices which automatically turn red by the end of the day." This indicates (presumably to the temporary or part-time security guard) "that they should no longer be allowed access" to the facilities (Greig 1994, 22).

14. Benetton's U.S. sales fell 28 percent from 1987 to 1993 (*Forbes* May 24, 1993, 97), and according to one business magazine, the company has annual losses of $10 to $15 million in the United States (Levine 1996).

15. In 1932 the Ford Service Department and the Dearborn, Michigan, police force shot over fifty unemployed automobile workers who were demonstrating outside one of Ford's factories.

16. In this regard, Harvey's (1989a, 125) claim that "the symbolic initiation date" of Fordism was 1914—the year in which Ford introduced his much trumpeted Five-Dollar Day—is puzzling because Ford temporarily increased wages in 1914 not so much to promote Fordism as to cope with the fact that turnover among his workforce had reached the startling figure of 390 percent the year before (Sward 1968, 48–49; see also Dassbach 1991).

17. The Ford Foundation is today a liberally oriented agency that finances many programs for women and minorities, but as recently as the 1940s it worked closely with the CIA to develop "an effective American world-wide strategy" for an "Inter-University Study of Labor Problems and Economic Development" (Clarke 1992, 23ff).

18. For an overview of regulation theory, see Jessop (1988, 1990a, 1990b, 307–337; Amin 1994, 7–11). For a critique, see Bonefeld (1987).

19. The following was distilled from Aglietta (1979, 1982), Lipietz (1987), De Vroey (1984), Schoenberger (1987, 1988), Scott (1988), Gertler (1988), Scott and Storper (1986), Storper and Scott (1988, 1990), Oberhauser (1990), Hirst and Zeitlin (1991), Tickell and Peck (1992), and Lash and Urry (1994).

20. During the Fordist era, developed capitalist economies contained three quite distinct sectors of activity: (1) "public" or state run; (2)"monopolistic"; and (3) "competitive" (O'Connor 1973, 13–17). Whereas economic activity in the competitive sector is shaped largely through the market, the large corporations in the monopolistic sector dominate through property ownership and through their access to the legal and bureaucratic resources of the state. "Public industries" dominate largely through legal authority.

21. For a discussion of the relation between the treatment of women and the treatment of ethnic or immigrant workers in the United States and Germany, see Lash and Urry (1994, 171–191).

22. The concerns of First World feminists have for the most part little or nothing to do with the desperate problems facing women in the Third World. As Kipnis (1988, 165) has pointed out, "First-world feminists" have managed to be surprisingly resistant "to the dangerous knowledge that in a *world* system of patriarchy upheld by an international division of labor, unequal exchange and the International Monetary Fund we first-world feminists are also the beneficiaries."

Chapter 5

1. Marx (1967b, 23ff) calls financial capital "money capital."

2. A "globalizing world economy" is one of internal differentiation; "globalization," in this sense, "implies a degree of functional integration between internationally dispersed economic activities" (Dicken 1992, 1).

"Globalization" can thus be defined as (1) "a general growth in the volume of international trade," (2) "a shift of production from the most developed capitalist economies to the NICs," (3) "a huge increase in the level of financial flows at a global level," (4) "sharply increasing levels of Foreign Direct Investment," and (5) a sharp increase in the amount of world business conducted by transnational corporations (Wilks 1996, 100).

3. In the United States invisible earnings in 1988 were 39.7 percent of the total; in Japan, 30.1 percent (*Review of the Month* 1992).

4. Morgan Guaranty Trust Company, *World Financial Markets* (April 1991).

5. Japan's Ministry of International Trade and Industry is a good illustration of this principle. See Freeman (1987).

6. Other factors that attract foreign investment in the United States include a good system of communications and transport, a relatively well-educated and compliant work-

force, and, last but not least, the willingness of federal, state, and local governments to offer competitive packages of incentives to foreign investors.

7. Major TNC investors in China are Mitsui, Marubeni, Siemens, Coca-Cola, Motorola, IBM, Phillips, Volkswagen, TPL, and AT&T (*WIR* 1994, 68). Shanghai alone has attracted about 120 of the world's largest TNCs (70).

8. Living in China for six months during 1994, I never met or even heard of anyone who was able to conduct business without having to bribe government officials. The luxury goods prominently displayed in many large cities (e.g., the ¥9,088 [$1,049] bottles of Remy Martin Champagne Cognac that are sold in most department stores) are typically purchased as gifts for party officials without whose support little can be accomplished. A great deal of consumer spending inside China—it is impossible to find out how much, exactly—involves the private spending of public funds by governing officials. Many restaurants cater almost exclusively to bureaucrats who can entertain themselves and their guests at public expense. Meanwhile, most urban Chinese families spend about three-quarters of their income of about $50–60 a month purchasing a diet that most Americans would consider minimal at best. Because of out-of-control inflation (30–40 percent in 1993), real income for many people in China has been in decline for a number of years.

The Chinese government claims that about 10,000 Chinese workers die every year in industrial accidents. Given that official statistics in China are routinely manipulated, it is hard not to conclude that this figure significantly undercounts the true total. According to some estimates, there are about 120–200 million uprooted peasants in China today who are out of work or looking for work. Since 1992 the government has forced parents to pay tuition for children who attend public schools. Because many peasants can no longer afford such fees, absenteeism is on the rise.

Since the economy began to overheat in 1991, political controls have been tightened. Journalists are given strict, almost daily, instructions from the censors present in every newspaper office and every TV studio about what they can and cannot report and how their stories must be framed. In the week before the fifth anniversary of the so-called Tienanmen Square massacre of 1989, every People's Guard Unit (Mingbin) in every workplace in Shanghai was put on standby to safeguard against the unlikely possibility of renewed disturbances.

In light of all this, it is illuminating to cite the views of Gaines (1994, 56), managing editor of *Time* magazine, whose facile mode of commentary nicely reflects mainstream opinion in the United States: "China is setting loose an economic system in which individual effort will yield individual rewards, and it is the commonest truth of Western development that such a system creates the best conditions for individual liberties. Given its heritage and beliefs, America is obliged to encourage this process. In this light, opposition to MFN [most-favored nation status] for China . . . seems at best to be wrongheaded, and most likely a force for further repression."

9. In 1994 the state determined that the Samsung group should stay out of the automobile-making business so that the interests of Hyundai, Kia, and Daewoo would not be jeopardized by unwanted and "dysfunctional" market competition (*The Economist* June 11, 1994, 71).

Chapter 6

1. These claims seem quite at odds with recent empirical findings. Reviewing recent studies of inequality, Westergaard (1995, 137), for instance, concludes that "the material class structure has been hardening, not softening."

2. According to the National Commission on Employment Policy, created by Congress, in the 1970s younger men in their twenties started their working careers by making 39 percent less than men in their forties. But at the end of the decade as the young men moved

into their thirties, and the older men into their fifties, the younger group was only 3 percent behind. In the 1980s, however, young men failed to catch up. They began by making 46 percent less than men in their forties, but by the beginning of the 1990s they were still 21 percent behind (reported by Knight-Ridder News Service January 26, 1995).

3. As Braverman (1974, 424–447) has pointed out, official labor classifications have been continuously adjusted throughout the twentieth century to make it look as if the numbers of blue-collar "unskilled" workers were in steady decline.

4. Many "service" jobs have been successfully "industrialized" in the last three or four decades through application of factory methods of production to occupations such as restaurant work. Although this issue is peripheral to the main discussion, it does help make the point that official occupational categorizations often conceal as much as they reveal.

5. This point obviously echoes Braverman's (1974, 73) insight that whereas "the social division of labor subdivides *society*, the [Fordist] detailed division of labor subdivides *humans*."

6. For Weber, "market society" meant (1) a constant and highly competitive struggle between autonomous groups in the marketplace, (2) the rational calculation of prices under conditions of unrestricted competition, (3) formally "free labor" (i.e., work performed on the basis of freely contracted wage agreements) as distinct from fixed salaries or the like, (4) expropriation of workers from the means of production, and (5) private ownership of the means of production (Mommsen 1985, 251–252).

Weber defined market society in ideal-typical terms so that he could subsequently identify factors that impeded or blocked "pure" market relations (and hence class relations). Among other things, these include bureaucratic regulation and economic domination, e.g., the emergence of the kinds of "large industrial combinations, trusts, and monopolies" that were prevalent in Germany by 1914 (Mommsen 1985, 234).

7. The "service class" is internally differentiated on a number of dimensions that are rarely sorted out. These include type of employment (private versus public), level of expertise (professional versus nonprofessional), credentials (high versus low), and amount of bureaucratic authority exercised (minimal to extensive).

8. To complicate matters, some theorists describe the "service class" as a "new class" (see, inter alia, Galbraith 1958; Piccone 1978; Gouldner 1979; Berger 1979; McAdams 1987; Albertsen 1988; Kriesi 1989; Featherstone 1991; Inglehart 1990a; Betz 1992; Heuberger 1992; Hunter and Fessenden 1992; Kellner and Heuberger 1992).

9. This helps explain why Crook et al. (1992) get themselves in the tangle of suggesting that the service class both is and is not a "class" in the classical (Marxist/Weberian) sense of the term.

10. Whereas Featherstone (1991) and Betz (1992) concentrate on groups that *produce* "postmodern culture," Lash (1990, 20; emphasis supplied) draws attention to the "newer, post-industrial middle classes, with their bases in the media, higher education, finance, advertising, merchandising, and international exchanges that provide the *audience* for postmodern culture." In this sense, then (and almost in spite of himself), Lash manages to find a connection between class structure and postmodernism.

Chapter 7

1. Habermas (1975, 20) defines "civil society" (*bürgerliche Gesellschaft*) as "a sphere, free of the state" involving "commerce between private autonomous owners of commodities" and creating "goods-, capital- and labor-markets."

2. For some business commentators, the failure of the French socialist government from 1981 to 1983 to reflate France's currency unilaterally was a critical watershed.

3. This would suggest that the government bailout of Chrysler Corporation in 1980 was a holdover from the Fordist era. Would such a rescue mission be launched today?

4. This support for the rootless interests of the TNCs encourages the petite bourgeoisie to turn to a "savior" such as Ross Perot, the little Bonaparte from Texas.

5. In 1990 Thatcher met privately with Rupert Murdoch and personally approved his merger of Sky Television and British Satellite Broadcasting. This gave Murdoch monopolistic control of cable television in Britain. Murdoch subsequently gave Thatcher a $5.25 million advance for her memoirs.

By an odd coincidence, Murdoch also met privately with newly elected Speaker of the House Newt Gingrich in 1995 to discuss his interest in expanding his ownership of media outlets in this country. Shortly thereafter Gingrich signed a $4.5 million book contract with Murdoch's publishing company, HarperCollins.

6. In 1979 James Callaghan, the Labour leader whom Thatcher defeated, opined helplessly that he knew he was going to lose the coming election because he sensed, as he phrased it, "a 'sea-change' in British politics of a kind that occurred 'perhaps once every 30 years.' Voters had changed their minds about the sort of government they wanted," he declared, "and there was nothing that Labour could do about it" (*The Economist* June 11, 1994, 17). For Callaghan, the underlying causes of this shift in political sentiment were deeply mysterious. Like a character in a Greek tragedy, the last Labour prime minister of the postwar period decided he could never hope to resist what was already destined to happen.

7. According to the Bureau of Labor Statistics, Deutsche Bank Research, the mean hourly labor compensation in manufacturing (including benefits) in 1993 was $25.56 for Germany and $12.82 for Britain (cited in *International Herald Tribune* July 19, 1994, 9).

8. Numerous polls conducted during the Thatcher era showed fairly consistently that most people believed that Britain had become more Thatcherite than they wished. For details, see Riddell (1991, 77ff, 244). In November 1994 the Gallup polling organization found that about 8 percent of the British population claimed to support the policies of the government—the lowest approval rating ever recorded.

9. It takes about 1 million full-time U.S. workers to produce $42 billion worth of goods. In 1987 the U.S. trade deficit was $170 billion. Thurow (1987) has suggested that this deficit can be interpreted as the result of business taking more than 4 million workers out of export industries. By 1996 the total cumulative trade deficits since 1976 were $1.9 trillion. As Bartlett and Steele (1996, 33A) have suggested, this total represents the imported products that came into this country as a result of nearly 3 million manufacturing jobs having been wiped out.

10. In 1994 *relief* programs in this country absorbed less than 6 percent of the federal budget; the AFDC program, for instance, made up only 0.36 percent of the nation's GNP in 1987, *down* from 0.6 percent in 1972 (Marmor, Mashaw, and Harvey 1990, 85).

11. A similar result was achieved in Britain. According to Treasury statistics, public spending on housing, education, health, and social security actually increased from 53.4 percent to 57.1 percent of total public spending from 1978 to 1988 (cited in Riddell 1991, 128).

12. This would include programs such as AFDC that supposedly offer relief to nonworking mothers but that also help support networks of people who work full time or intermittently for minimal wages.

13. In 1995 a Republican-dominated House committee decided to keep the federal food stamp program—not because it would help the poor but because it might cut into the profits of agrobusinesses and grocery retail outlets. Nevertheless, the House Republicans did not hesitate to reduce nutrition programs for children. Other "welfare" programs that the Republicans promised to cut included Head Start, Meals on Wheels, grants and guaranteed loans for college students, shelters for runaway teenagers, aid for the homeless,

care for abandoned babies, literacy programs, funds for libraries, the Jobs Corps, public support for childhood immunization, health care for American Indians, aid to blighted communities, the national service program AmeriCorps, and the foster grandparents program.

14. According to one source, tax expenditures for corporate America at the end of the 1980s totaled more than $79 billion a year (Peachman 1988). In fiscal 1989 subsidies to corporate businesses totaled more than $15 billion (Office and Management and Budget 1989).

15. According to government statistics read into the parliamentary record by Jean Corston, Labour MP for Bristol East.

16. "Civil" and "vocational privatism" should not be confused with private feeling. "Privatism" basically refers to a process of depoliticization. A private feeling is one that is hidden from public scrutiny, i.e., kept secret.

17. In this sense Crook et al. (1992, 98–99) are right to conclude that "the autonomy of the state" is limited, but wrong to state that "citizen politics," or "new politics," the "new social movements," the "renaissance of grass-roots Civil initiatives, self-organized actions and self-governing bodies" "restrict its [the state's] regulative capacity."

18. Baudrillard, *De la séduction*, 19.

19. Here and in the next two points Habermas is citing arguments made by his colleague Niklas Luhmann.

Chapter 8

1. Clergy are one possible exception to this rule.

2. Citing Hansfried Kellner and Frank Heuberger, "Working Papers," 1987–1991. Like Gouldner, Martin tags the "New Professionals" the "New Class."

3. As numerous studies have repeatedly shown, the sorting and credentialing functions of the academy tend to reproduce and hence legitimate existing relations of inequality (see Jencks 1979, 1992; Goldthorpe and Marshall 1992; Coleman 1966; Rubinson 1986).

4. With the shrinkage of public money for "humanities" projects, "private" (or, more accurately quasi-public) foundations such as the Ford Foundation and the Rockefeller Foundation play an increasingly important role in steering the research activities of "humanities" scholars into areas associated with the NAPs. The Rockefeller Foundation Humanities Fellowships for 1995–1996, for instance, were designed specifically to "encourage programs that seek to comprehend the differences and interrelationships of cultures and involve direct community interaction." In general, the fellowships "are meant to serve scholars who are testing disciplinary boundaries or moving into newer fields of inquiry within the humanities." Two dozen appropriate areas of study were identified for 1995–1996. They are as follows:

Black or Afro-American Studies: (1) Culture and Development in Africa, (2) Race Relations and Black Culture, (3) Afro-American and African Studies.

Ethnic Studies: (1) South Asian Muslims, (2) Cuban Research, (3) Native Philosophy, (4) Caribbean Studies, (5) Latin American Studies.

Minority Aesthetics: (1) Black Music, (2) Mexican Art, (3) Latino Art Research.

Ethics and Social Rights: (1) Ethics and Public Life, (2) Social Equity and Cultural Rights, (3) Legal Humanities.

Urban Culture: (1) Urban Culture, (2) the Urban Experience, (3) Cartography of Urban Culture.

Lesbian and Gay Studies.

Performance Art.

Program in Age Studies.

Culture: (1) Media, Culture, and History; (2) Critical Analysis of Contemporary Culture; (3) the Formation of National Culture; (4) Citizenship, Nation, and Contemporary Urban Experience.

Class, Capital, Social Structure, Inequality, Globalization, Economic Restructuring, the State as an Instrument of Coercion, etc. Nothing funded.

5. Weberian bureaucracies are characterized by rationality and an emphasis on the efficacious performance of complex tasks. They have the following characteristics: (1) specialization and a clearly defined division of labor, (2) hierarchical authority that stems from an office, (3) carefully formulated and highly specific rules and regulations, (4) written communication, (5) formal social relationships, (6) hiring and promotion that are based on technical competence.

6. There is no (b).

7. Under extreme circumstances, colleges or universities that resist manipulation by public authorities are hit with severe penalties. Baruch College in New York was denied accreditation after the Middle States Association of Colleges and Universities determined that the college did not have the required mix of minority and nonminority faculty (*New York Times* April 5, 1990, B1).

8. Private colleges receive significant amounts of public revenue both directly and indirectly and are the beneficiaries of massive subsidies from the state, as well as from corporations, private businesses, and foundations. Private colleges are not, of course, regulated or taxed as "private businesses." Additionally, like faculty at public universities, most teachers in private colleges are trained at public expense.

9. In the 1990s while the American Sociological Association's (ASA) theory journal debated the end of sociology, *Footnotes,* the newsletter of the ASA, carried several articles that described administrative attempts to shut down sociology departments. No attempt was made to think about any possible connection between these two events.

10. According to Newman (1976), the boundaries around the university should be impenetrable. Yet what Newman was never able to acknowledge was that the "universalism" of the classical university was a function of the almost total lack of dissonance among the theorists, the teachers, and the consumers of education. The "classical university" was thus institutionalized by mechanisms of exclusion that would be insupportable today.

11. MacDonald (1993, 22) points out that not only government and educational organizations but also "hundreds of small firms and large corporations have hired 'diversity' consultants to ease racial tensions and improve the 'diversity profile' of their businesses." Sometimes private firms are coerced into hiring these consultants (as a consequence of being coerced into adopting affirmative action policies in the first place), but, as MacDonald suggests, many corporate managers are willing to accept that diversity training will enable them to manage their employees more effectively—especially (and predictably) those already hired under affirmative action policies. MacDonald (23) further notes that "Barbara R. Deane, editor of the industry newsletter *Cultural Diversity at Work,* estimates that approximately half of the Fortune 500 companies have 'someone with some responsibility' for diversity."

12. Most economic projections predict that over 60 percent of the workforce will be "minority" and female by the end of the first decade of the twenty-first century.

13. The "race norming" introduced by the Reagan administration adjusted the scores of about 16 million people who took civil service tests as part of their application for jobs in the public and private sector since 1981 (see Taylor 1992, 158).

14. Brown University, for instance, recently opened a new residence hall reserved exclusively for members of one "race": African American.

15. In 1971 when the federal government first sponsored affirmative action programs, 32.5 percent of blacks were below the officially designated "poverty line." In 1988, 31.6 percent of blacks were below this line. Throughout the 1980s, the number of blacks living in

poverty *rose*, at least until 1986 (*Current Population Report* [Bureau of the Census], series P–160, nos. 154, 157, 166; U.S. Department of Commerce 1986, 1989).

16. Some affirmative action programs seem designed to reinforce the impression that "minorities" cannot compete with nonminorities. For instance, only about 40 percent of applicants at Berkeley were admitted in 1990 exclusively on "academic grounds." The other 60 percent (mostly black and Hispanic) were admitted on the basis of "non-traditional criteria." As Adler (1991, 107) has noted, although "black enrollment more than doubled" over the last decade, "fewer blacks graduated from Berkeley last year than ten years ago." Adler suggests that Berkeley is eager to recruit minorities but shows little interest in retaining them once they have enrolled. He speculates that the reason that the black dropout rate has increased in recent years is because blacks must now compete with "super-qualified whites and Asians" (107). In 1995 the Regents of the University of California voted to shelve most affirmative action programs. The move was led by an African American who was himself the beneficiary of such programs.

Chapter 9

1. Some of the mundane mass-produced commodities of a generation past have now assumed a special significance or value never intended at their point of production. Thirty years on, nostalgia for the 1960s involves, among other things, a reevaluation of the first transistor radios; the first LPs; the "bubble cars"; the numerous, strange, mass-produced, brightly colored plastic fittings; the orange, globular "lava" bubble lamps. In the 1990s, yuppie collectors comb through garage sales looking for such discarded items. Once found, they are proudly displayed in the homes of those who show they have a special, ironic (and postmodern) sense of taste and distinction.

2. Adapted from Kathryn Petras and Ross Petras, *The Only Job Hunting Guide You'll Ever Need* (New York: Poseidon Press, 1989), chap. 2.

3. Reagan's "Morning in America" commercials, made by Phil Dusenberry, were also produced by the BBDO agency.

4. For a critique of those who evaluate the pathologies of the present purely in cultural terms, see Habermas (1981a, 7).

5. Some commentators have suggested that capitalism must now be recognized as a permanent condition (Fukuyama 1989). Whether or not this is true, it seems that "capitalism rather than communism . . . has turned out to be the permanent revolution" (Martin 1992, 122).

6. The characters in Shaw's (1996) *Heartbreak House*, first produced in 1919, clearly recognize that full individuality and selfhood cannot be developed without the individual first having access to money. For these moderns, however, money is the means to an end (self-fulfillment); the commodity form is a necessary evil, not an end in itself.

7. See Martin (1992) for an analysis of how qualitative market research in Britain recruited many of the social scientists who had failed to find an academic position following Thatcher's cuts.

References

Abercrombie, Nicholas, and John Urry. 1983. *Capital, Labour, and the Middle Classes.* London: Allen and Unwin.

Adler, Fred. 1991. "Politics, Intellectuals, and the University." *Telos,* no. 86:103–117.

Adorno, Theodor W. 1973; orig. 1966. *Negative Dialectics.* New York: Seabury Press.

_____. 1991. *The Culture Industry.* Ed. Jay M. Bernstein. London: Routledge.

Adorno, Theodor W., and Max Horkheimer. 1972; orig. 1944. *Dialectic of Enlightenment.* New York: Herder and Herder.

Agger, Ben. 1992. *The Discourse of Domination: From the Frankfurt School to Postmodernism.* Evanston, Ill.: Northwestern University Press.

Aglietta, Michael. 1979; orig. 1976. *A Theory of Capitalist Regulation: The U.S. Experience.* London: Verso.

_____. 1982. "World Capitalism in the Eighties." *New Left Review,* no. 136:5–41.

Aksoy, Asu, and Kevin Robins. 1992. "Hollywood for the 21st Century: Global Competition for Critical Mass in Image Markets." *Cambridge Journal of Economics* 16:1–22.

Albertsen, N. 1988. "Postmodernism, Post-Fordism, and Critical Social Theory." *Environment and Planning D: Society and Space* 6:339–365.

Alexander, Garth. 1994. "Bubble Bursts as Magic Hedge Loses Its Market Edge." *Sunday Times Business Section,* October 2, 4.

Alexander, Robert. 1989. "A Keynesian Defense of the Reagan Deficit." *American Journal of Economics and Sociology* 48:47–54.

Allen, Roy. 1989. "Globalization of the U.S. Financial Markets: The New Structure for Monetary Policy." In Richard O'Brien and Tapan Datta, eds., *International Economics and Financial Markets.* New York: Oxford University Press.

Althusser, Louis. 1971. "Ideology and Ideological State Apparatuses." In *Lenin and Philosophy and Other Essays.* New York: Monthly Review Press.

Amin, Ash, ed. 1994. *Post-Fordism: A Reader.* London: Basil Blackwell.

Anderson, Perry. 1988; orig. 1984. *In the Tracks of Historical Materialism.* 2d ed. London: New Left Books.

Anthony, Dick, and Thomas Robbins. 1990. "Civil Religion and Recent American Religious Ferment." In Thomas Robbins and Dick Anthony, eds., *In Gods We Trust: New Patterns of Religious Pluralism in America.* 2d. ed. New Brunswick, N.J.: Transaction Books.

Aronowitz, Stanley. 1988. "Postmodernism and Politics." *Social Text* 18:46–62.

Aronowitz, Stanley, and William DiFazio. 1994. *The Jobless Future: Sci-Tech and the Dogma of Work.* Minneapolis: University of Minnesota Press.

Aronson, Ronald. 1995. *After Marxism.* New York: Guilford Press.

Asante, Molefi Kete. 1992. "Afrocentric Systematics." *Black Issues in Higher Education* 9:16–22.

Atkinson J., and N. Meager. 1986. *Changing Working Patterns: How Companies Achieve Flexibility to Meet New Needs.* London: NEDO.

Banhan, John. 1994a. *The Anatomy of Change: Blueprint for a New Era.* London: Weidenfeld and Nicolson.

_____. 1994b. "A Future in the Fast Lane." *Sunday Times Business Section,* April 3, 8.

Banks, Stephen P. 1995. *Multicultural Public Relations: A Social Interpretation.* Thousand Oaks, Calif.: Sage.

Bartlett, Donald L., and James B. Steele. 1996. "American Dream Turns into Nightmare for Many." *Denver Post,* September 22, 31A–42A.

Bataille, Georges. 1988a; orig. 1949. *The Accursed Share.* New York: Zone Books.

_____. 1988b; orig. 1943. *Inner Experience.* Albany: State University of New York Press.

Baudrillard, Jean. 1975; orig. 1973. *The Mirror of Production.* St. Louis: Telos Press.

_____. 1981; orig. 1972. *For a Critique of the Political Economy of the Sign.* St. Louis: Telos Press.

_____. 1983a. *In the Shadows of the Silent Majorities.* New York: Semiotext(e).

_____. 1983b. *Simulations.* New York: Semiotext(e).

_____. 1986; orig. 1985. "The Year 2000 Will Not Take Place." In *Futur*Fall: Excursions into Post-modernity.* Sidney: Power Institute of Fine Arts.

_____. 1987a. *The Evil Demon of Images.* Sydney: Power Institute of Fine Arts.

_____. 1987b. "The Year 2000 Has Already Happened." In Arthur Kroker and Marilouise Kroker, eds., *Body Invaders: Panic Sex in America.* New York: St. Martin's Press.

_____. 1988a; orig. 1986. *America.* New York: Verso.

_____. 1988b. *The Ecstasy of Communication.* New York: Semiotext(e).

_____. 1988c. "Hunting Nazis and Losing Reality." *New Statesman* 115:15–17.

_____. 1989. "The End of Production." *Polygraph* 2–3:5–29.

_____. 1990a; orig. 1987. *Cool Memories.* London: Verso.

_____. 1990b; orig. 1983. *Fatal Strategies.* London: Pluto Press.

_____. 1990c; orig. 1979. *Seduction.* New York: St. Martin's Press.

_____. 1991. *La guerre du golfe n'a pas eu lieu.* Paris: Galilée.

_____. 1993a. "The Evil Demon of Images and the Precession of Simulacra." In Thomas Docherty, ed., *Postmodernism: A Reader.* Hertford, England: Harvester Wheatsheaf.

_____. 1993b; orig. 1976. *Symbolic Exchange and Death.* London: Sage.

_____. 1993c; orig. 1990. *The Transformation of Evil: Essays on Extreme Phenomena.* London: Verso.

_____. 1994; orig. 1992. *The Illusion of the End.* Cambridge: Polity Press.

Bauman, Zygmunt. 1987. *Legislators and Interpreters: On Modernity, Post-modernity, and Intellectuals.* Cambridge: Polity Press.

_____. 1992. *Intimations of Postmodernity.* London: Routledge.

Bell, Daniel. 1973. *The Coming of Post-industrial Society.* New York: Basic Books.

_____. 1990. *The Winding Passage: Essays and Sociological Journeys, 1960–1980.* Cambridge: Polity Press.

Bellah, Robert N. 1967. "Civil Religion in America." *Daedalus* 96:1–21.

_____. 1990. "Religion and the Legitimation of the American Republic." In Thomas Robbins and Dick Anthony, eds., *In Gods We Trust: New Patterns of Religious Pluralism in America.* 2d ed. New Brunswick, N.J.: Transaction Books.

Benjamin, Walter. 1973; orig. 1961. "The Work of Art in the Age of Mechanical Reproduction." In Hannah Arendt, ed., *Illuminations.* New York: Schocken Books.

Bennahum, David S. 1997. "Just Gaming: Three Days in the Desert with Jean Baudrillard, D. J. Spooky, and the Chance Band." *Lingua Franca* 7 (February):59–63.

Berger, Peter L. 1979. "The Worldview of the New Class: Secularity and Its Discontents." In Barry Bruce-Briggs, ed., *The New Class?* New Brunswick, N.J.: Transaction Books.

Berman, Marshall. 1982. *All That Is Solid Melts into Air: The Experience of Modernity.* London: Penguin Books.

Bernstein, Jay M. 1991. Introduction to Theodor Adorno, *The Culture Industry*. Ed. Jay M. Bernstein. London: Routledge.

Best, Steven. 1994a. "The Commodification of Reality and the Reality of Commodification: Baudrillard, Debord, and Postmodern Theory." In Douglas Kellner, ed., *Baudrillard: A Critical Reader*. Oxford: Basil Blackwell.

_____. 1994b. "Foucault, Postmodernism, and Social Theory." In David R. Dickens and Andrea Fontana, eds., *Postmodernism and Social Inquiry*. New York: Guilford Press.

Best, Steven, and Douglas Kellner. 1991. *Postmodern Theory: Critical Interrogations*. New York: Guilford Press.

Betz, Hans-Georg. 1989. "Post-modern Politics and the New Middle Class: The Case of West Germany." Paper presented at the Meetings of the Midwest Political Science Association, Chicago, Illinois, April.

_____. 1992. "Postmodernism and the New Middle Class." *Theory, Culture, and Society* 9:93–114.

Blake, William. 1979. "And Did Those Feet." In *The Norton Anthology of English Literature*. 4th ed. New York: Norton, 2:78.

Bluestone, Barry, and Bennett Harrison. 1982. *The Deindustrialization of America: Plant Closings, Community Abandonment, and the Dismantling of Basic Industry*. New York: Basic Books.

Blumenthal, Sidney. 1994. "Christian Soldiers." *New Yorker*, July 18, 31–37.

Bocock, Robert. 1993. *Consumption*. London: Routledge.

Bogard, William. 1986. "Reply to Denzin: Postmodern Social Theory." *Sociological Theory* 4:206–211.

_____. 1990. "Closing Down the Social: Baudrillard's Challenge to Contemporary Sociology." *Sociological Theory* 8:1–15.

_____. 1992. "Postmodernism One Last Time." *Sociological Theory* 10:241–243.

_____. 1993. "The Postmodern Once Again." *Sociological Theory* 11:241–242.

Bonefeld, Werner. 1987. "Reformulation of State Theory." *Capital and Class*, no. 33:96–127.

Bornstein, Kate. 1994. *Men, Women, and the Rest of Us*. New York: Routledge.

Bourdieu, Pierre. 1977; orig. 1972. *Outline of a Theory of Practice*. Cambridge: Cambridge University Press.

_____. 1984; orig. 1979. *Distinction: A Social Critique of the Judgement of Taste*. London: Routledge.

_____. 1990; orig. 1980. *The Logic of Practice*. Cambridge: Polity Press.

Bowles, Paul, and Xiao-yuan Dong. 1994. "Current Successes and Future Challenges in China's Economic Reforms." *New Left Review*, no. 208:49–77.

Boyer, Robert. 1986. *La théorie de la régulation: Une analyse critique*. Paris: La Découverte.

Braun, Denny. 1991. *The Rich Get Richer: The Rise of Income Inequality in the United States and the World*. Chicago: Nelson-Hall.

Braverman, Harry. 1974. *Labor and Monopoly Capital: The Degradation of Work in the Twentieth Century*. New York: Monthly Review Press.

Bumiller, Kristin. 1988. *The Civil Rights Society*. Baltimore: Johns Hopkins University Press.

Bürger, Peter. 1984. *Theory of the Avant-Garde*. Minneapolis: University of Minnesota Press.

Burnham, James. 1941. *The Managerial Revolution*. New York: Doubleday.

Cage, Mary Crystal. 1994. "Diversity or Quotas? Northeastern U. Will Accord Gays and Lesbians Preferential Treatment in Hiring." *Chronicle of Higher Education*, June 8, A13.

Calhoun, Craig. 1993a. "'New Social Movements' of the Early Nineteenth Century." *Social Science History* 17:385–428.

_____. 1993b. "Postmodernism as Pseudohistory." *Theory, Culture, and Society* 10:75–96.

Calhoun, Craig, Donald Light, and Suzanne Keller. 1994. *Sociology*. 6th ed. New York: McGraw-Hill.

Callinicos, Alex. 1989. *Against Postmodernism: A Marxist Critique.* New York: St. Martin's Press.

Cambell, Laurel. 1994. "Diversity in Workplace Is New Strategy of Business." *Commercial Appeal,* August 21, C3.

Campbell, Colin. 1987. *The Romantic Ethic and the Spirit of Modern Consumerism.* Oxford: Basil Blackwell.

Caplan, Joel H., and Sheila Stowell. 1994. *Theatre and Fashion: Oscar Wilde to the Suffragettes.* Cambridge: Cambridge University Press.

Carter, P., and N. Jackson. 1990. "The Emergence of Postmodern Management." *Management Education and Development* 21:219–228.

Chittendon, Maurice, and Claire Oldfield. 1995. "I'm All Right John." *Sunday Times,* January 29, 12.

Clarke, Simon. 1992. "What in the F–'s Name Is Fordism?" In Nigel Gilbert, Roger Burrows, and Anna Pollert, eds., *Fordism and Flexibility: Divisions and Change.* London: Macmillan.

Clegg, Stewart R. 1990. *Modern Organizations: Organization Studies in the Postmodern World.* London: Sage.

Coates, David. 1994. *The Question of U.K. Decline: The Economy, State, and Society.* New York: Simon and Schuster.

Cohen, Jean. 1985. "Strategy or Identity: New Theoretical Paradigms and Contemporary Social Movements." *Social Research* 52:663–716.

Coleman, James S. 1966. *Equality of Educational Opportunity.* Washington, D.C.: GPO.

Colford, Stephen W. 1992. "Ross Perot: A Winner After All." *Advertising Age,* December 2, 17–18.

Collins, Randall. 1979. *The Credential Society: An Historical Sociology of Education.* New York: Academic Press.

Cooper, R., and G. Burrell. 1988. "Modernism, Postmodernism, and Organizational Analysis: An Introduction." *Organization Studies* 9:91–112.

Cox, Harvey. 1984. *Religion in the Secular City: Toward a Postmodern Theology.* New York: Simon and Schuster.

Crook, Stephen, Jan Pakulski, and Malcolm Waters. 1992. *Postmodernization: Change in Advanced Society.* London: Sage.

Crozier, Michael J., Samuel Huntington, and Joji Watanuki. 1975. *The Crisis of Democracy: Report on the Governability of Democracies to the Trilaterial Commission.* Albany: State University of New York Press.

Dachy, Marc. 1990. *The Dada Movement.* New York: Rizzoli.

Dalton, Russell J., and Manfred Kuechler. 1990. *Challenging the Political Order: New Social and Political Movements in Western Democracies.* New York: Oxford University Press.

Daly, Ann, ed. 1992. "What Has Become of Postmodern Dance?" *Drama Review* 36:48–69.

Dassbach, Carl H.A. 1991. "The Origins of Fordism: The Introduction of Mass Production and the Five-Dollar Wage." *Critical Sociology* 18:77–91.

Davis, Mike. 1986. *Prisoners of the American Dream.* London: Verso.

De Vroey, M. 1984. "A Regulation Approach Interpretation of the Contemporary Crisis." *Capital and Class* 23:454–456.

Deal, Terrence E., and Allan A. Kennedy. 1982. *Corporate Culture: The Rites and Rituals of Corporate Life.* New York: Addison-Wesley.

Debord, Guy. 1991; orig. 1989. *Comments on the Society of the Spectacle.* London: Verso.

_____. 1994; orig. 1967. *The Society of the Spectacle.* New York: Zone Books.

Department of Social Security. 1990. *Households Below Average Income, 1981–1987.* London: Her Majesty's Stationery Office.

_____. 1993. *Households Below Average Income, 1979/80–1990/91.* London: Her Majesty's Stationery Office.

Derrida, Jacques. 1994. *Specters of Marx: The State of the Debt, the Work of Mourning, and the New International.* New York: Routledge.

Dicken, Peter. 1992. *Global Shift: The Internationalization of Economic Activity.* 2d ed. New York: Guilford Press.

Docherty, Thomas, ed. 1993. *Postmodernism: A Reader.* Hertford, England: Harvester Wheatsheaf.

Dorst, John Darwin. 1989. *The Written Suburb: An American Site, an Ethnographic Dilemma.* Philadelphia: University of Pennsylvania Press.

Dostoyevsky, Fyodor. 1961; orig. 1864. *Notes from Underground.* New York: Signet Books.

Douglas, Mary. 1986. "The Social Preconditions of Radical Scepticism." In John Law, ed., *Power, Action, and Belief.* London: Routledge.

Douglas, Mary, and Brian Isherwood. 1980. *The World of Goods.* Harmondsworth, England: Penguin Books.

Drucker, Peter F. 1983. "Squeezing the Firm's Midriff Bulge." *Wall Street Journal,* March 25, 14.

_____. 1986. "The Changed World Economy." *Foreign Affairs* 64:768–791.

Duggan, Lisa. 1995. "Queering the State." In Lisa Duggan and Nan D. Hunter, eds., *Sex Wars.* New York: Routledge.

Durkheim, Émile. 1915; orig. 1912. *Elementary Forms of the Religious Life: A Study in Religious Sociology.* London: Allen and Unwin.

_____. 1974; orig. 1924. *Sociology and Philosophy.* New York: Free Press.

Durkheim, Émile, and Marcel Mauss. 1963; orig. 1903. *Primitive Classification.* London: Routledge and Kegan Paul.

Eagleton, Terry. 1986. *Against the Grain.* London: Verso.

Eco, Umberto. 1984. "Postmodernism, Irony, the Enjoyable." In *Postcript to the Name of the Rose.* New York: Harcourt Brace Jovanovich.

_____. 1986. *Travels in Hyperreality.* New York: Harcourt Brace Jovanovich.

Eliot, Thomas Stearns. 1975; orig. 1919. "Tradition and the Individual Talent." In Frank Kermode, ed., *Selected Prose of T. S. Eliot.* New York: Harcourt Brace Jovanovich.

Esser, Josef, and Joachim Hirsch. 1994. "The Crisis of Fordism and the Dimensions of a 'Post-Fordist' Regional and Urban Structure." In Ash Amin, ed., *Post-Fordism: A Reader.* London: Basil Blackwell.

Ewen, Stuart. 1988. *All-Consuming Images.* New York: Basic Books.

Eyerman, Ron. 1994. "Modernity and Social Movements." In David B. Grusky, ed., *Social Stratification: Class, Race, and Gender in Sociological Perspective.* Boulder: Westview Press.

Fahri, Paul. 1994. "TV Tunes to Changing Times." *Denver Post,* December 1, 2A, 15A.

Featherstone, Mike. 1988. "In Pursuit of the Postmodern: An Introduction." *Theory, Culture, and Society* 5:195–216.

_____. 1989. "Postmodernism, Cultural Change, and Social Practice." In Douglas Kellner, ed., *Postmodernism, Jameson, Critique.* Washington, D.C.: Maisonneuve Press.

_____. 1990. "Perspectives on Consumer Culture." *Sociology* 24:5–22.

_____. 1991. *Consumer Culture and Postmodernism.* London: Sage.

Feher, Ferenc, and Agnes Heller. 1983. "From Red to Green." *Telos,* no. 59:35–44.

Findlay, John Niemeyer. 1962. *Hegel: A Reexamination.* New York: Collier.

Firth-Cozens, Jenny, and Michael A. West. 1991. "Women at Work: Reflections and Perspectives." In Jenny Firth-Cozens and Michael A. West, eds., *Women at Work: Psychological and Organizational Perspectives.* Philadelphia: Open University Press.

Fiske, John. 1994. "Radical Shopping in Los Angeles: Race, Media, and the Sphere of Consumption." *Media, Culture, and Society* 16:469–486.

Fix-Sterz, J., and G. Lay. 1987. "The Role of Flexible Manufacturing Systems in the Framework of New Developments in Production Engineering." In Werner Wobbe, ed., *Flexible Manufacturing in Europe.* Brussels: Commission of the European Communities.

Flammang, Janet, Denis R. Gordon, Timothy J. Luke, and Kenneth R. Smorsten. 1990. *American Politics in a Changing World.* Pacific Grove, Calif.: Brooks/Cole.

Folkerts-Landau, David. 1989. "The Internationalization of Financial Markets and the Regulatory Response." In Hans-Jürgen Vosgerau, ed., *New Institutional Arrangements for the World Economy.* Berlin: Springer-Verlag.

Foster, Hal, ed. 1985. *Postmodern Culture.* London: Pluto Press.

Foster, John Bellamy. 1988. "The Fetishism of Fordism." *Monthly Review* 40, no. 10:14–33.

Foucault, Michel. 1973; orig. 1966. *The Order of Things.* New York: Vintage Books.

_____. 1978; orig. 1976. *The History of Sexuality.* Vol. 1: *An Introduction.* New York: Vintage Books.

_____. 1980. *Power/Knowledge: Selected Interviews and Other Writings, 1972–1977.* Ed. Colin Gordon. New York: Pantheon Books.

_____. 1984. "What Is an Author?" In Paul Rabinow, ed., *The Foucault Reader.* New York: Pantheon Books.

_____. 1991; orig. 1981. *Remarks on Marx: Conversations with Duccio Trombadori.* New York: Semiotext(e)/Foreign Agent Press.

Fox, Nicholas J. 1993. *Postmodernism, Sociology, and Health.* London: Open University Press.

Fraser, Nancy, and Linda Nicholson. 1993; orig. 1988. "Social Criticism Without Philosophy." In Thomas Docherty, ed., *Postmodernism: A Reader.* Hertford, England: Harvester Wheatsheaf.

Freeman, Christopher. 1987. *Technology, Policy, and Economic Performance: Lessons from Japan.* London: Frances Pinter.

Freud, Sigmund. 1962; orig. 1930. *Civilization and Its Discontents.* Ed. James Strachey. New York: Norton.

Frug, Mary Jo. 1992. *Postmodern Legal Feminism.* New York: Routledge.

Fuchs, Elinor. 1983. "The Death of Character." *Theater Communications* 5:1–6.

Fukuyama, Francis. 1989. "The End of History." *National Interest* 16:3–18.

Gaines, James R. 1994. "Welcome to the Wild West." *Time International,* April 11, 56.

Galbraith, John Kenneth. 1958. *The Affluent Society.* New York: New American Library.

Gallop, Jane. 1987. "French Theory and the Seduction of Feminism." In Alice Jardine and Paul Smith, eds., *Men in Feminism.* New York: Methuen.

Gamble, Andrew, and Paul Walton. 1976. *Capitalism in Crisis: Inflation and the State.* London: Macmillan.

Gane, Mike. 1990. "Ironies of Postmodernism: Fate of Baudrillard's Fatalism." *Economy and Society* 19:314–333.

_____. 1993. Introduction to Jean Baudrillard, *Symbolic Exchange and Death.* London: Sage.

Gansler, Jacques S. 1988. *The Defense Industry.* Boston: MIT Press.

Gellner, Ernest. 1992. *Postmodernism, Reason, and Religion.* London: Routledge.

Gershuny, Jonathan I., and Raymond Edward Pahl. 1979. "Work Outside Employment." *New Universities Quarterly* 34:120–135.

Gertler, Meric. 1988. "The Limits to Flexibility: Comments on the Post-Fordist Vision of Production and Its Geography." *Transactions, Institute of British Geographers* 13:419–432.

Giddens, Anthony. 1990. *The Consequences of Modernity.* London: Polity Press.

_____. 1991. *Modernity and Self-Identity: Self and Society in the Late Modern Age.* London: Polity Press.

Gilbert, Nigel, Roger Burrows, and Anna Pollert, eds. 1992. *Fordism and Flexibility: Divisions and Change.* London: Macmillan.

Gitlin, Todd. 1980. *The Whole World's Watching.* Berkeley and Los Angeles: University of California Press.

_____. 1989. "Postmodernism: Roots and Politics." In Ian H. Angus and Sut Jhally, eds., *Cultural Politics in Contemporary America*. New York: Routledge.

Glassner, Barry. 1990. "Fit for Postmodern Selfhood." In Howard Becker and Michael Mc-Call, eds., *Symbolic Interaction and Cultural Studies*. Chicago: University of Chicago Press.

Glazer, Nathan. 1978. *Affirmative Discrimination: Ethnic Inequality and Public Policy*. New York: Basic Books.

"Globalization—to What End? Part 1." 1992. *Monthly Review* 43:1–18.

"Globalization—to What End? Part 2." 1992. *Monthly Review* 43:1–19.

Glyn, Andrew, Alan Hughes, Alain Lipietz, and Ajit Singh. 1990. "The Rise and Fall of the Golden Age." In Stephen A. Marglin and Juliet B. Schor, eds., *The Golden Age of Capitalism: Reinterpreting the Postwar Experience*. Oxford: Clarendon Press.

Goffman, Erving. 1959. *The Presentation of Self in Everyday Life*. Garden City, N.Y.: Doubleday.

Goldman, Robert. 1992. *Reading Ads Socially*. London: Routledge.

Goldman, Robert, and Steven Papson. 1994. "The Postmodernism That Failed." In David R. Dickens and Andrea Goldman, eds., *Postmodernism and Social Inquiry*. New York: Guilford Press.

Goldthorpe, John H. 1980. *Social Mobility and Class Structure in Modern Britain*. Oxford: Clarendon Press.

_____. 1982. "On the Service Class: Its Formation and Future." In Anthony Giddens and Gavin Mackenzie, eds., *Social Class and the Division of Labour*. Cambridge: Cambridge University Press.

Goldthorpe, John H., and Gordon Marshall. 1992. "The Promising Future of Class Analysis: A Response to Recent Critiques." *Sociology* 26:381–400.

Gomery, Douglas. 1989. "The Reagan Record." *Screen* 30:92–99.

Goode, William J. 1967. "The Protection of the Inept." *American Sociological Review* 32:5–19.

Gordon, David M. 1988. "The Global Economy: New Edifice or Crumbling Foundations?" *New Left Review*, no. 168:24–64.

Gorz, André. 1982. *Farewell to the Working Class: An Essay on Post-industrial Socialism*. London: Pluto Press.

_____. 1988. *Critique of Economic Reason*. London: Verso.

Gottdiener, Mark. 1985. "Hegemony and Mass Culture: A Semiotic Approach." *American Journal of Sociology* 90:979–1001.

Gottfried, Paul. 1993. "Up from McCarthyism?" *Telos*, no. 97: 105–109.

Gouldner, Alvin W. 1979. *The Future of Intellectuals and the Rise of the New Class*. New York: Oxford University Press.

Graham, Hugh Davis. 1990. *The Civil Rights Era: Origins and Development of a National Policy, 1960–1972*. New York: Oxford University Press.

Graham, Julie. 1991. "Fordism/Post-Fordism, Marxism/Post-Marxism: The Second Cultural Divide?" *Rethinking Marxism* 4:39–58.

_____. 1992. "Post-Fordism as Politics: The Political Consequences of Narratives on the Left." *Economy and Planning D: Society and Space* 10:393–410.

Gramsci, Antonio. 1971; orig. 1929–1930. *Selections from the Prison Notebooks*. New York: International Publishers.

Greensberg, Judith G. 1992. "Introduction to Postmodern Legal Feminism." In Mary Joe Frug, ed., *Postmodern Legal Feminism*. New York: Routledge.

Greenstein, Robert, and Scott Barancik. 1990. *Drifting Apart: New Findings on Growing Income Disparities Between the Rich, the Poor, and the Middle Class*. Washington, D.C.: Center on Budget and Policy Priorities.

Greenwald, John. 1994. "The Secret Money Machine." *Time International*, April 11, 20–23.

Greig, Geordie. 1994. "Office Workers Face a Harsh New World." *Sunday Times,* April 3, 22.

Gross, George. 1969. "France, May 1968." In Julian Nagel, ed., *Student Power.* London: Merlin Press.

Gross, Paul R., and Norman Levitt. 1994. *Higher Superstition: The Academic Left and Its Quarrels with Science.* Baltimore: Johns Hopkins University Press.

Guilbaut, Serge. 1983. *How New York Stole the Idea of Modern Art: Abstract Expressionism, Freedom, and the Cold War.* Chicago: University of Chicago Press.

Guth, James L. 1983. "The New Christian Right." In Robert C. Liebman and Robert Wuthnow, eds., *The New Christian Right: Mobilization and Legitimation.* Hawthorne, N.Y.: Aldine.

Habermas, Jürgen. 1975; orig. 1973. *Legitimation Crisis.* Boston: Beacon Press.

_____. 1981a. "Modernity Versus Postmodernity." *New German Critique* 22, 3–14.

_____. 1981b. "New Social Movements." *Telos,* no. 49:33–38.

_____. 1982. "A Reply to My Critics." In John B. Thompson and David Held, eds., *Habermas: Critical Debates.* Cambridge, Mass.: MIT Press.

_____. 1983. "Modernity—an Incomplete Project." In Hal Foster, ed., *The Anti-aesthetic: Essays on Postmodernism.* Port Townsend, Wash.: Bay Press.

_____. 1984; orig. 1981. *The Theory of Communicative Action.* Vol. 1: *Reason and the Rationalization of Society.* Boston: Beacon Press.

_____. 1987a; orig. 1985. *The Philosophical Discourse of Modernity.* Cambridge, Mass.: MIT Press.

_____. 1987b; orig. 1981. *The Theory of Communicative Action.* Vol. 2: *Lifeworld and System: A Critique of Functionalist Reason.* Boston: Beacon Press.

_____. 1989a. *The New Conservatism: Cultural Criticism and the Historian's Debate.* Cambridge, Mass.: MIT Press.

_____. 1989b; orig. 1962. *The Structural Transformation of the Public Sphere: An Inquiry into a Category of Bourgeois Society.* Cambridge, Mass.: MIT Press.

Hacker, Andrew. 1992. *Two Nations, Black and White, Separate, Hostile, Unequal.* New York: Ballantine.

Hadden, Jeffrey. 1990. "Conservative Christians, Televangelism, and Politics: Taking Stock a Decade After the Founding of the Moral Majority." In Thomas Robbins and Dick Anthony, eds., *In Gods We Trust: New Patterns of Religious Pluralism in America.* 2d ed. New Brunswick, N.J.: Transaction Books.

Hadreas, Peter. 1991. "Foucault and Affirmative Action." *Praxis International* 11:214–226.

Halperin, David M. 1995. *Saint Foucault: Towards a Gay Hagiography.* New York: Oxford University Press.

Hamelink, Cees J. 1986. "Is There Life After the Information Revolution?" In Michael Traber, ed., *The Myth of the Information Revolution.* London: Sage.

Harms, John, and Douglas Kellner. 1991. "Critical Theory and Advertising." *Current Perspectives in Social Theory* 11:41–67.

Harris, Louis. 1980. "Pollster Gives Conservative Groups Credit for Reagan Win." *Greenville News,* November 25, 3A.

Harrison, Bennett, and Barry Bluestone. 1986. *The Great American Job Machine: The Proliferation of Low-Wage Employment in the U.S. Economy.* Washington, D.C.: Joint Economic Committee.

_____. 1988. *The Great U-turn: Capital Restructuring and the Polarizing of America.* New York: Basic Books.

_____. 1990. "Wage Polarization in the U.S. and the 'Flexibility' Debate." *Cambridge Journal of Economics* 14:352–373.

Harvey, David. 1989a. *The Condition of Postmodernity.* Cambridge: Basil Blackwell.

_____. 1989b. "From Managerialism to Entrepreneurialism: The Transformation of Urban Governance in Late Capitalism." *Geografiska Annale* 71B:3–17.

_____. 1994; orig. 1987. "Flexible Accumulation Through Urbanization: Reflections on 'Post-modernism' in the American City." In Ash Amin, ed., *Post-Fordism: A Reader*. Oxford: Basil Blackwell.

Hassan, Ihab. 1987. *The Postmodern Turn: Essays in Postmodern Theory and Culture.* Columbus: Ohio State University Press.

Havel, Vaclav. 1992. "The End of the Modern Era." *New York Times,* March 1, A15.

Head, Simon. 1996. "The New Ruthless Economy." *New York Review of Books,* February 29, 47–52.

Hebdige, Dick. 1988. *Hiding in the Light: On Images and Things.* London: Routledge.

Hegel, Georg W.F. 1967; orig. 1821. *The Philosophy of Right.* Oxford: Clarendon Press.

Held, David. 1989. "The Decline of the Nation State." In Martin Jacques and Stuart Hall, eds., *New Times: The Changing Face of Politics in the 1990s.* London: Lawrence and Wishart.

Heller, Agnes, and Ferenc Feher. 1989. *The Post-modern Political Condition.* New York: Columbia University Press.

Hennessy, Rosemary. 1995. "Incorporating Queer Theory on the Left." In Antonio Callari, Stephen Cullenberg, and Carole Biewener, eds., *Marxism in the Postmodern Age: Confronting the New World Order.* New York: Guilford Press.

Hertsgaard, Mark. 1988. *On Bended Knee: The Press and the Reagan Presidency.* New York: Farrar, Straus and Giroux.

Heuberger, Frank W. 1992. "The New Class: On the Theory of a No Longer Entirely New Phenomena." In Hansfried Kellner and Frank W. Heuberger, eds., *Hidden Technocrats: The New Class and New Capitalism.* New Brunswick, N.J.: Transaction Books.

Hirsch, James S. 1995. "New Credit Cards Base Appeals on Sexual Orientation and Race." *Wall Street Journal,* November 6, B1, B7.

Hirsch, Marianne. 1989. *The Mother/Daughter Plot.* Bloomington: Indiana University Press.

Hirst, Paul, and Jonathan Zeitlin. 1991. "Flexible Specialization Versus Post-Fordism: Theory, Evidence, and Policy Implications." *Economy and Society* 20:1–56.

Hobsbawm, Eric. 1994. *Age of Extremes: The Short Twentieth Century, 1914–1991.* London: Michael Joseph.

Hochschild, Jennifer L. 1988. "Race, Class, Power, and Equal Opportunity." In Norman E. Bowie, ed., *Equal Opportunity.* Boulder: Westview Press.

Hollier, Denis, ed., 1988. *The College of Sociology, 1937–39.* Minneapolis: University of Minnesota Press.

Honneth, Axel, Eberhard Knödler-Bunte, and Arno Widmann. 1981. "The Dialectics of Rationalization": An Interview with Jürgen Habermas. *Telos,* no. 49:5–31.

Hoover, Kenneth R. 1987. "The Rise of Conservative Capitalism: Ideological Tensions Within the Reagan and Thatcher Governments." *Comparative Studies in Society and History* 29:245–268.

Howell, Chris. 1992. "The Dilemmas of Post-Fordism: Socialists, Flexibility, and Labor Market Deregulation in France." *Politics and Society* 20:71–99.

Huff, Daniel D., and David A. Johnson. 1993. "Phantom Welfare: Public Relief for Corporate America." *Social Work* 38:311–316.

Hughes, Robert. 1993. *Culture of Complaint: The Fraying of America.* New York: Oxford University Press.

Hunter, James Davison, and Tracy Fessenden. 1992. "The New Class as Capitalist Class: The Rise of the Moral Entrepreneur in America." In Hansfried Kellner and Frank W. Heuberger, eds., *Hidden Technocrats: The New Class and New Capitalism.* New Brunswick, N.J.: Transaction Books.

Hutcheon, Linda. 1986. "The Politics of Postmodernism: Parody and History." *Cultural Critique* 5:179–208.

Huyssen, Andrew. 1986. *After the Great Divide: Modernism, Mass Culture, Post-modernism.* Bloomington: Indiana University Press.

Ingelhart, Ronald. 1990a. *Culture Shift in Advanced Industrial Society.* Princeton: Princeton University Press.

_____. 1990b. "Values, Ideology, and Cognitive Mobilization in New Social Movements." In Russell J. Dalton and Manfred Kuechler, eds., *Challenging the Political Order: New Social and Political Movements in Western Democracies.* Cambridge: Polity Press.

International Monetary Fund. *International Financial Statistics Yearbook.* 1994. Washington, D.C.: International Monetary Fund.

Jacoby, Russell. 1994a. *Dogmatic Wisdom: How the Culture Wars Divert Education and Distract America.* New York: Doubleday.

_____. 1994b. "The Myth of Multiculturalism." *New Left Review,* no. 208:121–126.

Jacques, Martin, and Stuart Hall, eds. 1989. *New Times: The Changing Face of Politics in the 1990s.* London: Lawrence and Wishart.

Jameson, Fredric. 1984a. "Periodizing the 60s: The 60s Without Apology." *Social Text* 4:178–209.

_____. 1984b. "Postmodernism, or the Cultural Logic of Late Capitalism." *New Left Review,* no. 146:53–92.

_____. 1985. "Postmodernism and Consumer Society." In Hal Foster, ed., *Postmodern Culture.* London: Pluto Press.

_____. 1988a. "Cognitive Mapping." In Cary Nelson and Lawrence Grossberg, eds., *Marxism and the Interpretation of Culture.* Urbana: University of Illinois Press.

_____. 1988b. "Periodising the 60s." In *The Ideologies of Theory: Essays, 1971–1986.* Vol. 2. Minneapolis: University of Minnesota Press.

_____. 1989. "Afterword—Marxism and Postmodernism." In Douglas Kellner, ed., *Postmodernism, Jameson, Critique.* Washington, D.C.: Maisonneuve Press.

_____. 1991. *Postmodernism, or the Cultural Logic of Late Capitalism.* Durham, N.C.: Duke University Press.

_____. 1994. *The Seeds of Time.* New York: Columbia University Press.

Jamieson, Dale. 1991. "The Poverty of Postmodernist Theory." *University of Colorado Law Review* 62:577–596.

Jencks, Charles. 1987. *What Is Postmodernism?* 2d ed. New York: St. Martin's Press.

Jencks, Christopher. 1992. *Rethinking Social Policy: Race, Poverty, and the Underclass.* Cambridge, Mass.: Harvard University Press.

Jessop, Bob. 1988. "Regulation Theory: Post-Fordism and the State." *Capital and Class,* no. 34:147–168.

_____. 1990a. "Regulation Theories in Retrospect and Prospect." *Economy and Society* 19:153–216.

_____. 1990b. *State Theory: Putting the Capitalist State in Its Place.* University Park: Pennsylvania State University Press.

Jhally, Sut. 1990. *The Codes of Advertising: Fetishism and the Political Economy of Meaning in the Consumer Society.* London: Routledge.

Johnson, Haynes. 1991. *Sleepwalking Through History: America in the Reagan Years.* New York: Doubleday.

Kanter, Rosabeth Moss. 1977. *Men and Women of the Corporation.* New York: Basic Books.

Kaplan, E. Ann. 1987. *Rocking Around the Clock: Music, Television, Post-modernism, and Consumer Culture.* New York: Methuen.

Kariel, Henry S. 1989. *The Desperate Politics of Postmodernism.* Amherst: University of Massachusetts Press.

Karoly, Lynn A. 1989. "Changes in the Distribution of Individual Earnings in the United States: 1967–1986." Santa Monica, Calif.: RAND.

Kellner, Douglas. 1988. "Postmodernism as Social Theory: Some Challenges and Problems." *Theory, Culture, and Society* 5:239–270.

———. 1989. *Jean Baudrillard: From Marxism to Postmodernism and Beyond.* Stanford: Stanford University Press.

———. 1990. *Television and the Crisis of Democracy.* Boulder: Westview Press.

———. 1994. "Introduction: Jean Baudrillard and the Fin-de-Millennium." In Douglas Kellner, ed., *Baudrillard: A Critical Reader.* Oxford: Basil Blackwell.

Kellner, Hansfried, and Peter L. Berger. 1992. "Life-Style Engineering: Some Theoretical Reflections." In Hansfried Kellner and Frank W. Heuberger, eds., *Hidden Technocrats: The New Class and New Capitalism.* New Brunswick, N.J.: Transaction Books.

Kellner, Hansfried, and Frank W. Heuberger, eds. 1992. *Hidden Technocrats: The New Class and New Capitalism.* New Brunswick, N.J.: Transaction Books.

Kellogg, Paul. 1987. "Goodbye to the Working Class?" *International Socialism* 2:105–111.

Keynes, John Maynard. 1932; orig. 1925. *Essays in Persuasion.* New York: Harcourt Brace.

Kimball, Roger. 1990. *Tenured Radicals: How Politics Has Corrupted Our Higher Education System.* New York: Harper and Row.

Kipnis, Laura. 1988. "Feminism: The Political Conscience of Postmodernism?" In Andrew Ross, ed., *Universal Abandon: The Politics of Postmodernism.* Minneapolis: University of Minnesota Press.

Kitschelt, Herbert. 1990. "New Social Movements and the Decline of Party Organization." In Russell J. Dalton and Manfred Kuechler, eds., *Challenging the Political Order: New Social and Political Movements in Western Democracies.* Cambridge: Polity Press.

Knight, Al. 1995. "Affirmative Action Programs Stay a Step Ahead of the Posse." *Denver Post,* November 19, G1.

Kreutz, Henrick, and Gerhard Fröhlich. 1986. "Von der alternativen Bewegung zum selbstverwalteten Betrieb." *Mitteilungen aus der Arbeits und Berufsforschung* 19:553–564.

Kriesi, Hanspeter. 1988. "The Mobilization Potential of New Social Movements: Its Structural and Cultural Basis." In Hanspeter Kriesi, ed., *New Social Movements in Western Europe.* Gothenberg, Sweden: University of Gothenberg, Peace and Development Research Institute.

———. 1989. "New Social Movements and the New Class in the Netherlands." *American Journal of Sociology* 94:1078–1116.

Kroker, Arthur, and David Cook. 1986. *The Postmodern Scene: Excremental Culture and Hyper-aesthetics.* New York: St. Martin's Press.

Kroker, Arthur, and Marilouise Kroker, eds. 1988. *Body Invaders: Sexuality and the Postmodern Condition.* London: Macmillan.

Kroker, Arthur, Marilouise Kroker, and David Cook, eds. 1989. *Panic Encyclopedia: The Definitive Guide to the Postmodern Scene.* New York: St. Martin's Press.

Kumar, Krishan. 1978. *Prophecy and Progress.* Harmondsworth, England: Penguin Books.

———. 1995. *From Post-industrial to Post-modern Society.* Oxford: Basil Blackwell.

Laclau, Ernesto. 1990. *New Reflections on the Revolutions of Our Time.* London: Verso.

———. 1993; orig. 1988. "Politics and the Limits of Modernity." In Thomas Docherty, ed., *Postmodernism: A Reader.* Hertford, England: Harvester Wheatsheaf.

Laclau, Ernesto, and Chantal Mouffe. 1985. *Hegemony and Socialist Strategy: Towards a Radical Democratic Politics.* London: Verso.

Lash, Scott. 1990. *Sociology of Postmodernism.* London: Routledge.

Lash, Scott, and Jonathan Friedman, eds. 1991. *Modernity and Identity.* Oxford: Basil Blackwell.

Lash, Scott, and John Urry. 1987. *The End of Organized Capitalism.* Cambridge: Polity Press.

———. 1994. *Economies of Signs and Space.* London: Sage.

Lazare, Daniel. 1991. "Collapse of a City: Growth and Decay of Camden, New Jersey." *Dissent* (Spring):267–275.

Leiss, William. 1978. "Needs, Exchange, and the Fetishism of Objects." *Canadian Journal of Political and Social Theory* 2:1–27.

Leiss, William, Stephen Kline, and Sut Jhally. 1986. *Social Communication in Advertising: Persons, Products, and Images of Well-Being*. New York: Methuen.

Levin, Charles. 1981. Introduction to Jean Baudrillard, *For a Critique of the Political Economy of the Sign*. St. Louis: Telos Press.

Levine, Joshua. 1996. "Even When You Fail You Learn a Lot." *Forbes*, March 11, 58.

Lévi-Strauss, Claude. 1969; orig. 1949. *The Elementary Structures of Kinship*. Boston: Beacon Press.

Lipietz, Alain. 1986. "New Tendencies in the International Division of Labor: Regimes of Accumulation and Modes of Regulation." In Allen J. Scott and Michael Storper, eds., *Production, Work, Territory: The Geographical Anatomy of Industrial Capitalism*. Boston: Allen and Unwin.

_____. 1987. *Mirages and Miracles: The Crisis of Global Fordism*. London: New Left Review.

Lipin, Steven. 1994. "Bankers Trust Woes Spread to Money Unit." *Wall Street Journal*, December 8, A3–A4.

Lipovetsky, Gilles. 1994; orig. 1986. "May '68, or the Rise of Transpolitical Individualism." In Mark Lilla, ed., *New French Thought*. Princeton: Princeton University Press.

Luke, Timothy J. 1989. "Class Contradictions and Social Cleavages in Informationalizing Post-industrial Societies: On the Rise of New Social Movements." *New Political Science* 16–17:125–154.

Lukes, Steven. 1977. *Émile Durkheim, His Life and Work: A Historical and Critical Study*. London: Penguin Books.

Lunn, Eugene. 1982. *Marxism and Modernism: An Historical Study of Lukács, Brecht, Benjamin, and Adorno*. Berkeley and Los Angeles: University of California Press.

Lyotard, Jean François. 1984; orig. 1979. *The Postmodern Condition: A Report on Knowledge*. Minneapolis: University of Minnesota Press.

_____. 1991; orig. 1988. *The Inhuman: Reflections on Time*. Stanford: Stanford University Press.

MacDonald, Heather. 1993. "The Diversity Industry." *New Republic*, July 5, 22–25.

MacEwan, Arthur. 1991. "Why the Emperor Can't Afford New Clothes: International Change and Fiscal Disorder in the United States." *Monthly Review* 43:74–94.

Macpherson, Crawford Brough. 1965. *The Real World of Democracy*. New York: Oxford University Press.

MacShane, Dennis. 1993. "Revival of the Fittest." *New Statesman and Society*, October 22, 20–21.

Mandel, Ernest. 1978. *Late Capitalism*. London: New Left Books.

Marcus, Greil. 1989. *Lipstick Traces: A Secret History of the Twentieth Century*. Cambridge, Mass.: Harvard University Press.

Marcuse, Herbert. 1964. *One-Dimensional Man: Studies in the Ideology of Advanced Industrial Societies*. Boston: Beacon Press.

Marglin, Stephen A., and Juliet B. Schor, eds. 1990. *The Golden Age of Capitalism: Reinterpreting the Postwar Experience*. Oxford: Clarendon Press.

Markham, James. 1988. "Is America Perfect? (Is the Tongue in Cheek?)" *New York Times* (12 December), p. A4.

Marmor, Theodore R., Jerry L. Mashaw, and Philip L. Harvey. 1990. *America's Misunderstood Welfare State: Persistent Myths, Enduring Realities*. New York: Basic Books.

Marquand, David. 1989. "The Irresistible Tide of Europeanization." In Stuart Hall and Martin Jacques, eds., *New Times: The Changing Face of Politics in the 1990s*. London: Lawrence and Wishart.

Marsh, David. 1992. *The New Politics of British Trade Unionism: Union Power and the Thatcher Legacy.* London: Macmillan.

Marshall, Thomas Humphrey. 1973; orig. 1949. *Class, Citizenship, and Social Development.* Westport, Conn.: Greenwood Press.

Martin, Bernice. 1992. "Symbolic Knowledge and Market Forces at the Frontiers of Postmodernism: Qualitative Market Workers." In Hansfried Kellner and Frank W. Heuberger, eds., *Hidden Technocrats: The New Class and New Capitalism.* New Brunswick, N.J.: Transaction Books.

Martin, William. 1988. "Mass Communications." In Charles H. Lippy and Peter W. Williams, eds., *Encyclopedia of the American Religious Experience: Studies of Traditions and Movements.* Vol. 3. New York: Scribner's.

Marx, Karl. 1964–1972; orig. 1861–1863. *Theories of Surplus Value.* 3 vols. Moscow: Progress Publishers.

_____. 1967a; orig. 1867. *Capital.* Vol. 1. New York: International Publishers.

_____. 1967b; orig. 1885. *Capital.* Vol. 2. New York: International Publishers.

_____. 1967c; orig. 1894. *Capital.* Vol. 3. New York: International Publishers.

_____. 1978; orig. 1857–1858. "The *Grundrisse.*" In Robert C. Tucker, ed., *The Marx-Engels Reader.* 2d ed. New York: Norton.

_____. 1986; orig. 1843–1844. "Religion, Philosophy, and the Proletariat." In Frederic L. Bender, ed., *Karl Marx: The Essential Writings.* 2d ed. Boulder: Westview Press.

Marx, Karl, and Friedrich Engels. 1970; orig. 1845–1846. *The German Ideology.* London: Lawrence and Wishart.

_____. 1974; orig. 1848. *The Communist Manifesto.* New York: Washington Square Press.

Mathews, John. 1989. *Age of Democracy: The Politics of Post-Fordism.* Melbourne: Oxford University Press.

Mauss, Marcel. 1967; orig. 1925. *The Gift: Forms and Functions of Exchange in Archaic Societies.* New York: Norton.

McAdams, John. 1987. "Testing the Theory of the New Class." *Sociological Quarterly* 28:23–49.

McHale, Brian. 1992. *Constructing Postmodernism.* London: Routledge.

McIntyre, Richard. 1995. "Columbus, Paradise, and the Theory of Capitalist Development." In Antonio Callari, Stephen Cullenberg, and Carole Biewener, eds., *Marxism in the Postmodern Age: Confronting the New World Order.* New York: Guilford Press.

McKendrick, Neil, John Brewer, and J. H. Plumb. 1982. *The Birth of a Consumer Culture: The Commercialization of Eighteenth-Century England.* Bloomington: Indiana University Press.

McKinsey Global Institute. 1993. *Manufacturing Productivity.* New York: McKinsey Global Institute.

Middlemas, Keith. 1983. "Rout of the Tory 'Wets.'" *New Statesman,* June 17, 14–15.

Miller, Arthur. 1987; orig. 1949. *Death of a Salesman.* London: Penguin Books.

Miller, James. 1993. *The Passion of Michel Foucault.* London: Flamingo.

Miller, Mark Crispin. 1986. "Deride and Conquer." In Todd Gitlin, ed., *Watching Television.* New York: Pantheon Books.

Mills, C. Wright. 1951. *White-Collar: The American Middle Classes.* New York: Oxford University Press.

Mirowski, Philip. 1991. "Postmodernism and the Social Theory of Value." *Journal of Post-Keynesian Economics* 13:565–582.

Mishel, Lawrence, and Jared Bernstein. 1994. *The State of Working America, 1994–1995.* Washington, D.C.: Economic Policy Institute.

Mishel, Lawrence, Jared Bernstein, and John Schmitt. 1996. *The State of Working America, 1995–1996.* Washington, D.C.: Economic Policy Institute.

Mommsen, Wolfgang J. 1985. "Capitalism and Socialism: Weber's Dialogue with Marx." In Robert J. Antonio and Ronald M. Glassman, eds., *A Weber-Marx Dialogue.* Lawrence: University Press of Kansas.

Moore, Laurence. 1994. *Selling God: American Religion in the Marketplace of Culture.* New York: Oxford University Press.

Mort, Frank. 1989. "The Politics of Consumption." In Martin Jacques and Stuart Hall, eds., *New Times: The Changing Face of Politics in the 1990s.* London: Lawrence and Wishart.

Moskowitz, Milton, Michael Katz, and Robert Levering, eds. 1980. *Everybody's Business: The Irreverent Guide to Corporate America.* New York: Harper and Row.

Mouffe, Chantal. 1988. "Radical Democracy: Modern or Postmodern?" In Andrew Ross, ed., *Universal Abandon: The Politics of Postmodernism.* Minneapolis: University of Minnesota Press.

Müller-Rommel, Ferdinand. 1990. "New Political Movements and 'New Politics' Parties in Western Europe." In Russell J. Dalton and Manfred Kuechler, eds., *Challenging the Political Order: New Social and Political Movements in Western Democracies.* Cambridge: Polity Press.

Münch, Richard. 1994. *Sociological Theory.* Vol. 3: *Development Since the 1960s.* Chicago: Nelson-Hall.

Murphy, John W. 1989. *Postmodern Social Analysis and Criticism.* Westport, Conn.: Greenwood Press.

Murray, Fergus. 1987. "Flexible Specialization in the 'Third Italy.'" *Capital and Class,* no. 33:84–95.

Murray, Robin. 1989. "Fordism and Post-Fordism." In Martin Jacques and Stuart Hall, eds., *New Times: The Changing Face of Politics in the 1990s.* London: Lawrence and Wishart.

Nagel, Julian, ed. 1969. *Student Power.* London: Merlin Press.

Naisbitt, John, and Patricia Aburdene. 1990. *Megatrends 2000: Ten New Directions for the 1990's.* New York: William Morrow.

Nathan, Richard, and Fred Doolittle. 1984. "Reagan's Surprising Domestic Achievement." *Wall Street Journal,* September 18, 28.

Negt, Oskar, and Alexander Kluge. 1973. *Öffentlichkeit und Erfahrung: Zur Organisations Analyse von Burgerlicher und Proletarischer Öffentlichkeit.* Frankfurt: Suhrkamp Verlag.

Newfield, Christopher, and Ronald Strickland, eds. 1995. *After Political Correctness: The Humanities and Society in the 1990s.* Boulder: Westview Press.

Newman, John. 1976. *The Idea of a University, Defined and Illustrated.* Oxford: Clarendon Press.

Nightingale, Carl Husemoller. 1993. *On the Edge: A History of Poor Black Children and Their American Dreams.* New York: Basic Books.

Noble, Kenneth. 1986. "Study Finds 60% of 11 Million Who Lost Jobs Got New Ones." *New York Times,* February 6, A1.

Norris, Christopher. 1990. *What's Wrong with Postmodernism?: Critical Theory and the Ends of Philosophy.* Baltimore: Johns Hopkins University Press.

_____. 1992. *Uncritical Theory: Postmodernism, Intellectuals, and the Gulf War.* London: Lawrence and Wishart.

Oberhauser, Anne M. 1990. "Social and Spatial Patterns Under Fordism and Flexible Accumulation." *Antipode* 22:211–232.

O'Connor, James. 1973. *The Fiscal Crisis of the State.* New York: St. Martin's Press.

_____. 1987. *The Meaning of Crisis: A Theoretical Introduction.* Oxford: Basil Blackwell.

Offe, Claus. 1972. *Strukturproblem des kapitalischen Staates.* Frankfurt: Surhkamp Verlag.

_____. 1984. *Contradictions of the Welfare State.* Ed. John Keane. London: Hutchinson.

_____. 1985a. *Disorganized Capitalism.* London: Polity Press.

_____. 1985b. "New Social Movements: Challenging the Boundaries of Institutional Politics." *Social Research* 52:817–868.

Oliver, Melvin L., and Thomas M. Shapiro. 1990. "Wealth of a Nation: A Reassessment of Asset Inequality in America Shows at Least One-Third of Households Are Asset Poor." *American Journal of Economics and Sociology* 49:129–151.

Organization for Economic Cooperation and Development. 1986. *Flexibility in the Labour Market: The Current Debate.* Paris: OECD.

Paarlberg, Robert L. 1988. *Fixing Farm Trade: Policy Options for the United States.* Cambridge, Mass.: Ballinger..

Parsons, Talcott. 1951. *The Social System.* New York: Free Press.

_____. 1966. *Societies: Evolutionary and Comparative Perspectives.* Englewood Cliffs, N.J.: Prentice-Hall.

_____. 1967. *Sociological Theory and Modern Society.* New York: Free Press.

_____. 1969. *Politics and Social Structure.* New York: Free Press.

Peachman, Joseph A. 1988. *Federal Tax Policy.* Washington, D.C.: Brookings Institution.

Persinos, John F. 1994. "Has the Christian Right Taken over the Republican Party?" *Campaigns and Elections* (September):21–24.

Peters, Tom J., and Robert H. Waterman. 1982. *In Search of Excellence: Lessons from America's Best-Run Companies.* New York: Harper and Row.

Pfeil, Fred. 1986. "Postmodernism and Our Discontent." *Socialist Review* 16:125–134.

_____. 1988. "Postmodernism as a 'Structure of Feeling.'" In Cary Nelson and Lawrence Grossberg, eds., *Marxism and the Interpretation of Culture.*

Piccone, Paul. 1978. "The Crisis of One-Dimensionality." *Telos,* no. 35:43–54.

_____. 1991. "Artificial Negativity as a Bureaucratic Tool? Reply to Roe." *Telos,* no. 86:127–140.

_____. 1993. "Scapegoating Capitalism." *Telos,* no. 97:85–96.

Pierson, Paul. 1994. *Dismantling the Welfare State? Reagan, Thatcher, and the Politics of Retrenchment.* New York: Cambridge University Press.

Pilger, John. 1995. "Natural Born Partners." *New Statesman and Society,* March 10, 26.

Piore, Michael J., and Charles F. Sabel. 1984. *The Second Industrial Divide: Possibilities for Prosperity.* New York: Basic Books.

Piven, Frances Fox, and Richard A. Cloward. 1982. *The New Class War: Reagan's Attack on the Welfare State and Its Consequences.* New York: Pantheon Books.

Plant, Sadie. 1992. *The Most Radical Gesture: The Situationist International in a Postmodern Age.* London: Routledge.

Platten, David. 1986. "Postmodern Engineering." *Civil Engineering* 56:84–86.

Pollert, Anna. 1988. "Dismantling Flexibility." *Capital and Class,* no. 34:42–75.

Ponterotto, Joseph G., J. Manuel Casas, Lisa A. Suzaki, and Charlene M. Alexander. 1995. *Handbook of Multicultural Counseling.* Thousand Oaks, Calif.: Sage.

Popcorn, Faith, and Lys Marigold. 1995. *Clicking: Sixteen Trends to Future Fit Your Life, Your Work, and Your Business.* New York: HarperCollins.

Porphyrios, Demetri. 1989. "Architecture and the Postmodern Condition." In Lisa Appignanesi, ed., *Postmodernism: ICA Documents.* London: Free Association Books.

Postman, Neil. 1986. *Amusing Ourselves to Death.* New York: Penguin Books.

Poulantzas, Nicos. 1978. *State, Power, Socialism.* London: Verso.

Power, M. 1990. "Modernism, Postmodernism, and Organization." In John Hassard and Denis Pym, eds., *The Theory and Philosophy of Organizations: Critical Issues and New Perspectives.* London: Routledge.

Price, Joyce. 1994. "Cultural Diversity Required at HUD." *Washington Times,* February 11, A1.

Qu, Yingpu. 1994. "Industry Maintains Double-Digit Growth." *China Daily Business Weekly,* May 29–June 4, 8.

Rabinow, Paul. 1986. ."Representations Are Social Facts: Modernity and Postmodernity in Anthropology." In James Clifford and George E. Marcus, eds., *Writing Culture: The Poetics and Politics of Ethnography.* Berkeley and Los Angeles: University of California Press.

Renner, Karl. 1978; orig. 1953. "The Service Class." In Tom Bottomore and Goode, eds., *Austro Marxism*. Oxford: Clarendon Press.

Rheingold, Howard. 1991. *Virtual Reality*. New York: Summit.

Richardson, Michael. 1994. *Georges Bataille*. New York: Routledge.

Riddell, Peter. 1991. *The Thatcher Era and Its Legacy*. Oxford: Basil Blackwell.

Rieff, David. 1991. *Los Angeles: Capital of the Third World*. New York: Simon and Schuster.

Riesman, David. 1970; orig. 1950. *The Lonely Crowd: A Study of the Changing American Character*. New Haven: Yale University Press.

Ritzer, George. 1997. *Postmodern Social Theory*. New York: McGraw-Hill.

Robertson, Pat. 1982. *The Secret Kingdom: A Promise of Hope and Freedom in a World of Turmoil*. Nashville, Tenn.: Thomas Nelson.

Roderick, Rick. 1986. *Habermas and the Foundations of Critical Theory*. London: Macmillan.

Rogin, Michael Paul. 1987. *Ronald Reagan, the Movie*. Berkeley and Los Angeles: University of California Press.

Rosenau, Pauline Marie. 1992. *Post-modernism and the Social Sciences: Insight, Inroads, and Intrusions*. Princeton: Princeton University Press.

Rothblatt, Martine. 1995. *The Apartheid of Sex: A Manifesto on the Freedom of Gender*. New York: Crown.

Routledge, Paul. 1995a. "Privatised Power Bosses Give Themselves £72m in Shares." *Independent on Sunday*, February 12, 1.

_____. 1995b. "Proper Jobs Vanish as New Work Goes to Part-Timers." *Independent on Sunday*, March 19, 6.

Rowthorn, Bob, and Andrew Glyn. 1990. "The Diversity of Unemployment Experience Since 1973." In Stephen A. Marglin and Juliet B. Schor, eds., *The Golden Age of Capitalism: Reinterpreting the Postwar Experience*. Oxford: Clarendon Press.

Rubinson, Richard. 1986. "Class Formation, Politics, and Institutions: Schooling in the United States." *American Journal of Sociology* 92:519–548.

Ruccio, David F. 1991. "Postmodernism and Economics." *Journal of Post-Keynesian Economics* 13:495–510.

Rustin, Michael. 1989a. "The Politics of Post-Fordism: or, the Trouble with 'New Times,'" *New Left Review*, no. 175:54–77.

_____. 1989b. "The Trouble with 'New Times.'" In Martin Jacques and Stuart Hall, eds., *New Times: The Changing Face of Politics in the 1990s*. London: Lawrence and Wishart.

Sabel, Charles F. 1994. "Flexible Specialization and the Re-emergence of Regional Economies." In Ash Amin, ed., *Post-Fordism: A Reader*. Oxford: Basil Blackwell.

Saunders, Stonor. 1995. "Modern Art Was CIA 'Weapon.'" *Independent on Sunday*, October 22, 12.

Sayer, Andrew, and Richard Walker. 1992. *The New Social Economy: Reworking the Division of Labor*. Oxford: Basil Blackwell.

Schiller, Herbert I. 1989. *Culture Inc.: The Corporate Takeover of Public Expression*. New York: Oxford University Press.

Schlucter, Wolfgang. 1981. *The Rise of Western Rationalism: Max Weber's Developmental History*. Berkeley and Los Angeles: University of California Press.

Schmitter, Philippe, ed. 1979. *Trends Towards Corporatist Intermediation*. London: Sage.

Schoenberger, Erica. 1987. "Technological and Organizational Change in Automobile Production: Spatial Implication." *Regional Studies* 21:199–214.

_____. 1988. "From Fordism to Flexible Accumulation: Technology, Competitive Strategies, and International Location." *Environment and Planning D: Society and Space* 6:245–262.

Schoonmaker, Sara. 1994. "Capitalism and the Code: A Critique of Baudrillard's Third Order Simulacrum." In Douglas Kellner, ed., *Baudrillard: A Critical Reader*. Oxford: Basil Blackwell.

Schwartz, Martin D., and David O. Friedrichs. 1994. "Postmodern Thought and Criminological Discontent: New Metaphors for Understanding Violence." *Criminology* 32:221–246.

Scott, Alan. 1990. *Ideology and the New Social Movements.* London: Unwin Hyman.

Scott, Allen J. 1988. *New Industrial Spaces: Flexible Production Organization and Regional Development in North America and Western Europe.* London: Pion.

Scott, Allen J., and Michael Storper, eds. 1986. *Production, Work, Territory: The Geographical Anatomy of Industrial Capitalism.* Boston: Allen and Unwin.

Seidman, Steven. 1991. "The End of Sociological Theory." *Sociological Theory* 9:131–146.

_____. 1994a. *Contested Knowledge: Social Theory in the Postmodern Era.* Oxford: Basil Blackwell.

_____. 1994b. "Symposium—Queer Theory/Sociology: A Dialogue." *Sociological Theory* 12:166–175.

_____. 1995. "Why Postmodernism?: Steve's Story." In Steven Seidman and Linda Nicholson, eds., *Social Postmodernism: Beyond Identity Politics.* Cambridge: Cambridge University Press.

_____, ed. 1994. *The Postmodern Turn: New Perspectives in Social Theory.* Cambridge: Cambridge University Press.

Seidman, Steven, and Linda Nicholson, eds. 1995. *Social Postmodernism: Beyond Identity Politics.* Cambridge: Cambridge University Press.

Shaw, George Bernard. 1996; orig. 1919. "Heartbreak House." In *Selected Plays.* New York: Gramercy.

Simmel, Georg. 1911. *Philosophische Kultur.* Leipzig: Kröner.

_____. 1978; orig. 1907. *The Philosophy of Money.* London: Routledge and Kegan Paul.

Simon, William. 1996. *Postmodern Sexualities.* London: Routledge.

Slansky, Paul. 1989. *The Clothes Have No Emperor: A Chronicle of the American 80s.* New York: Simon and Schuster.

Smith, Barbara Hernstein. 1988. *Contingencies of Value: Alternative Perspectives for Critical Theory.* Cambridge, Mass.: Harvard University Press.

Soja, Edward W. 1989. *Postmodern Geographies: The Reassertion of Space in Critical Social Theory.* London: Verso.

Solomon, Robert C. 1990. "Nietzsche, Postmodernism, and Resentment: A Genealogical Hypothesis." In Clayton Koelb, ed., *Nietzsche as Postmodernist: Essays Pro and Con.* Albany: State University of New York Press.

Squire, James. 1992. "When You See Perot, You See Perot." *New York Times,* June 5, A20.

Stearns, William, and William Chaloupka, eds. 1992. *Jean Baudrillard: The Disappearance of Art and Politics.* New York: St. Martin's Press.

Storper, Michael, and Allen J. Scott. 1988. "The Geographical Foundations and Social Regulation of Flexible Production Complexes." In Jennifer Wolch and Michael Dear, eds., *Territory and Social Reproduction.* London: Allen and Unwin.

_____. 1990. "Work Organization and Local Labor Markets in an Era of Flexible Production." *International Labour Review,* no. 129:573–591.

Sward, Keith. 1968. *The Legend of Henry Ford.* New York: Atheneum.

Sweezy, Paul M. 1994. "The Triumph of Financial Capital." *Monthly Review* 46:1–11.

Tarrow, Sidney. 1989. *Struggle, Politics, and Reform: Collective Action, Social Movements, and Cycles of Protest.* Ithaca: Cornell University Press.

Taylor, Frederick Winslow. 1911. *The Principles of Scientific Management.* New York: Norton.

Taylor, Jared. 1992. *Paved with Good Intentions: The Failure of Race Relations in Contemporary America.* New York: Carroll and Graf.

Thatcher, Margaret. 1993. *The Downing Street Years.* New York: HarperCollins.

Therborn, Göran. 1978. *What Does the Ruling Class Do When It Rules?* London: Verso.

_____. 1995. *European Modernity and Beyond: The Trajectory of European Societies, 1945–2000.* London: Sage.

Thomas, Arthur Jr. 1991. *Beyond Race and Gender: Unleashing the Power of Your Total Work Force by Managing Diversity.* New York: American Management Association.

Thompson, E. 1982; orig. 1967. "Time, Work-Discipline, and Industrial Capitalism." In Anthony Giddens and David Held, eds., *Classes, Power, and Conflict.* Berkeley and Los Angeles: University of California Press.

Thurow, Lester C. 1987. "A Surge in Inequality." *Scientific American,* no. 256:30–37.

Tickell, Adam, and Jamie A. Peck. 1994. "Searching for a New Institutional Fix: The *After-Fordist* Crisis and the Global-Local Disorder." In Ash Amin, ed., *Post-Fordism: A Reader.* London: Basil Blackwell.

Touraine, Alain. 1969. *La sociétié post-industrielle.* Paris: Editions Denoël.

Tucker, Robert C., ed. 1978. *The Marx-Engels Reader.* 2d ed. New York: Norton.

Turner, Bryan S. 1988. *Status.* Milton Keynes, England: Open University Press.

_____. 1993. "Baudrillard for Sociologists." In Chris Rojek and Bryan S. Turner, eds., *Forget Baudrillard?* London: Routledge.

United Nations. 1993. *United Nations World Economic Survey.* New York: United Nations.

_____. 1994. *World Investment Report: Transnational Corporations, Employment, and the Workplace.* Geneva: United Nations.

United States, Department of Commerce, Bureau of the Census. 1986. *Statistical Abstract of the United States.* Washington, D.C.: GPO.

_____. 1989. *Statistical Abstract of the United States.* Washington, D.C.: GPO.

_____. 1991. *Statistical Abstract of the United States.* Washington, D.C.: GPO.

United States, House of Representatives, Ways and Means Committee. 1990. *Green Book: Background Material and Data on Programs Within the Jurisdiction of the Committee on Ways and Means.* Washington, D.C.: GPO, 1069–1145.

Urry, John. 1989. "The End of Organized Capitalism." In Martin Jacques and Stuart Hall, eds., *New Times: The Changing Face of Politics in the 1990s.* London: Lawrence and Wishart.

Van der Pijl, Kees. 1984. *The Making of an Atlantic Ruling Class.* London: Verso.

Vaneigem, Raoul. 1962. "Basic Banalities I." *Internationale Situationniste,* no. 7 (April):90.

_____. 1994; orig. 1967. *The Revolution of Everyday Life.* 2d ed. London: Left Bank Books.

Veblen, Thorstein. 1979; orig. 1899. *The Theory of the Leisure Class.* New York: Penguin Books.

Viénet, René. 1992; orig. 1968. *Enragés and Situationists in the Occupation Movement in France, May '68.* London: Rebel Press.

Vogel, David. 1981. "The 'New' Social Regulation in Historical and Comparative Perspective." In Thomas K. McGraw, ed., *Regulation in Perspective.* Cambridge, Mass.: Harvard University Press.

Wallerstein, Immanuel. 1982. "The USA in Today's World." In Marlene Dixon, ed., *World Capitalist Crisis and the Rise of the Right.* San Francisco: Synthex.

_____. 1990. "Antisystemic Movements: History and Dilemmas." In Samir Amin et al., eds., *Transforming the Revolution: Social Movements and the World System.* New York: Monthly Review Press.

Waters, Malcolm. 1989. "Collegiality, Bureaucratization, and Professionalization." *American Journal of Sociology* 94:945–972.

Weber, Marianne. 1975; orig. 1926. *Max Weber: A Biography.* New York: Wiley.

Weber, Max. 1946; orig. 1918. "Science as a Vocation." In Hans H. Gerth and C. Wright Mills, eds., *From Max Weber: Essays in Sociology.* New York: Oxford University Press.

_____. 1949. *The Methodology of the Social Sciences.* New York: Free Press.

_____. 1951. *The Religion of China.* New York: Free Press.

_____. 1958; orig. 1904–1905. *The Protestant Ethic and the Spirit of Capitalism.* New York: Scribner's.

_____. 1969; orig. 1925. *The Theory of Social and Economic Organization.* New York: Free Press.

_____. 1974. "Politics as a Vocation." In Hans H. Gerth and C. Wright Mills, eds., *From Max Weber: Essays in Sociology.* New York: Oxford University Press.

_____. 1978. *Economy and Society.* 2 vols. Berkeley and Los Angeles: University of California Press.

Weiner, Richard R. 1981. *Cultural Marxism and Political Sociology.* Beverly Hills, Calif.: Sage.

_____. 1987. "Must Social Democracy Always Lead to Corporatism? The Legacy of the New Deal and the 'Social Contract.'" *Current Perspectives in Social Theory* 8:239–277.

Weinstein, Deena. 1992. *Heavy Metal: A Cultural Sociology.* New York: Lexington.

Westergaard, John. 1995. *Who Gets What? The Hardening of Class Inequality in the Late Twentieth Century.* Cambridge: Polity Press.

Whitley, Richard. 1990. "East Asian Enterprise Structures and the Comparative Analysis of Forms of Business Organization." *Organization Studies* 11:47–74.

Wilkerson, Isabel. 1988. "Two Decades of Decline Chronicled by Kerner Follow-Up Report." *New York Times,* March 1, A1.

Wilks, Stuart. 1996. "Class Compromise and the International Economy: The Rise and Fall of Swedish Democracy." *Capital and Class* 58:89–111.

Williams, Raymond. 1976. *Keywords.* London: Fontana.

_____. 1977. *Marxism and Literature.* Oxford: Oxford University Press.

Williamson, Judith. 1986. "An Interview with Jean Baudrillard." *Block,* no. 15:16–19.

Willmot, Hugh. 1992. "Postmodernism and Excellence: The De-differentiation of Economy and Culture." *Journal of Organizational Change Management* 5:58–68.

Wolff, Richard D. 1995. "Markets Do Not a Class Structure Make." In Antonio Callari, Stephen Cullenberg, and Carole Biewener, eds., *Marxism in the Postmodern Age: Confronting the New World Order.* New York: Guilford Press.

Woolf, Virginia. 1955; orig. 1927. *To the Lighthouse.* New York: Harcourt, Brace and World.

World Bank. 1991. *World Development Report.* New York: Oxford University Press.

_____. 1993. *World Tables.* Baltimore: Johns Hopkins University Press.

_____. 1994. *World Tables.* Baltimore: Johns Hopkins University Press.

_____. 1995a. *World Development Report.* New York: Oxford University Press.

_____. 1995b. *World Tables.* Baltimore: Johns Hopkins University Press.

Wuthnow, Robert. 1988. *The Restructuring of American Religion: Society and Faith Since World War II.* Princeton: Princeton University Press.

_____. 1989. *The Struggle for America's Soul: Evangelicals, Liberals, and Secularism.* Grand Rapids, Mich.: Eerdmans.

Young, T. R. 1991. "Chaos and Social Change: Metaphysics of the Postmodern." *Social Science Journal* 26:289–306.

Zinn, Howard. 1980. *A People's History of the United States.* New York: Harper and Row.

About the Book and Author

History Without a Subject presents a broad-ranging discussion of the topic of postmodernity. Beginning with an analysis of how changes in the global economy are affecting the lives of ordinary Americans, this book suggests that the postmodern condition in this country can be likened to the balkanization of culture and society and the "Brazilianization" of politics and the economy.

Arguing that global trends are now more determining than nationally based institutions and organizations, David Ashley traces connections between the postmodern condition and the following developments: the American obsession with consumerism and debt; the loss of security and confidence in the work place; the "culture wars"; the declining quality of education; the loss of "public" intellectuals and debate about public interests; the bipartisan acceptance of many New Right policies; and the resurgence of ethnic and racial mistrust and division.

Postmodernization is associated by Ashley with the removal of barriers that previously afforded Americans a certain autonomy from the rest of the world. As a result, not only are jobs now taken from the first world to the third world but also, and increasingly, third-world conditions are produced in the heart of first-world nations such as the United States. *History Without a Subject* argues that these globalizing processes have yet to be understood by the people whose lives they are transforming—thus the title of the book.

David Ashley is professor of sociology at the University of Wyoming.

Index